"Hanna Reichel has written the best book on theological method in a generation. With rigor, creativity, and compassion, Reichel makes an often-dull topic exciting, even effervescent. This book accomplishes the seemingly impossible: it makes Barthians want to read queer theology, and it makes queer theologians want to read Barth."

—Vincent Lloyd, Professor, Villanova University

"Method will not save theology. It can't even save itself. But Hanna Reichel's brilliant book invites us to a better theology on the other side of methodological absolutes. Through careful attention to Marcella Althaus-Reid and Karl Barth, *After Method* diagnoses, undoes, and transcends some of the deepest divisions in the field of theology today. Reichel's book is not just a preface to theology; it is a major theological event in itself."

—Ted A. Smith, Charles Howard Candler Professor of Divinity, Candler School of Theology, Emory University

"Lucid and elegant, *After Method* clears and creates a much-needed space for creative play in contemporary theology. Reichel deploys conceptual design theory as a potential solution for all the ways theologians have (wrongly!) believed method can save us (or, at least, save our discipline). This approach is not to give theologians another supposedly stable method to copy but, rather, to invite us into a stance of epistemological humility. *After Method* liberates theology toward the methodological promiscuity it so desperately needs and liberates us poly-methodologists toward the forms of playful accountability we so desperately desire. Reichel's work will be cited by any genuinely innovative theological project for years to come!"

—Natalie Wigg-Stevenson, Associate Professor of Contextual Education and Theology, Emmanuel College, Toronto School of Theology

"At a time of disciplinary ferment and self-scrutiny in theology, Reichel raises a series of searching questions about its purposes, practitioners, audiences, and effects. In challenging familiar curricular distinctions, they gesture toward a more integrated and pragmatic approach that seeks to serve the church more effectively. Replete with insights, this creative study deserves widespread attention."

—David Fergusson, Regius Professor of Divinity, University of Cambridge

"Few, if any, in the academy today are equipped to engage the range of theological and theoretical interlocutors as Reichel has in this book. With great clarity and wisdom, *After Method* forges a groundbreaking path. Conversant in Reformed, Lutheran, queer, and Latin American liberation theologies, Reichel offers both an insightful introduction to methodological differences across a range of theological perspectives and a stunning exposure of their similar commitments and pitfalls. *After Method* further develops a new theological discourse and vocabulary where queer ideas and lives are not fringe exceptions but are brought to bear on the most powerful and formative proposals in Christian faith. We need this book!"

—Lisa D. Powell, Professor, St. Ambrose University

"Reichel's *After Method* offers a breathtakingly virtuosic programmatic orientation for theology today to attend courageously to the reality of God. This is constructive theology at its best, infused with deep systematic theological commitments to the Protestant doctrine of justification and deftly deploying queer theory to discover grace outside the fixed walls of organized existence. With fierce clarity Reichel challenges theologians to practice theology with an open-minded honesty and expansive vision for an 'otherwise' in our challenging times."

—Christine Helmer, Peter B. Ritzma Professor of the Humanities, Northwestern University

"This book is pathbreaking. Reichel is indeed after method—in many ways. Convinced that method cannot save, as many mistakenly believe, there remains the hope that it can still deliver valuable affordances. The book's argument is therefore designed—intentionally, skillfully, artfully, playfully, care-fully, craftily, logically, insightfully, authoritatively—as a conceptual guide on such a way to do better theology. It shows ways to do theology that will be less violent, less complicit in falsehood, and less arrogant and self-assured than much of what we know and do. It offers an intriguing invitation to come along on this way of doing theology—to journey together with others, often strange and unexpected faces, including outsiders; to experience the surprise of recognizing much that seem so familiar yet now suddenly new and exhilarating once more, like law turned into life, swords into plowshares; to become sensitive to false promises of trails in the forest leading nowhere or worse, to destruction; to richly receive that alien grace that awakens hope for what may become possible and provides reorientation in the dense forest. For those of us doing theology—whether in church, academy, or public life—this guide on how to get along—and how not to get along!—will offer much discernment and delight on our shared journey. Many readers may feel strangely reassured, comforted, and at home—yet also somehow subverted, even shocked, and strangely surprised with every twist and every turn: the route was clearly designed with that in mind and for that purpose. This book is simply trailblazing—in so many ways."

—Dirk J. Smit, Rimmer and Ruth de Vries Professor of Reformed Theology and Public Life, Princeton Theological Seminary

"In this rich, energetic, and wide-ranging account, Reichel argues for a thoroughgoing reconception of theological method. Reichel calls for diverse and creative queer destabilization rather than theological attempts to maintain control and focus on one's own righteousness. Weaving together constructive and systematic approaches and calling on theology to try not to save itself via methodological immaculacy, Reichel remains committed to an irreducible grounding in the reality of God and the world, and hope for chastened yet expectant futures."

—Susannah Cornwall, Professor of Constructive Theologies, Director of the Exeter Centre for Ethics and Practical Theology, University of Exeter

"Reichel is assuredly not the only one who is restless and longing for a different kind of theology, and in grappling with and pursuing that longing—in cruising that longing—they have given a great gift to the rest of us. Rejecting the terms of the methodological conflict between systematic and constructive theologies, Reichel promiscuously engages both, proposing a messy, indecent (queer) reorientation. *After Method* offers, dare I say, a better (approach to) theology—precisely as it promises nothing of the sort."

—Brandy Daniels, Assistant Professor of Theology, Co-Director of Gender, Women, and Sexuality Studies, University of Portland

"What if critical reflection on theological method, on the possibility of theological knowledge, offered something more than a cleared throat, a sharpened knife, or a soul in despair? What if, indirectly, almost accidentally, it yielded real theological substance—hints of sin and grace, shadowy images of Christ and salvation, a stammering witness to the eschatological itinerancy of a Christian life? What if these methodological reflections unmasked the sinful folly of every theology that tries to redeem itself, epistemologically speaking, by whatever method? And what would a theology look like that resisted the temptation to save itself, that broke free of the standard options—systematic or constructive, dogmatic or liberationist, truth-tracking or justice-seeking—by making each contend with each? Funded by a resolute theological realism and an antipositivist account of truth and value, could this nonconforming theology bear witness to God's queer grace? Hanna Reichel poses these questions and many more in this brilliant, important, provocative book."

—John R. Bowlin, Robert L. Stuart Professor of Philosophy and Christian Ethics, Princeton Theological Seminary

"Weaving between and together systematic and constructive theologies, Karl Barth and Marcella Althaus-Reid, the dogmatic and the liberationist, Reichel casts an exciting vision for what is possible when theologians are freed from their enthrallment to method. Where methodological dogmatism has reinforced divisions within theology and estranged theologians from the God they want to describe, Reichel's 'desoteriologized' understanding of method draws on design theory to help theologians find a way back to describing our messy reality and the God who exceeds all attempts at naming. *After Method* is energizing and challenging in the best way."

—Natalie Carnes, Professor of Theology, Baylor University

"Reichel's work brims with creativity and provocation, asking readers to consider again the design, use, and affordances of Christian doctrine. By insisting that theologians attend carefully to the ethos of the development and deployment of doctrine, this study invites us all to do better by both our subject matter—the God of the gospel—and all those who matter to our God."

—Philip G. Ziegler, Professor of Christian Dogmatics, University of Aberdeen

"*After Method* is many things at once: an impassioned rejection of the tired binary of 'systematic' and 'constructive' theology; an extended love letter to a deliciously odd theological couple; a guide for traversing the landscape of Christian thought without becoming lost in methodological cul-de-sacs. Even more, *After Method* is an erudite, humane, and imaginative example to us all. Reichel showcases a mode of reflection wherein responsiveness to context, attention to the grace of revelation, and the imperative of liberation are no longer treated as competing goods but entangled obligations—or, better, opportunities—whose negotiation can foster the emergence of 'better theology.'"

—Paul Dafydd Jones, Professor, University of Virginia

After Method

After Method

Queer Grace, Conceptual Design,
and the Possibility of Theology

Hanna Reichel

WESTMINSTER
JOHN KNOX PRESS
LOUISVILLE · KENTUCKY

© 2023 Hanna Reichel

First edition
Published by Westminster John Knox Press
Louisville, Kentucky

23 24 25 26 27 28 29 30 31 32—10 9 8 7 6 5 4 3 2 1

Scripture quotations are taken from the New Revised Standard Version Updated Edition. Copyright © 2021 National Council of Churches of Christ in the United States of America. Used by permission. All rights reserved worldwide.

Quotations from Karl Barth's "The Word of God as the Task of Theology, 1922" are © Amy Marga, 2011, *The Word of God and Theology*, translated by Amy Marga, T&T Clark, an imprint of Bloomsbury Publishing Plc. Used with permission.

Book design by Sharon Adams
Cover design by Kevin van der Leek Design Inc.
Cover art by Jacob van Loon. Used by permission.

Library of Congress Cataloging-in-Publication Data is on file at the Library of Congress, Washington, D.C.

ISBN: 9780664268190

Contents

Part III: How (not) to do better (*tertius usus legis*)

Acknowledgments

The question of theology has accompanied me for a while now, and in conversations across a variety of different contexts. If this book is an attempt to reconcile them and make sense of myself across them, it reflects not a definite conclusion, let alone a final word, but rather my ongoing participation in these conversations.

In this effort, I am primarily indebted to my students, who have kept challenging, stretching, and inspiring me in these past years to spell out my understanding of theology in response to the many questions they have raised. The students of the Doing Christian Theology course have pushed me to think harder about the value of different approaches to the theological task, different modes and styles of engagement, and the need to be able to attend to forms of critique and construction that do not neatly fit into the categories afforded by the inherited theologies and their frameworks. A highly energetic study group titled "Is an anti-racist theology possible?" has challenged my epistemological commitments in light of the (more-than epistemic) exclusions they effect. The students in my Theologies of Order and Chaos and Feminist Epistemologies courses have helped me reexamine our doctrinal constructions with an eye to their affordances and materialized ethics. These classes also became spaces for experimenting and playing with theological method in redesigning theology in diverse epistemic ecologies. Wes Willison first introduced design theory into my theological imagination and inspired my explorations on the topic. Micah Cronin challenged me to take queer grace—the queerness of grace and the grace found in queerness—more seriously than either Barth or queer negativity alone will. The intellectual conversation with PhD candidates Samuel Davidson, Charles Guth III, Rochhuahthanga Jongte, Heather Ketchum, Gary Burl McClanahan, Mary Nickel, Eric Tuttle, and Nicola Whyte, and their own wrestling with how to do theology in attention to pressing contemporary issues and epistemological challenges has been a constant source of learning and insight to me.

Colleagues have offered community along the way. John Bowlin, Mark Taylor, and Jonathan Tran read early versions of my proposal and provided helpful corrections and encouragement. Eric Barreto, David Chao, Keri Day, Lindsey Jodrey, Erin Raffety, Nate Stucky, Linn Tonstad, Ben Menghini, and Micah Cronin read chapters and supplied critical and constructive feedback. David Fergusson, Julia Enxing, and Henco Van der Westhuizen invited me to present and discuss the emerging book with their research seminars. Mark Jordan gave me back my faith in humanity at a crucial moment. Dirk Smit has throughout reminded me to go beyond the "sharpening of knives," while also modeling what it means to take the work that theology *does* (beyond what it *says*) seriously as a material rather than merely methodological question. Michael Welker has been a steadfast inspiration toward an unapologetically realistic theology in disciplinary as much as in interdisciplinary conversations.

I am immensely grateful to all those who have helped me get the work *done* and into this final shape. To Brandy Daniels and Elaine James for writing accountability sessions. To Ulrike Guthrie for developmental editing and attention to voice and composition. To Samuel Davidson and Eric Tuttle for editorial assistance. To Ben Menghini for pointing me to the cover art, to Jacob van Loon for his permission to use it. To Princeton Theological Seminary for financial and institutional support. To Bob Ratcliff, Daniel Braden, and José Santana, who have thoughtfully accompanied the completion, publication, and marketing with Westminster John Knox Press. To Ulrike Bornecke for love and childcare when I was wrapped up in wrapping up. To Moritz Menacher, who patiently provided moral and logistical support because, in his own words, "I know that if you don't finish this, you'll be insufferable." To Joshua and Junia who were puzzled that even as I had written so many words, they might not be the right words yet.

The sustained and sustaining conversation with Benedikt Friedrich and Thomas Renkert has been the intellectual *ecclesiola* that has nurtured this book more than anything else. Among many other things, Benedikt Friedrich has kept pushing against my temptations toward negativity, insisting on a theological commitment to the "better" even after critiques of progress and teleology, while Thomas Renkert's ingenious theorizations of salvaging, labor, and care have provided much-needed nuance for the "third use" of method. Their companionship has stretched and expanded my theological imagination and enriched my own journey as it coalesced into this book. It is dedicated to them.

Introductions

"WE NEED BETTER THEOLOGY!" DO WE, NOW?

Good theology is pleasing to God and helpful to people.

—*Karl Barth*[1]

Bad theology kills.

—*Kevin Garcia*[2]

Selah.

—*the psalmist*

We need better theology! That statement, while providing the motivation for this book, comes with baggage: optimism, naiveté, and problematic assumptions. Let us unpack some of that baggage.

Better? First, the call for *better* theology indicates that things are *bad* in theology. Theology is in crisis and has been for a while, and this is hardly surprising since a lot of the work theology is doing in our world is highly problematic. In short, *better* theology is needed because there is a lot of *bad* theology out there.

Bad theology, some will say, is at work in unreflective, uncritical, and ahistorical forms of faith. Bad theology is at work in excessive optimism about human rationality and scientific objectivity. Bad theology is at work in the

---

1. Karl Barth, *Evangelical Theology: An Introduction* (Grand Rapids: Eerdmans, 1979), 196.
2. Kevin Garcia, *Bad Theology Kills: Undoing Toxic Belief & Reclaiming Your Spiritual Authority* (Independently published, 2020).

promises of earthly prosperity or transcendent rewards in exchange for unwavering belief. Bad theology is at work in the projection of overly human sentiments onto our images of God. Bad theology is at work where any political movement is directly and unequivocally identified with the work of God in history.

Bad theology, others will say, is at work in systems of oppression, injustice, and discrimination. Bad theology is at work where suffering is justified as God's will. Bad theology is at work in the identification of bodies, desires, and feelings with sin. Bad theology is at work in myths of universal progress, betterment, and respectability. Bad theology is at work in all the "us-vs.-them" myths from Christian exceptionalism to imperialist white supremacist capitalist ableist cisheteropatriarchy and extractivism.

Any individual claim in these litanies might be debated, of course, but bad theologies exist, and need to be addressed, because, as Kevin Garcia puts it starkly, *Bad Theology Kills.* This claim is not so much a proposition as it is a diagnosis. "Bad theology" is not the subject to which the action of killing is (correctly or incorrectly) predicated; *that* a theology is bad is the verdict passed upon it in discernment of its fatal effect. This may sound simplistic. But "bad theology kills" is still one of the most compelling shorthands for diagnosing bad theology that I have found and not far from the Gospel warning, "Thus you will know them by their fruits" (Matt. 7:20):[3] If it bears bad fruit, it is a bad tree. If they behave like "ravenous wolves" (Matt. 7:15), they are bad prophets. If it kills, it is bad theology. Whatever else can be said about a theology, if it has systemically harmful and potentially even fatal consequences, then there must be something wrong with it. We need better theology.

Need? We are living in a world in ruins, to a not insignificant extent caused by ruinous theologies. Bad theologies are not only a problem for the vocational theologians, for those working in diverse ministries, not even only for those who believe in them. Believers and unbelievers, nonhuman animals and the creation at large are affected and wounded by many a bad theology and are thus in deep need of *better* theology.

In light of the atrocities with which theology, especially in the dominant forms of Western Christianity, continues to be entangled, we might also ask (as many do today): Do we *need* theology at all? Would the world not be better off *without theology* altogether? But while we might de-institutionalize critical practices of reflecting on implicit theologies, that does not mean they will go away; they will just remain unexamined. Theology is always already there, explicitly or implicitly. It is operative not only in our faith commitments but also in our cultural practices, political structures, and societal systems—and

---

3. Unless otherwise indicated, all Scripture quotations follow the NRSVue translation.

it is not going anywhere. In the so-called West alone, centuries of critique, speculations about secularization and post-secularization, societal and demographic changes, and postmodern disillusionment have not done away with theology, nor will the work of the critic achieve that in the future. The question therefore is not *whether* we need theology or whether we could just as well do without it. The question is *which* theologies will be operative and *to what uses* they will be put.

This is not to say that theology will save the world, or even make it better. It is to say that all leveling to the ground or rebuilding itself also has implicit or explicit theological shapes that might be subjected to analysis and discernment. How do we live in these ruins, if not by attending to their distinctly theological formation? What can we rebuild from the rubble? Can we at least remove some of the theological bullets that have been shot at people and are bleeding them out? In which theological swords may we recognize repurposed plowshares, and which devices of war might we yet be able to turn into instruments of peace?

Theology? But what is even meant by *theology* here? The litanies above do not exclusively point to reflective systems of belief in the scholarly or disciplinary sense of that word. They certainly are not all explicitly laid out in dogmatic treatises, nor do they necessarily remain within what Western Protestantism has considered sound doctrine. But if theology is concerned with God and with the shape of the relationship between God, self, and world, then a lot of cultural formations and political commitments contain implicit assumptions that are distinctly theological and might benefit from explicit forms of theological reflection.

People are always already engaged in articulating these implicit theologies in words and deeds, in practices and habits, in conversation and conflict with those around them. Implicitly or explicitly, they wrestle with assumptions and experiences, with conflicting interpretations and ambiguous implications, and often articulate their own position over and against other implicit theologies in a deliberate attempt to mitigate what they perceive to be "bad theology." They do so through practical demonstrations, performances and liturgies, through textual reasoning and faithful inquiry, through verbal, emotional or physical violence, through reflections on practice and culture, through apologetic or ecumenical, polemical or irenic conversation across difference, and, *sometimes*, even through methodologically disciplined scholarship. The shape of the life of any person expresses and generates, implicitly or explicitly, distinct beliefs about God, self, world, and the shape of their relationship—and these beliefs in turn have real effects on our being in the world, for better or worse; they *matter* not only existentially and spiritually but also materially, ethically, politically, culturally, and ecologically.

Theology is thus not the domain of a distinct professional class or educational elite but done by all who pursue *better* understanding, clarification,
reflection, and critique. Alongside the "priesthood of all believers" that the
Reformers claimed, we might thus also postulate a common "theologianhood" to which neither baptism nor a confession of faith marks a determinate
threshold. But there are also those persons who make the examination of the
theological dimension of our existence their vocation. The Reformers conceived the relationship between the priesthood of all believers and ordained
ministry as a division of labor that allows for a more focused, educated, and
reflective proclamation of the Word, and more intentional administration of
sacraments. We might also conceptualize the relationship between a general
theologianhood and professional theologians as such a division of labor: some
people specialize in asking these questions intentionally and intensively, invest
time and resources to train for this purpose, and sustain this inquiry over significant periods of their lives.

The professional theologian thus does not own theology. The professional
theologian is merely the person who comes late to a conversation that is
already going on. That person's work will partly attempt to make an intervention in ongoing conversations, partly engage in meta-observation about these
conversations, partly catch up on its minutes, partly attempt to fine-tune and
restructure such conversations, moderating escalating arguments and misunderstandings and doing the kind of damage control that will allow them to sustain the conversation. The professional theologian is the person who devotes
time and training to explicit reflection on how to do theology *well*—even as
what that means might be subject to debate.

We? In my claim that *we need better theology*, the "we" is thus twofold. In
one sense, this book arises out of the firm conviction that the world at large
is affected by all sorts of bad theology and needs, deserves, and longs for *better* theology. Maybe this is true even of God: regardless of where we stand on
divine passibility, even God might deserve, and crave, *better* theology. In this
sense, the aim of the book is as broad as can be.

But both the road this book sketches and the audience with which it con-
verses are much narrower than "God and the world." After all, it is not my
intention to save the world, or to save it alone. The ambition to save and be
the savior is but another iteration of bad theology, as is the ambition of the
comprehensive scope. Many who should be in this conversation remain unaddressed, and much that needs to be said is not articulated here. Others will be
better able to make these other kinds of interventions, address these other audiences, and say these other things. I believe, however, in local responsibility.

One of the possible "we"s in need of better theology are thus the (professional) theologians. "We need better theology" is then not a grandiose claim

but rather the self-conscious utterance that those of us whose professional role it is to tend to the shape of theology need to do *better* in light of its haunted and haunting state. But even such doing better is not for our own, the professional theologians', sake at the end of the day. Instead, it asks what is demanded of us where we stand, for the sake of God and the world.

Better? The aspiration toward a *better* theology, too, might sound optimistic, defiant, or even self-assuredly triumphant—but it is intended as a simple comparative, relative to wherever we find ourselves. I am wholeheartedly convinced of the necessity to fight bad and death-dealing theologies, and equally convinced that theology has something better to offer. I am, however, for reasons that will become clearer soon, quite skeptical of our ability to perform the exorcism Garcia calls for, and to achieve "good theology."

The Christian language of salvation and repentance that has surfaced throughout this section is not a rhetorical one: At the heart of my argument lies the conviction that sin affects the work of the theologian as it does all human enterprises. The theologian is not alone in such a diagnosis. Critical theorists like Adorno and Horckheimer famously also maintain that "there can be no right life in the wrong one."[4] While *metanoia* is always needed, it can never be "achieved" once and for all but is a perpetual movement in which all of Christian life, including the work of the theologian, unfolds. Justification and sanctification are ongoing; they can never become a linear progress or simple progression, let alone reach perfection.

The call to do *better theology* emerges from the insight into bad theology while recognizing that theology will never be perfect and maybe not even unequivocally good. The question can never be, What is the *right* theology? or even How does one do theology *rightly*? Nor is "better" here meant to indicate an essential quality, rather, it is a relational and comparative one. Never determined once and for all times, it can only be discerned contextually. Instead of trying to achieve "good theology"—whether as "correct" theology in correspondence with the truth, or as methodologically justified "rightly done" theology, or as ethically perfected "morally excellent" theology—Garcia's call reorients us to start with and attend to problematic effects. Instead of attempting to do justice to dominant methodological standards of orthodoxy or orthopraxy, we might ponder: Maybe it is the theology that is not doing justice to reality—neither to the divine reality it purports to testify to, nor to the human reality of actually living people. Maybe adherence to method does not get us closer to the truth or to justice, to union with God or to community with one another. Maybe we ought to seek specific, limited, local improvement for

---

4. Theodor W. Adorno, trans. E. F. N. Jephcott, *Minima Moralia: Reflections from Damaged Life* (London: Verso, 2010), 42, translation adapted.

specific ills, rather than delude ourselves in striving for the perfect form or perfect content. This wrestling marks the book.

At the end of the day, this is therefore less a book on theological method than a book on the ethics of doing theology *after method*—a call for "doing better" even as we know we will never "be good." Nevertheless, recognizing our sin and in gratitude for grace, we are called to "go forth and sin no more" (John 8:11) wherever the insight into a particular sin has dawned.

ACCIDENTAL THEOLOGY:
LESSONS FROM UNBELONGING

Theology always emerges out of concrete experiences, and much theological insight happens to us by accident. A theological term for this might be "grace." The variation of "We need better theology" that I was handed when I started teaching at Princeton Theological Seminary (PTS) was the charge "We need a better *Intro to Theology* course." It quickly became clear to me and the colleague who were charged with this task that in the face of longstanding division and discontent in the department, the implicit task was to *do better*.

Known as a bulwark of faithful Reformed Theology, PTS is more recently aspiring to be a progressive spearhead and training ground for people far beyond the Presbyterian Church (U.S.A.). The department had a long history of fervent disagreement and hard-baked divisions between different claims to the "right" theology, both within approaches and between "doctrinal" theology and "cultural" theology, between "historical" and "constructive," between "dogmatic" and "political" approaches. For more than a decade, several attempts to redesign the introductory course had led to nothing but further divisions. It had also added considerable confusion to the students whenever two co-teaching professors flatly contradicted one another or openly denounced each other's approaches as wrong. I have heard several accounts of de-conversions not just from the faith but also from a vocation to theology of those who got caught between the fronts: taken aback by the polemical and combative discursive culture they encountered, and disabused by professional gatekeepers of the calling they felt to intellectual work, these students were eventually deprived of their desire to seek deeper understanding in theological inquiry.

As my colleague and I envisioned a new introductory course, we knew that any adaptation of the existing syllabi would only lead to more turf wars—who had now gotten their way, who had gained or lost ground. So, instead, we started from scratch. One of the first things we implemented was an initial reflection paper, in which the students reflected on the understanding of theology with which they arrived at Princeton: what they understood theology to be and do, and in what ways they were already part of theological conversations. Across the responses, two things stood out. First, the majority of students were absolutely baffled by (and slightly panicking over) the prompt to think of themselves as active practitioners of theology. Second, a significant number of students had strongly negative associations with the term theology: it stood for something rigid and judgmental, or something abstract and academic, in either case, something both intimidating and alienating. These associations obviously were not caused by our local feuds. They had more to do with a broader perception of theological culture that students seemed to share across diverse geographical, educational, and denominational backgrounds.

Their responses caught *me* by surprise. This was, after all, a cohort of seminarians, and *Princeton* seminarians at that: in short, highly qualified, highly motivated graduate students, self-selected and admissions-curated, all faithful, professing Christians, passionate about serving God and the world, and seeking study and training to equip themselves for such work. How could it be that for so many of them, the term "theology" itself engendered only negative images, and that most of them felt uneasy with being identified as theologians?

Diving further into their responses suggested layers of answers. Many of these young people associated "theology" with things that had actively hurt and scarred them or their communities: women had been told they could not use their gifts to serve in the ways they felt equipped, queer and trans folx had had their desires and identities denounced as sin, people of color had had their experiences and perspectives denied, first-generation academics had experienced theology as a realm of class privilege and gate-keeping. Beyond these experiences, there was a widespread perception that theology was theoretical and academic—not simply abstract and irrelevant to live issues, but actively hostile to people who did not have the correct answers, did not speak the right language, and, scandalously, were *asking questions*.

In response to such experiences, students felt acutely that theology was not *for them* in at least a twofold sense: It did not invite them to participate in its endeavor but actively excluded them, and it did not offer them anything life-giving, illuminating, or rewarding. At the same time, these very students were wrestling deeply with theological interpretations of their experience, their churches, and their Scriptures—they just did not see this work as "doing theology," let alone understand themselves as theologians.

Increasingly, I came to recognize, in the sentiments among my students and in the divisions of my guild, the characteristics of a good family fight in which everyone is always losing. And yet, in these same tensions I also strangely found myself. Strands that had long been disjointed in my own formation and my own biography suddenly stood in such stark contrast that, paradoxically, I began to reconcile them for the first time.

Long before I ever read a theological book in my life, I was formed in a theology that I only learned to spell out, put into technical terms, and associate with particular schools of thought much later. While such is true for seemingly everyone, this is the shape this in-formation took for me:

As a child, I grew up in the tumultuous heart of Caracas, Venezuela, and as a young adult, I worked in the barrios of the Gran Buenos Aires in grassroots organizations loosely shaped by a militant liberationist Catholicism. Before I had ever parsed Luther's "justification by faith through grace alone," I had seen the futility of righteousness and the failure of works. I knew the violence and agony that myth inflicts on those who experience themselves as "unable" to "make it." Before I studied colonial history, I knew the brutal footprint the church had left on the Americas and of the complicated complicity of salvation and domination. Long before I was familiar with the concepts of Liberation Theology, I felt in my bones that a loving God cannot be satisfied with promising spiritual or transcendent peace, but aches and groans for justice and flourishing of all people in this life. Long before I had read Barth's Romans commentary, I knew that only a God who was *totaliter aliter* could save the world and that any grace worth its name necessitated a whole lot of judgment to set things right.

Were these what, with Juan Luis Segundo, I would later learn to call "pre-theological commitments,"[5] emerging from my personal relationships with people who lived at the margins of global neoliberal capitalism, a commitment that there must be something more for them? Would these pre-theological commitments later simply set me up for alignment with certain theological positions over others? Or was my experience deeply informed by implicit theologies that had trickled down from dogmatic conceptions through teaching and preaching and become habits of mind, hermeneutic lenses, and practices of solidarity of the ecologies and communities that shaped my understanding? Or had I simply stumbled upon the same fallenness of the world, the same need for redemption, and the same grace of God that theologians in all ages have recognized in diverse expressions and simply formulated in different ways?

But why think of these interpretations as mutually exclusive? If we are serious about the God we profess, then there can be no pre-theological experience; at most, there may be a pre-*theologized* experience, always already experience of and in and with God's world, its unredeemed shape as well as its glimpses of salvation. And if we are serious about the God we profess, then doctrine, on the other hand, is not an abstract self-contained truth about eternal states but speaks about the world as it really is. Nor can it be unidirectionally operative

5. Juan Luis Segundo, *Liberation of Theology* (Maryknoll: Orbis, 1976), 39.

from theology to reality, as if theology was there first to then be applied to real life. It always emerges out of concrete experiences of misery and grace in the world, articulates their interpretation, and needs to remain legible and re-translatable as such.

From my own experiences, I knew in my gut that theology *mattered*—for better and for worse, that theological differences make a difference, and that different experiences engender different theologies. On the one side, I saw how, defiantly or quietly, a fierce spirituality drove the community organizers I worked with—most of them themselves illiterate, uneducated, and living in extreme poverty—in their work to not only survive but also to build movements with and for others and to build a better future that they might never live to see. Did their belief sustain them in the face of the everyday grind, disappointment, betrayal, violence, and historical hopelessness? Or did their experience somehow fund this stubborn faith and the commitment to a wholly other God who was wondrously at work in the vulnerable life all around them? On the other side, I balked at how the church hierarchy in Argentina had been hopelessly complicit in the dictatorship. Had their theology not protected them from the seductions of power and fear, or had their privileged position generated a theology that justified it, even saw in their survival a greater good over the lives that they abandoned and betrayed? In any case, theology *mattered*: It was part of the differences that made a difference, for better or for worse.

What drove me to study theology, then, was a desire to understand more clearly that mattering, as well as to understand why it could take so widely divergent shapes in roughly the same context as well as convergent expressions across different experiences. I knew I could read up on historical, political, sociological, cultural backgrounds, but I needed the discipline of theology, as reflection about God and the world and everything in between in their interconnectedness, to make sense of this reality at large. I needed theology as a grammar of faith to better articulate the reality, convictions, and commitments from which I came. And I needed theology as critical normative intervention to be able to speak back to them, to have a word to offer them, to find resources with which to confront these realities, to resist them and . . . to change them.

And, roughly speaking, this is still how I understand the intellectual practice of doing theology in an academic setting: as the specific movement of parsing out, articulating more precisely, and critically reflecting on the shape and the meaning of the relationship between God and the world that is *already there*, and of the words and images that people are *already* employing to describe it. One may associate this movement with the traditional vision of *fides quaerens intellectum*, or a "making it explicit." At the same time, that parsing out, organizing, and reflecting also serves a specific pedagogical and preparatory function: to understand something better that will then be put to use in practice. The aim of understanding lived theological interpretations better will also identify needs for clarification and intervention and prepare for the same. One may associate this movement with the traditional vision of theology as a *scientia practica*, or a "making it implicit" once more, forming understanding into practices, habits, and frames of mind.

I started studying theology because I wanted to go into ministry, to make a concrete difference in the world. I came from community organizing and went straight to classes in Hebrew Bible and Practical Theology because of the prophetic traditions and because of concrete skills in which I was interested. From there, I was drawn to doctrine, because I became intrigued in the nuances of what those texts and practices witnessed to, how it all made sense, how it all belonged together. From there, I migrated further to what the Germans called *Fundamentaltheologie*, i.e., something like the philosophy of science for theology, and what in the English-speaking world is often summarized under the vague term "theological method." What prompted this move to further abstraction was the increasing need to reflect more deeply out of a desire to be able to do theology *better*.

As my trajectory went from practical questions to more theoretical territory and yet the next meta-level, I accidentally became a theologian. I say accidentally, because I had never set out to make theology a career, I had always considered theology as a resource for a practice, a language and imaginary of this practice, an equipment and preparation for a practice. But I discovered that *doing theology* itself was also a practice—an intellectual practice of doing things with words, with mental images, with texts, with traditions, with experiences, with cultures.

I fell in love with the practice of doing theology, the textual discernment and reasoning, the wrestling with critical questions, the development of thought in conversation, and, most importantly, the teaching: accompanying people who wanted to make a difference on the ground in people's lives, equipping them to articulate their experience in theological terms, and in turn to be able to *use* theology to speak back to their experience. Even so, my movement into further abstraction perfectly embodied the systematic, the theoretic, and the meta, and I became a professional theologian. And as such I discovered that there was not only a need to theorize for *better* practice, there was also a need for a *better* practice of theory, in order to do reality justice, both practically and theoretically, ethically and epistemically.

I began my academic study of theology in West Germany in the 2000s. The formation I received there somehow made quite different explicit connections from the ones with which I had arrived from my lived experience of theological communities in Argentina. They were so different that I (much like my students later at Princeton Theological Seminary) did not see them as participating in the same conversation, nor did I think of contrasting them as distinct theological styles or approaches. This possibility only surprised me in hindsight, much later.

In the West German academic context, the systematic paradigm of doing theology reigned supreme. Other, more "engaged," more "contextual," or more "experiential" approaches were eyed as latently or manifestly ideological, as more interested in justice or ethics than in truth, and thus ultimately "less academic" and "not sufficiently theological." Indeed, "the theological" was practically identified with the systematic method, and detached, "objective" reasoning with scholarly rigor.

In my formal theological training, I was taught that any passion for justice and social change was works-righteousness (the utmost heresy from a Lutheran perspective!) and that concern for the ultimate has to relativize and override any penultimate concerns, lest the latter become idolatries. I was taught that, yes, bad things had happened in the history (and present) of the church, but that these bad things were *abuses* of theology or a *lack* of theology in the first place. Such bad consequences therefore were "downstream" consequences of being *insufficiently* theological. Theology determined practice, not the other way around, and it was impossible for good theology to have bad consequences.

Theology obviously mattered here, but the guild assumed that one had to start with theology, and get it right, and that then all else would follow. The concern for practice, for implications, for consequences was often suspect—an ideological trap that would lead to projection *upstream*, and thus result in bad theology. If there was an alternative to such rigorous systematic theology, it could not consist in engaged scholarship, but only in something even more "meta," more "objective," supposedly less ideological because even less committed to the dogmatic content it studied: the historical approach to theology that confined itself to reconstructing rather than being constructively involved in the theological grammar. From that vantage point, even the commitment to the faith of the church, let alone to the existence of the God it proclaimed, would seem naive and unscientific.

On the other hand, despite the relative aloofness of twenty-first-century German theology, I was aware that strongly engaged theologies existed: liberation theologies, feminist theologies, post- and decolonial theologies, and queer theologies. But in turn it seemed as if such "contextual" approaches had nothing but disdain for systematic theology: denouncing it as not only complicit in systems of oppression but also hopelessly their product, their mouthpiece, and their puppet. I found myself time and again deeply resonating with both their critiques and with their practical investments, which I perceived as fundamentally driven by *theological* concerns and insights. I also found myself grieving that no small number of these latter approaches actively distanced themselves entirely from doctrinal commitments.

Ironically, it was only at Princeton Theological Seminary, a flagship seminary of the Reformed tradition with a reputation for academic rigor, an institution that prided itself on seamlessly integrating "faith and scholarship," and a "Reformed and Ecumenical" identity, that for the first time I was able to articulate my two histories—my formative experiences and my academic education—as one. Here I felt the tensions between both "sides" so acutely, here the wars between different approaches were so existential, and here I found myself weirdly so alone time and again identifying with both "sides" concurrently, that I counterintuitively gave up trying to make sense of their manifest, hostile, and live divisions, decided to give up trying to "get it," and decided instead to focus on the "doing" of theology—despite the theologians.

I confess that to this day I do not understand the distinction and division between liberation theology and systematic theology. I do not understand the distinction and division between contextual and doctrinal theology, between constructive and historical theology, or between dogmatics and ethics. I do not understand the distinction and division between practice and theory that the guild both celebrates as a hallmark of rigor and practitioners in the church lament.

This book, then, presents my deliberate refusal to understand the distinctions and divisions that all sides have tried to teach me for so long. I have given up trying to understand them. In fact, I no longer desire to understand them. Instead, I insist on reading them together. I take my legitimation from a resolute theological realism: If God is real, and if this is God's world, these divergent and often conflicting fields can only be different responses to that same reality, different testimonies to it. At worst: mutual misunderstandings. At best: a division of labor.

This refusal to understand the divisions grows out of my experiences of unbelonging throughout my life: existentially committed to, but not firmly rooted in, appreciative of but not identifying with any of the places, the schools of thought, the genders, the cultures I have traversed, having found in all of them great value and insight, yet in none of them my origin or destination, my happiness or my home. This book, then, embarks on an exercise in deliberate, even strategic misunderstanding out of faithfulness to this shared reality and out of commitment to do the kind of theology that *matters*.

I did not only become a theologian by accident, I also wrote this book by accident. In summer 2020, I was invited by an international journal to contribute an article on the nature and the task of theology for its anniversary edition. As I started writing, the frustration of the state of the field, the insight from my colleague's and my wrestling to design a better introductory course for our students, and the disjointed bits and pieces of my own theological biography suddenly started to coalesce. I began articulating my conviction that we are always already engaged in doing theology, and that much depends on doing theology in such a way that it makes room for the suffering, wrestling, and joy of real people in their concrete experiences, and in such a way that it makes space for grace. When I had written the first 30,000 of the 5,000 words assigned, I realized that this was more than an article. This would need to become a book.[6]

Maybe it is deeply ironic that out of frustration with methodological divides, I would add another book on method, against method. Maybe my attempt to bridge systematic and liberationist theology, theological and ethical commitments, Reformed and queer trajectories will make little sense to anyone but me, and the attempt to speak in "both" of these languages will result in alienation from both. But maybe I am not the only one who is dissatisfied with these disciplinary divisions, who is not able to make their home in any paradigm or method because important things immediately slip out of sight, and who is haunted by the feeling that in all their differences, these approaches point to a shared reality and wrestle with it in their own ways. Maybe I am not the only one who is restless and longing for a different kind of theology, one that would stop being overly concerned with method, and instead attend to the questions that *matter*. If that happens, I would not consider it an accident. I would consider it grace.

UN/JUST METHOD: HOW DO WE KNOW . . . CHRIST?

What does it mean to know God? *"Hoc est Christum cognoscere, beneficia eius cognoscere"*[7] ("to know Christ means to know Christ's benefits") was Philipp Melanchthon's claim in his *Loci Communes*, the first "Systematic Theology" in the sense of the modern genre, and, incidentally, the first proposal of theological method in the Reformation.[8]

---

6. Chapters 1, 2, 3, 7, 8 of this book expand the sketch in Hanna Reichel, "Conceptual Design, Sin and the Affordances of Doctrine," *International Journal of Systematic Theology* 22, (2020): 538–61.

7. Philip Melanchthon, *Commonplaces: Loci Communes 1521* (Saint Louis: Concordia, 2014).

8. Melanchthon himself called his *Loci* "mea methodus," Philipp Melanchthon, *Opera Quae Supersunt Omnia*, ed. Karl Gottlieb Bretschneider, CR 1 (Halle: Schwetschke, 1834), 366. Luther also referenced the book as such: *"Methodus tua gratissima est; nihil est, quod mea penuria tuas opes hic moneat; prospere procede et regna,"* Martin Luther "Nr. 428 Luther and Melanchthon. Wartburg,

In his introduction, Melanchthon cautions against speculation about the nature of God. It is through his works that Christ is known, through the benefits he imparts to us, through the use to which he is put. Only by understanding how Christ benefits us are we able to articulate both grace and sin, only from there to draw out true knowledge of God and of the human being, and only from there can insights into the nature of Christ and the nature of God be formulated. Melanchthon's programmatic dictum became a shibboleth of Protestantism.[9] Barth judged,

> With particularly painful clarity we are faced here by the rift which divides the Evangelical Church. Those who are at loggerheads here can neither understand nor convince one another. They not only speak another language; they speak out of a different knowledge. They not only have a different theology; they also have a different faith.[10]

Should theology be fundamentally concerned with who God *is* in Godself or with what God has done *for us* in history? Should Christology be done "from above" or "from below"? Is the primary purpose of theology *noetic* or *ethical?* These questions signal some of the variations the rift has taken in the meantime, running through debates as diverse as the ones between Erasmus von Rotterdam and Martin Luther,[11] between Rudolf Bultmann and Karl Barth, and, in our day, between doctrinal and liberationist theologies.

The tragedy of the divide is, of course, that it is false—both ontologically and epistemically speaking. Both "sides," respectively, have typically asserted its falsity—maintained that who God is *is* no other than God for us, that the work of Christ is no other than who Christ *is*, that the economic Trinity *is* the immanent Trinity. Both sides have also maintained that Christ is definitive for our knowledge of God and for our knowledge of ourselves, i.e., that who God is *is* revealed in Christ's work for us. What remains as divisive is the order in which different parties want to read the equation, its sequence or direction, in other words: What has divided theologians is the question of *how to proceed*: theological method.

---

9 September 1521," In *WAB 2 (1520–1522)*, ed. Joachim Karl Friedrich Knaake, 382–87, (Weimar: Böhlaus, 1931), 382: 3–4.

9. Cf. the very informative study by Jan Bauke-Ruegg, "'Hoc est Christum cognoscere beneficia eius cognoscere': Melanchthons 'Loci Communes' von 1521 und die Frage nach dem Proprium reformatorischer Dogmatik. Ein Lektüreversuch." *Neue Zeitschrift für Systematische Theologie und Religionsphilosophie* 42, no. 3 (2000).

10. Karl Barth, *Church Dogmatics I.1: The Doctrine of the Word of God*, ed. G. W. Bromiley and T. F. Torrance (Edinburgh: T&T Clark, 1936), 425.

11. Wilhelm Maurer, "Melanchthons Anteil am Streit zwischen Luther und Erasmus," *Archiv für Reformationsgeschichte* 49, (1958): 89–115.

The insistence on the direction of the reading is not trivial. Much is at stake, because much can go wrong. In any given variation of this conflict, both sides have seen fundamental theological commitments endangered by the one-sidedness of the respective other. But what if we read Melanchthon's *Hoc est* as strictly pointing to the epistemic *site* of theology: the incarnate word of God in Christ, which as such is both God's self-revelation (who God is) *and* good news (what God is for us)? The starting point itself thus already includes a bi-directional definition, and bi-directional consequences. Only by knowing Christ are we able to recognize his benefits. But also, it is from Christ's work that we see who Christ really is. Only by knowing Christ and the grace found in him are we able to understand our own situation of misery and sin. But also, our experiences of misery and grace are what points us to Christ. Only by knowing Christ are we able to talk about who God the Father and the Spirit are. But also, our Trinitarian theology allows us to delineate properly what we see happening in Christ.

In Melanchthon's own theology we can observe an intricate web of mutual, and at times "irritating identifications"[12] of different theological touch points and insights with one another, raising the question whether all of theology is ultimately only tautology and rhetoric. This, however, is precisely where the *beneficia Christi* develop their force: functioning as the one concrete, irreducible anchoring point of theological reflection. They are where heaven touches earth, and thus the starting point, end point, and point of return of all theological reflection. "Knowing Christ through his benefits" thus describes the core of the knowledge to which Christian theology points.

But *how* do we know Christ and his benefits? Of course, this is again where theological approaches differ. By reading and interpreting the Scriptures, say some. By experiencing the grace of Christ in our lives, say others. Both of these are important routes. Without in any way challenging either of them or their necessary conspiration, this book takes a different route. It looks at theological method. More precisely, it looks at the issues that ensue when theology tries to establish itself by way of method, and it tries to draw out the precise shape of these problems theoretically and theologically. Rather than trying to deduce an "adequate" method from the subject matter of theology—which ultimately means presupposing a certain theology, deducing a method from it, by way of which we then reinforce the presupposed theology—I will look at the problems that ensue when we try to establish one. Rather than investigating christological claims directly, we look at the conditions of the possibility of our knowledge on the ground, or rather, as it will turn out, at the factual disarray of such pursuit.

---

12. Bauke-Ruegg, "Hoc est Christum cognoscere," 288–90.

I then ask what these findings imply, theologically. By investigating the shape of epistemological issues, the book thus takes an explicitly anthropological, even anthropopragmatic approach: It starts with the human being and the conditions under which we attempt to gain knowledge, rather than with God. Its wager, however, is that if the *beneficia Christi* are real, they will not simply solve our problems at the end of the day, but they have always already responded to the condition in which we find ourselves. Thus, those benefits will already assert themselves in the shape of the problem that we draw out. In short, the wager is that at the end of this epistemological, anthropological road, something like an implicit Christology will come into view. Rather than presupposing that we know who Christ is and what the nature of Christ's benefits are, we will trust that examining in depth the shape of the problems as they present themselves to us—while not giving us a complete account of Christ by any means—will nonetheless give us an inverse shadow image of the *solus Christus* that the Reformation has asserted.

Some more clarifications are in order. First, on terminology. Throughout this book, I use the language of "Systematic Theology" and "Constructive Theology." I understand these terms not as descriptions, much less as definitions of differing approaches, and more as the discursive *framing devices* as which these terms function in a lot of contemporary discussions to categorize existent theological approaches according to main theological and epistemic commitments and resultant methodological frameworks. At least in the European, USian, and Latin American theological contexts I have inhabited, the categories of "Systematic Theology" (or "doctrinal theology," "dogmatics," "classical theology" etc.) and "Constructive Theology" (or "Liberation(ist) Theology," "Contextual Theology," etc.) function as boundary drawings: positively identifying main commitments that characterize a given theological approach and negatively marking an "other" who thereby is denounced as "not sufficiently theological" or "not sufficiently critical," respectively. Definitions might characterize the one as primarily "truth-seeking," the other as primarily "justice-seeking"; the one as primarily indebted to the doctrinal tradition of creeds, confessions and theological deliberation of confessional churches, the other as primarily indebted to the contextual experiences and struggles of particular communities; the one as primarily organizing faith-claims into rationally defensible systems, the other as primarily disrupting dominant structures with subjugated knowledges.

These categories are types at best, and caricatures at worst. Even as many theological approaches would identify themselves strongly with one or the other term, many—and I would say, the *better*—versions of "both" would understand these two sets of commitments and concerns to not be mutually exclusive and indeed rather intertwined. Throughout this book, I attempt to demonstrate that the *best* versions of what is typically considered "Systematic Theology" and the best versions of what is typically considered "Constructive Theology" can come to remarkably similar insights about the shape of truth and justice, and can function as allies to each other in their pursuit. I am not saying that they necessarily do or have to, only that it is possible for them to work this way, and that personally, I find doing so to be mutually beneficial in service to the project of "better" theology.

Throughout the book, I will thus use the terms "Systematic Theology" and "Constructive Theology" strictly and strategically to frame "types" for heuristic and diagnostic purposes—not to give a nuanced or accurate account of any individual actually existent position. My wager is that doing so will help identify the particularities of different theological *epistemes* operative within different theological methodological frameworks. To remind the reader of this typological rather than descriptive use, I capitalize "Systematic Theology" and "Constructive Theology."

In order to traverse the width of the divide, I choose such main interlocutors as will typically be conceived as exclusively representing one "side" with even a significant hostility against the other. Karl Barth and Marcella Althaus-Reid figure as exemplars of the systematic and constructive commitments in doing theology, respectively. Presumably, both would object to this categorization, but as per common practice, dead authors do not get a say with regard to the conversations in which they participate. They are chosen not so much as "representatives" of Systematic Theologians and Constructive Theologians, but because both distinguish themselves by a reflexive, self-critical deployment of the respective paradigm as well as a certain levity (which their respective followers often curiously lack): Their complete commitment to their *Sache* at the same time gives them all the liberty of not taking themselves or their method too seriously.

With his monumental and authoritative oeuvre, Karl Barth represents one of the pre-dominant dogmatic "systems" of Western theology. Barth's theology is marked by his firm but not uncritical commitment to the Scriptures, by a thorough appreciation and engagement with the history of doctrine in the ecumenical church, its creedal and doctrinal consensuses, and by a Christocentric commitment which allows him to reorganize a lot of the language he has inherited in "reforming" ways. Importantly, he is a theological "realist"—and critical of theological idealism as idolatry (primarily identified in the elevation of religious experience). His theology is thus decidedly post-critical: It takes the major modern critiques of epistemology and religion into account and even radicalizes them—the intellectual critique of Kant, Hegel, Feuerbach, as well as the existential, political, and theological disillusionments with modernity in the wake of World War One. As such, Barth's Systematic

Theology is rather post-systematic than pre-modern. It continues to function as a theological "grammar" in many branches of Protestantism and beyond.

In its scandalous irreverence, Marcella Althaus-Reid's critique of theology's dominational entanglements continues to be one of the most critical intersectional proposals in Constructive Theology. Her queer-feminist, materialist, decolonial intervention is equally indebted to and critical of liberation and feminist theologies, expanding and radicalizing them in decisive ways. Marked by a syncretistic mix of high theory, folklore, and sexual storytelling "from below," her radical critique of dominant theologies is always in service of liberation—queer and indigenous people's as much as God's own. Her approach is thus similarly post-critical and committed on the constructive side as Karl Barth's is on the systematic one. I therefore lift the two of them up as standing for the best work the respective "types" have to offer, striving to demonstrate how, despite obvious and undeniable differences, the contrived types are not antagonistic projects.

In line with its primary commitment to coherence and unity, the Systematic side will primarily be represented by one theological system, namely constructed from within Barth's theology and the theology of the Reformation he adopts. In line with its primary commitment to experience and struggle, the Constructive side will be better represented by a variety of voices than by a single interlocutor. A less unified archive will serve to contribute important insights and invectives on the Constructive side, with particular attention given to interlocutors from (post-)Liberationist theology and queer theory—without any pretension or aspiration that they should individually or collectively represent the Constructive "side," just like Barth obviously cannot speak for Systematic Theology at large.

Importantly, I will read both Barth and Althaus-Reid, both the Systematic and the Constructive, both the doctrinal and the queer approach, as deeply rooted in a theological realism and pursuing decidedly *theo*logical projects, that is, as speaking of (1) the scandalous reality of the wholly other God, (2) the true humanity of the human being, and (3) the relationship between them. I will read both of them as attempting to speak truth by doing justice to these realities. Construing a common ground this way will allow to better distinguish the different scientific epistemes with differing frameworks of accountability and theological "quality control."

This book, then, is written from a dual commitment: to the reality to which Systematic Theology at its best tries to witness, and to the reality to which Constructive Theology at its best tries to do justice. In short: to God and the world, to both of their stubborn, slippery, challenging realities, to the transcendence and immanence of both. Working toward a *constructive* way of taking such difficulty into account *systematically*, this book, not only in its argument, but even in its structure and its language, will thus perform an experiment, a kind of Feyerabendian wager. Following Feyerabend's studies in the history of science, it will assume that any attempt of doing justice to these realities (whatever that may mean) can only be achieved by *breaking* with method rather than by following it, and that such bold procedure can never be justified in advance, only rationalized in hindsight in light of its insights.[13]

Making "both sides'" contentions against one another my business, this book then is as much a lived Constructive Theologian's as it is a trained Systematic Theologian's self-reflection and self-critique. It assumes and points out the impossibility of doing theology *rightly*—and moves beyond it. Organized as a conversation in two voices—the Systematic-theological, dogmatic, confessional voice, prominently represented by Karl Barth, and the Constructive-theological, queer, decolonial voice, prominently represented by Marcella Althaus-Reid, the book wagers that beyond all their difference, there might be significant overlaps in the theological and material *realities* to which they ultimately testify and to which they are committed, and that in the interference patterns between them, constructive insights might thus emerge. Identifying with central commitments of Systematic and Constructive theological work, respectively, and disregarding their supposed mutual exclusiveness, it draws on the theology of the Reformers as much as on queer critique, and eventually hazards a foray into design theory and philosophy of information. Through a material-historical contextualization of the different paradigms and through a doctrinal assessment of epistemic sin, the redemptive potential of any methodological program is thoroughly called into question. But the recognition that no method may be able to "save" theology does not mean that we cannot do "better" than we are doing at any given time and place. By refusing the appearance of epistemic incommensurability produced by adherence to differing methodological programs, the book harnesses the best insights Systematic and Constructive Theologies have to offer in their mutual critique and gestures toward a "better" theology—one that relies on localized close feedback-loops instead of universal truth-aspirations.

Claiming and drawing out the architectural metaphor operative in both constructive and systematic approaches, the book plays with an understanding of theological work as *conceptual design*, responsibly ordering and structuring given materials for a purpose. A more realistic *adaequatio ad rem* for theology results. On the one hand, such an understanding of theological work heightens the stakes and demands the expansion of theology's critical standards to encompass not only cognitive and logical criteria but also the practical effects

13. Cf. Paul Feyerabend, *Against Method: Outline of an Anarchistic Theory of Knowledge*, ed. Ian Hacking (London; New York: Verso, 2010).

and uses of doctrine in an ethic of affordances. On the other hand, the honesty, humility, and solidarity generated through the failure of method liberates theology to a more playful and tentative cruising of different approaches. Equally demanding and self-relativizing, the resultant ethos is better able to do justice to the reality of the world and the reality of God than doctrinal orthodoxy or methodological orthopraxy.

This book is a book on theological method, or more precisely, an intervention against method on theological grounds. The shared name that a dogmatic and a queer account have for this problem is that of "law." Both approaches develop nuanced accounts of the problem of law and its theological significance. The law that is complicated between the two accounts is method as "law" of theology—a law that indeed quite in keeping with the structure devised by the Reformers can serve in a first "use" to navigate human finitude and curb sin, can secondly function as a mirror of sin that drives the believer into despair, and thus prepares them to accept an external grace that is already there, yet thirdly retains an orienting function in the life of the believers, in sanctification rather than justification.

The book is thus divided into three parts: "Part I: How (not) to get along" examines the epistemic deadlock between Systematic Theology and Constructive Theology, in which they mutually identify one another as "bad theology" according to their different, and ultimately incommensurable, methodological paradigms (chapter 1). A "provincializing" analysis sheds light on their strong reaction as due to constraints and requirements in different epistemic ecologies and puts the two approaches in relative solidarity with one another without resolving their conflicting standards. Their different contextual navigations of the problems presented by divine ineffability and human finitude is both prompted and challenged by the fallenness of theology itself. Marcella Althaus-Reid's indictment of T-theology's decency is complemented by Barth's threefold account of the sin of theology. A *primus usus legis*, or first use of method can be discerned in the disciplining and punitive functioning of mitigating different forms of bad theology in keeping with different epistemic requirements (chapter 2).

"Part II: How (not) to lose hope" takes the reader on a tour through the failure of theological method that drives theologians of both Systematic and Constructive varieties into despair. Structured around Barth's three (impossible) ways of doing theology as sketched in *The Word of God as the Task of Theology*, and drawing on Liberation theology and queer theory for Constructive-theological complements, this part demonstrates how attempts to achieve perfection by way of method can serve as a mirror of sin and either lead into despair or also to the insight of the need for grace—the traditional *secundus usus legis*. Challenged to radical honesty about its own failure to achieve "good theology" and its ongoing and ineradicable complicity in forms of "bad theology," theology has to realize methodically that method cannot save it (chapter 3).

But impossibility is not all there is: Theology always already comes from realities of divine grace and queer holiness, which become revelatory as they resist and exceed its articulations. They prompt a theological realism that takes both sin and grace seriously and follows God's own movement to "become real." Queer grace results in a twofold commitment to the reality of God and the reality of real human beings. It spells out stubborn excess, messy solidarity, and indecent honesty as the queer virtues that obtain when applying the reality principle to faith, love, and hope (chapter 4). Driven by grace beyond despair toward a third use of the law, the distinction between law and gospel—which structures the conception of the book as a whole—is subsequently critically examined and partially redesigned through several interpretive loops on Kafka's parable, *Before the Law,* making use of some helpful metaphors from design theory in the process (chapter 5).

"Part III: How (not) to do better" experiments with theological method *after* method as a kind of *tertius usus legis,* third use of the law. Design theory becomes a particularly fecund interlocutor in my own pursuit as a shared reference between "systems" and their "construction." No longer invested in the attempt to save itself, justify itself, or to conclusively establish its own righteousness, a use of method *after method* is re-oriented to the "outside" of any theory and its "outsiders." Such a queer use may consequently draw on diverse methodologies. It will "cruise" hermeneutical circles without an ultimate commitment to any one of them—recognizing them as means rather than ends, to be used rather than enjoyed in themselves, and aspire to "sideways" rather than "upward" growth (chapter 6). It reflects on the uses of doctrine and its conceptual affordances and investigates several case-studies for constructive conceptual redesign through this lens. It inquires into the possibility of user-oriented hermeneutics, learning from outsiders and "misfits," and allows for the "queer use" of doctrine in remedial practices of repurposing and recycling that might turn swords (like the doctrine of sin, or atonement theology) into plowshares (chapter 7). Finally, it more systematically draws out the resonances between design theory and theology through the central metaphor of conceptual design as the construction of habitats, suggesting the use-orientation of design to guide a method *after method* that is pragmatic and subtle, materially and ecologically grounded, attentive and caring (chapter 8). A conclusion loops back to Paul Feyerabend's epistemic anarchism as well as to the lens of the *beneficia dei* as opened up in the introduction.

PART I

How (not) to get along
(primus usus legis)

Chapter 1

"Bad theology!"?

"THOUGH THIS BE CRISIS, YET THERE IS METHOD IN'T."

What is theology about? God, theologians will typically maintain in one variation or another. Looking at theological discourse, one might however get the impression that the main topic of theology is—theology itself. Instead of talking about God, theologians talk about *how* to talk about God. Instead of exploring the nature of God, time and again they conceptualize the nature of theology: its task and its purpose, its use and its relevance in the world, its method and the state of the field. In short, one might almost get the impression that theology is in some kind of crisis. After all, no one reflects on "the state of" anything unless the state of things is a mess, and no one reflects on "how" to do anything unless how to do it is not intuitively clear.

For starters, Christian theology finds itself in a *crisis of relevance*: The much-belabored decline of mainline churches, shifts in global demographics and power dynamics, the pluralization of the public sphere, the privatization and politicization of religion, along with institutional crises in the churches as well as higher education make it unsurprising that interest in the academic reflection of Christian teaching seems to have waned in recent decades. Under pressure to justify its continued existence under new circumstances, and prompted to reinvent itself, theology turns to method.

Second, Christian theology suffers from a *crisis of identity*. If in the Protestant West theology as an academic field was once defined as "Systematic Theology" and typically subdivided into dogmatics and ethics, these disciplines have now become decentered and complemented by a broad range of other approaches, often characterized as contextual, liberationist, political, constructive approaches. Apart from inner diversification, theology is also facing increasing competition as site of reflection on religious thought and religious histories. If once the West equated religion with "the" Christian religion and academic reflection on it with the faith-based discipline of theology, interest in multiple religious traditions proliferates, and religious studies has become the primary site of their engagement. The discipline thus finds itself under pressure to rearticulate its scope and purpose to gain a sense of control over its diversification, relationships to neighboring disciplines, and divisions of labor.

Third, Christian theology is in a *moral crisis*. From different directions, concerns are being raised about theology's historic complicity in structures of domination and oppression from patriarchy to colonialism. Such critique does not merely constitute an external attack on the discipline's legitimacy, but rather results in feelings of "moral injury": Confronted with the fact that the discipline has been "perpetrating, failing to prevent, or bearing witness to acts that transgress deeply held moral beliefs and expectations," it struggles with shame and guilt, cognitive dissonance and self-consciousness, all of which are "deleterious in the long-term, emotionally, psychologically, behaviorally, spiritually, and socially."[1] The moral crisis further exacerbates the other crises: Whether and how theology's relevance and identity can be restated is complicated by the nagging doubt if theology is a good that *ought* to be saved.

"Systematic Theology is 'bad theology'" could be the in-a-nutshell summary of a prominent form this moral crisis takes today. This charge is substantiated by a broad range of empirical as well as theoretical work in social sciences and cultural studies that point to historical and conceptual links between systematicity's rational, objective, and dispassionate ordering and violence, injustice, and domination. While such interventions, often broadly referenced as "critical theory," might have rather loose genealogical relation to their name-sake Frankfurt School, they share its attention to the functioning of power in its structural effects and reflect on its inextricable role in scientific method. Such critical approaches have drawn attention to evil's bureaucratic order and systematic execution to procedural perfection in the Holocaust; environmental catastrophes in the wake of the Anthropocene's efficient reorganization of ecological habitats for the purpose of extractivism, convenience, and management; to how historical origin accounts and biological taxonomies have produced racialized hierarchies and legitimated dehumanization, enslavement, eugenics, and genocide; to how scientific systematizations of the world have otherized geographic regions, cultures, and nations, marking them

---

1. Brett T. Litz et al., "Moral Injury and Moral Repair in War Veterans: A Preliminary Model and Intervention Strategy," *Clinical Psychology Review* 29, no. 8 (2009): 695–706, 16.

as inferior to Western norms and available for economic exploitation and dispossession; to the epistemically constructed universality of Western knowledge as advancing colonial and imperial aims; to the male subjectivity operative in abstract rationality, and the systemic oppression women experience in patriarchal systems by being cast into normalized gender roles, often with religious legitimation; to cisheteronormative pathologization of sexual minorities and gender-nonconforming bodies as "deviant" from supposedly "natural" (social/biological/divine) order; and to how norms categorize and rank bodily and mental functions of individuals into a disability/ability systems effectively diminishing the full humanity of those perceived as "deficient" by its norms.

Such a motley catalog of grievances does not necessarily imply that systematicity is solely or primarily responsible for any or all of these ills, and what precisely is meant by "systematicity" might need further specification. But to say the least, over a range of disciplines, attention to material effects and epistemic conditionings has highlighted the powerful and ambivalent effects of systematicity. Within theological study, critical reckonings with systematicity, its material effects and epistemological entanglements have thus accompanied the emergence of Black and Latin American Liberation Theologies, of Feminist and Womanist Theologies, of Post-Holocaust Theology and Ecotheologies, of Postcolonial and Decolonial Theologies, of Queer and Crip Theologies, and so on.

As multifaceted and diverse as such critical approaches are, Systematic Theologians often subsume them under labels such as "Contextual Theologies" in light of their commitment to specific communities and their experiences; as "Political Theologies" by virtue of their explicit transformative agendas; or as "Liberation" or "Liberative Theologies" in reference to their commitment to work for justice of oppressed groups and marginalized communities. Such "lumping together" deserves critical scrutiny of its own: It once more engages in systematic ordering with more-than-epistemic effects, effectively relegating those so labeled to a shared periphery vis-à-vis the then unmarked, neutral, objective, and normalized-normative theology of the mainstream center.

Of course, such "lumping together" also works in the other direction, as systematizing approaches to theology might be subsumed under labels like "historical," "classical" or "traditional" theology in light of its dominant position in the past; as "dogmatic" or "doctrinal" theology by virtue of its self-declared subject matter; as "Eurocentric" or "Western theology" in light of its genealogies, and so on. With reference to such discursively antagonistic formations we might thus even outright define Constructive Theology by its critical posture vis-à-vis the viability and legitimacy of Systematic Theology, by its mindfulness of the contextual and actively constructive nature of theological work, including its own, and reflection on the power dynamics involved in doing theological work, including its own. While such a broad definition will generate a wide range of critiques, three distinct yet overlapping charges against Systematic Theology from Constructive Theology, thusly defined, tend to emerge: its unexamined contextual commitments, its systemic complicity, and its bad effects.

In this chapter, I lay out a typical range of criticisms that Constructive Theologies will raise against Systematic Theology, and a typical range of responses from Systematic Theology. Thus sketching out a typology of criticisms and counter-criticisms as they arise from different debates, the exercise serves to demonstrate that the respective invocation to method as criterion of "good theology" is not conducive to constructive conversation and insight, but almost necessarily perpetuates mutual illegibility and apologetic self-immunization and sustains a sense of crisis.

THE HARDCORE NATURE OF DECENCY, OR: SYSTEMATIC THEOLOGY AS "BAD THEOLOGY"

> An Indecent Theology must go further in its disrespect for the inter-pellative, normative forces of patriarchal theology.
> —*Marcella Althaus-Reid*[2]

Its denunciation as "T-Theology" by Marcella Althaus-Reid may be one of the most thorough, pointed, and biting critiques of Systematic Theology. An exemplary proponent of the Constructive Theology "type" for the task at hand, she draws on contextual and marginalized experience and examines the power structures that theology engenders and sanctions. Her queer theology is both in continuity with and criticism of feminist theologies, her postcolonial stance in both continuity with and criticism of liberation theology. In sustained engagement of ideological construction as well as their sexual and economic analyses, Althaus-Reid pays particular attention to the epistemological underpinnings and real-life effects of Systematic Theology while never veering from material engagement into meta-analysis.

It will be apparent to even the most casual reader that Althaus-Reid's Constructive Theology—which she aptly calls "Indecent Theology"—explicitly and unapologetically centers sexuality. But, Marcella Althaus-Reid claims, "[t]here is more to Queer theology than sexuality, because there is more to

---

2. Marcella Althaus-Reid, *Indecent Theology: Theological Perversions in Sex, Gender and Politics* (London: Routledge, 2000), 95.

sexuality than sex."[3] Her provocative opening question whether theology ought to be done with or without underwear starts from the material disconnect between Systematic Theology's idealized accounts of human beings and the indigenous lemon vendors in the streets of Buenos Aires.

A dictum often attributed to Oscar Wilde—another deeply antinomian thinker—sketches in a nutshell the dynamic Althaus-Reid leverages: "Everything is about sex—except sex, sex is about power." The materiality of sexuality is at the center of her attention because it also grounds other relations of power and domination—gendered relations, colonial relations, economic relations, class relations, racialized relations, ecclesial relations of power. When Althaus-Reid presses a "sexual analysis" of theology, it is a matter of discerning how all these relations are structured around sexual hierarchies and sexual logics of exchange. As sex is identified as the undergirding dimension of material existence, of unequal exchange logics, and of power dynamics at large, it has to be critically reflected on "not because Christianity depends on who marries whom or when," but because of the Church's teachings on sexuality betray the "pattern of hierarchical thinking and its structures of power"[4] that underlies much of its doctrinal constructions, as well. By embarking on a "sexual analysis," then, Marcella Althaus-Reid aims *not only* at an analysis of sex but at a comprehensive and critical analysis of *everything—by way of* the sexual lens.

Such ambition explains what would otherwise seem like a wide, less-than-well-defined, and even meandering use of "sex," its meaning ranging across sexual activity and practice, desire and sexual orientation, through the biological materiality of sex, to gender and its performance. In this way, it becomes clear that sex has to do with the ordering of bodies, and not only of bodies: also of desires, of exchange logics, of relationships, of power. At times, it seems difficult to pinpoint where sex "ends." This, of course, is precisely the point: "sex" here is not at all meant to delimit a specific sphere of existence; instead, it aims to address human existence in all its dimensions. As an ordering that is often structured in hierarchical and normative ways, it implicitly touches on broader questions of love and of justice—what is good and what is just. As an ordering that frames and informs material existence, it touches on broader questions of epistemology and ontology—what is true and what is real. And where its ordering includes God in relationship to human beings or deploys God-talk in order to order human relationships, it becomes explicitly theological. Critical examination through the lens of sexuality is thus

3. Marcella Althaus-Reid, "Outing Theology: Thinking Christianity Out of the Church Closet," *Feminist Theology* 27 (2001): 57–67, 67.

4. Marcella Althaus-Reid, "Class, Sex and the Theologian," in *Another Possible World*, ed. Marcella Althaus-Reid, Ivan Petrella, and Luiz Carlos Susin, Reclaiming Liberation Theology (London: SCM, 2007), 31.

warranted in order to understand theology's own complicity in sexual/power dynamics. A "sexual analysis" of theology has much to tell us about its implicit commitments regarding truth, justice, God, reality.

Crucially, sex is not only theologically relevant where it explicitly comes into view, say, as a field of theological ethics among others ("not because Christianity depends on who marries whom or when").[5] Understanding Althaus-Reid this way would miss the epistemological and ontological point of her analysis. The delimitation of something like "sexual ethics" already starts from a ground loaded with presuppositions and assumptions that Althaus-Reid refuses to accept. But hers is also not *merely* a critique of implicit assumptions and their potentially "bad effects," of unavowed sexual/power dynamics in ecclesial and theological structures. Althaus-Reid insists that her interest is indeed also *theological* in the strictest sense.

Sex is about love, and power, and exchange logics; sex is about allowing what is real to be true and about finding grace and freedom in such truth. Therefore, sex has implicitly been about themes at the heart of theology all along, and Althaus-Reid's sexual theology is a committed form of intellectual and material discipleship:

> Let us never forget that lovemaking and working for justice go well together when we are engaged in the real struggle for the *alternative* project of the Kingdom of God, which is a transgressive and pro-vocative project: a Queer Kingdom whose order means a dis-order to heteropatriarchal economics and closeted Christian theology alike.[6]

From such strategically disrespectful self-positioning, Althaus-Reid raises several issues with Systematic Theology. The first is that Systematic Theology has failed to understand the material and epistemological significance of "sex" for theology and thus traditionally excised it from the delimitation of its field. It has thereby not only missed out on important insights regarding sex and sexuality but also on important insights regarding its very objects. Althaus-Reid's radical claim is that a theology that fails to include a sexual material analysis will be *epistemologically unable to get at either the reality of the human being or the reality of God*. Therefore, Althaus-Reid pushes for a truly *realistic theology*—in the full breadth of that term—where taking the true sexual nature of things into account can become an epistemic and material force for truth as well as for liberation, both for God and for the human being.

If the first problem might thus consist in the fact that Systematic, "T-theology" Theology has not been sexual *enough*, since it has not paid explicit

---

5. Althaus-Reid, "Class, Sex and the Theologian," 31.
6. Althaus-Reid, "Outing Theology," 67.

enough attention to sexuality, the second problem is that at the same time, it has been *too* sexual. Ironically, despite (or maybe because of?) its disregard of sexuality, theology has *not* been as sexless or sexually neutral as it presents itself. For all its systematicity, theology has not been systematic enough: It has never systematically reflected on the ways in which unspoken assumptions, sexed hierarchies, and power dynamics manifestly underlie and inform its doctrinal constructions.

In ontological assumptions about sexuality and gender, sex is indeed at work in the constitutive backdrop of theological production and invariably reproduces dominant structures of power. Disavowing its sexual entanglements, marking sex as either completely foreign to its investigation, or else integrating it as merely a subfield of ethics, Systematic Theology has effectively made the de facto existent assumptions unaddressable, moving them beyond critique by moving them beyond articulation. The real power effects have thus remained masked and all-the-more powerful precisely as sex has been denied theological attention. The apparent lack of attention, then, may not be a bug as much as a feature: Althaus-Reid finds the disciplinary episteme as we know it to be the effect of the strategic and systematic disavowal of its own sexual dimension, i.e, its own ordering activity, its oppressively normalizing effects, and its hierarchical structure, with self-reifying effects.

Rather than entering into conversation with what Systematic Theology *says* about God, Althaus-Reid thus looks at what Systematic Theology *does* through a sexual analysis: the material effects on sexed bodies it engenders and the patterns of theologically condoned relationships that are established in real life in effect. From the sexual analysis of what theology *does*, it becomes clear that it not only sexualizes everything but also promotes very specific sexual patterns of unequal relationships as "discourses on power have been systematised, classified and organised in Systematic Theology."[7] Whether it be due to unconscious projection or strategic deployment, sexual hierarchies and logics of exchange organize what is said doctrinally about God and God's relationship to the world. This creates manifest inconsistencies in the Christian message, which go unexamined as long as there is no sexual analysis of theology itself. Because theology disavows sex and presents its substance as being about spiritual rather than material matters, it masks the "indecent" core of what it is *effectively* about. Also in this second sense, then, a more *realistic theology* is necessary: one that examines the all-too-real power structures, assumptions, and effects of theology and their ramifications in the real lives of actually existing people.

Althaus-Reid draws the comparison between Systematic Theology and "softcore" pornography. Softcore porn ostensibly develops a story line, and

---

7. Althaus-Reid, *Indecent Theology*, 23.

pretends as if the recurring sexual activity emerging in its wake is completely incidental and not even worth commenting on. This parallel spells out her critique: Systematic Theology's lack of transparency about its sexual constructions actively conceals the ideologies operative in it, removing them from the surface, from articulation, and from critical engagement. The sexual ramifications of decent, sanitized, de-sexualized doctrine can only be addressed under the threat of shame and self-incrimination. As in softcore pornography, surface "decency,"[8] i.e., decency of form and appearance, of what is explicitly addressed and what is addressable is essential in this construction: It serves both to self-legitimate the surface and to render invisible what is happening in, with, and under the surface discourse. What the production effectively *does* cannot be addressed on the surface of what it *says*.

The formal decency of soft-core porn correlates with the formal apparatus and self-understanding of Systematic Theological method: It unfailingly redirects any critical engagement back to the level of the story (the doctrinal loci) and the apparent requirements of the plot (the systematic structure) as to what will happen next, making it impossible to challenge its logic or even to address what is effectively happening under its guise. In theology and in soft-core pornography, decency thus not only formally renders the discussion well-ordered, it also disciplines where one looks and where one looks away, what comes into view, what can be discussed, and what will be ignored even as one powerfully feels its effects. Decency thus engenders a carefully curated naiveté and innocence at the surface, which in turn produces strategic ignorance as an epistemological effect.

Therefore, those who play by Systematic Theology's rules—this is Althaus-Reid's critique of Feminist and Liberation Theology too—will always end up replicating the same effects without the ability to critically examine them. Precisely by way of its formally decent logic that ensures its legibility and recognition, then, Systematic Theology functions as "a totalitarian construction of what is considered as 'The One and Only Theology'" whose doctrinal truths and their sexual, racial, and political manifestations precede the discussion and thus cannot be disputed.[9] Contrary to appearances, then, theology has never started with a "pure" quest for understanding, with power only coming into play secondarily, or sexual effects only obtaining in practice. Rather, it starts with the material outcomes that have already been preconceived by the ideology, and then exerts power to form an epistemological apparatus that will guarantee the stability of these outcomes. The "pure" doctrinal intellectuality is the carefully constructed effect of veiling its material presuppositions. No

8. Althaus-Reid, *Indecent Theology*, 24.
9. Marcella Althaus-Reid, *The Queer God* (London: Routledge, 2003), 172, fn. 3.

amount of examination of the surface story, however in depth, will get us to the material conditions from which it emerges and which it reproduces.

The full implication of the analogy between Systematic Theology and soft-core pornography goes beyond the insinuation that there are unacknowledged sexual commitments in doctrinal formulations, which, while true, can almost be taken for granted as something that even a casual reading of Christian doctrine and practice would demonstrate. As in the case of softcore porn, the full implication of the analogy is that *both the sex and the theology are bad*. The problem is twofold: (1) as long as theology is not sexual theology, it is not sufficiently *theological*; (2) as long as theology is not sexual theology, it is still about sex, but *uncritically* so, with all kinds of bad effects it cannot address. Only a truly realistic theology—one that attends to the real lives of real human beings rather than their idealized, sanitized, dematerialized versions, and one that explicitly examines the real and material ramifications of theology instead of its ideality—can begin to gesture toward something like a better theology (the possibility of better sex is beyond the purview of this study). The surface—the story, the content that Systematic Theology is ostensibly about—not only *does* things that it does not acknowledge, it also does *not* do what it says it does—namely, in the case of theology, tell us anything true about God. At least, it tells us more about our own desires and projections than it does about divine realities. As in softcore porn, the reality is that the surface story has never been the function nor the organizing logic of what happened in this production, it is at best underdeveloped, at worst a smoke screen. Effectively, then, "theology is not about theology," but about sex, "a sexual ideology performed in a sacralising pattern: it is a sexual divinised orthodoxy (right sexual dogma) and orthopraxy (right sexual behaviour) . . . an arbitrary sexual theory with divine implications."[10] Thus, God has become a function of heteronormative theology and its orthodox decency, a guarantor of the sexual order it promotes and of its unquestionability. The question of who God really is, on the other hand, has been systematically *excluded* from theological consideration. In order to get to this God, the surface story first has to be undone.

Systematicity, Althaus-Reid discerns, constructs a closet. An image from queer experience, the closet signals both imprisonment and concealment, is an existential and an epistemological condition. The closet restricts freedom of movement and articulation as well as understanding. Closeting keeps deviancy from the system's rules out of sight, pathologizes and effectively neutralizes it, and at the same time forecloses the possibility of recognizing the failure and violence of the system. The closet reinforces epistemic predominance, because it conceals that the doctrinal system and reality are not coextensive,

10. Althaus-Reid, *Indecent Theology*, 87.

and that the system is an artificial, active ordering with exclusionary effects rather than an accurate reflection of a supposedly "natural" order of things.

We do not have to read Althaus-Reid's critique as an indictment or ideology critique; we can simply read it as a perceptive account of reality—of what happens in people's lives as an effect of Systematic Theology: Systematic Theology effectively closets everyone who does not fit into a preconceived cisheteronormative identity and performance. Regardless of author intent, theological constructions like hypermasculine God-clouds who have sex with virgins or virginal purity as blueprint for faithful humanity *function* as a matrix of compulsory and highly violent heterosexual decency. But, as Althaus-Reid never fails to remind us, "life is less static than theological systems."[11] Life, as can quickly be seen when examining the sexual lives of the poor, full as they are of promiscuity, precarious relationships, sex work, and all kinds of unfulfilled desires, is marked by the intersection of different kinds of materialities and constraining forces, stubbornly "refuses to fit . . . into different compartments"[12] of any system.

Althaus-Reid presents a thick description of the material reality of the poor in all their folkloric queerness and theological syncretism. She relentlessly demonstrates how the doctrines defended by Systematic Theology invalidate, marginalize, and suppress their experience and render it indecent, turning real life into something that needs to be shamefully hidden, never spoken about, and only lived out behind closed doors. The fact that no one meets this normative order's aspirational standards is a feature, not a bug: Systematic Theology's sexual ideology "makes of every courageous human being a Queer, indecent person,"[13] where everyone is closeted into isolated states of perceived deviancy, an indecency that cannot show itself, moralizing everyone into marginalization, into dependency on forgiveness through the system, and into the epistemological neutralization by way of invisibility.

But Althaus-Reid does not stop at the "bad effects" of Systematic Theology. Even more outrageously, she claims that they are problematic for a thoroughly *theological* reason: They closet *God*, as well. God's nature, abundant and uncontainable by neat and economical categories; God's love, which goes beyond all norms and rationalities; and God's grace, which is indecent in its refusal to mete out according to merit-based logics; all are systematically confined and restricted, normalized and sanitized by Systematic Theology's operation. In light of this analysis, Althaus-Reid provocatively proposes the need for an "Indecent Theology," a theology that refuses to play by the rules

---

11. Althaus-Reid, *Indecent Theology*, 108.
12. Althaus-Reid, *The Queer God*, 2.
13. Althaus-Reid, *Indecent Theology*, 120.

established by Systematic Theology. Its indecency has several layers. There is the obvious surface indecency of its language, its choice of stories and images, its disrespectful and provocatively sexualizing interpretations of doctrine and Christian practice. But that surface indecency—provocative and thought-provoking as it might be—is the least of it. Indecent theology wagers that "what cannot be made indecent in theology is not worth being called theology" lest its doctrinal terms "only have meaning in a determined heterosexual economic system."[14]

Indecent theology is thus an active exercise in in-decenting, out of commitment to God and the world against their heteronormatively restrictive orderings. "Lifting the skirts" of decent theological production and "undressing" the layers of oppression it engenders becomes an epistemic practice that "forces a Soft-Core Porno Theology (namely, Systematic Theology) to assume its real hard-core nature and to come out with the crudeness of its sexual constructions."[15] That is, Indecent Theology shows how "indecent" T-theology's "decency" in reality is—and holds against it the indecently, unorthodoxly real experience of actual people. Strategically disorderly, queer theology uses "de-stabilizing categories because they confront the so-called normality of Systematic Theology with the eyes of the people whose lives are less co-opted into the sexual regulations of the system, and therefore have more possibilities of radical practices reflected in theology, as an art of understanding the sacred in the midst of human relationships."[16] "Indecent" realities—material, non-idealized, honest—thus become both the critical mirror for theology's constructions and serious epistemic resources for that which lies beyond heteronormative and economic orders and power structures, and to which theology ought to be committed.

By indecenting sexual orders, Althaus-Reid's queer version of Constructive Theology performs a kind of critical meta-systematicity: countering the always hegemonic tendency inherent in theological systematicity (or really any positively normative project!) in an all-out effort to liberate both God and the human being from the confining closets by which they are restricted: "Queering theology is the path of God's own liberation, apart from ours, and as such it constitutes a critique to what Heterosexual Theology has done with God by closeting the divine."[17]

This, then, is the full dialectic: Indecent Theology is about sex, but sex is about . . . everything, because the "sexual construct is at the base of theology and economics at the level of what is desirable and the strategies for

14. Althaus-Reid, *Indecent Theology*, 69.
15. Althaus-Reid, *Indecent Theology*, 93, parentheses in the original.
16. Althaus-Reid, "Outing Theology," 63.
17. Althaus-Reid, *The Queer God*, 4.

achieving that including counting the costs."[18] Making sex explicit allows the Indecent Theologian to get to the base level, and therefore to the truth of things: power and epistemology, logics of exchange and the alienness of grace, love, and freedom, and that which ultimately does not fit in any system: God and humanity. It allows the theologian to stop concealing that desire and flesh, the messiness of incarnation and people's real lives have something to do with theology. For all its queerness, such a theology plays it remarkably straight; and for all its indecency, it is disarmingly honest.

In sum, Althaus-Reid presents a relentless and realistic account of the material conditions and effects of theology, not so much as an ideology critique but as a taking account of what lies beyond its internal cognitive structure, what such a theology *does* underneath of what it *says*. Her critique refuses to play by Systematic Theology's methodological rules, and it crosses over an assumed divide between concepts and effects, between cognitive and material issues, between knowledge and power. Recognizing with Audre Lorde that "the master's tools will never dismantle the master's house,"[19] Althaus-Reid decides "not to demolish Liberation Theology *a la Europea* (in a European academic fashion)" but instead to question the "hermeneutical principles which led liberationists to be indifferent to the reality of lemon vendors in the first place."[20]

Althaus-Reid disregards Systematic Theological method, well, almost systematically. She rarely cites Scripture or tradition, and she seems blissfully uninterested in "understanding" Christianity's doctrinal or historical narratives on their own terms. Instead, she harnesses momentum from a combination of intersectional positionings and theory engagements, draws on the lives of lemon vendors and cross-dressers, on folklore and sexual stories, and develops less sanitized, more honest accounts of human and divine reality. Althaus-Reid questions not the propositional content of theological claims, their logical coherence, their consistency with Scripture, tradition, and other intellectual commitments but the way such theology has tended to function in the marginalization of vulnerable populations. At the root of her constructive engagement is the implicit functioning of theology, the effects it produces.

The radicality of Althaus-Reid's critique takes its cue from what she diagnoses as the shortcoming of feminist and liberationist critiques: while seeking to start their reflection with the marginalized and poor, these predecessors remained invested in the legibility of their critiques by the standards of the

---

18. Althaus-Reid, *The Queer God*, 176–77.

19. Althaus-Reid, *Indecent Theology*, 40, quoting Audre Lorde, "Age, Race, Class, and Sex: Women Defining Difference," in *Words of Fire: An Anthology of African-American Feminist Thought*, ed. Beverly Guy-Sheftall (New York: The New Press, 1995), 291.

20. Althaus-Reid, *Indecent Theology*, 5.

theology they were critiquing. Against the "decency" of Feminist Theology and Liberationist Theology, Althaus-Reid insists that we "must go further in [our] disrespect"[21] not simply against individual claims or positions but against the epistemological frameworks that enable them in order to liberate both God and the human being from the chokehold of T-theology.

A first site of Constructive Theology's divergence from Systematic Theology is, then, the calling-out of the latter's real-life implications and "bad effects" in the experience of different communities. Althaus-Reid examines the impacts that theological notions of Mary's virginal purity have on the possibility of self-assertion and defense of queer people on the streets of Buenos Aires, the effects that divine hypermasculinity has in neoliberal globalized contexts. On the grounds of such analysis, Althaus-Reid finds the underlying notions of incarnation or divine fatherhood irredeemably problematic.

The critique of Systematic Theology's bad effects of course gives rise to questions of intent and questions of responsibility. Any number of bad effects may be attributed to ignorance, misuse, or misapplication of theology. But as the critique centers on effects, it remains mostly uninterested in historical causation or malign intent. Instead, it highlights structural patterns in the way the doctrine has tended to function, what we might call its conceptual affordances (a notion that will be explained in depth in chapter 7). Althaus-Reid's critique points to a systemic complicity of Systematic Theologies with misogynistic, racialized, and colonial domination and with ongoing neoliberal exploitation through the theological validation of hypermasculine structures of subjugation. Beyond issues of intent and responsibility, the question remains if and why Systematic Theology's critical methodological apparatus is unable to prevent or even recognize its systemic complicities and recurrent bad effects. And not in all cases can we suggest that bad results are obtained from a less-than-rigorous employment of systematic-theological method. The suspicion arises: If it consistently and persistently inflicts harm, this might indicate not a failure of applying Systematic Theology's method, but its efficient functioning: not a bug but a feature. To put it in more classical terms: maybe there's "method in the madness"—which raises the question what kind of "madness" is in this method. The Constructive Theologian will point out that the more rigorous employment of Systematic Theological method never breaks the spell: the issues called out have been justified and defended doctrinally long after the intellectually rigorous and philosophically critical standards of Systematic Theology proper had been developed. One of the first observations in the study of harmful effects will thus regard the sociology of theological inquiry: The harmful effects have a (not all that) curious tendency to obtain

21. Althaus-Reid, *Indecent Theology*, 95.

for groups who are not typically represented in Systematic Theology's author-ship; in Althaus-Reid's case: not just women and the poor, but poor women from indigenous and colonized communities, and the queer and gender-non-conforming poor in the cityscapes of neoliberal globalization.

The Constructive Theologian points out how such gaps of representation mean that certain experiences form the regular backdrop of Systematic The-ology's imagination, while others do not come into view and do not inform its conceptual work. Such a testimonial gap will lead to what Miranda Fricker calls "testimonial injustice"[22]—a tendency to discredit divergent testimonies on the basis of the critics' identity or their lack of fit with what counts as knowl-edge in the field. In this way, testimonial injustice over time generates and reinforces what Fricker calls "hermeneutic injustice": the lack of hermeneutic resources for marginalized experiences to articulate or even understand them-selves in the language and imagination available to them. At best there ensues a lack of attention, lack of fit, and lack of relevancy of Systematic Theological work to "outsider" experiences. At worst, it perpetuates the marginalization of, discrimination against, or even outright rejection of these agents and their experiences as theologically valid, testimonially reinforcing the cycle of her-meneutic injustice. At the same time, hermeneutic injustice leads to the per-petuation of material injustice—political, economic, sexual, racial—against marginalized communities, with theological support.

As the bad effects, so the systemic complicity turns out to have *epistemological* roots in the unexamined contextuality of Systematic Theology. The insights into testimonial and hermeneutic injustice challenge Systematic Theology's self-understanding as methodically rational, objective, neutral, and universal. Time and again, the articulation of a marginalized community's theologi-cal perspectives and experiences, including their experience *with* Systematic Theology, has thus demonstrated Systematic Theology's epistemological bias, revealed the contingency of underlying assumptions in Systematic Theolo-gy's method and framework, and rendered alternative rationalities plausible. The fact *that* Systematic Theology's methodological paradigm is contextually dependent and has cultural, historical, intellectual particularities neither sur-prises nor makes it suspect *per se*, least of all to the Constructive Theologian who will typically insist on such contextual embeddedness and particularity of all theology. However, it is the *unreflected nature* of its contextuality and the con-ditions of its knowledge production that for the Constructive Theologian mark Systematic Theology as intellectually subpar and practically problematic.

In her sexual analysis, Marcella Althaus-Reid calls such a theology "vanilla." In classifications of sexuality and ice cream, vanilla is the basic or

---

22. Miranda Fricker, *Epistemic Injustice* (Oxford: Oxford University Press, 2007), esp. 9–29.

plain variety that appears to have no particular flavor at all. However, that is an illusion. Beyond its unadventurous implication, "vanilla," names an insufficient critical self-examination that results in a lack of or even a false consciousness. The risk aversion with which vanilla types are associated, their choice to perform within the established scripts of decency, might thus have less to do with their lack of trying different approaches, and more with the avoidance of claiming their particularity as their own: "Vanilla Theology is the realm of the decisions made for us by others, like Sexual Systematic Theology."[23] Systematic Theology is vanilla insofar as it disavows its—actually existent—particularity. Rather than coming out of the closet with it, it instead claims a flavorless, universal, objective normality from which all (other) flavors are framed as deviations.

Althaus-Reid's sexual analysis of Systematic Theology thus not only uncovers the heteronormative and patriarchal ideologies that effectively function under the surface of "purely" doctrinal and spiritual claims and calls out the systemic complicity of Systematic Theology in its recurrent bad effects. She goes further and homes in on the underlying epistemological issue: Systematic Theology's unavowed particularity and contextuality, its unacknowledged commitment to certain cultural understandings of sexuality and their unquestionably "right" ordering that form the root of its theological constructions. The unacknowledged nature of these epistemic conditionings makes them effective in the first place as well as immunizes them against critique.

To make it very clear: Such a critique does not primarily insinuate that order as such is bad and that systems as such are oppressive. What it draws out is, as Melvin Kranzberg famously claimed of technologies at large, that they are not "neutral":[24] There is always an element of active force exerted by them that generates particular effects and needs to be accounted for in theology's self-reflection. Like any other technology, systematicity's method of cognitive coherentism (drawn out further in chapter 2) might carefully curate its innocence, but it certainly is not harmless.

Even as the analysis might start with bad effects, it is ultimately on the grounds of method that Constructive Theology has to consider Systematic Theology "bad theology." It is Systematic Theology's method that facilitates the veiling of Systematic Theology's particularity and contextuality, and thus immunizes its strategic effects from critique—that is the Constructive Theologian's fundamental contention against Systematic Theology. Constructive Theology therefore does not necessarily decry any kind of ordering, but it asks critically "whose order" and "what kind of ordering" are effected by way of

23. Althaus-Reid, *Indecent Theology*, 89.
24. Melvin Kranzberg, "Kranzberg's Laws," *Technology and Culture* 27, no. 3 (1986): 544–60.

theological concepts, and it pushes for expanding the analysis to take the contextual conditioning, power dynamics, and real-life effects of cognitive systems into account, instead of merely assessing their inner coherence and explanatory potential. It challenges theology to reflect self-critically on contextual commitments, discern systemic complicity, and prevent bad effects.

Through the lens of a sexual analysis that at times might seem like a playful tapestry of random anecdotes, wild connections, and free fabulation, Althaus-Reid draws together much contemporary suspicion of Systematic Theology in her analysis: its monopolization into "T-the one and only" possible version of T-truth, including the policing of its boundaries that becomes T-totalitarian, with subsequent systematic complicity in bad effects, all of which is fundamentally due to an underlying epistemic issue that is produced by and in turn enables Systematic Theology's methodological framework.

As can be seen in Althaus-Reid's exemplification of the Constructive Theology *type*, the three overlapping criticisms of bad effects, systemic complicity, and unavowed contextual commitments result in increasing suspicion of Systematic Theology's method: It is not neutral toward the world it purports to describe; its conceptual order has contextual conditions and material effects that in turn produce epistemological constraints. At best, cognitive systematization seems to be insufficiently equipped to prevent bad effects and discern systemic complicity as well as to understand its own entanglement in contextual commitments. At worst, theology's pious method is but a cover-up for neo-colonial, patriarchal, and cisheteronormative power plays.

AUTOIMMUNE REACTIONS, OR: CONSTRUCTIVE THEOLOGY AS "BAD THEOLOGY"

> It might be thought that the statement, "Look how they love one another!" . . . might apply pre-eminently to theologians. But, in fact, theologians are nearly proverbial for their zealousness about all that they continually have in their hearts and on their lips to say against one another, and for what they put in black and white against one another with deep mistrust and a massive air of superiority.
>
> —*Karl Barth*[25]

> I am by nature a gentle being and entirely averse to all unnecessary disputes . . . but in the church we are concerned with truth. . . . And truth is not to be trifled with.
>
> —*also Karl Barth*[26]

25. Barth, *Evangelical Theology*, 139.
26. Emil Brunner and Karl Barth, *Natural Theology: Comprising "Nature and Grace" by Emil Brunner and the Reply "No!" by Karl Barth* (Eugene: Wipf & Stock, 2002), 67.

To such typical critiques articulated by Constructive Theologians against Systematic Theology, Systematic Theology shows a range of reactions that might roughly be clustered or typologized along the following lines.

Nonengagement. First of all, wide segments of Systematic Theology do not interact seriously with Constructive Theology's critiques as exemplified here. A work like *Indecent Theology* fails to register on many a Systematic Theologian's radar precisely *because* it does not adhere to Systematic Theology's methodological paradigm and thus remains a disciplinary "outsider." The price of freedom is illegibility.

Where Constructive Theological critiques *have* registered within Systematic Theology, they have often elicited various kinds of irritated, paternalizing, and domesticating responses. The primary issue here is not gatekeeping as such. It is that the disciplinary and confessional standards of Systematic Theology—central to its method—immunize the discipline against critique in self-reifying ways while in turn dismissing Constructive Theology as "bad theology."

Dismissal as heretical. Even before considering its methodological credentials, Systematic Theologians might disavow the Constructive critique as simply being theologically wrong, i.e., "heretical": Althaus-Reid's Mary is not the one of the Gospels, the bisexuality of her Jesus is not Chalcedonian, and her kenotic theology of orgies does not map onto traditional trinitarian patterns of *perichoresis*. Freely using notions from the Christian tradition, queering and "indecenting" them, she is at best unconcerned with whether her position is coherent with "orthodox" Christian faith and at worst explicitly invested in "per/verting" it. Systematic Theologians will charge Constructive Theologians further with replacing "theological" standards with "ideological," "political," or "ethical" ones. Ironically, this both confirms the Constructive Theologian's claim that "orthodoxy" and "theological method" function as tools of epistemic policing of the system's internal logics by establishing what is allowed to count as "proper" theology, and at the same time prevents the Systematic Theologian from hearing this critique.

Rejection of critique. Next, Systematic Theologians might hear but reject the claim that their theology is about anything but the content of its theological claims. They will insist that their theology indeed *is* about theology, and not about sex or power, and feel offended by the suggestion otherwise, as if such description of their "aboutness" necessarily insinuates strategic scheming or hidden agendas, when the Constructive Theologian might simply be pointing to what they see materially happening around and through the intellectual production of Systematic Theology, unaccounted for by Systematic Theology itself.

Refusal of responsibility. Then again, Systematic Theologians might acknowledge some of the concerns voiced by the Constructive Theologian but refuse to consider the subject's matter at hand their business. They will claim that theology is concerned with higher, perennial truths, not with marginalized experiences: say, with Trinitarian relations, not with street vendor's underwear, with the natures of Christ, not the rosaries of cross-dressing salsa dancers that, according to Systematic Theology's methodological starting points and principles, cannot be sources of theological insight. Cisheteropatriarchy and neoliberal neo-imperialism may be pressing issues, but they are pressing issues for *other fields,* by definition not part of Systematic Theology's subject matter, and therefore not part of its purview. Systematic Theologians might even express some degree of solidarity with the concerns raised. But, framing them as un- or extra-theological, they refuse to admit them as critique of systematic-theological claims let alone method. How very unfortunate indeed, the Systematic Theologian might exclaim, if language about God the Father elicits traumatized reactions from poor women, but there's really nothing to be done about this, divine fatherhood is simply the adequate way of stating Trinitarian filiation, there is ample scriptural evidence for it, it is central to the tradition and a matter of consensus in the ecumenical church, and it has no intention of harming women. Women will just have to understand that the doctrine is about who God is and has nothing to do with human gender, even if women—completely unrelatedly (Systematic Theology will say)—suffer under patriarchal systems. Once more, this response amounts to a self-immunization of Systematic Theology against the issues raised, while Constructive Theology precisely challenges such a neat separation of fields as historically contingent, theologically untenable (*who God is* might undermine these very boundaries), or even part of a strategic functioning of power

Mere misuse. Another variation of a self-immunization response is the minimization of the issue to "mere" misuse or bad application—downhill from the question of right doctrine. The Systematic Theologian might embrace the critique, acknowledging and even lamenting the problem. Yes, they will recognize, the claim to the lordship of Christ played a violent role in colonial expansion and supremacism, but that is an issue of its practical application, not of its theological content. Yes, Mariology valorizes standards of purity, but the fact that poor women are rarely in conditions to emulate them and thus face stigmatization does not mean that the doctrine itself is not perfect, true, and good. Systematic Theologians thus delegate the issue to ethics or practical theology, divesting doctrine of responsibility.

Dismissal as instrumentalizing theology. Further, the Systematic

Theologian might lash back and accuse the Constructive Theologian of not being interested in theology, of only using theological language to further their political agenda. The Constructive Theologian, they will claim, is randomly or strategically reinterpreting theological fragments to fit into their ideological worldview without interest in truth or continuity with traditional interpretation. Since political commitments are explicitly acknowledged by the Constructive Theologian (as part of their method), the Systematic Theologian will frame them as intellectual biases that discredit the scholarly validity and theological authenticity of the Constructive Theologian's argument. Systematicians will thus charge Liberationist Theology with being Marxist ideology, and Feminist Theologies with being forms of syncretistic paganism, rather than as being "properly theological." Immunizing themselves in this way, Systematic Theologians will thus reciprocate the charge of unexamined contextuality—and therefore ideological false consciousness—and will retreat to stylizing their own position once more as that of unbiased, disinterested, politically neutral objectivity—precisely what Constructive Theologies are calling into question—while charging their critic in turn with ideological interests.

From conditional recognition to pigeonholing. Alongside such dismissals, refusals, and counterattacks, we might find responses that grant conditional recognition for "different voices." They will acknowledge the Constructive Theologian as engaged in theological work while pigeonholing their reach and relevance contextually. Such conditional recognition will limit the feminist critique to voicing "women's issues," the queer critique to "identity politics," and the postcolonial critique to folkloric contributions—as if the systems of belief they address and the insights they produce were only relevant to specific groups. Constructive Theologies will be allowed to keep their "idiosyncrasies" as long as they accept their marginalized and confined positioning, exoticized as deviating from disciplinary norms, and neutralized against the logic and dominance of Systematic Theology. Special appointments and whole subdisciplines like Feminist, Queer, and Postcolonial Theologies might be allowed to form, where they will be free to develop alternative methodologies and insights. In reality, such conditional recognition functions like reservations, isolating the contribution as pertaining only to a particular constituency and limiting the scope of its impact to a circumscribed domain while continuing business as usual in the larger world of theology. To put it more pointedly: banning heretics or giving them "a room of their own"[27] in a specially conceived sub-field may just be two different ways of putting them into a box,

---

27. Thus the title of Virginia Woolf's feminist classic, which unironically demands such space in Virginia Woolf, *A Room of One's Own* (London: Hogarth; Harcourt), 1929.

even if it now is a broom closet instead of a coffin. The fundamental epistemological critiques that Constructive Theologies offer Systematic Theology are
thus once more effectively neutralized.

Inclusion. Going further in recognition, while effectively continuing to
neutralize the Constructive critique, is the response of inclusion, integration,
and assimilation. We could also call this response the domestication strategy.
Systematic Theologians might embrace the concerns and insights articulated
and welcome other approaches into the field—as long as those voices conform to the established disciplinary standards. They can enrich the theological choir but not call the musical arrangement as such into question. This
is Althaus-Reid's contention against the "decency" of contextual theologies:
Liberation Theology will be included in the theological conversation as long
as its Christology operates within Chalcedonian definitions and its political
vision conforms to proper eschatological deferment of societal transformation; Feminist Theology will be celebrated as long as it reinterprets classical
Trinitarianism to carve out proper human submission to the divine; Queer
Theology will be allowed to exegete Gregory of Nyssa with a bit more nuance
than before.

In turn, Constructive Theologians have long called out "the problem with
inclusion,"[28] which among other things commodifies Constructive Theologies and co-opts them into the dominant paradigm: "Terrible is the fate of
theologies from the margin when they want to be accepted by the centre!"[29]
Their theological and ethical critique of the rules according to which theology
is constructed will then be assimilated into another version of that "which has
been believed everywhere, always, by all." Going back to Vincent of Lérins,
this standard definition of dogma unironically invisibilizes how the "everywhere," "always," and "all" have (dare we say: "at all times"?) been subject to
intense power struggles, frequently ending in the physical removal or extinc-
tion of differing perspectives to uphold the consensus of the remaining "all."

Conversion. Of course, there *do* exist a variety of responses by Systematic
Theologians that embrace critiques from Constructive Theologies head-on
and translate them into new methodological and epistemological criteria for
the work of theology. They might recognize that a theology that has endemic
fatal effects for minoritized groups is at odds with central claims of the gospel of the living God and cannot claim to adequately represent this God's
truth. They might abandon all hope in the positive possibility of theology
and re-envision the theological task as one of perpetual ideology critique and

28. Althaus-Reid, "Class, Sex and the Theologian," 25.
29. Marcella Althaus-Reid and Lisa Isherwood, "Thinking Theology and Queer Theory,"
Feminist Theology 15, no. 3 (2007): 302–14, 304.

self-critique. Or they might establish additional standards of scholarly rigor within Systematic Theology, such as explicitly recognizing the contextual and constructive nature of the endeavor, accounting for the social location of its subjects, and multiplying attention to layers of intersectional justice concerns. In turn, such more affirming responses will typically become subject to the same set of responses sketched above—from denunciation as heresy to inclusion—by the self-styled defenders of Systematic Theology. That is, the same immunization will ensue, only one step further down the chain of reception. Would you be surprised if I told you that this has already happened to me, and that it will certainly be part of Systematic Theologians' response to this book?

EPISTEMIC INCOMMENSURABILITY

Truth is not to be trifled with.

—Karl Barth[30]

The one and only thing that can maintain the liberative character of any theology is not its content but its methodology.

—Juan Luis Segundo[31]

The truth will set you free.

—John 8:32

Whether the responses sketched in the previous section are well-meaning but hapless, or whether they are strategic and malign is beside the point of my inquiry. I am neither interested in polemics nor in resolving mutual misunderstandings or misconstruals on individual points. I am rather puzzling over the fact that Systematic Theology's methodological apparatus seems to be unequipped to process the questions about its own contextuality, its functioning, and its effects: Constructive Theology's critique remains illegible to it. In what seems de facto to amount to something like an allergic reaction, Systematic Theology's immune system identifies the irritation caused by Constructive Theology almost by reflex as a contaminant and works either to eject it altogether or to neutralize its critical potential.

Throughout the range of responses, Systematic Theology seems unable to see Constructive Theology as anything other than a deficient mode of Systematic Theology: not intellectually rigorous enough, not objective and unbiased enough, not presenting a sufficiently plausible and defensible account

---

30. Brunner and Barth, *Natural Theology*, 67.
31. Segundo, *Liberation of Theology*, 39–40.

of orthodox Christian faith, and not measuring up to standards of biblical interpretation and creedal adherence. On the other side, Constructive Theology, too, will see Systematic Theology as insufficiently rigorous: lacking in its critical apparatus, failing to subject its own methodology and practice to self-critical examination, and therefore being ideologically blindfolded. Dismissing Systematic Theology as deficient Constructive Theology, Constructive Theology thus similarly immunizes itself against the theological insights and truth-claims of Systematic Theology. Both will charge one another with attending insufficiently to reality as it really is (divine or human), with a lack of adequacy to truth, and with a lack of fit with other truth commitments. Both will charge one another with being ideological, citing explicit articulation of a political agenda on the one side and uninterrogated assumptions and unavowed biases on the other.

In short, a stalemate ensues by measuring each other according to a different epistemic standard of *what counts* as critical and rigorous scholarship, in which every side is performing well by its own standards and finds the other lacking. Both will feel methodologically *justified* in dismissing the other's critique. And it becomes apparent that this stalemate is not an unfortunate misunderstanding that could be resolved by more good will or dialog on the individual material points: it is due to a fundamental incommensurability between epistemes. I use the term *episteme* in the sense coined by Michel Foucault:

> as the strategic apparatus which permits of separating out from among all the statements which are possible those that will be acceptable within . . . a field of scientificity, and which it is possible to say are true or false. The episteme is the "apparatus" which makes possible the separation, not of the true from the false, but of what may from what may not be characterised as scientific.[32]

In this vein, understanding Systematic Theology and Constructive Theology as different epistemes means attending to the ways in which their different methodological apparatuses regulate what constitutes good scholarship. By doing so, they also predetermine what can come into view as an insight, a potential piece of knowledge in the first place.

In what follows, I will be using the adjective "epistemic" in a technical sense as "relating-to-an-*episteme*," *not*, as might otherwise be assumed, as more generally "relating-to-knowledge" (for which I will instead use the adjective "epistemological")—since precisely how knowledge might be established and what should count as such will be contentious between different epistemes.

---

32. Michel Foucault, *Discipline and Punish: The Birth of the Prison* (New York: Random House, 1977), 197.

Readers who are disinclined toward Foucault can mentally substitute Thomas Kuhn's use of "epistemic paradigm" or "scientific paradigm" for the purposes at hand.[33]

Strictly speaking, one would need to distinguish a methodological framework from the epistemic paradigm to which it responds, and individual methods as the concrete tools by which such methodology is applied.[34] However, theological discourses tend to deploy the term "method" broadly as a shorthand that includes methodological frameworks and even epistemic paradigms as a whole. In this book, *method* will thus most often not refer to individual steps in a theologian's work, but to the larger framework that determines how their methodological toolbox will be stocked.

As we have seen in Althaus-Reid, Constructive Theology not only acknowledges its epistemic incommensurability with Systematic Theology, it also often intentionally performs it for critical purposes, i.e., out of dissatisfaction with the critical tools afforded by Systematic Theology. Indeed, Constructive Theology typically emerges where a different episteme, one that centers experience, contextuality, and subjugated knowledges, is deployed. Its "outsider within" perspective is what first allows for the foundational critique of Systematic Theology.[35] The Constructive Theologian recognizes that "the master's tools can never dismantle the master's house": The critical insights of Constructive Theologies cannot be achieved on Systematic Theology's terms and are often actively obstructed by it, even as (or because?) they ultimately call it into question. Constructive Theologians who, like Althaus-Reid, refuse to formulate their critique within the standards of Systematic Theology thus (to differing degrees) also accept that a certain illegibility will be the price for their integrity.

This in turn leaves Systematic Theology at a loss. It has at its disposal a sophisticated apparatus of coherentist standards between philosophical reasoning, biblical exegesis, and the history of doctrine that enable it to justify its truth-claims on par with other rationally grounded truth-seeking endeavors. It is extremely capable of explicating the webs of meaning that underlie individual items of belief and of reinterpreting inherited formulas to make sense of them in changing times. It is highly successful in presenting Christian belief-claims about ultimate truths, truths that are neither empirically nor logically strictly

---

33. Thomas S. Kuhn, *The Structure of Scientific Revolutions* (Chicago: University of Chicago Press, 1962).

34. For such a clarifying distinction, cf. Sandra G. Harding, ed. *Feminism and Methodology: Social Science Issues* (Bloomington: Indiana University Press, 1987).

35. As theorized by Black feminist sociologist, Patricia Hill Collins, "Learning from the Outsider Within: The Sociological Significance of Black Feminist Thought," *Social Problems* 33, no. 6 (1986): S14–32.

demonstrable as nonetheless rationally intelligent, justified, and plausible. It does so by establishing their comprehensive unity, internal coherence, and consistency with truth-claims outside of theology. It is, however, *epistemically unequipped* to process Constructive Theology's criticisms of Systematic Theology's unexamined epistemic commitments, systemic complicity, and bad effects, because these criticisms operate on a different plane: Constructive Theology does not target the plausibility of systematic-theological truth-claims or refute any of its arguments. It does not debate its consistence with tradition, or Scripture, across denominations, or its internal coherence. It might not even be articulated in terms of claims about ultimate truths in the first place. The critiques articulated by Constructive Theology thus remain *illegible* by Systematic-Theological standards and may even fail to register entirely as critique. Systematic Theology will thus not respond to the critical input, but only to the interruption and irritation of Systematic Theology's own functioning that Constructive Theology indeed represents. Without being able to render it into coherent terms, Systematic Theology thus only snaps, "What's this noise?"[36]

Constructive Theologians, in turn, often abandon altogether the faith commitments Systematic Theologians have developed. For them, Systematic Theology also becomes illegible and unable to afford theological insight and resources for constructive engagement with God and the world. Without being able to discern constructive potential in Systematic Theology, Constructive Theologians will dismiss it wholesale as dead and death-dealing.

Assessed by one another's methodological apparatus, both paradigms can only see in one another forms of "bad theology." When that happens, the typology sketched earlier turns into straw-people in deadlock antagonisms, organized along something like the following lines: Systematic Theology is interested in eternal truth, Constructive Theology in temporal justice; the former committed to objective and universal claims, the latter to subjective and contextual experience; one makes the reality of God its starting point, the other the real lives of real people; one is interested in spiritual, the other in material things; one is interested in the content of theological truth-claims, the other in their functioning and use—not what theology *says*, but what theology *does*. A more rigorous use of theological method does nothing to overcome this deadlock; it only exacerbates it.

Not infrequently, the incommensurability between epistemic paradigms seems to function as a *status confessionis*, where for both different paradigms, everything is at stake. While Systematic and Constructive Theologians may

---

36. Cf. Spivak's definition of subalternity as an epistemological condition, the discursive impossibility to make oneself heard, Gayatri Chakravorty Spivak, "Can the Subaltern Speak?," in *Marxism and the Interpretation of Culture*, ed. Cary Nelson and Lawrence Grossberg (Basingstoke: Macmillan, 1988), 271–313.

not be formulating confessional statements on method, the question of theological method de facto becomes the site where "true faith" is negotiated and distinguished from "heresy," effecting communal identity constitution at the price of exclusion and otherization. Principles of theological method serve to establish oneself as orthodox and "good"—epistemically justified, theologically adequate, grammatically well-formed—while ostracizing other approaches as fundamentally endangering the faith. But it is not the truth of the gospel that is at stake in theological method—what is at stake is epistemic self-justification.

It might be worth pondering whether the incommensurability of paradigms indeed necessitates their antagonism. Maybe the allergic reaction Systematic Theology displays to Constructive Theology is in fact an autoimmune reaction—wrongly identifying part of the theological organism as a contaminant and treating it like an attack on the system when it is a member of the same body. On the grounds of theological method, both "sides" see in one another only "bad theology." The scholarly production of both "sides" functions as a confessional practice of calling out and mitigating wrong teachings. Might there be possibilities of acknowledging that different epistemes bring into view different aspects of reality, and account for them in different ways in response to different concerns?

While I am not interested in an integration of both paradigms into a successor episteme, the three parts of this book suggest three readings that allow us to turn the antagonistic relationship into relative solidarity without diminishing its conflictual potential: (1) Both Systematic and Constructive Theology are attempts to mitigate different forms of "bad theologies" (*primus usus legis*); (2) both ultimately lead to a self-conscious realization of the impossibility of achieving "good theology" by way of method (*secundus usus legis*); and (3) in their recognition of divine grace, both can be used constructively to guide the pursuit of "better" theology (*tertius usus legis*).

Toward the first point, a "provincializing" account will put the different paradigms into the historical contexts of their respective epistemic ecologies. This puts both into perspective and challenges their disciplinary hold over one another. Even as such temporalization remains in danger of lending itself once more to hierarchical thinking, a theological reading can discern relative value in either paradigm's investment in damage control vis-à-vis different possibilities of "bad theology." A *primus usus legis* that the Reformers traditionally ascribed to the political and civic functioning of the law thus allows for a fuller appreciation of the important contextual work that both paradigms are doing respectively, without falling into the temptation of integrating them into a new, supposedly "comprehensive" epistemic paradigm.

Chapter 2

Provincializing theology, or:
Solidarity under the law

In a time when Third World theologians have made contextuality a hermeneutical key, it is sad to notice how contextuality has remained linked to the geographical more than the epistemological.

—*Marcella Althaus-Reid*[1]

The Christian community . . . exists in total dependence on its environment and yet also in total freedom in relation to it. Neither its dependence nor its freedom is partial; they are both total . . . all religious language is also and indeed primarily non-religious, having in itself no less but also no more to do with what the Christian community has to say than non-religious.

—*Karl Barth*[2]

PROVINCIALIZING SYSTEMATICITY

Why is it so difficult for Systematic Theology and Constructive Theology to "hear" one another? It might be because their epistemic paradigms are listening and responding to different interlocutors. The Argentinian Constructive Theologian Ivan Petrella muses,

Modern theology had the skeptic, the person who denies belief in God, as its main interlocutor, and giving reasons for religious belief as its main goal, while liberation theology has the non-person, the person whose humanity is denied by the prevailing social order, as its

1. Althaus-Reid, *The Queer God*, 25–26.
2. Karl Barth, *Church Dogmatics IV.3,2: The Doctrine of Reconciliation*, ed. Geoffrey W. Bromiley and Thomas F. Torrance (Edinburgh: T&T Clark, 1962), 734–35.

51

interlocutor, and liberation as its goal. This shift in standpoint from the concerns of a rich minority to those of a poor majority is liberation theology's epistemological break from modern religious thought. The epistemological break leads to a kind of conversion within the discipline of theology in which the world is now looked at differently.[3]

Petrella's assessment elucidates Systematic Theology's investment in an objective, coherent, and universal framing as a response to a particular challenge in a particular epistemic context. The characterization of *epistemic conversion* imbues the historical analysis with a theological interpretation of its own, to which we will return later. For now, I want to draw out a possible epistemic contextualization of Systematic Theology as indicated by Petrella.

In *Provincializing Europe*, postcolonial theorist Dipesh Chakrabarty analyzes how Europe has constructed itself as the center of world history. Setting its own particular development as a universal measure becomes a self-justifying move. Any other trajectories will subsequently be read in terms of lag behind Europe's ideal case. This conceptual set-up reinforces Europe's hegemony and superiority on epistemological grounds while rendering its particularity invisible.

A similarly provincializing analysis can demonstrate how in Western modernity, the notion of systematicity became the epitome of rationality that would henceforth justify itself as the universal standard for truth-seeking endeavors, measure all scientific paradigms by its own particular values, and erase the traces of the contextual embeddedness of this self-understanding's particularities. Systematic Theology's self-understanding is a rather particular development of Western, predominantly Protestant theology, developed in a series of permutations between the double demands posed by the ecclesial institutionalization of the Reformation and the academic rise of rationalism as the new framework for science or academic inquiry. Dogmatics as a "system" of teachings, in the sense of "a structure of principles and their consequences, founded on the presupposition of a basic view of things, constructed with the help of various sources of knowledge and axioms, and self-contained and complete in itself,"[4] was only fully developed in the seventeenth century, when in the Western world "science" became, as philosopher of science Nicholas Rescher notes, "virtually by definition—a branch of knowledge that systematizes our information in some domain."[5]

---

3. Ivan Petrella, "Theology and Liberation: Juan Luis Segundo and Three Takes on Secular Inventiveness," in *Another Possible World*, ed. Marcella Althaus-Reid, Ivan Petrella, and Luiz Carlos Susin, 162–77 (London: SCM, 2007), 174–75.

4. Karl Barth, *Church Dogmatics I.2: The Doctrine of the Word of God*, ed. G. W. Bromiley and T. F. Torrance (Edinburgh: T&T Clark, 1956), 861.

5. Nicholas Rescher, *Cognitive Systematization: A Systems-Theoretic Approach to a Coherentist Theory of Knowledge* (Oxford: Blackwell, 1979), 22.

While every post-apostolic age has developed forms of "conceptual reconstruction of Christian teaching,"[6] this took a variety of shapes in different times. Early Christian intellectual productions were often doxological or parenetical. Scholastic theology was typically driven by rhetorical, dialectical forms. Presented in collections of sentences and their commentaries, and culminating in formidable "sums" of theological knowledge, its organization by way of syllogistic argumentation and deductive reasoning drove it toward increasing logical clarity and coherence.

The Reformation marked a stark departure from the logics of dogma. Its reorientation to Scripture and revelation put theological knowledge on a supernatural if not necessarily anti-rational foundation, and its application of the soteriological problem to epistemology extended a certain antisystematicity to the organization of theological knowledge: If, in the inflection of Luther's *Heidelberg Disputation*, God's cruciform revelation defied what might be said about God on the basis of reason, and if, in the Reformed inflection, *finitum* remained constitutively *incapax infiniti*, then theology could never justify itself by means of rational principles or methodological procedure. A distinctly anti-systematic impulse is at work in Martin Luther's "occasional," rhetorical theological production as well as in the *loci*-method developed by Philipp Melanchthon. At the same time, the Reformation's critical epistemology also turned method into a theological *problem* in ultimately insoluble ways. Paradoxically, its anti-methodological impulse necessitated reflection on theological method in an unprecedented manner and contributed to its ever-expanding treatment in theological reflection ever since.[7] With the transition from an inner-catholic Reform movement into its own ecclesial and academic institutions, the Reformers' need to articulate their insights in form of a normative and defensible body of teaching grew from a polemical and intellectual one to a political and pedagogical one.[8] Protestant scholasticism emerged between the heritage from the Reformers' late medieval formation and the humanism and rationalism developing in the European Renaissance.

Even as "reason" started being played increasingly against "faith," and its critical deployment called ecclesial authority and dogmatic orthodoxy into question, theologians were at the forefront of those who developed systematicity into the standard of scientificity. During high and late Protestant

---

6. John Webster, "Introduction: Systematic Theology," in *The Oxford Handbook of Systematic Theology*, ed. John Webster, Kathryn Tanner, and Iain R. Torrance, 1–15 (Oxford Handbooks. Oxford: Oxford University Press, 2007), 3.

7. Cf. Richard Muller, who calls the development of theological prolegomena "the central issue of post-Reformation theology." Richard A. Muller, *Post-Reformation Reformed Dogmatics*, vol. 1: Prolegomena to Theology (Grand Rapids: Baker, 1987).

8. Muller, *Post-Reformation Reformed Dogmatics* 1:34.

scholasticism, reason with its systematizing capacities transitioned from a point of contact with revelation, lingering at its threshold, to a normative guide.[9] The Calvinist theologian and philosopher Bartholomaeus Keckermann was allegedly the first to use "systema" in a monograph title. Keckermann, who also invented the "analytic method" of theology, is typically credited with coining the term "Systematic Theology."[10] Keckermann was infatuated with encyclopedic ordering of knowledge, including but not limited to his *Systema SS Theologicae*, 1602. He published a wide range of "systems" of physics, astronomy, logics, ethics, geography, and rhetorics, culminating in his 1613 *Systema systematum* as an encyclopedic account of the different branches of science. Further developed by Johan Franz Buddeus a century later,[11] systematic method had to satisfy two central requirements:

1. it deals with its subject matter comprehensively, i.e., it takes into consideration all that is necessary to salvation;
2. it explains, proves, and confirms (*explicit, probet, atque confirmet*) its content in detail.[12]

As historical theologian Richard Muller argues, the innovation Protestant scholasticism displayed in developing this methodology was precisely geared to preserve doctrinal continuity with the Reformation and the larger church, its orthodoxy. Neither an irrational fideism nor a merely formal rationalism, it replaced Aristotelian dialectics and metaphysics with the fine-tuning of doctrinal systematicity "on a high technical level and in an extremely precise manner by means of the careful identification of topics, division of these topics into their basic parts, definition of the parts, and doctrinal or logical argumentation concerning the divisions and definitions . . . with mastery of the tools of linguistic, philosophical, logical, and traditional thought."[13] This method allowed theology to both persist in an environment increasingly dominated

9. Johannes Reinhard, *Studien zur Geschichte der altprotestantischen Theologie* (Leipzig: Deichert, 1906), 102.

10. Joseph S. Freedman, "Keckermann, Bartholomaeus," in *Encyclopedia of Renaissance Philosophy*, ed. Marco Sgarbi, 1–4 (Cham: Springer, 2016).

11. Protestant scholastics Johann Wilhelm Baier, Georg Calixt, and Johann Andreas Quenstedt do increasingly make use of the language of systematicity, but without developing it into a fully-fledged theological methodology. Cf. Friederike Nüssel, *Bund und Versöhnung: Zur Begründung der Dogmatik bei Johann Franz Buddeus*, Forschungen zur Systematischen und Ökumenischen Theologie, vol. 77 (Göttingen: Vandenhoeck & Ruprecht, 1996).

12. Cf. Johann Franz Buddeus, *Isagoge Historico-Theologica Ad Theologiam Universam Singulasque Eius Partes* (Leipzig: Fritsch, 1727), 303, as presented by Wolfhart Pannenberg, *Systematic Theology* (London; New York: T&T Clark, 2004), 1:18.

13. Muller, *Post-Reformation Reformed Dogmatics*, 1:18.

by a practically if not nominally atheistic rationalism, and to insist on its own rational, scientific status under its conditions.

With Buddeus's dual requirement of comprehensiveness and coherence,[14] Systematic Theology reached its first full-fledged form roughly at the same time as the comprehensive, hierarchical taxonomies of Carl Linnaeus's *Systema Naturae*.[15] Like other contemporary scientists, Linnaeus understood himself to be reflecting the ingenious order of God's creation in his method. Self-confidently, he would assert, "*Deus creavit, Linnaeus disposuit*"—God has created, Linnaeus has systematized.[16]

From its inception, systematicity displays a tendency not only toward the organization of thought but also ultimately of the material world as well: It has therefore been called "amphibious" in this dual applicability to bodies and concepts.[17] As postcolonial and other Constructive-theological critiques would point out much later, it was this crossing-over between cognitive and material ordering that allowed for science to operate in the threefold extension of understanding, prediction, and control over nature that such systematicity to the glory of God intertwined. By aspiring to encompass everything into overarching structures, systematicity promised to establish mastery over the natural world by leaving nothing unaccounted for, no "blind spots" on the map of knowledge, no ungoverned territory. Where truth and goodness and beauty were seen as fundamentally rational and essentially co-extensive, systematicity lent itself to the aspiration that human rationality would be able to order the world by ordering the knowledge about it. Such aspiration at ordering the created world went hand in hand with its colonial ordering, not only in a metaphorical way: Linnaeus sent his most promising students—whom he called "apostles"—into all the world. Descriptively integrating flora and fauna from different parts of the globe into Linnaeus' account, they rendered his *Systema* ever more comprehensive while at the same time amplifying its usefulness as well as its actual global use. In this vein, Linnaeus also famously integrated human beings into a comprehensive biological account of species as primates,

14. Nüssel pinpoints the transition from Protestant orthodoxy and its analytic loci method to Enlightenment and Neo-Protestantism and its systematic method already in the work of Buddeus. She calls attention to the complex apologetic endeavor in which, far from being a simple embrace of rationalistic tendencies, the adoption of systematic method as a form of "theological self-enlightenment" afforded theological resistance to the fully-fledged rationalism of a Christian Wolff (Nüssel, *Bund und Versöhnung*, 77:11, 86)

15. Carl von Linné, *Systema Naturae* (Weinheim: Cramer, 1964), [1735].

16. Linnaeus' first biography shows this widely cited motto as Linné's coat of arms on its frontispiece, cf. Dietrich Heinrich Stoever, *The Life of Sir C. Linnaeus; to Which Is Added a List of His Works, and a Biographical Sketch of the Life of His Son*, tr. Joseph Trapp (London: White, 1794).

17. Rescher, *Cognitive Systematization*, 127.

establishing race as a biological classification to translate taxonomies of simi-
larities and differences into hierarchies.

Perfected by philosopher-theologians Gottfried Wilhelm Leibniz and
Christian Wolff, systematicity not only became the "hallmark of science"[18] for
individual disciplines but also increasingly aspired to integrate all domains of
knowledge into a *sciencia universalis.* Any discipline, including theology, would
soon be effectively validated as authentically scientific by its ability to demonstrate its inclusion into a comprehensive and cohesive system of human
knowledge.[19] In this perfect science of everything, claims to knowledge would
have to conform to the following principles:

- wholeness (unity and integrity),
- completeness (comprehensiveness),
- self-sufficiency (independence),
- cohesiveness (connectedness of the parts with one another),
- consonance (no internal discord),
- architectonics (a well-integrated structure, generally in a hierarchic ordering),
- functional unity (having a unifying rationale or telos),
- functional regularity (lawfulness),
- functional simplicity (elegance, harmony, balance, structural economy),
- mutual supportiveness (of the components), and
- functional efficacy (adequacy to a common task).[20]

The philosophy of Immanuel Kant as the mature theorization of systematicity also represents its epistemological turning point from a mode of organization
to a criterion of truth. Kant continued to emphasize systematicity as a requirement of scientificity: "A systematic unity is what first raises ordinary knowledge to the rank of science, that is, makes a system out of a mere aggregate of
knowledge, architectonic [the art of constructing systems] is the doctrine of the
scientific in our knowledge."[21] As his *Critique of Pure Reason* established the limits
of reason to confirm the *adequatio intellectu ad rem* traditionally required of knowledge, systematicity, however, also acquired a distinctly *epistemological* function:
"the unity of the manifold modes of knowledge under one idea . . . makes it
possible for us to determine from our knowledge of the other parts whether
any part be missing, and to prevent any arbitrary addition."[22] Hegel effected

---

18. Rescher, *Cognitive Systematization*, 22.

19. Rescher, *Cognitive Systematization*, 23.

20. Rescher, *Cognitive Systematization*, 10–11, the whole chapter presents a highly instructive
overview of the history of systematicity in Western philosophical thought.

21. Immanuel Kant, *Critique of Pure Reason*, Bohn's Philosophical Library (London: Bell,
1897), A832=B860.

22. Kant, *Critique of Pure Reason*, A833=B861.

the final step in the "transition from system as organizer of what is accepted to that of system as arbiter of what is acceptable."[23] Rather than maintaining that the real should also be rational, he now postulated, in his account of the self-development of the Spirit, that the rational *is* the real. In order to count as real, reality now had to conform to the logic of the system.

Systematicity, which started as a principle of well-ordered presentation of existing knowledge, thus quickly served explanatory and justificatory purposes and eventually graduated to a speculative modeling device in the active building of knowledge. Turning the challenge of Kant's critique into a virtue, it became the solution to the problem of epistemology as such: The system may remain unjustifiable by the inability to establish positive correspondence with external reality, but precisely for that reason it is therefore now self-justifying.[24]

The trajectory painted shows, first, Systematic Theology as a particular response to a particular epistemic ecology in which systematicity became all but synonymous with scientific validity. Neither the only possible shape of intellectual reasoning nor the culminating point of all theological development, systematicity emerges from the intensive negotiation between theology's subject matter and the epistemic ecology of Western Enlightenment philosophy. After magisterial and dogmatic authority were increasingly under pressure, after the confessional fragmentation in the wake of the Reformation rendered the institutional unity of the church and its doctrinal teachings unfeasible, after theology's particular object had become more than ever an epistemological problem, and when systematicity started demonstrating its use in the domination of the natural world and the conquest and governance of new territories and human races, the Christian faith, too, increasingly looked to human reason, with its appeal to comprehensive and universal applicability, as the arbiter of truth. When appeals to dialectics and Aristotelian method lost traction, yet the "correctness" of theological truth-claims could not easily be proven logically or empirically, the adherence to procedural, methodological requirements became paramount to securing the validity of Christian faith-claims.

What marked Systematic Theology beyond other pragmatic organizational schemes was that the systematic structure and method itself now justified orthodoxy's faith-claims as rational *and therefore* viable—according to the requirements of the particular epistemic ecology that theology found itself in. That is, to speak of Christian teaching as "a conceptual articulation of Christian claims about God and everything else in relation to God, characterized

---

23. Rescher, *Cognitive Systematization*, 66, calls this the "Hegelian Inversion."
24. Rescher, *Cognitive Systematization*, 42.

by comprehensiveness and coherence"[25] became the strategic response of a
scripturally and ecclesially committed theology to its contemporary primary
interlocutor: Enlightenment rational coherentism.

Fierce internal debates about the new method's alleged practical atheism
accompanied theology's transition from Protestant scholasticism to rationalism. Despite today's often almost synonymous usage of terms like "doctrine,"
"dogmatics," and "Systematic Theology," the methodology of Systematic
Theology had a decidedly *anti-dogmatic* edge: Rather than simply expositing
"that which has acquired ecclesial definition and approval," theology became
now "especially interested in the scope, unity, and coherence of Christian
teaching," "especially concerned to coordinate their subject matter with what
is held to be true outside the sphere of Christian faith."[26] Still, systematicity perfected tendencies inherent in the pursuit of orthodoxy: the necessity to
articulate biblical faith and its merits rationally and coherently, to explore all
its ramifications, to defend it against doubt and critique, to teach it to subsequent generations, in short: to navigate the unsystematic, systematically. The
unity of the world as God's creation, reason's capacity to function as *sensus
divinitatis*, and the necessary coherence of all truth in God's mind may be cited
to defend systematicity on theological grounds.

In an increasingly formalized mode of presentation, insights derived from
Scripture or collections of faith-claims into *loci* became organized according
to overarching logics like the history of salvation or the human being's faith
journey, and ever more closely interwoven with one another. In its ratio-
nalization of faith-claims along the lines of the epistemic context, theology
increasingly excised subjective elements in favor of the most objective account
and translated historical particularities into the most universal pattern conceivable. The emergent conceptual structures articulated faith commitments
and quickly became objects of faith themselves: subject to almost confessional
debates around method.

Second, explicating the epistemic ecology to which it is fitted should not
prematurely be seen as a way of discrediting or refuting Systematic Theology
as contextual and therefore limited, primarily apologetic or strategic. Rather,
in drawing out the particularity of Systematic Theology, a provincializing
analysis also helps to make sense of the historical success of this paradigm. To
apply Chakrabarty's reflections on Europe to the (undoubtedly Eurocentric)
project of Systematic Theology,

> [t]he project of provincializing [Systematic Theology] cannot be a
> project of cultural relativism. It cannot originate from the stance that

25. Webster, "Introduction," 2.
26. Webster, "Introduction," 1.

the [scientific standards] that help define [Systematic Theology] as the modern are simply "culture-specific" and therefore only belong to the [Western, white, academic, male] cultures. For the point is not that Enlightenment rationalism is always unreasonable in itself, but rather a matter of documenting how—through what historical process—its "reason," which was not always self-evident to everyone, has been made to look obvious far beyond the ground where it originated. If a language, as has been said, is but a dialect backed up by an army, the same could be said of the narratives of "modernity" that, almost universally today, point to a certain "[Systematic Theology]" as the primary habitus of the modern.[27]

With its abstract rationality and formalized method, systematicity may not *be universal*, but it *is universally applicable*—and that was one of its primary advantages in the political and intellectual "evolution" of Western hegemony. Systematicity lent itself to the aspiration of incorporating and conceptually controlling any and all otherwise disjunct subject matters, both intellectual and material, by achieving internal coherence. It effectively relied on *and* generated the continuous cognitive space that became key in the imperial ordering of the world, thus "proving" itself politically and justifying itself epistemologically.[28] Rescher calls the conviction of the synoptic systematicity of all knowledge "one of the great formative ideas of Western civilization."[29] Like Europe in Chakrabarty's account, Systematic Theology might thus be "an imaginary entity, but the demonstration as such does not lessen its appeal or power."[30] By coining its own methodology in congruence with the epitome of Western scientific standard, Systematic Theology secured for itself "a place in the sun" of Europe's success story and presented itself as coextensive with theological knowledge as such.

Third, in the face of rising faith-vs.-reason contentions, Systematic Theology presents itself as the pursuit of *better theology* over against expressions of theology were rendered as irrational, authoritarian, pre-modern, intellectually inferior, historically contingent, and practically limited in their application and use. Systematic Theology, in the words of an exemplar of post-Hegelian systematicity, "ascertains the truth of Christian doctrine by investigation and

27. Dipesh Chakrabarty, *Provincializing Europe: Postcolonial Thought and Historical Difference* (Princeton: Princeton University Press, 2000), 43, replacing Chakrabarty's use of "Europe" with "Systematic Theology" throughout.

28. For a decolonial critique of such notions, cf. e.g., Enrique D. Dussel, *Philosophy of Liberation* (Maryknoll: Orbis, 1985); Walter Mignolo, *The Darker Side of Western Modernity: Global Futures, Decolonial Options*, Latin America Otherwise: Languages, Empires, Nations (Durham: Duke University Press, 2011).

29. Rescher, *Cognitive Systematization*, 26.

30. Chakrabarty, *Provincializing Europe*, 43.

presentation of its coherence as regards both the interrelation of the parts and the relation to other knowledge."[31] In all their historic difference, theological "systems" like those of Buddheus, Schleiermacher, or Pannenberg mark what Systematic Theology, methodologically, is able to do *better*: render Christian faith legible according to the standards of European Enlightenment coherentism, conversant with the state of the art developments in other fields of inquiry and demonstrating non-contradiction with insights from the natural and historical sciences, thereby substantiating its own plausibility vis-à-vis them.

Self-reflective versions of Systematic Theology have always been critically aware of the apologetic impulse inherent in their methodology, if not necessarily of its epistemic contextuality. They have been painstakingly conscious of the finitude and limitations of the reason by way of which they organize its subject matter and have typically understood systematicity as an auxiliary device, a limited strategy for navigating the particular epistemological issues presented by the fundamentally a-systematic and ir-rational (or reason-transcending) nature of its subject matter, as well as of the conditions of sin and finitude under which human understanding operates (a matter to which I will return shortly): Systematicity, then, is less a tool of mastery than a damage control strategy of intellectual peacekeeping with other fields of knowledge and serves to avoid certain known forms of bad theology. In this sense it can be read as an epistemological variation on the *primus usus legis*.

Better versions of Systematic Theology have thus tended to hold systematicity lightly. They have been transparent about their own extra-systematic preconditions—material, historical, and theological—conceptualizing them as revelation, tradition, and Scripture, and only secondarily employed reason to "make sense" of them. Systematic Theology has pointed to the particularity of Christ and Christian existence before eschatological closure, intrinsically limiting any accommodation of Christian theological reflection by way of "systematicity."[32] As a *scientia practica*, it has reflected on historically existent church tradition and practices, rather than "inventing" them speculatively. Barth's reminder of the necessity of "irregular dogmatics" alongside "regular dogmatics" can be seen as an example of such consciousness as well as an active attempt to disidentify himself from the rationale of systematicity, which he continued to execute in practice with great mastery.[33] The old expression *fides quaerens intellectum* has in recent decades been revived to articulate such a self-conscious understanding of Systematic Theology.[34] Even as, at its worst,

31. Pannenberg, *Systematic Theology*, 1:21–22.

32. Cf. Otto Weber, *Foundations of Dogmatics*, vol. 1 (Grand Rapids: Eerdmans, 1981), 1:60–61.

33. Cf. Barth, *CD I.2*, 277–78.

34. Barth's famous study on Anselm and, a couple of generations later, Dan Migliore's textbook of the same names have been highly influential in that vein: Karl Barth, *Fides*

systematicity becomes all-controlling and hegemonic, suppressing difference and punishing deviation, at its best, systematicity might simply be a methodology to be employed reflectively, pragmatically, and humbly as a standard for *relatively best* intellectual practice under the conditions of Western modernity.

Fourth, thus, as the provincializing account draws out Systematic Theology's success story as entangled into the hegemony of Eurocentric reason, it also can be set into a network of epistemological wrestling in which it was neither the first nor the final knot. This opens up room for further investigation as well as for imagining alternatives.

A SERIES OF INSULTS? REVISITING THE SYSTEMATIC-CONSTRUCTIVE TYPOLOGY

Whoever is not with me is against me.

—*Matt. 12:30*

Whoever is not against us is for us.

—*Mark 9:40*

Ecological thinking is not simply thinking about ecology or about the environment: it generates revisioned modes of engagement with knowledge, subjectivity, politics, ethics, science, citizenship, and agency, which pervade and reconfigure theory and practice alike. . . . ecological thinking is about imagining, crafting, articulating, endeavoring to enact principles of ideal cohabitation.

—*Lorraine Code*[35]

In 1917, Sigmund Freud proclaimed boldly that human self-confidence had suffered three major "insults" through scientific revolutions: First, the Copernican turn in cosmology revealed that the earth is not the center of the universe. Second, the evolutionary insights of Darwinism foreclosed any anthropocentrism in the natural sciences. Finally, Freud's own theory of the libido revealed that the Ego was not even "master in its own house."[36] Differ-

---

Quaerens Intellectum: Anselms Beweis der Existenz Gottes im Zusammenhang seines theologischen Programms, Forschungen zur Geschichte und Lehre des Protestantismus, vol. 3 (München: Kaiser, 1931); Daniel L Migliore, *Faith Seeking Understanding: An Introduction to Christian Theology* (Grand Rapids: Eerdmans, 1991).

35. Lorraine Code, *Ecological Thinking: The Politics of Epistemic Location* (Oxford: Oxford University Press, 2006), 24.

36. Sigmund Freud, "Eine Schwierigkeit der Psychoanalyse," *Imago: Zeitschrift für Anwendung der Psychoanalyse auf die Geisteswissenschaften* 5 (1917): 1–7.

ent commentators have since extended Freud's list by further paradigm shifts. The modern history of theological epistemology, too, might be written in as a series of insults: One critical revolution after another has increasingly challenged our confidence in human capabilities to attain the kind of knowledge to which theology has traditionally aspired, necessitating recalibrations and the development of damage control strategies in theological method.

The advent of historical critique undermined theological claims to eternal truths and relativized them to contingent outcomes. After the initial shock at the "ugly ditch"[37] this historical critique laid bare, which seemed to make any perennial truth-claims nonviable, theology (as well as biblical scholarship) realized that these critiques allowed them to recognize forms of "bad theology" and mitigate them methodologically: To avoid uncritically projecting contemporary ideas into texts and artifacts, theology developed a methodological apparatus to take the historicity of its own claims into account. At times, theologians even turned this new-found critical capability into an apologetic virtue to trump the secular sciences and establish their own religion's "relative absoluteness."[38]

Immanuel Kant's famous "all-crushing" critiques demonstrated the limitations of pure reason to know—not just God but at the end of the day really any "thing in itself." After the initial shock wore off, theologians have by and large accepted this critical relativization as inviting them to avoid "bad theologies" that attempted to metaphysically prove the existence of God. As laid out above, theologians thus resorted to a coherentist methodology to establish the intellectual viability of theological claims—or else they heeded Kant's prompt further and shifted the domain of theology from that of "pure reason" to that of "practical reason" or ethics, or, following Schleiermacher's subsequent turn, to that of affect and aesthetics.

Radical criticisms of religion, e.g., its denunciation as projectionism by Ludwig Feuerbach, have shed doubt on how much theologians' claims say about God, rather than merely expressing something about the nature of the human being. The advent of psychoanalysis demoted religious claims further to symbols of the subconscious or understood them as existential coping strategies with contingency. Once more, theologians by and large adopted the criticism and used it to identify and excise projectionist forms of "bad theology." Some, like Karl Barth and Dietrich Bonhoeffer, even radicalized secular critiques of religion theologically, conceptualizing them as an idolatry critique that is part and parcel of the task of theology itself. Even so, they at the same

37. This much-cited expression goes back to Gotthold Ephraim Lessing, *Lessing: Philosophical and Theological Writings* (Cambridge: Cambridge University Press, 2005), 87.

38. Cf. Ernst Troeltsch, *The Absoluteness of Christianity and the History of Religions* (Louisville: Westminster John Knox, 2005).

time reasserted theology's scholarly nature as hyper-criticality by the standards of critiques of religion.

More instantiations of such epistemic game changing "insults" to theological epistemology, with subsequent methodological innovations for quality management and mitigation of newly discerned "bad theologies," could easily be furnished. Such epistemic adaptations are not limited to modernity, either. We might interpret medieval mysticism as a model to recognize and respond to the problem posed by divine ineffability and the epistemic inadequacy of human speech, and an attempt to avoid the overconfidence and hubris that for them marked cataphatic approaches as "bad theologies." We might conceive conciliar theology as well as the development of an authoritative magisterium as methodologies that navigate the problems posed by the specific limitations of human reason, attempting to mitigate "bad theologies" by communal reasoning, expert councils, and strictly ordered procedures. Even the invention of the biblical canon might arguably be understood as a hermeneutic strategy to cope with the problem posed by the elusiveness of divine revelation, and its boundaries were famously drawn to mitigate what "bad theologies" the church saw sprouting from the proliferation and unregulated use of diverse testimonies.

In every epoch, theology has developed its methodology for scholarly theological reflection along the development of its major contemporary intellectual paradigms. Such correspondence need not be understood as a sell-out to the respective zeitgeist or as mere apologetics. It speaks to the reflective decision to do theology—in all its relativity—responsibly, and thus responsively, holding it accountable to the highest critical standards—in all their historical relativity—that the respective epistemic contexts have to offer. As Marcella Althaus-Reid notes, "The theoretical framework of interpretation which theology uses varies in time, or at least, it should. New awakenings of consciousness challenged previous ones."[39] Differences in theological method are adaptations to different epistemic ecologies. They respond to different epistemological problem analyses, leveraging the respective critical insights afforded in pursuit of relatively *better* theology.

All theological method can be understood as damage management strategies of whatever can be diagnosed as "bad theology" by the epistemological lights of the times. More positively, we might conceptualize method as exercises in "fitting" theology to the requirements discerned in its respective epistemic ecologies. Althaus-Reid's observation of such contextual dependence might thus simply be seen as an application of the Reformed *ecclesia semper reformanda* in theological epistemology. Rather than perceiving shifting

---

39. Althaus-Reid and Isherwood, "Thinking Theology," 306.

epistemic contexts as a series of insults, the theologian might see in them gifts
and invitations to greater (self-)awareness. While deepening the awareness of
theology's epistemological fragility, every new round of critical consciousness
has given theology new tools to continue embarking on its already impossible
task with new *instrumentaria,* a bit more humbled, a bit more ennobled, a bit
more in solidarity with other human truth-seeking endeavors.

Despite initial denunciations, it is not surprising that literally every one of
the epistemic challenges mentioned has since largely been recognized by theologians as instead allowing for a deepening and sophistication of theological
inquiry by its increasing critical self-awareness. Systematic Theologians might
thus yet recognize the rise of critical theory in sociology and cultural studies as
a new round of epistemological destabilization that presents a new "awaken-
ing of consciousness," which in theological terms we might also appreciate as
increasing hamartiological realism.

Systematic Theology and Constructive Theology are, then, *both* ecologically fitted ways of doing theology. Their respective methodologies respond to
the challenges and requirements posed by the respective epistemic ecologies
they inhabit. Contextually alerted to different potential forms of "bad theology," both paradigms try to contain them and aim at doing "better" with the
epistemic standards their respective ecologies afford them. Rather than seeing Systematic Theology and Constructive Theology as competing with each
other for scholarly validation and intellectual rigor, it might be more generative to regard them as fundamentally concerned with a similar, and truly
theological task: the old task of saying what can be said about God, the world,
and the human being, while methodically accounting for the fundamental
limitations of human abilities to do so. But both "what can be said" and which
"fundamental limitations" of such an endeavor are recognized and addressable, as well as what comes into view as relatively "better" ways of doing
theology is conditioned by the challenges and requirements of the respective
epistemic ecologies. We might thus typologize these two paradigms in light of
our provincializing analysis as follows:

Drawing on forms of rational coherentism, Systematic Theology identifies
incoherent, illogical, and self-contradictory accounts of belief as intellectually
inviable forms of "bad theology." In its epistemic fitting, Systematic Theology
recognizes that beliefs which are sustained *merely* by tradition ("has always
been believed that way") or authority ("because the church/pope/bible says
so") as insufficient and even dangerous forms of theology and aims at mitigating those dangers methodologically. An orientation to systematicity arises
both from external challenges to the Christian faith—Enlightenment criticisms of dogma and church authority. Even so, it fleshes out deep theological
commitments about the unity of the world and the rationality of God: that the

truth that God *is*, is one, coherent, plausible, and intellectually defensible—because God is good, but also because of this God's fundamental will to community and communication, as affirmed in revelation and salvation history, because of God's unchanging faithfulness to Godself and creation, because of God's desire to be known by God's creatures, and because of the participation in God that eschatologically fulfills true creaturehood. Therefore, rational coherentism is not simply an apologetic move to defend faith-claims against their "cultured critics"—even as such apologetics may at times be found—but developed as necessary (if never sufficient) for *theological* reasons, as a methodology that tries to do justice to the truth theology is called to articulate, reflect on, and maybe even proclaim: If it is not rationally coherent, it is indeed "bad theology."

At its best, Systematic Theology has always recognized the limitations of reason and coherentism to describe the particular objects of theology. Deeply attuned to biblical witness and ecclesial tradition and discerning the reality of God through them, it has relativized its own best efforts and intellectual constructions. It has found its strength in a vision of divine truth that is geared toward human participation and understanding. It has employed its systematic methodology freely in an attempt to "begin again with the beginning,"[40] to resist the inevitable sedimentations of its systematizations. The proposal in the latter chapters of this book recognizes the ongoing value of such a pursuit and draws out pointers toward such an "at its best" of Systematic Theology.

Drawing on diverse strands of critical theory, Constructive Theology in turn identifies as intellectually and theologically unviable forms of "bad theology" approaches that monopolize dominant experiences and perspectives into objective truth, that are harmful to marginalized communities, and complicit in structures of domination and hegemony. In its epistemic fitting, it recognizes that beliefs that are sustained merely universally, without reflection on their contextual presuppositions, commitments, and biases, as intellectually deficient and dangerously hegemonic forms of theology, and aims at mitigating those dangers methodologically.

An orientation to critical contextuality arises from external challenges to the Christian faith—critiques of its imperial and patriarchal complicities. Even so, it fleshes out deep theological commitments about the incarnated nature of God's truth: that the truth that God *is*, is good, liberative, just, and merciful—because God is good, but also because of this God's fundamental will to community in justice and peace, as affirmed in God's acts of solidarity and liberation in salvation history and the incarnation, because of God's unchanging faithfulness to Godself and creation, because of God's desire for

---

40. Barth, *CD I.1*, xi.

the flourishing of God's creatures, and because of the participation in God that eschatologically fulfills true creaturehood. Therefore, critical contextuality is not merely an apologetic move to defend faith-claims against those who criticize them as ideological—even as such apologetics may at times be demanded—but developed as necessary for theological reasons, as a methodology that tries to do justice to the truth theology is called to articulate, reflect on, and maybe even proclaim: If it kills, it is indeed "bad theology."

At its best, Constructive Theology has always recognized the limitations of experience and plural perspectives to achieve an effective critique of theological idolatry. Deeply attuned to the real lives of real people and discerning the reality of God in them, it has been decidedly iconoclastic of its own projections and ideological tendencies. It has found its strength in a vision of divine life that is geared toward justice and human flourishing. It has employed its constructive methodology freely in an attempt to "maintain the liberative character"[41] of theology, to resist the inevitable sedimentations of its own constructions. And again, the proposal in the latter chapters of this book recognizes the ongoing value of such a pursuit and draws out pointers toward such an "at its best" of Constructive Theology.

Rearticulating the typology of Systematic and Constructive Theology according to their epistemic-ecological fitting allows us to also look at the impasse between them differently: In their attunement to the critical awakenings of different paradigms, Systematic and Constructive Theology's respective methodological solutions might simply not gain purchase in a different epistemic ecology, or might there even be seen as part of the problem. But the fact that each approach navigates epistemic-ecologically specific insights does not mean that they are determined externally; it means that "external" critiques—the critical consciousness afforded by the respective epistemic ecology—resonate with "internally" held convictions—theological requirements. Where these requirements meet, they inform the pursuit of *better* theology. The fitting of the pursuit of better theology to an epistemic ecology is thus never simply apologetical, it is also profoundly polemical (to reference the traditional modes of theological engagement in pursuit of truth): It is a complex negotiation between a theological articulation and its epistemic context that is conditioned as much by the requirements of the one as of the other.

Systematic and Constructive Theology are not opponents, then, let alone competitors, even as they also do not necessarily complement one another neatly. Indeed, Systematic Theology and Constructive Theology are not even "two sides" of one theological debate: they respond to different "external" interlocutors, and make theology legible to them, respectively. But insofar as

41. Segundo, *Liberation of Theology*, 40.

they do take an "apologetic" stance, insofar as it is by way of method that they justify their work vis-à-vis different epistemic challenges, their divergence indeed pulls the rug out from one another. If method moves from a navigation of ecological requirements to self-justification, theology's whole existence stands and falls with it—for both of them. Thus, the mutual critiques and "auto-immune" reactions parsed out in chapter 1 ensue. Yet, if we relegate method from the existential status of establishing oneself as "good," to a pragmatic status of ecological fitting in mitigation of "bad theologies," then Systematic and Constructive Theologies can work in relative solidarity with one another, providing one another with constructive mutual irritation and encouragement to push their respective critical awareness further.

Systematic Theology is already a critical and self-critical endeavor that points to divine ineffability and the finitude of human understanding. Constructive epistemic paradigms flesh out the conditions under which human knowledge construction operates, criticizing objective rationality from insights into historical contingency and the embodied conditions of knowledge construction, its contextual dependence and communal testimonial negotiation, as well as, crucially, the play of power in all of these. They do not invalidate human rationality and reasoning, but point out its possibilities as well as its limitations, its temptations and entanglements within a broader horizon of factors that play into the construction of knowledge. The Constructive-theological diagnosis of Systematic Theology's complicity in structural violence and oppression might be taken as midwifing the birth of theological consciousness regarding not simply its finitude but its entanglement in the sin that affects all of human existence.

If by sin we mean a tragic human condition of alienation and distortion of right relationship, one that in its effects undermines trust, destroys the ability to love and be loved, and deprives of hope,[42] that produces suffering and further self-entanglement, then such sin also affects the work of the theologian. Like any other methodology, systematicity is not necessarily *bad*, but like any other methodology, it remains complicit in sin. If systematicity was the tool to mitigate the incoherences attending dogmatism and the irrationalities attending authority structures, then critiques that call into question the aspirational universality, objectivity, self-sufficiency, neutrality, and innocence of Enlightenment's celebrated reason and demonstrate Systematic Theology's own hegemonic functioning do not only refute it but even refute it on its own terms. They ask pointedly if Systematic Theology might have become just

42. This tryptic, a negative to the Pauline theological "virtues," follows Sigrid Brandt's systematization of theological and biblical conceptions of sin, cf. Sigrid Brandt, "Sünde: Ein Definitionsversuch" in *Sünde: Ein unverständlich gewordenes Thema*, ed. Sigrid Brandt et. al., 13–34 (Neukirchen-Vluyn: Neukirchener, 1997).

another iteration of the irrational and authoritarian "bad theologies" it set out to fight. The intellectual conditions upon which Systematic Theology built its self-justification have become questionable, even self-defeating: While they offer intellectual mechanisms that navigate divine ineffability and human finitude methodologically, they do not sufficiently ponder the weight of sin, Anselm's *quantum ponderis peccatum*. By unmasking pervasive unrecognized bias, complicity in power struggles, and self-deception, Constructive Theologians allow Systematic Theology to realize how much more self-critical it needs to become.

The conclusion to be drawn from such recognition is not that it is hopeless to do theology at all, but that such hope does not come from ourselves. Faith knows that only confronted by an Other, only confronted with the real possibility of a different world, do we gain insight into our sin as sin, and only thus our situation changes. In science as in religion, awakenings of consciousness push for conversion, make the need for transformation undeniable and inescapable. There can be no falling back behind critical insight once reached. Drawing on Petrella's earlier analysis, for Systematic Theology to be saved from its self-induced "sanctioned ignorance,"[43] an epistemic conversion needs to take place; Systematic Theology needs to recognize Constructive Theology's critique as confronting us with our own sinful condition.

Epistemological sin does not afflict Systematic-theological method alone. It equally entangles the Constructive theologian, as well as any other pursuits of knowledge. Systematic Theology might also push Constructive Theology to become more self-critical, avoid parochialism, invest in cross-contextual communicability, and attend to the ambivalences of wedding epistemological and political projects. Zooming out further from different approaches to theology, we will find that the crises—or awakenings of consciousness—brought about by epistemic paradigm changes have afflicted all knowledge endeavors. In many modern turns, theology has been the first target of critiques that subsequently challenged broader intellectual, cultural, and societal assumptions in other areas of inquiry. If theology has always struggled with the fact that its *object of knowledge* was outside its reach, in the critical revolutions from Kant to our days, human ability to speak positively about things in themselves and confirm philosophical claims by way of establishing their correspondence with reality has been contested more broadly. If theology has long challenged the aptitude of the human *subject of knowledge* for deeper truths, critique has since challenged the objectivity and universality of reason as not just finite but complicit in structures of domination, hegemony, and exploitation.

---

43. Gayatri Chakravorty Spivak, *A Critique of Postcolonial Reason: Toward a History of the Vanishing Present* (Cambridge; London: Harvard University Press, 1999), 2.

Maybe more than ever before, theology as an intellectual endeavor is in the same boat as all human pursuits of knowledge, as they are increasingly becoming aware of their limitations and entanglements, theologically speaking: their finitude and sin. Rather than perceiving critical challenges from other knowledge-seeking endeavors as threats or competitors in the pursuit of truth, theology would do well to take seriously its deep solidarity with the precarity of all human attempts at understanding. With its hamartiological lens on the condition of all human faculties, theology might even have a unique critical perspective, as Part II will lay out.

PRIMUS USUS METHODUS: DAMAGE CONTROL AND EPISTEMIC PEACEKEEPING

God does not need our good works, but our neighbor does.
—*Martin Luther*[44]

Lege enim disciplina externa et honestas contra feros et indomitos homines utcunque conservatur.
—*Solida Declaratio Fidei*[45]

In the meantime, I will offer a theological lens on the problem of method as discerned so far. The human impossibility of conclusively and unequivocally achieving "the good" was framed by the Reformers as the problem of justification by works of law. While they vigorously denied that the law affords a method to achieve perfection or salvation, they maintained its ongoing importance before, toward, and after sovereign divine grace. They famously formulated a threefold use of the law, which, I argue, can also be applied to the "law" of method:

1. *primus usus legis*: the political or civil use of the law in limiting sin and violence in the fallen earthly society;
2. *secundus usus legis*: the pedagogical and theological use of the law for believers, in which God's command confronts them with their shortcomings and, leading them to despair about their own capacities, prepares them to lean on God's grace instead;
3. *tertius usus legis*: to the believer, the law once more affords concrete guidance for life without turning into an instrument of self-justification.

44. Luther as referenced by Gustaf Wingren, *Luther on Vocation* (Eugene: Wipf & Stock, 2004), 10.
45. Paul Timothy McCain et. al., eds. "The Formula of Concord, Solid Declaration (1577)," in *Concordia: The Lutheran Confessions – A Reader's Edition of the Book of Concord*, 503–620 (St. Louis: Concordia, 2007), VI.1.

In its *primus usus*, the law is a profoundly human institution that does not extend to Christians alone, but recognizes the fundamental needs of human beings for living in community while navigating the fallenness of the world. Rather than aim at the achievement of the good, it implements minimal standards and norms for sustainable coexistence and mitigates the bad by drawing boundaries between what is acceptable and unacceptable conduct. It does not require individuals under the law to subscribe to particular belief commitments. Its rules and regulations are not authorized by divine revelation but are discerned internally by general standards of human rationality, or else function externally through rewards and punishments. Neither are they enforced divinely, but by the worldly authorities of the day, in all their mundanity. Defending these boundaries with force as necessary, the political use of the law remains complicit in and dependent on the violence it seeks to limit.[46]

In an epistemological version of such a *primus usus legis*, the law of method establishes the *disciplina externa et honesta* for theology that reproves sin and teaches good works through external threats and promises.[47] While method may not be able to justify theology once and for all, that does not affect its contextual use and practical necessity in drawing boundaries against "bad theology," limiting their occurrence, and mitigating their damage in contextual discernment, thus allowing for relative possibilities of conviviality and peace. Such a use is not to be despised: Serving both the love of God and of neighbor, it is a genuinely *good* use of the law.

As the laws regulating political and civil existence are neither specifically Christian in their origin or application, theology also does not possess a methodology of its own. It does not have privileged epistemic access to the world. Working under the same conditions as all human pursuits of knowledge, theology has always had to rely on the language, method, and criteria of rigor of its respective intellectual environment. This is a variation on the trope that "all theology is contextual."

The Constructive Theologian reminds us, "In a time when Third World theologians have made contextuality a hermeneutical key, it is sad to notice how contextuality has remained linked to the geographical more than the epistemological."[48] But the Systematic Theologian, too, recognizes the "total dependence [of theology] on its environment . . . for all its freedom it is bound to it, oriented on it, determined and conditioned by it."[49] Yet the dialectic of this total dependence and the sovereignty of the subject matter of

---

46. Cf. John Calvin, *Institutes of the Christian Religion*, ed. John T. McNeill, tr. by Ford Lewis Battles (Philadelphia: Westminster Press, 1960), 4:20.15.
47. McCain et al., "Formula of Concord," IV.1; V.18.
48. Althaus-Reid, *The Queer God*, 25–26.
49. Barth, *CD IV.3*, 1961, 734–35.

theology means that in practice, it has substantial freedom to use, in each time and place, the relatively suitable language, grammar, and style of its epistemic ecology. Rather than perceive its condition in terms of lack, Barth understands it as the "royal freedom" of theology.[50]

Just as no method can "save" theology, no method is fundamentally opposed to it. As in the *usus civilis legis*, method's standards are not proper to theology: they are "borrowed" from logics, linguistics, hermeneutics, archeology, sociology, and so forth. They establish a minimal code of conduct that allows for coexistence because such standards adjudicate what counts as "good conduct" even in the absence of shared belief. Method mediates recognition and legitimacy by mundane criteria that do not rely on divine revelation or intervention. This allows theology to defend its boundaries without the need to create agreement about its content. As in the *usus civilis legis*, method is not enforced by specifically theological institutions, but by the authorities, institutions, and discourses that govern the scholarly community at large. In its first, civil use, method strives for a relatively peaceful coexistence of theology with other intellectual practices and fields of inquiry in a religiously pluralistic or even secular world, and for minimal standards of justice and equity.

Its *primus usus* thus finds theological method in relative solidarity with the conditions of all human knowledge pursuits under the conditions of finitude and fallenness, negotiates their coexistence, and is geared toward limiting "bad theology" more than toward achieving "good" theology. The contestations between different theological methodologies or epistemes can be read as due less to differences about what constitutes theology positively, as to contextual differences in the requirements for good governance: What are the respective forms of "bad theology" in need of damage control? What are the contextual requirements for peaceful coexistence between theology and its epistemic environment? And which hermeneutic and conceptual apparatuses lend themselves to its establishment and defense?

The classification as *primus usus* of theological method establishes the ongoing need for this "political" functioning of boundary management for the possibilities of communal coexistence, while also recognizing the preliminary, imperfect, and complicit nature of all such attempts. This function of method will remain important as a practice of intellectual peacekeeping with the epistemes of the day and between different theological trajectories in a deep solidarity that is grounded in the precarity and finitude of all participants, far beyond the reach of "the theological," per se.

In the negative solidarity under the law in its first use, theologians of diverse stripes will insist on the indivisibility of the discourse into a theological and

---

50. Barth, *CD IV.3*, 739.

non-theological, as well as into an orthodox (or orthoprax) and heterodox realm. Rather than justify ourselves by way of method and ostracizing one another in turn, we are called to constructively attend to the critical insights even of those who themselves are no longer interested in a conversation, taking responsibility not only for our own biases but also responding to the biases of the other in order to strive for the possibility of coexistence in discursive communities.

Conceptualizing methodology within a theological understanding of "the law" thus firmly resists theology's urge toward self-immunization and self-justification by way of theological method. The disagreements between the different epistemic paradigms drawn out earlier are disagreements over the right form of government, not disagreements over the gospel. Neither approach is methodologically self-sufficient, but that does not mean that either of them is not "theological" enough, respectively. They might remain incommensurable, but their incommensurability is due to the contextual requirements they respond to in navigating different epistemic ecologies and in the attempt to mitigate different phenomena of "bad theology." Where contestations between them turn into full-blown confrontation, we might do well to remember that the Reformers recognized the law as good insofar as it limits sin but developed acute sensibilities against its use for moral self-justification. The law of method, too, becomes problematic when it mistakes epistemic governance for the kingdom of God. And it reaches its limits and has to concede its failure when it aspires beyond mitigation of ills to justification and beyond damage control to salvation.

Even as intellectual peacekeeping seems like a task that will not leave theology underemployed in any foreseeable future, this same task also brings into view a deeper disillusionment over what method can do for theology. The imperfection and precarity of methodological adjudication and the insights into its irreducible complicity in the evils it strives to mitigate invariably lead to frustration. But in the despair over the failure of method, the theologian might be disabused of the hubris of self-justification and prepared for the grace we have needed all along. In short, the *secundus usus legis* comes into view.

PART II

How (not) to lose hope
(secundus usus legis)

Chapter 3

Crisis and method

"THOUGH THIS BE METHOD, YET THERE IS CRISIS IN'T."

As theologians, we must speak of God. But we are humans and as such cannot speak of God. We need to know both the "must" and the "cannot," and precisely in this way give God the glory. Everything else is child's play in comparison.

—*Karl Barth[1]*

All theology claims to be a form of soteriology.

—*Jon Sobrino[2]*

Jesus said to him, "Why do you call me good? No one is good but God alone."

—*Mark 10:18*

Mark narrates the story of a young man searching for the *right way:* "As [Jesus] was setting out on a journey, a man ran up and knelt before him, and asked him, 'Good Teacher, what must I do to inherit eternal life?' Jesus said to him, 'Why do you call me good? No one is good but God alone'" (Mark 10:17–18). These verses lead into the well-known parable of the rich young man, challenged to give away all his possessions to the poor, and then come and follow

---

1. Karl Barth, "The Word of God as the Task of Theology, 1922," in *The Word of God and Theology*, ed. Amy Marga, 171–98 (London: T&T Clark, 2011), 177, modified translation.
2. Jon Sobrino, *The Principle of Mercy: Taking the Crucified People from the Cross* (Maryknoll: Orbis, 1994), 37.

Jesus. The story reports that the young man "went away grieving, for he had many possessions," leading Jesus to reflect, "How hard it will be for those who have wealth to enter the kingdom of God!"

I am struck by the little verse-and-a-half that leads into this story. The young man's pursuit of the kingdom is not superficial. He is an engaged and avid believer. As Jesus cites the law at him, the young man impatiently professes having kept the commandments since childhood, no small feat. If there is a critique of wealth in this passage, it is not the usual judgment of exploitation, oppression, or moral corruption. Rather, the young man's wealth seems to be the hallmark of the believer's abundant life, not only economically but morally impressive.[3] And Jesus recognizes and reciprocates his passion; in terminology not used elsewhere in the Gospel, Mark here "states that Jesus loved (*egapesen*) someone."[4] The young man is such an exemplar of discipleship that commentaries note, "If this man, with every advantage and indication of being near the kingdom, cannot be saved, then who can?"[5]

Yet the young man is restless, even as he has fulfilled the law. "Good teacher," he entreats, only to have Jesus snap at him, "why do you call me good? No one is good but God alone." Everything else in the story is a development of this initial, direct, visceral response, at the danger of distracting from it. The rebuke seems unwarranted. The young man *wants* to do right, he seeks further wisdom and advice, and he seeks it in the right place.

Maybe this is precisely the problem: the orientation to perfection and fulfillment, the fixation on "the good." What could be a greater good than eternal life and the care of the poor (a challenge that the story in no way diminishes or abrogates but rather keeps in place)! But maybe this orientation to achieving the good (we might think of Sarah Ahmed's thoughtful investigation of what orientations *do*[6]) leads the young man astray precisely by insisting on an ever-straighter path. This path is *not* a dead-end, we might even say that it is *unfortunately* not a dead end. Maybe Jesus's musing about the difficulty for this young man to enter the kingdom does not insinuate that he will never give away his many possessions. Maybe the issue is rather that the young man has *so many* resources that he can *keep* giving away almost indefinitely, without coming to an end to stop, reorient, and turn around. When there is still something more one can do, it is easy to deceive oneself into thinking that doing *more* is *doing good*. The problem with resources is that they can so easily fill the gap of that which is not attainable, not achievable—eternally deferring the insight that "No one is good but God alone."

3. Cf. M. Eugene Boring, *Mark: A Commentary*, New Testament Library (Louisville: Westminster John Knox, 2006), 296.

4. Boring, *Mark*, 295.

5. Boring, *Mark*, 296.

6. Sara Ahmed, *Queer Phenomenology: Orientations, Objects, Others* (Durham: Duke University Press, 2006).

Might the story be applicable to material, intellectual, and institutional resources in the pursuit of "good theology," as well? Maybe the parable faces us with an even greater challenge than to employ all our intellectual resourcefulness in attaining good theology, by finding the right method, or by trying yet one more method. The greater challenge is to give up our pursuit of "the good" as something we can locate and allocate. "Why do you call me good?" is neither a reminder of Jesus's humanity nor a pun about his true divinity ("Jesus *is* good because he is, after all, the *God* who is 'good alone'"). "No one is good but God alone" radically confronts the Christian's *best* desire as also our greatest temptation. The parable pushes back against this urge, while in no way abandoning or diminishing the ethical demand. Method cannot save us, but "for God all things are possible" (Mark 10:27).

Theology as a discipline has been busy for decades, frantically searching for *just* the right way, *just* the angle, *just* the methodological innovation or restoration that would solve its crises of identity and relevance, heal its sense of moral injury, and confer meaning, relevance, and integrity. Theology is ready to keep investing time, effort, and its remaining ecclesial and societal standing, into demonstrating the rightness of its approach—a readiness that can be discerned across a whole breadth of vigorously maintained, fiercely committed, and mutually conflicting approaches. But maybe this is a misdirected desire?

Where crises have been diagnosed, a turn to methodological reflection has often been the move to address them, engendering remarkable scholarly productivity. Pronouncements of crisis may thus not be indications of lack as much as a method of choice to generate a sense of relevance, identity, and moral purpose for a precarious field in the first place; it is a way to keep doing something more, something else, in order to hopefully, eventually, do the good.

But the pronouncement of crisis is hardly new, not confinable to the contemporary stand-off between Systematic and Constructive Theology. A twofold crisis of relevance and identity was already diagnosed by Jürgen Moltmann half a century ago.[7] Another half a century earlier, "crisis" was the watchword that became eponymous for dialectical theology,[8] preceded further by a number of earlier turns of the epistemological-methodological spiral; different awakenings of critical consciousness, some of which we traced in the last chapter. For decades, groundbreaking works have more often been occupied with redefinitions of theology and proposals in method than with doctrine. Reflection on the nature and task of the theological project has gained ever more ground

---

7. Moltmann, *The Crucified God*, ch. 1.

8. Cf. Friedrich Gogarten, "Die Krisis unserer Kultur [1920]," in *Anfänge der dialektischen Theologie*, ed. Jürgen Moltmann, 2:101–21 (München: Kaiser, 1963); Barth, "The Word of God as the Task of Theology."

within theological reflection for centuries,[9] culminating in the suspicion that "with the prolegomena *everything*" might already be "said."[10] Laments over the "de-substantialisation"[11] of theology worry that the preoccupation with method means that "*the* problem of the contemporary systematic theologian" becomes "actually *to do* systematic theology."[12]

A deeper sense of crisis might thus arise from the ongoing state of crisis in which the discipline seems to have found itself for as long as it can remember. To invoke the late Walter Benjamin, "That things continue this way—*that* is the catastrophe."[13] As the suspicion emerges that the sense of crisis is coextensive with the discipline itself, we might ask, is crisis (and which crisis?) really the problem, and method the site at which to address it? What if method has never been a solution, but at the end of the day, is itself a crisis-producing machine? And what if "crisis" is not a problem to be solved after all, if the ongoing crisis-mode and the succession of crises is even the way in which the discipline justifies and legitimates itself in the first place?

Karl Barth had famously little patience for any of the particular crises decried by his contemporaries or attempts to solve them methodologically. Still, the question of method was central to many of the heated debates he sustained with contemporaries, on scriptural hermeneutics, natural theology, or the *analogia entis* question. A remarkable portion of his work revolves around the impossibility of doing theology, of doing it rightly. Dialectical theology is driven by the existential dilemma that there is no methodologically securable standing ground, and that theology thus has to be deconstructed time and again.

Of course, Barth rarely begins method, and he does not identify theology's perceived "impossibility" with its lack of relevance, self-definition, or moral integrity. Instead, he insists on identifying "the real crisis" behind the crises of his time as the particular subject matter of theology: the wholly Other God. The epistemological gap between us and God is both an ontological and a hamartiological one. Method thus has to fail, for theological reasons.

Of all human knowers, the theologian might be uniquely cognizant of the fact that their object of inquiry can never be grasped epistemologically, and that there is something *wrong* with the human being even beyond the limitations

9. Wolfhart Pannenberg, *Systematische Theologie* (Göttingen: Vandenhoeck & Ruprecht, 1991), 1:37.

10. Barth, "The Word of God as the Task of Theology," 198.

11. Notger Slenczka, "Flucht aus den dogmatischen Loci: Das Erbe des 20. Jahrhunderts. Neue Strömungen in der Theologie." *Zeitzeichen*, no. 8 (2013): 45–4847, my translation.

12. David Tracy, *Blessed Rage for Order: The New Pluralism in Theology* (New York: Seabury, 1975), 238.

13. Walter Benjamin, "Charles Baudelaire. Ein Lyriker im Zeitalter des Hochkapitalismus, Zentralpark 1937," in *Gesammelte Schriften*, ed. Rolf Tiedemann and Hermann Schweppenhäuser, 1:509–690 (Frankfurt am Main: Suhrkamp, 1991), 683, my translation.

posed by our finitude. Why this should be the case remains utterly inexplicable, but it appears that individually as well as collectively, historically and in our own lives, human beings both suffer from and exacerbate alienation from God, fellow humans, ourselves, and the world. Even applying the best of human faculties, neither we nor the cognitive systems we produce will ever be "pure" or "innocent," but will always *also* generate tendencies that exacerbate this alienation. The theologian calls this condition "sin," and means more than misbehavior, bad intentions, or harmful actions. "Sin" is no moralizing indictment but the diagnosis of the tragic and inextricable quality of human self-entanglement, self-perpetuating and escalating as it undermines trust, destroys the ability to love and be loved, and thwarts the potential for hope.[14]

The Reformers explicitly extended their account of sin to theological epistemology, maintaining that sin affects the human being in their totality, not exempting any faculty, corrupting the soul as much as the flesh, cognition as much as desire.[15] Divine ineffability and human finitude will relativize what method can achieve, marking human understanding as incomplete but not fundamentally negate it. Sin, by contrast, will twist and turn human understanding into something ontologically void but devastating and destructive in its effects. Finitude might make human insight *insufficient*; sin will make it *wrong*.

In his *Church Dogmatics,* Barth develops a threefold phenomenology of sin as hubris, sloth, and falsehood, which also applies to theology's attempt to master its object by way of method. But already his programmatic essays in the 1920s declare the "*defeat* of *all* theology and of *every* theologian," its impossibility of theology by way of whichever method.[16] From its inception, theology is caught in a double bind of necessity and impossibility, characterized in famously dialectical form: "As theologians, we must speak of God. But we are humans and as such cannot speak of God. We need to acknowledge both our 'must' and our 'cannot,' and precisely in this way give God the glory."[17]

Theology must respond to a command which in the first place requires it to admit its inherent incapability to respond. Neither does the command meet an inherent ability to respond to it, nor can any response do the command justice. When theology responds, and thus heeds the command, it performatively transgresses its creaturely boundaries. When it instead acknowledges these boundaries and stays silent, it fails to live up to its task. Theology cannot

14. Cf. Brandt, "Sünde."

15. The theology of the cross developed by Luther in his *Heidelberg Disputation* pinpoints the effects of sin beyond the flesh, extending to human reason and will, thus necessitating a theological epistemology that takes sin into account. For a full-blown critique of theological epistemology on this basis see Jürgen Moltmann, *The Crucified God: The Cross of Christ as the Foundation and Criticism of Christian Theology* (New York: Harper & Row), 1974.

16. Barth, "The Word of God as the Task of Theology," 197.

17. Barth, "The Word of God as the Task of Theology," 177, revised translation.

escape that bind. Indeed, its very task becomes a "plight" such that "[e]very-
thing else is child's play in comparison."[18]

Barth investigates three possible responses to this dilemma, although he
announces from the outset that "All three end up with the insight that we
cannot give the answer."[19] The first, positive, and the second, negative way of
doing theology are dismissed as overly optimistic about human capacities, but
even the third, dialectical approach—which people subsequently identified
with Barth's "school"—does not fundamentally overcome the impossibility of
theology by way of its method; at best, it navigates it.

The dilemma laid out in Barth's programmatic essay, *The Word of God as the
Task of Theology,* is a critical self-reflection of the Systematic Theologian. But
Constructive Theologies have identified similar dilemmas in the century since.
In this chapter, I thus use Barth's threefold impossibility to parse out the apo-
ria of all attempts to achieve and justify "good" theology, enriching them with
parallels from Constructive Theological conversations. Broadly, the dilemma
will look something like this:

- Frustration with the fact that the theologian ultimately *"cannot"* live up to
  our task unmasks the hubris in positive approaches: Flights to the intellectual purity of orthodoxy or the ethical purity of orthopraxy by way of
  method can neither guarantee the truth nor the justice of any theology, and
  attempts to do so only lead into inhumanity.
- The demand that the theologian still *"must"* continue with our task unmasks
  the sloth in radically negative approaches: Flights to sophisticated medi-
  tations on the impossibility of theology, to critique and self-critique, and
  to refusal and negation still fall into inverse forms of Prometheanism or
  attempts to maintain one's own integrity at the expense of the entanglement and complicity with the world.
- Hitting the rock bottom of methodological hopelessness, the theologian
  might learn from dogmatics to understand the aspiration to secure success
  by way of method as an intellectual form of self-justification and works-
  righteousness. From queer theory and design theory, the theologian might
  in turn learn to *"give God the glory"* by using method *after method* as a form of
  serious, subversive, and self-relativizing *"child's play."*

THE HUBRIS OF DOGMATISM

Despite Barth's identification of the first, "positive" approach with "dogmatic" theology, the modes of speech and the epistemological assumptions it
references can be embodied by both Systematic and Constructive theologies.

18. Barth, "The Word of God as the Task of Theology," 177.
19. Barth, "The Word of God as the Task of Theology," 186.

Systematic-theological versions of "positive" theology display an epistemological optimism that the church's faith can be spelled out in a (relatively) conceptually coherent and comprehensive body of dogma, confident that human reason and experience are able to discern (relative) truth from falsehood, find (relatively) adequate models that convey theological insight, and are thus able to get theological reflection closer to truth. On the positive foundation of biblical testimony and church tradition, as well as confident in the ability of reason, experience, and conversation to make sense of them, they make positive claims about God, the world, and the human being—including positive claims about divine ineffability and human finitude!

Constructive-theological versions of a "positive" approach can be found in theologies of hope[20] or liberation[21] that insist that God is positively on the side of the oppressed, that "another world is possible."[22] These proposals embody an epistemological optimism that a critical praxis in engagement with the world will allow us to come to the (relatively) right political and theological insights and advance the (relative) materialization of the better world promised by faith. Born in an explicit pushback against Western dogmatic orthodoxy (as an epistemic paradigm, not necessary with regard to its content), theologies of hope and liberation are not naive in their quest. They emerged out of a commitment to the concrete material struggles of disenfranchised and oppressed communities, taking these as an epistemological starting point, generative for theological reflection itself, rather than merely an ethical ramification of doctrinal thought. Often framed as an emphasis on orthopraxy instead of orthodoxy, their optimism is a critical and reflective one, best captured by Juan Luis Segundo's famous remark that "the one and only thing that can maintain the liberative character of any theology is not its content but its methodology."[23]

Despite all insight that a commitment to "right teaching" does not guarantee any particular outcome in congruence with it, positive approaches in Constructive Theologies have maintained both the positive ideal of Liberation as such and the commitment to "right practice" as unequivocally aligning with this goal, just like positive approaches to Systematic Theology have maintained optimism about achieving "right teaching" in the first place. Substituting a Constructive method for a Systematic one takes little away from the inherently positive (or "dogmatic") character: Methodologically-secured orthodoxy and methodologically-secured orthopraxy equally embody a

20. Following Jürgen Moltmann, *Theology of Hope: On the Ground and the Implications of a Christian Eschatology* (Minneapolis: Fortress, 1993).

21. Following Gustavo Gutiérrez, *A Theology of Liberation: History, Politics, and Salvation* (London: SCM, 1973).

22. Thus the oft-invoked slogan of the *World Social Forum* that emerged from Liberationist advocacy "from below" against neoliberal globalization.

23. Segundo, *Liberation of Theology*, 39–40.

general confidence in the human ability to discern right from wrong, better from worse, and to make progress along these ideals.

Marcella Althaus-Reid's attack on "T-theology," the self-veiling "decency," its coercive effects, and its complicity in intersectional structures of domination (see chapter 1) can easily be read as a Constructive-theological account of epistemological sin, and it is directed against Systematic Theology as much as against the positive versions of Liberation and Feminist Theology. Karl Barth's critique of epistemological sin is no less scathing: Even the best of all theology remains "a dubious and equivocal phenomenon," susceptible to "misunderstanding, deception, falsification and corruption."[24] The incommensurable difference between creator and creature measures the epistemic limitation of any "positive" approach. This foundational difference marks any attempt to talk definitively about God as undue overreach, slipping into hubris. Theological system-building is a case in point, where the theologian heroically advances the truth of God to the point of mastering, controlling, and overriding it. Confident of having identified the site and content of God's truth, the theologian

> sets up a theoretical and practical system of truth . . . . He is so active in the cause of truth that compared with him Jesus Christ the true Witness seems to be only a waif and bungler who must surely be glad that He has found a patron and advocate to support Him so skillfully and powerfully.[25]

Such hubris need not be self-serving and self-elevating; it might be done wholly in service to the seriousness of the task. Like the heroic figure of Dostoevsky's Grand Inquisitor, who casts out Jesus Christ because the freedom announced by him is more demanding than beneficial for the human being, the Systematic Theologian steps into the place of God with his aspiration of providing a clearer, tidier, *better* version of God's word. In the positive presentation of the truths of theology, the theologian "nostrifies" and "domesticates" this truth, putting it into a form that renders it bearable and comprehensible, manageable and executable. Hubris thus tips into falsehood, of which Barth says,

> Nothing is more dangerous than the falsehood in which [the theologian] manages, or at least tries and thinks that he [*sic!*] manages, to use the truth to silence the truth, or the true Witness, by finding for Him a place, by championing Him, by making Him its Hero, Example and Symbol, yet all the time patronising, interpreting, domesticating,

---

24. Karl Barth, *Church Dogmatics IV.3: The Doctrine of Reconciliation*, ed. Geoffrey W. Bromiley and Thomas F. Torrance (Edinburgh: T&T Clark, 1961), 376.
    25. Barth, *CD IV.3,* 436.

acclimatising, accommodating, and gently but very definitely and significantly correcting Him.[26]

The highest reverence for the supremacy of God, promoted systematically, can function as an ideological construct to render God's demand innocuous. It introduces an image, a "substitute God"[27] in piously conceptualized form, rendered coherent and congenial with what the theologian already knows to be true. The hubris of theology thus turns into falsehood as, with all methodological justification, the theologian fails to do justice to God's freedom and actively obscures it. She puts God into the box of a theological system and replaces God's free and sovereign grace with the systematic tracing of its underlying logic, thus actively "neutralizing," "smoothing," and "eliminating" the promised "liberation of man by and for the free God."[28] Nothing is allowed to happen that is not accounted for by the positive dogma.

But the *falsehood* does not start where theology misapprehends or misconstrues the truth. Factual error, as well as disagreement over what should count as truth, are widespread but undramatic implications of human finitude. Sin is a different category. Barth illustrates his treatment of sin as falsehood with Job's three friends and insists: What they *say* about God is not incorrect; it is the best any Systematic Theologian could offer. Yet what the friends *do* by the way they *wield* that truth over Job means that their very correct theology becomes in effect "the continuation, development and even the fulfillment of the satanic assault"[29] with which Job is stricken! By trying to speak God's truth to Job, and by insisting on possessing the theologically correct account of truth, they turn their truth into falsehood because the way in which they use that truth does not correspond to its—arguably theologically correct—content. With their positively correct theology, they immunize themselves against the real, concrete, and existential demand in front of them: Job's wrestling with God.

The problem with the dogmatic approach does not start where it gets God's truth *wrong*. Even and *especially* where theology gets it *right*, convinced of its possession of the truth, it turns the truth of God into an idol. Pointing to its own possession of the truth, it indulges in hubris about the possibility of human understanding, the sufficiency of human intellect and language, the progress and perfectability of knowledge, about the human's capacity to move beyond Feuerbachian projection when talking about God, about the possibility to root out error and bias by one's own lights—and in turn about its entitlement and

26. Barth, *CD IV.3*, 505.
27. Barth, *CD IV.3*, 450.
28. Barth, *CD IV.3*, 448.
29. Barth, *CD IV.3*, 453.

right to wield the thus discerned truth, apply it, put it to use. By stepping up to speak God's truth—whether in the form of magisterial dogma or prophetic socioeconomic critique—the theologian puts her word in the place of God's word and herself in the place of God. This inversion of right relationship that results in epistemological self-justification is the target of Barth's famous, and often misunderstood, critique of religion.[30]

Interestingly, Barth sees as the ultimate issue with "dogmatic" or "positive" speech of God not the overstepping of creaturely boundaries, but its *inhumanity*. Even more than the epistemological hubris, Barth critiques that the positive approach flouts the humanity of the human being and ignores the humanity of God altogether. As illustrated by Job's friends, the human "question about God is abolished by this kind of answer," and an answer that does not reach the human, does not become answer "for us" is no answer *at all*. In turn, "God alone [German *an sich*, i.e. as God in and for Godself, not as the God of the human being] is not God"—"The God who becomes human is [G]od." But in their positive, definitive, objective talk about God, "Dogmaticians do not speak of *this* God."[31] Failing to do justice both to its divine object and the human subject, such a theology, then, has radically missed its *subject matter*. It betrays that it has understood *nothing*.

Straightforward positivism has, of course, long been critiqued theologically. The more reflective versions not only of progressive but even of the more doctrinally conservative schools recognize that positive doctrine is theologically impossible. If Barth's theological critique was directed theologically against the epistemological optimism of both classical and modern liberal-theological ideas of reason, such disillusionment has only further progressed in the century since his programmatic manifesto. Human reason and its capacity for enlightenment and progress (another term that curiously straddles the boundary between the historical and the noetic, the political and the epistemological) have been thoroughly called into question as bound up with coloniality and whiteness. Such critiques of "positive" approaches not only affect Systematic Theology. Both orthodox- and orthoprax-based optimisms have become increasingly questionable. If generations of Liberation Theology felt empowered and inspired by a *Theology of Hope*[32] and a *Theology of Liberation*,[33] the very notions of "hope" and "liberation" have in the meantime been critiqued as

---

30. Thickly palpable already in Karl Barth, *The Epistle to the Romans*, tr. Edwyn C. Hoskyns (Oxford: Oxford University Press, 1968), he develops it most extensively in Karl Barth, *Church Dogmatics IV.3: The Doctrine of Reconciliation*, ed. Geoffrey W. Bromiley and Thomas F. Torrance (Edinburgh: T&T Clark), 1961, sec. 17.

31. Barth, "The Word of God as the Task of Theology," 187, emphasis mine.

32. Moltmann, *Theology of Hope*.

33. Gutiérrez, *A Theology of Liberation*.

depending on the same modernist optimism, the same dogmatic positivity with all its limitations as well as complicities as its Systematic-theological counterparts. Maybe, the "dogmatic" theologian might admit, we cannot ever get to "truth" or "justice," but maybe we can, in incremental steps, inch our way toward them, asymptotically getting closer even if we self-critically acknowledge that an ultimately unbridgeable gap will always remain between our best pursuits and the thing itself. Alternatively, maybe we cannot give one positive, comprehensive account of the truth, but different approaches might positively complement one another into a fuller picture.

Over the past half century, Liberationist Theologies, too, have been deepening their critique and self-critique through intersectional analysis, which not only complexified but also brought to light ineradicable ambiguities of "positive" approaches. To name but a few examples: In her womanist study, *Sisters in the Wilderness*, Delores Williams demonstrates that theological hope in liberation may not only be unrealistic, and therefore in the long-term an unsustainable struggle, but also that it has historically been partially counterproductive for Black women, in particular. It has resulted in heroic cries for self-empowerment that resonated widely with Black masculinities but were easily frustrated in history's more ambiguous outcomes. And it has advocated for redemptive suffering and patterns of surrogacy that further increase Black women's plight, now with theological justification.[34]

In a similar critique, Joseph Winters points out that while a belief in the possibility of progress has been central to many struggles and movements of resistance and transformation, it paradoxically also reifies myths of American exceptionalism and structurally "operates to establish and justify racial hierarchies," thus remaining dependent on and subservient to the very structures it denounces.[35] In the face of its historical abuses and structural ramifications, political theologian Vincent Lloyd concludes that "hope is not a virtue."[36] Latinx theological ethicist Miguel De la Torre calls for *Embracing Hopelessness*[37] in light of the overwhelming evidence of racialized discrimination and violence, neoliberal global exploitation, and climate apocalypse, that positive theology, both in its doctrinal and in its liberationist optimism, has "continually stood on the wrong side of history."[38]

34. Delores S. Williams, *Sisters in the Wilderness: The Challenge of Womanist God-Talk* (Maryknoll: Orbis, 1993).

35. Joseph R. Winters, *Hope Draped in Black: Race, Melancholy, and the Agony of Progress* (Durham: Duke University Press, 2016), 10.

36. Vincent Lloyd, *The Problem with Grace: Reconfiguring Political Theology* (Stanford: Stanford University Press, 2011).

37. Miguel A. De la Torre, *Embracing Hopelessness* (Minneapolis: Fortress, 2017).

38. De la Torre, *Embracing Hopelessness*, 2.

In the positivity marked by *hope*—where the strife for understanding and betterment, and the belief in the possibility of a different world come together in an optimism in theology's capacity to "get it right"—De la Torre sees yet another "quest for universal meaning in history" that only brutalizes those on its underside, justifies and placates current suffering, fosters demobilizing complacency and engenders racialization, supremacy, and exceptionalism.[39] In her own critique, Marcella Althaus-Reid writes,

> We perhaps need to demythologize liberation theology as a naive the-
> ology, but more than that, we need to demystify it . . . . More than
> trying to affirm liberation theology as a theology based on a premise
> of equality, we need to understand that no theology can escape the
> epistemological characteristics of its time, even if it intends to oppose
> them.[40]

Critiques of "positive" approaches, whether in dogmatic theologies or theologies of hope, thus oddly concur in their denunciation of its inhumanity. Like Barth, Marcella Althaus-Reid postulates that the liberation of God and the liberation of the human being go hand in hand. As for Barth, so for Miguel de la Torre the commitment to the reality of God and to the reality of the human being is what precludes the continuation of positive, "dogmatic" approaches to theology:

> With all my heart, soul, mind, and body, I wish to become intoxicated
> with the simplicity of unquestionable and uncomplicated faith. But to
> do so would be an insult to the vast majority of humanity scraping by
> at the margins of society, and an insult to an absent God in whom I
> grudgingly choose to believe, regardless of whether said God exists.[41]

What might traditionally be construed as "ethical" vs. "dogmatic" arguments or what might be framed as Systematic-theological vs. Constructive-theological commitments are conjoined: For the sake of God *and* for the sake of the human being, the positive approach is inviable. Practically and theoretically, quests for "the good" in theology cannot escape spirals of despair, afflicting not only the Systematic Theologian in her attempt to speak of God rightly but also the Constructive Theologian in his attempt to realize the material correlate of this God's word in liberation, right relations, justice, and peace. Flights to truth under the banner of orthodoxy and flights to praxis under the banner of orthopraxy—as if either could be established beyond ambivalence,

---

39. De la Torre, *Embracing Hopelessness*, 25.
40. Althaus-Reid, Marcella, Ivan Petrella, and Luiz Carlos Susin, eds., *Another Possible World* (London: SCM, 2007), 27.
41. De la Torre, *Embracing Hopelessness*, 154.

equivocation, and complicity—are merely versions of evading the problem of theology. Praxis is just as ambivalent and equivocal as theory, historical optimism as brittle as noetic optimism, and on both "sides" the political and the epistemological are deeply intertwined.

From Black to Womanist, from Feminist to Queer, from Liberationist to Post- and Decolonial approaches, Constructive Theologies have by and large become ever more (self-)critical over the past decades. The participation of new constituencies in Western academic reflection resulted in attention to hitherto unaccounted factors in critique and self-critique. Every new wave of theoretical and intersectional critique, we may hope, adds to the critical awareness of the theologian and to her critical toolbox. Surely, at least such an accumulation of cautions and restraints might count as a form of epistemic progress, if progress in critique only? The "dogmatic" theologian who strives toward a "better" theology will not simply replace any one paradigm with another but will continue to self-critically take new and more critical challenges into account in her positive attempt to speak about God *rightly*.

The critiques we have briefly visited, however, also raise cautions with regard to deflated, incremental, yet still "straight"-forward aspirations to progress: If, as they have shown in so many inflections, the notion of progress itself is deeply and structurally complicit in historic violence and human hubris, particular shifts of critical consciousness that were critical gains in certain respects easily become critical losses in other respects. The first and maybe crucial insight of intersectionality was that dimensions of oppression and injustice cannot be treated additively but are in complex ways mutually constitutive and exacerbate one another. As demonstrated by Kimberlé Crenshaw, Black women's plight is not simply the addition of gender- and race-based discrimination, nor will it be attended to automatically by the advancement of Feminism and Black Liberation.[42] As drawn out in Delores Williams as well as Marcella Althaus-Reid's interventions, different critical perspectives do not necessarily complement one another, they also call one another into question theoretically and are practically sometimes in contradiction to one another, even as they might be building on one another in important ways.

Ironically, progress in critical awareness has thus engendered ever more pessimism regarding the possibility of progress itself, recognizing the inextricable complicity of struggles for understanding and liberation in injustice. To maintain, like Segundo did, that "the one and only thing that can maintain the liberative character of any theology is not its content but its methodology"[43] is

42. Kimberlé Crenshaw, "Demarginalizing the Intersection of Race and Sex: A Black Feminist Critique of Antidiscrimination Doctrine, Feminist Theory and Antiracist Politics," *University of Chicago Legal Forum*, no. 1 (1989): 139–67.

43. Segundo, *Liberation of Theology*, 39–40.

too optimistic about methodologically secured orthopraxy—which turns out to be epistemologically and politically every bit as ambivalent, complex, and complicit as optimism in orthodoxy's methodological securement of truth. The idea that progress (whether political or epistemic) could be achieved by ever increasing degrees of inclusion, or that different theological approaches might be integrated into a kind of pan-intersectional paradigm is quickly disillusioned both in theory and practice.

But not only is pan-intersectionality—or comprehensive integration of the whole range of Constructive-theological concerns and critiques in a kind of super-Systematic Theology—an *impossibility*. The question, we might say with Barth, is also whether it is *desirable*,[44] since it reproduces the need for recognition according to a prevailing symbolic system that produced the exclusion in the first place. The theological insight that the attempt to mitigate sin leads to the reproduction of sin on the next level resonates with the queer insight that "the Symbolic can only win."[45] Every integration will proceed according to a rule that puts conditions on qualifying approaches to be *legible* by these standards in order to become *eligible*. In light of these *structural* demands that pit theories and theologies against one another even within well-meaning agendas of integration and inclusion, queer theologian Linn Tonstad points out, "The demand for symbolic recognition is itself the problem."[46] Rather than aiming toward greater inclusion, the task of the theologian might thus be "to focus our attention on the non-integrability that structures every subject and every social order—that is, on the impossibility of inclusion, and the destructive effects of aiming at it."[47]

If the positive ideals of Systematic and Constructive Theologies are thus thoroughly frustrated, might it be more promising to think in terms of *shifts* of critical consciousness rather than their accumulation in absolute terms, to pursue "better theology" by way of critique rather than positive assertion, and thus to frame theology's task not as the achievement of "good theology" or the positive integration of more, however relative, insight toward that end, but instead of ever new rounds of critique—*semper reformanda* as a perpetual movement of negation?

---

44. Karl Barth, "Wünschbarkeit und Möglichkeit eines allgemeinen reformierten Glaubensbekenntnisses. 1925," in *Vorträge und kleinere Arbeiten 1922-1925*, ed. Hinrich Stoevesandt, 19:604–43. GA. (Zürich: TVZ, 1990).

45. Lee Edelman, *No Future: Queer Theory and the Death Drive*, Series q (Durham: Duke University Press, 2004), 26.

46. Linn Marie Tonstad, "The Limits of Inclusion: Queer Theology and Its Others," *Theology & Sexuality* 21, no. 1 (2015): 1–19, 2.

47. Tonstad, "The Limits of Inclusion," 1–2.

THE SLOTH OF CRITIQUE

How *not* to do theology might at this point be relatively easier to ascertain than *how to do theology*. If historically, negative theology might have been mystical and rather apolitical, and critical theologies might have been rather optimistic in their conviction that the successive elimination of wrongs might accumulate into epistemic capital, Barth compellingly discusses the long theological tradition of *apophaticism* together with contemporary practices of *critique* as "negative" ways of doing theology. Contemporary Constructive Theologies similarly combine critique and negativity in the attempt to find alternative ways through the complexity of positivity's epistemological, theological, and political entanglements.

No mere subjective mood, negativity presents itself as the realism appropriate to the theological disillusionments of the twentieth and early twenty-first centuries. Whether melancholically redressing "hope draped in black,"[48] pessimistically calling for "embracing hopelessness,"[49] or fervently advocating a radical stance of refusal, negativity has become an existentially and intellectually compelling theological option, both epistemologically and politically.

Despite a theoretical predilection for the "positive," Barth finds, "*We* stand more deeply in the 'No' than in the 'Yes,' deeper in criticism and protest than in naivety."[50] The reality of the wholly Other marks first and foremost a boundary for any human attempt to epistemologically grasp, master, and own God or politically appropriate and instrumentalize theological insight.[51] The divine judgment under which this puts humanity translates seamlessly into a theological habitus of negation: Barth's Romans commentary and dialectical writings manifest a comprehensive and relentless critique of "religion"—a sometimes misleading term that for Barth is less a descriptor of actually existing faith-based practice or institutions than a verdict over the possessive, self-elevating hubris of any theological mastery, including his own.

---

48. Winters, *Hope Draped in Black*.

49. De la Torre, *Embracing Hopelessness*.

50. Barth, *The Word of God and Theology*, 60, similar in *RomI*, 216, *RomII*, 486 (for some obscure reason rendered as "Our negations submerge us more deeply than do our affirmations," in the translation of Edwyn Hoskyns, Barth, *Romans II*, 1968, 462), and *GDII*, 244.

51. Some have maintained that it was Barth's insistence on God's alterity as radical negation of the human being that allowed Barth to also be "uniquely alert politically": Christian Link, "Bleibende Einsichten von Tambach" in *Karl Barth in Deutschland*, ed. Michael Beintker, Christian Link, and Michael Trowitzsch, 333–46 (Zürich: TVZ, 2005). Others have debated how uniquely alert he really was, e.g. with regard to the "Jewish question": Hermann E. J. Kalinna, *War Karl Barth "politisch einzigartig wach"? Über Versagen politischer Urteilskraft* (Münster: LIT, 2009). However far Barth's judgment may or may not have extended historically, it is clear that he has explicitly founded his political stances of resistance on his theological base conviction.

The strength of the negative approach is that it takes theology's impossibility seriously and translates it into the rigor of critique. "The only thing we are *certain* of, that which we can *demonstrate*, is always only the negation, the negativity of the human," Barth posits.[52] Theology, then, can "in no way be about the building up of the human but must fundamentally be about helping in the deconstruction of [human] existence."[53] Barth is quite aware that not only positive modes of doing theology but also pledges to radical negativity will continue to engage in theological projection and self-affirmation. Negativity might even be particularly prone to hubris. But no getting-it-right, whether in our dogmatic claims or in our critique, can provide the human being with an epistemological "standing-place in the air."[54] Critique has to continue to tear down the illusion of having found such a ground in whatever positive or negative insight or method. No simple negativity is demanded but "to move from one negation to the next."[55]

Barth was a master of such relentless movement. When his Romans commentary—already a scathing intervention against the state of the discipline—was favorably received, he revised it thoroughly until no doubt could remain about its antagonism.[56] Many of Barth's salient contributions perform critical negations of the very tasks set before him, to the (strategic?) disappointment of his audience: When religious socialists invited him to lay out the task of *The Christian in Society*, he disabused them harshly of the idea that this might refer to *them*, and swept the rug of activist energy out from underneath them.[57] When asked to speak to the crisis of preaching, he insisted that what they experienced was not yet the real crisis, which was moreover wholly without solution.[58] When the Alliance of Reformed Churches invited him to discuss perspectives for a unified Reformed Confession, he denied both the necessity and desirability of such a pursuit.[59] Barth executed relentless public judgment on not only prominent theological figures but also on his teachers and even his closest friends and once-allies, despite their (often surprisingly long-sustained)

---

52. Barth, "The Word of God as the Task of Theology," 189.
53. Barth, "The Word of God as the Task of Theology," 188.
54. Barth, *Romans II*, 94.
55. Barth, "The Word of God as the Task of Theology," 188.
56. Barth explains that what necessitated the revision was "a careful consideration of the manner in which the first edition of this book has been received. I am bound to say that the more favourable reviews have been most valuable in compelling me to criticize myself. Their praise has caused me such dismay that I have had sometimes to express the matter otherwise, sometimes even to adopt an entirely different position" (Barth, *Romans II*, 4).
57. Karl Barth, "The Christian in Society," in *The Word of God and Theology*, ed. Amy Marga, 31–70 (London; New York: T&T Clark, 2011).
58. Barth, "The Word of God as the Task of Theology."
59. Barth, "Wünschbarkeit und Möglichkeit eines allgemeinen reformierten Glaubensbekenntnisses. 1925."

attempts to remain in constructive conversation with him. What stands out, however, is the closeness of the critiqued positions to his own. Rather than pushing back against egregiously but also relatively obviously problematic positions, Barth would target whom and what he perceived to be "far more dangerous . . . because he is so much nearer to the truth."[60] His interventions might thus be read as forms of extended self-critique, methodological second-guessing, and refusals to turn his own insights into a "positive" mode of theological thought.

Although the "dialectical" Barth more obviously reveled in negation, even the mature, "dogmatic" Barth will primarily define the task of theology as critique.[61] And even where his contributions were framed positively rather than negatively, and politically more than theologically, the movement they performed tended to be "against the stream," negative counter-movements to dominant assumptions and public opinion. His insistence on the sovereignty of God and the Lordship of Christ was developed in close contrast to the claims to sovereignty and absolute power in Nazi Germany. His "No!"[62] to natural theology aimed at cutting off the possibility of claiming divine authority for human cultural, religious, and political achievements. When the waves of National Socialism rose high, Barth resisted the urge to imbue even theological resistance with pathos and pleaded instead to "do theology as if nothing had happened."[63] He sparked controversy when he encouraged international military action against Germany, but after the war he—equally controversially—was an ardent advocate of reconciliation. As a Western theologian, he critiqued Western anticommunism as well as NATO rearmament, but when prompted to condemn communism in the East, he refused with the remark that there was no need to join the already existent choir of critique, and, when approached for pastoral support by pastors in the East, he commanded them to stay at their post.[64] Even in his last academic lectures, Barth spoke of God's revolt against the disorder of the world as a radical negation in service of an even greater affirmation, while also continuing to resist the identification of this revolt with any actually existing revolutionary or political movement— negating even the possibility of performing this negation positively by human means.[65] The later Barth's (re)turn to a "positive" mode of speech should thus not distract from the movements of negation he continued to perform.

60. Barth, *Romans II*, 478.
61. Barth, *CD I.1*, 4.
62. Brunner and Barth, *Natural Theology*.
63. Karl Barth, *Theological Existence To-Day!: (A Plea for Theological Freedom) [1934]*, tr. R. Birch Hoyle (Eugene: Wipf & Stock, 2012).
64. Karl Barth, "Brief an einen Pfarrer in der DDR," in *Offene Briefe 1945–1968*, ed. Diether Koch, 35:401–39. GA. (Zürich: TVZ, 1984).
65. Barth, *CD IV.4*.

In the meantime, many versions of Liberation Theology previously committed to positive visions articulate practical and theoretical disillusionments with hope, humanity, progress, and other "positive," "dogmatic" ideals and radically renounce the conditions that afford them no hope. In light of the impossibility of bringing about the kingdom of God, the frustration with continued systems of oppression, the insurmountable intersectional complexities and complicities, the lack of unequivocal progress, many have announced an end of hope, or even advocated "hopelessness" as a more radical stance, one that is more realistic even as it also immunizes itself against the experience of failure, one that gains conceptual independence from the possibility of achieving the better worlds imagined. Queer negativity will serve as the Constructive-theological conversation partner in this section, but negative turns can also be found in afropessimism, ecopessimism, various intersectional feminisms and decolonial approaches.

As uncompromising as Barth's "No" against any positive possibility is Lee Edelman's anti-futuristic manifesto of "queer negativity."[66] And as insistent on the need for critical undoing as Barth's *Romans Commentary* is Kent Brintnall's conception of queer theology's all-consuming "conflagration."[67] Where Barth's negativity comes from the crisis of theological positivity in the wake of its cooptation into Christian militarism and nationalism, queer negativity comes from the crisis of positive advocacy for queer rights and its cooptation into political pragmatism. Where Barth comes from the self-revelation of divine alterity that bridges the unbridgeable gap out of God's desire to be with and for the human, queer theologians lift up apophatic and erotic notions of God as divine yearning. Both parties put their hope-beyond-hope in that which remains ever outside of symbolic and political representation, epistemically bound to illegibility and politically, to exclusion. Both have a similar response: that of radical negation.

Having become almost synonymous with queer negativity, "No future!" is both a sobering assessment of the predicament for queers in society, and a rallying cry that boldly defies society's normalizing and oppressive imperative. Edelman's intervention confronts the apologetic impulse of queer people who would demonstrate to a cisheteronormative society that—contrary to prejudices—their existence and desires are *not* socially corrosive, *not* undermining the traditional family, etc. That impulse is misdirected, Edelman avers. The conservatism of the political as such goes far beyond political agendas who lift up some historically contingent form of life; it rests on "reproductive

---

66. Edelman, *No Future*.

67. Kent L Brintnall, "Desire's Revelatory Conflagration," *Theology & Sexuality* 23, no. 1–2 (2017): 48–66.

futurism." While reproductive futurism often invokes the figure of the child and a collective responsibility "for the children," its anti-queer mechanism goes deeper than its surface promotion of the cisheterosexual nuclear family, as it rests on the need to achieve social cohesion by way of a self-sustaining exclusion of alterity, and the perpetuation of its conditions.

While, as Edelman concedes, "nothing intrinsic in the constitution of those identifying as [LGBTQIA+] predisposes them to resist the appeal of futurity, to refuse the temptation to reproduce, or to place themselves outside or against the acculturating logic of the Symbolic,"[68] society will perceive their desire and existence as a disruption of the social order. And society is not altogether wrong: Queer desire exceeds proffered societal norms and it persists in its *jouissance* beyond and despite the imperative of any identity, law, or meaning. Edelman thus resorts to Freud's and Lacan's notion of the "death drive" to name "what the queer, in the order of the social, is called forth to figure: the negativity opposed to every form of social viability."[69] Edelman coins the term "*sinthomo*sexual" to signify the symbolic identification of the homosexual as the symptom and site of disruption of reproductive futurism's societal ordering.

As queer desire thus figures a rejection of the future, there can be no future for queers. Pursuing politics of integration and respectability, assimilation and pragmatism is futile. Queers will never be able to conclusively and comprehensively legitimate themselves and their lives under conditions that organize societal cohesion around the exclusion of the un- and anti-reproductive queer. Advocacy for LGBTQIA+ rights is misdirected in that it feeds into cisheteronormative logics: attempting to demonstrate that one is "not anti-social" (*not* a criminal, *not* a pedophile, *not* adulterous, *not* contagious, and so forth) only reifies a system that is built on the exclusion of the "anti-social" element—even if some might successfully evade the predication of anti-sociality, others will not.

Queer negativity thus challenges queers to abandon any hope of respectability and inclusion, and to move "beyond apologetics"[70]—a remarkably Barthian sentiment. Where the ideality of "the human" is itself recognized as an exclusionary, normalizing, and violent order, the attempt of establishing and justifying one's humanity or even subjectivity has to be abandoned. Queer negativity calls queers to embrace the role of disruption that society will read them as figuring in any case, and to head-on pronounce: "Fuck the social order and the Child in whose name we're collectively terrorized; . . . fuck

---

68. Edelman, *No Future*, 17.
69. Edelman, *No Future*, 9.
70. Tonstad, *Queer Theology: Beyond Apologetics* (Eugene: Cascade, 2018).

Laws both with capital ls and with small; fuck the whole network of Symbolic relations and the future that serves as its prop."[71]

Queer negativity thus refuses the price at which salvation is always bought in the economies of future-orientation. In recognition of the impossibility of escaping the symbolic order, Edelman demands a political suicide that refuses any notion of an afterlife in favor of a radical intervention in the here and now: "Not that we are, or ever could be, outside the Symbolic ourselves; but we can, nonetheless, make the choice to accede to our cultural production as figures—*within* the dominant logic of narrative, *within* Symbolic reality—for the dismantling of such a logic and thus for the death drive it harbors within."[72] Its anti-redemptive eschatology calls for an ultimate sacrifice of the queer: not saving oneself at the expense of those who will not or cannot "pass," not trading the hope for a better future for an imperfect now, instead forsaking "*all* causes, *all* social action, *all* responsibility for a better tomorrow or for the perfection of social forms,"[73] and thus ultimately, their own legibility and recognition within "the recognizably human."[74]

Embracing queer negativity "can have no justification if justification requires it to reinforce some positive social value; its value, instead, resides in its challenge to value as defined by the social, and thus in its radical challenge to the very value of the social itself."[75] Queer negativity thus marks "the 'other' side of politics":[76] negation and refusal accede to one's own negation by the logic of the political. Queer negativity does not advocate a different "positive" vision of "the good" or an alternative future, instead it insists "that the future stop here."[77]

This is not only a radical—and potentially violent!—stance, it is also as clear-sighted about its own nonviability as Barth's "impossible possibility" of negation without ground, aware that it will be dismissed "as an irresponsible, because unworkable, approach."[78] Equally theoretically exhilarating and practically unsustainable, both negations are not driven by critique for critique's sake. Their insistent "No" is, to use Barth's phrase, authorized by an even bigger "Yes"—even if this yes remains permanently elusive, radically transcendent, or constitutively eschatological. Similarly, in its negation of all that is seen by society as good and holy, queer negativity is marked by a pronounced ethical impetus, a commitment to what Edelman names as truth,

71. Edelman, *No Future*, 29.
72. Edelman, *No Future*, 22.
73. Edelman, *No Future*, 101.
74. Edelman, *No Future*, 101.
75. Edelman, *No Future*, 6.
76. Edelman, *No Future*, 7.
77. Edelman, *No Future*, 31.
78. Brintnall, "Desire's Revelatory Conflagration," 51.

"where truth does not assure happiness, or even . . . the good. Instead, it names only the insistent particularity of the subject, impossible fully to articulate and 'tend[ing] toward the real.'"[79]

The ethical and the theological converge in such an alterity beyond the differences our symbolic, religious, and political orders can figure, a "wholly Other." Its refusal (to play the game of politics, to believe in rewards in exchange for sacrifice or in incremental societal and self-improvement) may be less a symptom of hopelessness than of faithfulness. The non-transactional, non-redemptive persistence articulates a profound commitment to truth and to "the real." Edelman muses, "Such queerness proposes, in place of the good, something I want to call 'better,' though it promises, in more than one sense of the phrase, absolutely nothing."[80]

If the "human" as a category thus moves from a salvific figure to a hamartiological predicament, promise and hope lie in that which exceeds "the human." But what is "outside" the recognizably human? Queerness, in this logic. In another logic, God. In an intriguingly close parallel to Barth's doctrine of election in which all humanity is elect in Jesus Christ who is the only reprobate, Edelman's queer becomes the reprobate by illegibility, an almost messianic figure. Both proposals are driven by a commitment to that which remains outside of the symbolic order, exceeding it and violently excluded by it. Their difference might be split by Marcella Althaus-Reid's postulate that "Queerness is something that belongs to God, and . . . people are divinely Queer by grace."[81]

Kent Brintnall draws out such resonances between queer and theological negativity, albeit in a more apophatic register than Barth's Christocentrism or Althaus-Reid's sexual theology. With Pseudo-Dyonisius, Brintnall conceptualizes God primarily by way of desire, divine yearning that generates movement in Godself and into the very act of creation, a creative and creating yearning that calls forth existence without ever providing "a presence that could support, sustain, or ground the self."[82] In that sense, homosexuality and God, the excess that puts God beyond human grasp and the excess that homosexual desire figures in a cisheteronormative society, share certain characteristics. All "coordinates by which we know ourselves, the categories through which we name ourselves . . . are undone by the movement of desire that gets named as (homo)sexuality—or God."[83]

79. Edelman, *No Future*, 5.
80. Edelman, *No Future*, 5.
81. Althaus-Reid, *The Queer God*, 34.
82. Brintnall, "Desire's Revelatory Conflagration," 56.
83. Brintnall, "Desire's Revelatory Conflagration," 57.

Brintnall's mystic eroticism connects apophatic theology to critique of language, symbolic order, norms, and law, and harnesses them for ideology critiques that bridge theological, epistemological, and political categories. He writes,

> The longing to name, to classify, to order: the longing to know, describe, understand; the longing to channel desire toward appropriate objects in a proper fashion; these ubiquitous human longings demand that we draw distinctions, adopt rules, impose prohibitions. They feed and are fed by exclusion, denial, opposition. To be human is to participate in these practices. To be human is to be caught in the antagonisms that make the self and the social possible. To be human is to constrain and be constrained by a violent order.[84]

In its commitment to that which lies beyond what can be named, apophatic theology strives for intentional divestment from the pursuit of naming and defining and negates the very ideals of the good and the human: "We cannot be human without being implicated in violence, but we can allow the violence to sunder our violent attachment to being human. Strengthening the forces that loosen our grip; this must become (queer) theology's object."[85]

In light of the hubris (Barth) and violence (Brintnall) of symbolic orders, including the theological, choosing that queer—that is: unnameable—space of negation and excess beyond any name, refusing to strive for "the good" or anything that can be declared "good" in the eyes of whatever law or method, may just constitute a *better* alternative: *Better* not in a sense of attaining any higher value, but in its sustained commitment to the real beyond the law, in all its unjustified and unjustifiable persistence, and even in its gesture toward an ethics that lies beyond the economy of any morale. This commitment to the particularity of what *is* over and against any notions of what *ought to* be, what can be named, what can be invested with meaning, what can become legible and integrated into a logical, political, or redemptive economy, this commitment marks the ethics of queer negativity.

It also positions the proposal squarely in our question about theological epistemology and method. In a passage rife with theological and epistemological overtones, Edelman writes: "Truth, like queerness, irreducibly linked to the 'aberrant or atypical,' to what chafes against 'normalization,' finds its value not in a good susceptible to generalization, but only in the stubborn particularity that voids every notion of a general good."[86] Both proposals see a dynamic, ongoing movement of perpetual "undoing" as the negative

---

84. Brintnall, "Desire's Revelatory Conflagration," 57.
85. Brintnall, "Desire's Revelatory Conflagration," 57.
86. Edelman, *No Future*, 6.

approximation of the "better"—without the illusion that at the end of such a movement something like a positive core will remain. If others have likened negative approaches to the work of a sculptor who chips away all rock that conceals a hidden form, Brintnall radicalizes the image: "The One is perpetually beyond; it is that which exceeds; it is unknowable yearning, unclassifiable movement. The One should be likened, then, not to the sculpture, but to the hammer swing. The clearing away radiates beauty; there is no shimmer to be revealed."[87] Brintnall demands that theological work, too, must engage in such a relentless movement—beyond either positive categories or dialectical antagonisms in radical negation. Out of faithfulness both to "the One" who, beyond naming, beckons in creative yearning, and to the human being's liberation from the constraints with which we bind ourselves, Brintnall envisions an undoing of all categories of identity and politics. Challenging the assumption that politics must rest on antagonism, exclusion, and therefore, ontological violence, he provocatively concludes, "Queer theology must demand an end to war, not to sue for peace, but to spark an all-consuming conflagration."[88]

In their bleak assessment of human impossibility and the impossibility of humanity, Barth's and Edelman's "No!"'s resonate with one another. If Barth's negation starts from an existential theological insight and draws out political ramifications from there, queer negativity starts from an existential political insight and draws out epistemological ramifications from there. Queer negativity aligns itself with theology's suspicion that attempting to achieve "the good" is not only impossible but violent, and that attempts at justifying oneself by way of its pursuit need to be refused—for the sake of both God and the human being whom no method can do justice, whom no method can render justified. In both proposals the (anti-)methodological and the (anti-)political are intricately intertwined in the envisioned movement of *undoing*, hammer swing after hammer swing, deconstruction after deconstruction, critique after critique.

There is something very appealing in such radical negativity, both theoretically and viscerally. Assuming the groundless stance (the queer, the critic, the prophet)—whether in apophatic forms of unsaying or in all-consuming critical conflagrations—promises the critic a position that is conveniently independent, and appealingly superior, beyond the ambiguities and complicities that invariably attend positive negotiations of method, politics, and ethics. The division of the world performed by negation is "oddly reassuring in its envisioning queerness as radically disruptive of heteronormative society and, indeed, of the world of established meaning," as Tim Dean writes, "it lets us know which side the

---

87. Brintnall, "Desire's Revelatory Conflagration," 57.
88. Brintnall, "Desire's Revelatory Conflagration," 59.

queers are on and how much potential queerness has."[89] The resort to refusal and negation may thus be expressions of despair but also covert re-assertions of agency and moral authority in a complex world. Such moves betray a surprising *optimism*—not only about the auto-deconstructive effect of the symbolic order but also about the potential of the subject (the queer, the theologian) to undo the very forces that constitute her. Negativity may not be all that effective at escaping the hubris with which it charges the positive, dogmatic approach; and both Edelman's and Barth's positions have often been charged with arrogance. If the positive approach arrogates to itself the position of talking about God objectively and definitively, the negative approach arrogates to itself the position of executing God's judgment.

Its nonviability may not be the only issue with the negative approach—what serious politics, after all, have ever been viable? We must also ask, is negation not self-defeating and ineffective? Does it, for all its emphasis on drive, movement, excess, and even force, ultimately not tread in place? The "not speaking" to which traditional apophatic theology calls and the "unsaying" contemporary forms of critique are demanding and rigorous. At the same time, their result might look eerily similar to the most conservative option: remaining silent.

Queer negativity is no mere acquiescence to the positive symbolic order, nor are Barth's counter-cultural invectives. But Edelman is aware that "such refusals perform, despite themselves, subservience to the law that effectively imposes politics as the only game in town"[90] and Barth acknowledges that "the busy activity of tower-building may long ago have passed from those who affirm to those who negate."[91] There is at times an almost Girardian sense in Edelman's call to negativity: Embracing the anti-social position means embracing a structurally necessary position for the symbolic order that allows it to reify itself by excluding the anti-social queer. Edelman is aware of this irony in which "the Symbolic can only win." However, he is confident that a kind of auto-deconstruction operative in this victory. An excess that prevents the ultimate realization of the symbolic order always remains present as its condition: "For the division on which the subject rests can never be spirited away . . . . The *structural position* of queerness, after all, and the need to fill it remain."[92] But is this an overly confident, "a false sense of liberation"?[93]

89. Timothy James Dean, "An Impossible Embrace: Queerness, Futurity, and the Death Drive," in *A Time for the Humanities: Futurity and the Limits of Autonomy*, edited by James J. Bono, Tim Dean, and Ewa Plonowska Ziarek, 122–40 (New York: Fordham University Press, 2008), 127.
    90. Edelman, *No Future*, 26.
    91. Barth, *Romans II*, 464.
    92. Edelman, *No Future*, 26–27.
    93. Dean, "An Impossible Embrace," 38.

The despair and heroism that mark the two sides of negation's coin might betray a particular fragility: Where the illusion of being self-sufficiently in control of one's methodological pursuits crumbles, the impression emerges that *nothing* remains. Negation's refusal to be complicit in ongoing forms of violence gives way to either detachment or counter-violence. Both options are invigorating but also more invested in maintaining one's own intellectual and existential purity than keeping faith to the messy reality they observe. The refusal to play the game of politics is also the refusal of saving what is salvageable. There is a *temptation*—in the explicitly theological sense—in negation that consists in ensuring one's own purity. Despite its very demanding nature, the stance of negation is ultimately a way of keeping one's hands clean, and a heroism quite in juxtaposition to the self's undoing it demands. Barth himself calls the ensuing posture of critique and refusal, in its "Titanism of revolt and upheaval," "far more dangerous" than the hubris of positivity, precisely because it "is so much nearer to the truth."[94]

We might want to question the part in us that finds the radicality of the approach appealing. Barth's pronouncements of crisis at times resonated in nationalist and anti-modern circles, and the charge that there is something fascist about this rhetoric has haunted his interpretation—Barth's well-documented and consistent anti-fascist politics notwithstanding.[95] Similarly, a certain virility animates Edelman's critique; his anti-sociality trades in heroic and exceptionalist posturing, which has resulted in the description of queer negativity as "the gay white man's last stand."[96] The alleged non-position of queer negativity and the self-undoing it advocates are only feasible from a position of relative detachment—a privilege that many queers of color, queers of non-male genders, queers living in economic precarity or with disability do not have and for whom "giving up on futurity is not an option."[97] The optimism about critical ability thus turns into a matter of privilege, "of the conditions under which subjective destitution as an 'ethical act' becomes a feasible option."[98]

94. Barth, *Romans II*, 478.

95. Franz Tügel, later bishop in the Nazi church, reports experiencing Barth's commentary on Romans as a "Stahlbad"—a baptism of steel: Franz Tügel, *Unmögliche Existenz! Ein Wort wider Karl Barth* (Hamburg: Agentur des Rauhen Hauses, 1933), 9. Dieter Schellong framed such resonances of Barth's ideas on the right as "success out of misunderstanding": Dieter Schellong, "Alles hat seine Zeit: Bemerkungen zur Barth-Deutung," *Evangelische Theologie* 45, no. 1 (January 1985): 61–80. Still, such misunderstandings have persistently accompanied Barth's overtly and outspokenly anti-fascist theology, recently once more rehearsed by Paul Silas Peterson, *The Early Karl Barth: Historical Contexts and Intellectual Formation, 1905–1935*, Beiträge zur historischen Theologie, vol. 184 (Tübingen: Mohr Siebeck, 2018).

96. José Esteban Muñoz, "The Antisocial Thesis in Queer Theory," *PMLA* 121, no. 3 (2006): 819–28, 825.

97. Cf. Jack Halberstam's endorsement on the cover of Muñoz, *Cruising Utopia*.

98. Mari Ruti, "Why There Is Always a Future in the Future," *Angelaki - Journal of The Theoretical Humanities* 13, no. 1 (2008): 113–26, 116.

Negation alone is both *too much* and *not enough*: It is a superhuman—inhumane—demand for actually existing persons in their needs and desires, relationships and commitments. It undermines any positive relation to a livable world, any hope for a livable future, any struggle for survival. The political, metaphysical, or literal "suicide" referenced by both Edelman and Barth is not a way out, especially not for those whose lives are deeply entangled with lives around them in relations of care. It fails to do justice to the human being and denies the reality of the God who became human.

The charge of "inhumanity" might ring hollow against positions that straightforwardly renounce "the human" as a redemptive category—but it might be legitimate to ask, will the call to negation not be counterproductive to the humanity at which both camps arguably attempt to get, if by other means (or names)? To riff on Barth's famous interjection against historical criticism, "Would that the critical theologians were more critical!"[99]

Impossibility is not *all* there is, it is not even the primary reality even if felt acutely. Lingering on it constitutes epistemological *sloth*: failure to attend to the fullness of reality and embrace the partial freedom it affords. Impossibility might be an existentially felt truth, but its expression succumbs to rhetorical hyperbole: Theology *exists*, after all, quite undeniably, and proliferates in numerous forms. What does *not* exist is a pure and wholly uncompromised positionality. The wholly unredeemed state into which negation escapes is a nonexistent purity. The claim that there is "no future" for queers (or any other *sinthome* of negativity) is just as hyperbolic: There is, of course, "always a future in the future."[100] The queer insistence "that the future stop here"[101] is bold and radical, but reality-denyingly pretentious. The question is not whether there is a future or no future (and much less can one simply take a decision in that regard); the question is rather *what kind of future* it will be, and for whom.

Constituencies who have historically existed in the messiness of only partial agency, constrained by external forces and structural limitations, have long developed strategies beyond escapism or resignation. In her critique of Liberation and Feminist Theology's ultimate optimism about their ability to dismantle T-theology from within, Marcella Althaus-Reid already demanded that theology must go "further in its disrespect"[102] than the preservation of decency would permit. Against white myths of progress and betterment, Black theorists leverage melancholy rather than hope or pessimism.[103] Against the heroism of Black liberation as much as against the nihilism of afropessimism,

99. Barth, *Romans II*, 1968, 8, Hoskyn's translation adapted by me.
100. Ruti, "Why There Is Always a Future in the Future."
101. Edelman, *No Future*, 31.
102. Althaus-Reid, "Outing Theology," 95.
103. Winters, *Hope Draped in Black*.

Womanist theologians argue for quality of life and survival.[104] Queer and crip theorists advocate "monstrous" forms of belonging that allow for living together "in ruins."[105]

Radical negativity is simply another ideality. At its tipping point, the sin of *hubris* becomes indistinguishable from the sin of *sloth*: the arrogation of a humanly impossible superior position goes hand in hand with the rejection of the demand that the humanity of God places on us. Whatever frustration with the state of the world might be vocally articulated by negation, in its effective and performative denial of realities divine and human it turns into *falsehood*.

THE FALSEHOOD OF DIALECTICS

Barth does not stay in a posture of negativity. Clear-sightedly he states already in *RomII*, "Anti-religious negation has no advantage over the affirmations of religion. To destroy temples is not better than to build them."[106] The negative approach, he avers, is even most inadequate of the three, since it overlooks the primacy of the divine "yes" over the divine "no." Both the free God and the liberated human being in their historical reality and concreteness of their real existence remain outside its gates.

There is nothing redemptive about negation, Edelman maintains, just as Barth notes that negation does not *solve* anything. The sharpest critique can only demonstrate that "the *human* has again become human. And that is not a salvific event."[107] This adamant insistence on its own non-redemptiveness on which both negativities land might just be their surprisingly *positive* contribution. In its persistent, ongoing movement, negativity might be less nihilistic than it acknowledges: Its hammer swings articulate and sustains an insistence that "this world is not enough."[108] Radical negativity might even be a form of lament, unmasking the questionability of the answers provided and insisting that the question about grace, about salvation, about God have not been answered, precisely as it refuses their economies. Refusing to provide answers itself, its embrace of excess keeps open the quest for grace, the quest for meaning, the quest for survival, the quest for justice, the quest for truth. In this, negativity signals that it, too, is *not enough*. It can only time and again open

104. Williams, *Sisters in the Wilderness*.
105. Sharon V Betcher, "Crip/Tography: Disability Theology in the Ruins of God," *JCRT* 15, no. 2 (2016): 98–115.
106. Barth, *Romans II*, 136.
107. Barth, *Romans II*, 190.
108. José Esteban Muñoz, *Cruising Utopia: The Then and There of Queer Futurity*, Sexual Cultures (New York: New York University Press, 2009), 1.

the space for an annihilation *or* salvation that it cannot bring about. It points beyond itself. It is, in short, in need of grace.

In *The Word of God as the Task of Theology*, Barth concludes that the best the theologian *can* do is a combination of positive and negative approaches: "Only along this narrow cliff ridge can we walk."[109] Such a dialectic can never have closure; it can only be performed as ongoing movement. Its dynamic character carries over from the negative approach, but rather than perpetual deconstruction, the movement now becomes a balancing act. The dialectical theologian has no additional method at her disposal. Knowing about different methodologies' respective weaknesses, she out-maneuvers them momentarily in a meta-methodological oscillation. In constant danger of falling down either side of the cliff, the dialectician can only keep balance if she keeps moving—offsetting any (dogmatic) step to one side with a (critical) step to the other side in perpetuity, never lingering.

Barth's own theology at the time performs this technique in masterful sophistication. Watching it is as breathtaking as it is exhausting. He proceeds in immaculately tailored series of artful self-deconstructions and relentless betrayal of the audience, writing only to cross out again, making positive statements only to pull out the rug from underneath them, performing one loop of self-critical self-relativization of his own possibility of speaking after another.

The dialectical theologian tries to embody the best of the positive and the negative approach and to let their respective weaknesses offset each other. However, all the caveats against both approaches still hold. The dialectical approach does not get any closer to the truth, it only avoids the ossification of the errors inherent to the individual approaches. Even as it is thoroughly demanding, it, too, only moves between different questions instead of focusing on the answer. In all its frantic movement, dialectics might be less an art of mastery than of failure, not successfully balancing between two abysses, but falling down *both* of them.

In addition, the "meta" positioning of the dialectical approach and the inbuilt reflectivity on the different methods it employs make it even more prone to presumption and self-preoccupation. Having intellectually risen above the simple positive or negative approaches and working methodologically to mitigate its own sin, the dialectical approach is subject to a second-order *hubris*. It fails most where it is successful in its self-critique and self-relativization since this only allows it to performatively prevail, to assert its own relative truthfulness, to justify itself by way of method. Its ingenious methodology of precarity makes the dialectical theologian in addition subject to a second-order *sloth*. The possibility of doing theology comes out of the (alien) objectivity of grace,

109. Barth, "The Word of God as the Task of Theology," 191.

not out of the subjective despair over one's impossibility. In the face of the reality of God's incarnation, God's revelation, a continued concern about the impossibility of theology, and methodical attempts to navigate or solve such impossibility, only marks blatant unbelief. Constant preoccupation with one's own plight and how to navigate it by way of method is, as Barth maintains, *not* the task of theology. The self-preoccupation that marks all method is most pronounced in the dialectical approach.

Finally, the dialectic theologian's sophisticated movement, her complex rhetorical architecture, her play with the expectations of the reader, her triumph over her own self-entanglement, her trumping of positive and negative approaches by holding conflicting insights comes closest to the appearance of performative mastery of its subject matter that Barth diagnoses as the particularly theological form of sin: *falsehood*. Barth rejects the dialectical approach with special emphasis, since it is the one that *by* fully acknowledging its own impossibility devises a way out of the impossibility: It turns navigating the impossibility into a method. This is the pinnacle self-contradiction: Lying by saying the truth.

The aspiration to *better* theology by way of method only lead deeper into performative self-contradiction. Theology cannot escape its own complicity in the problem it describes—which also applies to its own articulation of that very problem. At the end of his indictment of all theological method, Barth grumpily concludes, "I hardly dare to hope . . . that no one will approach me after this and ask: 'So, what should we do now? . . .' I have no suggestions for you." Barth insists that the *sine qua non* for theological work is the recognition of the insurmountable impossibility of the task, to the point that if we are still asking what to do *now*, we still have not gotten to this breaking point: the conversion of method.

Either theology is beyond saving, or only a God can save theology. The freedom announced by God, according to Barth, shatters the work of the theologian since it means "liberation from all the presuppositions conditioning and limiting God and himself. It means liberation from every arbitrary presupposition and therefore from himself."[110] From such alien and demanding freedom, theological method provides (illegitimate) refuge. It can only achieve such relief *from God* by way of "elimination of the freedom of God and man, this depriving of the confrontation of God and man of all force and tension by the notion of an order overruling and comprehending them both."[111]

Looking beyond obvious differences in language, imagery, and the contextual direction of their relative critiques, Barth's account of the falsehood of theology's systematizing appropriation, nostrification, and neutralization of

110. Barth, *CD IV.3*, 447.
111. Barth, *CD IV.3*, 448.

God, and Althaus-Reid's charges against T-theology's closeting of the divine (as discussed in chapter 1) turn out to be surprisingly congenial—including their yearning for liberation from such predicament. Both denounce any theology that tries to justify itself by way of method, thus preserving its own integrity, intellectual purity, and appearance of decency. Barth more explicitly interprets what he sees through a doctrinal lens, while Althaus-Reid draws out the implications further and more concretely than Barth does. Barth comes to the fallenness of theology through his own struggles with the (im)possibility of doing theology, while Althaus-Reid discerns its distorting force from its material effects in the lives of the poor and the queer. Barth's hamartiology provides a three-fold taxonomy of how sin warps the human being's relationships to God, fellow human beings, and their self into ontologically void, yet nevertheless actively destructive, relations; Althaus-Reid fleshes the pathology of sin out in sexual stories and unveiling per/versions of doctrine and piety. Systematic and Constructive theologies converge in their diagnosis of epistemological sin at the root of the problem of method.

Method cannot save us. This is an existential experience, a historical fact, and a theological diagnosis. Method cannot take away anything from the foundational impossibility of theology that is marked by the Otherness of God on the one hand, and by humanity's entanglement in sin on the other. Neither hope nor despair, neither active negation as radical critique nor silence as radical refusal, neither flights to transcendence nor flights to self-righteousness provide a way out of theology's dilemma. Epistemic relativism, too, would be a form of epistemological sloth: Simply allowing a diversity of approaches and perspectives as if all stances were equal renounces the theologians responseabilities. What the pursuit of method to its bitter end apparently *can* do is lead the theologian to this very insight: Theology will never be able to get it "right," not simply due to limits of human understanding but due to its sinful distortion of truth into falsehood, its hubris and self-conceit, as well as its sloth and resistance to "become real." The attempt to overcome its fundamental impossibility by way of whichever method can only drive us into despair. This, however, might be recognized as a particularly *theological* use of (the law of) method, its second, *usus elenchthicus sive paedagogicus*.

Far from being futile, embracing such failure might be surprisingly generative. Queer negativity might object to being read through a theological lens, but Barth's is the same existential anxiety over which Luther agonized, the theological problem of justification, extended into the register of theological epistemology.[112] Barth's dialectic keeps oscillating between despair over

112. For Barth's theological alignment with Luther's doctrine of justification and anthropology see, e.g., George Hunsinger, "Barth and Luther," in *Wiley Blackwell Companion to*

the irresolvable impossibility and the comfort he takes in the reality of divine grace. Such insight does not absolve the theologian from the need of proceeding in some well-reflected way. Neither the difficulty of discerning the spirits, nor that of taking concrete and specific stances are spared to us simply because there is no unequivocal ground on which to stand. But it does deprive method of any redemptive potential and pathos, and opens the door for a new understanding of the labor that theology does and does not do, even as it might never amount to "a work" in Luther's sense. The search for redemption by way of method is unfeasible because it is misdirected. The problem of theological method turns out to be the noetic version of the problem of justification, with its corollary in Christian ethics. Something like revelation comes into view on the other side of this door: alien and queer grace, the precondition on which the theologian's wrestling has rested all along.

Karl Barth, ed. George Hunsinger and Keith L. Johnson, 461–72. Wiley Blackwell Companions to Religion (Chichester: Wiley Blackwell, 2019), 466–67; Shannon Smythe, "Barth on Justification," in *Wiley Blackwell Companion to Karl Barth*, ed. George Hunsinger and Keith L. Johnson, 291–301, Wiley Blackwell Companions to Religion (Chichester: Wiley Blackwell, 2019), 291; Jeff McSwain, *Simul Sanctification: Barth's Hidden Vision for Human Transformation* (Eugene: Pickwick, 2018).

Chapter 4

Realism, or: Queer grace[1]

The Yes cannot be heard unless the No is also heard. But the No is said for the sake of the Yes and not for its own sake. In substance, therefore, the first and last word is Yes and not No.

—Karl Barth[2]

Much time and attention has been devoted by liberation and Feminist Theologies to the structures of sin, but little consideration has been given to the structures of sanctity.

—Marcella Althaus-Reid[3]

HOPEFUL REM(A)INDERS: FROM SIN TO SANCTITY

In his reflection on the failure of any method to fully "get" (at) reality, philosopher of science Paul Feyerabend cautions,

"[i]t is very important not to let this suspicion deteriorate into a truth, or a theory, for example into a theory with the principle: things are never as they seem to be. Reality, or Being, or God, or whatever it is that sustains us cannot be captured that easily. The problem is not why we are so often confused; the problem is why we seem to possess useful and enlightening knowledge."[4]

---

1. I owe the term "queer grace," and the reorientation it indicates, to Micah Cronin, "Queer Grace: An Essay on the Task of Queer Theology," *Theology & Sexuality* (forthcoming).

2. Karl Barth, *Church Dogmatics II.2: The Doctrine of God*, ed. Geoffrey W. Bromiley and Thomas F. Torrance (Edinburgh: T&T Clark, 1957), 13.

3. Althaus-Reid, *The Queer God*, 142.

4. Feyerabend, *Against Method*, xvi.

Impossibility is not all there is. Failure and frustration are not all there is. Reality persists despite our deepest existential frustrations and our most sophisticated theoretical refusals. Neither God nor queerness are all negation. Negativity is only an overspill of their positive excess in a world that fails to accommodate them.

"Much time and attention has been devoted . . . to the structures of sin, but little consideration has been given to the structures of sanctity,"[5] Marcella Althaus-Reid points out thoughtfully. Much time and attention has been devoted by Barth, despite himself, to human impossibility, to the critique of religion as the bound-to-fail human attempt at mastering the divine, to denouncing the hubris, sloth, and falsehood inevitably at work in the efforts of the theologian. Much time and attention has been devoted, by Althaus-Reid herself, to the material critique of T-theology, to revealing the hard-core sexual and economic nature of theological constructions and getting at its conditions of production and their ceilings with regard to epistemology as much as with regard to justice. Barth's stress on the "infinite qualitative difference"[6] effectively hamartiologizes the epistemic problem of theological method. Althaus-Reid's stress on the sexual and material nature of all theology effectively renders any positive theological project deeply enmeshed in ideological constructions. Have we, too, given too little consideration to the structures of sanctity?

For both of these theologians, the issues they critique are neither the only nor the primary, let alone the ultimate reality. Indeed, their critiques are only possible because they come from a different reality that challenges the state of things as we factually encounter them. For the theologian, this always-excluded reality that remains beyond all our efforts and their frustrations is the reality of God. For Althaus-Reid, "God the stranger"[7] persists outside our ideological constructions, knocking at their gates, breaking into the closets that fail to consider "to what excesses God takes God's love for humans."[8] Barth in turn always emphasized the ontological superiority and primacy of the divine "yes" over the divine "no," of reality over possibility, and of the concreteness of *who God is* in Jesus Christ over any abstract concept of God. Even the "crater," which was Barth's favorite image for the negation produced by divine revelation, has a determinate shape.[9] It is the imprint of a concrete, material, and specific reality.

---

5. Althaus-Reid, *The Queer God*, 142.
6. Barth, "First Commandment," 10.
7. Althaus-Reid, *The Queer God*, 171.
8. Althaus-Reid, *The Queer God*, 23.
9. Barth, *Romans II*, 29, 36, 65, et passim.

In addition, for the queer (and for many others who receive unequal consideration by this world's symbolic and political orders), an experiential sign of this always-excluded reality that remains beyond all our efforts and their frustrations, is the fact that we exist. And continue to exist. We find grace and joy, every day, despite—or, we might have to say: *in, with, and under* all impossibility and nonviability. Whatever else may be true about the world we live in and about our (in)capacity to change it for the better—*that* joy is stubbornly real too!

The appropriate theological term for these glimpses of reality that cannot be explained and yet are undeniably *real* might be "grace." They surprise us at the margins of any system in our most aspirational as well as in our most hopeless hour. They interrupt both our optimism and our pessimism, unsettle and reorient us. They are signs of an external reality, which comes to us and keeps giving itself to us despite our inabilities to do them justice. Both in divine queerness and in the queerness we encounter in the real lives of real people, in the resistance to our constructions that both of these offer, we find "parables" and "sign-posts"[10] of revelation—which is both an epistemological and an ontological opening—and thus hope, rather than merely frustration and despair.

If the queer/theologian *cannot* abandon their post despite the nonviability of any method, it is not because of some abstract task or some misplaced sense of duty—who, after all, could impose such duty on anyone? If the queer/theologian *cannot* abandon their post, it is because there is a reality that cannot so simply be denied or abandoned. Hubris, sloth, and falsehood are not all there is. *In, with, and under them*, something else "remains," glistens, beckons. The frustration of the theologian gives way to the revelation that reality is already there. What *remains* beyond all our assertion and critique is the reality of God, who can never be conclusively captured by any system, and the reality of people, who fail to fit neatly into the compartments afforded by any description, taxonomy, normality, ideality—signs of a stubborn, messy, excessive . . . and revelatory reality.

QUEER HOLINESS

As theology remains committed to divine and human truths, Pilate's question "what is truth?" (John 18:38) betrays its apparently neutral and detached reasoning as an illusion. Just as Pilate's question is never innocent, truth is never purely epistemic. What truth one finds depends on the sites one pays

10. Barth, *Romans II*, 129 et passim.

attention to, depends on one's commitments to the realities one comes from and goes back to. The formulation of the task and the method of theology are themselves a theological task; they are not independent of the object and the content of theology, and theological rigor consists primarily in commitment to its particular objects. The Barthian demands that the adequacy of any method be measured by its correspondence to its particular object, that is: its faithfulness in response to it. The Queer-Liberationist adds that such correspondence cannot be merely conceptual or "idealistic." Both agree that it is never the *thatness* but always the *whatness* of reality, divine and human, in their incarnational intertwinement, that is crucial and determinative for theological inquiry.

Throughout his theology, Barth insists vehemently that it is the determinate shape of the reality of God that matters, not an ideal, abstract, or principled notion of a divine being. God is not the ultimate, the infinite, the paradox, not a projection of a highest faculty or reason, not an abstract principle or an unmovable mover. God is who God reveals Godself to be in Jesus Christ: the concrete other in, with, and for the concrete other human being. Christ is the "one Archimedean point"[11] that can alone fund not just theological method but ultimately redemption, salvation, life, and ethics. Jesus Christ is the starting point and the point with which theology must begin again and again, Barth avers. But, of course, Jesus Christ is no mathematical point, no mere geometric indication of location. Jesus Christ is a human being in history. Even as the early Barth seems radical in the relentless dialectical application of this principle into shattering any constructive theological movement, he insisted that Christ's humanity can only be understood as his co-humanity, his fellowship and solidarity with human beings that also turns human beings toward one another. The later Barth's positive theology spells out further that Christ is true human being for others; the Lord who in priestly kenotic substitution becomes servant, the servant who in royal option for the poor is elevated, and the true prophetic witness who struggles victoriously against the reality-twisting falsehood of sin.[12] Theological realism gains its specific shape from this double commitment to divine and human reality as one and the same commitment, an ontological reality with epistemological and ethical ramifications.

Liberationist Jon Sobrino reminds the theologian that it "is an option whether to look at the truth of things or not."[13] The nonchalant English "option" softens the blow of the Spanish *opción*, as if there were several options

11. Karl Barth, *Church Dogmatics III.2: The Doctrine of Creation*, ed. Geoffrey W. Bromiley and Thomas F Torrance, tr. Harold Knight (Edinburgh: T&T Clark, 1960), 132.
12. Cf. Barth, *CD IV.1*; Barth, *CD IV.2*; Barth, *CD IV.3,1*.
13. Sobrino, *The Principle of Mercy*, 33.

between which theology could equally choose. *Opción* implies a fundamental decision: not a choice, but a commitment. It is *the* option that theology has to take if it is to follow God's *opción*, God's decision, self-determination, and sustained commitment to *becoming real* that we see reflected in the being and life of Jesus Christ. What Systematic theologians calls "election"—in Barth's version, God's divine self-determination to be God with and for the human being—Liberation theologians call God's "*opción*" for the marginalized—in political as much as epistemological commitment.[14]

Marcella Althaus-Reid would, of course, caution us: there is nothing that would prevent the formulaic commitment to "theological realism," whether in a Barthian or a Liberationist inflection, from becoming another principle. The invocation of "the reality of God," of "the real lives of real people," or of "the whatness of God in Jesus Christ" do not protect theology from idealistic temptations. The Liberationist as much as the Systematic Theologian's "Jesus is not about Jesus,"[15] she will remind us. This is both a critical and a positive statement: The theologians' Jesus is never about Jesus, always about something else as they tend to fetishize him and project ideological normalizations onto Jesus as a discursive origin and anchor point, requiring renewed theological critique. But "there is no pure, incorruptible and unique, coherent Jesus"[16] (not even the "systematically deviant Jesus"!)[17] who could be recovered behind their constructions, because Jesus is not about Jesus in a positive sense too: he does not coincide with himself in what is not only an elusive fluidity, but even more, an excessive, kenotic movement directed outside of Godself.

Wary of speculative tendencies to ideology and idolatry, both Barth and Althaus-Reid insist on starting with the determinate, incarnated reality of the divine and the human over abstract conceptions of either. Barth's demand of concretion in theology remained, however, by and large vexingly abstract (with some exceptions, as when he would insist on the Jewishness of Jesus, and with some more concrete abstractions, as when he would define Jesus' humanity as co-humanity). Maybe Althaus-Reid's unruly, *concrete* concreteness can flesh out and complement Barth's clean-shaven postulate for theological concreteness. Reading them together, I interpret her demand for a truly material theology and his demand for a truly theo-logical theology into a call for a thoroughly *realistic* theology. Such a theological realism takes its cues

---

14. On the qualities of Barth's doctrine of election as a theological ontology for Liberation Theology's option for the poor, see the excellent dissertation of Rochhuahthanga Jongte, "The Being of the Electing God: The Relevance of Karl Barth's Doctrine of Election for a Liberationist Theological Ontology," PhD thesis, Princeton Theological Seminary, 2023.

15. Althaus-Reid, *Indecent Theology*, 108.

16. Althaus-Reid, *Indecent Theology*, 110.

17. Althaus-Reid, *Indecent Theology*, 112.

from that which it recognizes as even *more real* than the reality of sin: the revelatory, excessive, messy, kenotic, indecent, and honest reality of God and real
people. If Barth urges us to resist the temptation to abstraction and objectivity,
Althaus-Reid reminds us to resist the temptation of ideality and perfection.

Grace is not clean, straight, or immaculate. Holiness is not purity—even if
these categories have come to be conflated in certain modern imaginaries and
faith cultures. Althaus-Reid draws out the inherent ambivalence and queerness of holiness. Holiness points to a status of being sacrosanct, inapproach-
able, ineffable—as traditionally ascribed to God. But we can identify similar
"structures of holiness" every day in those we discursively and materially *otherize*. If Althaus-Reid muses that queer holiness is "always the holiness of the
Other,"[18] such otherness is no merely formalistic definition. Both God and
other Others are strangers at the gates of our ethics, politics, and economies
of exchange. The holiness Althaus-Reid points toward lives outside the law:
Even as it might be marginalized and excluded by it, it also possesses a certain
unruly and disruptive freedom from it that keeps kicking. Althaus-Reid challenges the theologian to find "Queer holiness" not in a sanitized, transcendent
ideal, but in all the messiness, plurality, and abiding ambiguity of real people's
lives, in their revelatory disruptiveness of norms, ideals, and laws. Conscious
of the limited and fallen nature of our constructions, "Queer holiness" testifies
to divine grace even in the hells we inhabit and from which we cannot redeem
ourselves by whatever method.

Obviously, Althaus-Reid is not invested in outlining a typology or phenomenology of holiness. But if we were to hash out some contours of grace—discerning their features without determining their outline—themes of revelation
in excess, of indecenting honesty, and of kenotic solidarity would surface, even
as they remain carefully undertheorized and unsystematized in her writing.

If we recognize that "Queerness is something that belongs to God, and
that people are divinely Queer by grace,"[19] then the sites of excess, solidarity, and honesty allow us to glimpse divine grace in the messy and unruly,
mundane and quotidian, failing and marginal pockets of life that exist in the
here and now, despite any and all efforts to clean them up, and practices of
excess, solidarity, and honesty allow us to reflect divine grace theologically.
Negatively, the epistemological and material commitment of a realistic theology thus attends to moments that run counter, to whatever imperfect degree,
to the realities of hubris, sloth, and falsehood. Positively, theological realism
may find in the excessiveness of real-life commitments a queer realization—
an unruly and messy invitation of *becoming real*—of divine faithfulness against

18. Althaus-Reid, *The Queer God*, 154.
19. Althaus-Reid, *The Queer God*, 34.

sloth; in the messiness of real-life solidarity the theologian may find a queer realization of divine kenosis against hubris; and in the indecency of calling reality by its name, the theologian may find a queer realization of divine revelation against falsehood.

REVELATION'S EXCESSES (EXCESSIVE FAITHFULNESS)

Any epistemological project must be committed to saying something true about reality. But—to slightly catch Pontius Pilate off guard—what is reality? We encounter a paradoxical phenomenon. Reality is that which imposes its truth unavoidably; real is what hits you over the head, so to speak. At the same time, if the real is that which is true independently of our observation of and reflection on it, if it is to be the authentic, unchangeable, external truth, it is also, as Edelman's reference Jacques Lacan was fond of observing, impossible. While giving rise to thought and action, reality remains "what resists symbolization absolutely."[20] We are cut off from any direct relationship to the real with our entrance into symbolic orders, language, representation, meaning, and imagination. Without denying that insight and knowledge can be found through symbolic representation, that which resists symbolization continues to confront us epistemologically. Persistent, it remains "glued to [the symbolic's] heel, ignorant of what might exile it from there,"[21] it continues to assert itself where our symbolic orders fail and where our materiality resists integration. The real is revelatory and excessive. It exposes the limits of language and representation, it throws their functioning into stark relief, and it indicates the undeniable existence of truth that is infinite and absolute, as it remains beyond our control and beyond our grasp. The real is thus also inherently traumatic: It is, by definition and by experience, that which cannot be integrated into the symbolic orders of our lived experience or meaning-making, even as it pushes them to frantic and diffuse activity. The failure of method to get to reality is thus not merely a negative verdict on any particular system of truth, or methodology of ascertaining it, but a negation of its possibility.

How to go on under conditions of hopelessness to ever *achieve* the truth, epistemologically or materially? By giving up hope, say some of the proposals we have studied in chapter 3. Their response is provocative as it expresses an existential, visceral sentiment. It is also strategic, as it seeks to avoid the illusions, complicities, and idealizations of "hope," "progress," and "achievement" in

20. Jacques Lacan, *The Seminar of Jacques Lacan: Book 1, Freud's Papers on Technique, 1953–1954*, ed. Jacques-Alain Miller, ed. John Forrester (New York: Norton, 1991), 66.
21. Jacques Lacan, *Écrits* (Paris: Seuil, 1966), 25.

their historic appropriations. Similar to De la Torre's opting for hopelessness over hope's cruel optimism, and Edelman's opting for refusal over the price of redemption by futurity, Barth calls on the theologian to "break, not with impiety, but with the *piety*"[22] of the systems of truth they have inherited. Such strategic hopelessness, refusal, or impiety is everything but faithlessness. De la Torre calls it "not despair, but perseverance,"[23] just like Barth talks about the theologian's need to "persevere" in their labor even as it remains unredeemed by method.[24] There is a kind of resignation[25] that—out of faithfulness to what is real over faithfulness to idealities—persists in its commitment beyond the question of success.

Going back to the Pauline semantic, we might also say: If in light of the violence and complicities, the illusions and delusions of both progress *and* radical negation, it earlier seemed as if all hope was lost, we might also be reminded that not *all* is lost when hope is lost. In Paul's theological imaginary, hope is but one of three virtues, and not even "the greatest of them" (1 Cor. 13:13). Not all is lost when hope is lost. In fact, not *even* (a theological understanding of) hope is lost when hope (in progress, success, and achievement) is lost: The belief in universal improvement, undebatable advancement, irrevocable betterment that has often been called "hope," might have been erroneously identified as such. Hope as a theological category is not so much the belief that things will get better, might get better, or can get better once we do the right thing. The hope we have invoked has pointed to the fact that what we see and understand may not be all there is to reality, while also feeling acutely that what is "is not enough"[26]—a sentiment that I want to call theological even as it is shared by religious and non-religious thinkers. The theological realism that is demanded of us is not a principle, it has an anti-docetic and anti-methodological commitment to take reality seriously as it resists us, time and again.

If, with notions of progress and betterment, whether epistemological or existential, theological or political, we give up hope, *something* always remains "outside" any symbolic order, outside any political project of inclusion or epistemic pursuit of understanding, outside the grasp of any method or system, constituting its boundary as much as its condition, its revelation as well as what demands our commitment in faith and love. This is where queer and theological analysis overlap, calling this outside "queerness" or "God," respectively.

22. Barth, "The Word of God as the Task of Theology," 183.
23. De la Torre, *Embracing Hopelessness*, 141.
24. Barth, "The Word of God as the Task of Theology," 173.
25. For a constructive theological appraisal of "resignation," cf. Benedikt Friedrich, "Gottes Resignieren," in *Verletzt Fühlen: Systematisch-theologische Perspektiven auf den Zusammenhang von Verletzung und Emotion*, ed. Lisanne Teuchert, Mikkel Gabriel Christoffersen, and Dennis Dietz, 219–43 (Tübingen: Mohr Siebeck, 2022).
26. Muñoz, *Cruising Utopia*, 1.

Queer theology is a realistic theology that starts where these two analyses are read together.

Faithfulness to the reality of God and that of human beings demands practicing care for them in active resignation against their idealizations as well as their overly apophatic dismissals. In all its ineffability, reality is also hermeneutical and generative: Reality gives rise to thought, prompts reflection, directs our attention to the margins, the excesses, the failures, the misfits as places where something real asserts itself and prompts renewed reckoning with this experience. It might only enter our experience by way of a certain negativity—as that which eludes, exceeds, and disrupts our imaginary and symbolic orders. Such negativity can and has been turned into epistemological practices to get at "the real."[27] Negativity, as we have seen, can also be deployed as an ideology critique of positivity.

But the failure of method to get to reality, truth, or justice should not primarily engender skepticism and relativism, at least not the kind of relativism that is thinly veiled nihilism, as if thus *nothing* can be said or done in any case. Whatever "shows itself" at these limits has also undeniable positivity by virtue of its resistance to integration. The failures and limits of our epistemic and ethical, theological and political system are the imprint of a reality that ultimately refuses to fit into our categories, however subtle and smart we contrive them. Method's failures bear witness to the truth of this reality. Reality leaves a trace, which Barth might call "craters" and which Althaus-Reid might call queerness. The determinate form of our epistemological failures and limitations affords positive insights.

Queer grace appears in God's excessive reality. Queer holiness is the stubborn insistence on an existence, an unrelinquishable excess of reality beyond the law, despite the law, before the law. Even as Marcella Althaus-Reid acknowledges that queer bodies and lives are not in and of themselves

---

27. A similar intuition is at work in basic hermeneutic guidelines such as the "difference criterion" in historical-critical exegesis. The quest for the "historical Jesus" was a (highly questionable) search for the "authentic" core of Jesus' own proclamation and historical existence under layers of interpretation and redaction. To distinguish between authentic and inauthentic elements, scholars concluded that whatever elements of Jesus' discourse and practice were irreducible to and inexplicable from his own or the Gospel writers' social, intellectual, and religious context were most likely authentic since there was no rationale to make them up, by the standards of their context, they were unintuitive, vexing, disruptive. They thus resisted integration and excision even in testimonies by and large hostile to them. Of course, the difference criterion never postulated that *only* such inexplicable, irreducible elements were authentic, it can merely pick out those elements that defy integration as indicators of reality as entry points into the subsequent web of interconnected elements in otherwise continuity with surrounding traditions and contexts. But it successfully leveraged the insight hermeneutically that what does not fit into our categories, what exceeds our economies of reason, what cannot be integrated into a system, points to truth.

any more or less holy than other lives or bodies, they are the site where such queer holiness may appear and become effective—that is, disruptive—in our world. While queerness does not necessarily imply holiness, holiness is always attended by a certain queerness.[28] Holiness appears in the unrepresentable, ungovernable, lingering difference between justice and law, between love and law, which becomes manifest in unorthodox relationships and heterodox fellowships, gives glimpses of a material reality that persists on the outside of all the options and alternatives, idealities and concretions provided by the law. The lives and loves of queer people can thus become revelatory, and "pedagogic": sites where the real appears, parables of the kingdom, as "love that exceeds institutions."[29] Rather than representing closure and comprehension, theology's designs, too, are called to "represent the resurrection of the excessive in our contexts."[30]

In defiance of a hubris that wants to master knowledge, and a sloth that indulges in epistemological abdication, theological realism demands that we meet the reality of God and the lives of real people where they exceed—and thus resist—the idealizing constructions of theology and our methodological control. They attain revelatory quality: uncovering the material truths of our constructions but also the truth of the real that escapes and defies them. Accountable to reality as it reveals itself, stubbornly exceeding language and reason, purity and ideality, laws and compulsory normativities, theology is called to an equally *excessive faithfulness* to the multiformity and ambivalence of what it encounters. In its pursuit of saying something true about reality, theology is called to attend to, seek out, and inhabit spaces and practices of excess, and to privilege sites of disruption, failure, and marginalization. It is called to an excessive commitment to the margins and failures of our political, religious, and symbolic systems, and to the marginalized, misfitting, illegible, stubbornly real people it finds at their gates, Christ among them.

INCARNATION'S MESSINESS (MESSY SOLIDARITY)

Any epistemological project must be committed to saying something true about reality, we said. It might appear that we have introduced a twofold reality: the reality of God and the reality of people, which both individually trouble our attempts at understanding, systematizing, and devising categories or other orders into which to fit. But these are of course not two disjunct realities.

---

28. Althaus-Reid, *The Queer God*, 143.
29. Althaus-Reid, *The Queer God*, 171.
30. Althaus-Reid, *Indecent Theology*, 200.

The epistemological faithfulness to these two is no more a bifurcation of the theologian's loyalty, than the Great Commandment's love of God and love of neighbor are additions of distinct, and possibly rivaling objects of love. They do not constitute a theologically problematic division of desire and will, nor do they divide attention and care as if these were competing goods. Considering who God *is* and what it *implies* to love one's neighbor, only by committing to both can either one of these commands be honored. These two loves are inextricably intertwined to the point of being co-constitutive, and their ethical intertwinement is preceded by their ontological one. The term theologians have used for this ontological intertwinement that grounds our epistemology as well as our ethics, is "incarnation."

Liberation Theology already formulated a "reality principle" to further materialize Barth's or other Systematic Theologians' christological starting point. The "thatness" of Christ's humanity as affirmed by the councils must, Jon Sobrino insisted, be specified as to its historical "whatness": its faithfulness to the God who is faithfully determined to be in enfleshed fellowship and solidarity with suffering humans against the forces of inhumanity. Quite in keeping with Barth's theological realism, Sobrino's "reality principle" is first and foremost grounded in God's own self-determining "will to reality," and beyond that, in God's incarnationally manifest and salvific "will to become real in the flesh of not just anyone but of the poor and the victims."[31] God's commitment to be fully real, fully with and for human beings, is God's quite determinate commitment to humanity in the twofold sense: not only of the assumption or acquisition of an abstract human nature but also as "pathos for humanity" that works toward the concrete overcoming of concrete inhumanity.[32] The world as it *actually* is, both for Sobrino and for Barth, is not simply to be equated with "reality" in a theological register. Like God, the theologian, too, is charged with "becoming real" to overcome this world's present suffering.

Marcella Althaus-Reid finds God in the lengths God goes in God's love for people, and she is surely down for "getting real." She invokes the classical language of kenosis to describe a "love that exceeds institutions (as God exceeds Godself in Christ and the trinity)."[33] But wary of the easy romanticization and sanitation of such love in the registers of mercy and charity, hers is a fiercely erotic expression of self-emptying and self-undoing, God pouring out Godself, almost (?) masochistically. Not that the erotic could not also be idealized—which is why in Althaus-Reid's account, the grounding of her

---

31. Jon Sobrino, *Christ the Liberator* (Maryknoll: Orbis, 2001), 297.
32. Sobrino, *Christ the Liberator*, 287.
33. Althaus-Reid, *The Queer God*, 171.

theological realism in intersectional material analysis remains critical. Paying attention to ambivalences, obscenities, and contradictions introduced by economic, cultural, imperial, and gendered logics, helps at least to trouble an all-too-easy equivocation of any, even libertine or queer, sexuality with a new salvific ideality.

Before the twofold commitment to the reality of God and the reality of human beings issues a twofold ethical demand, it presents an ontological description of who God is in Jesus Christ: In his being, his teaching, and his acts, the "Bi/Christ" (as Marcella Althaus-Reid calls him) challenges the primordial binary construction in theology: that which puts God and the human being in opposition, and the commitment to one of them as exclusive of the other. Transgressing the economies of mono-directional love and desire, the Bi/Christ defies the commonplace association of bisexuality with vagueness, confusion, and lack of commitment. Instead, he radicalizes commitment and love in a way that constitutively exceeds the measure of the law, any law. He is the "Un/Just Messiah" insofar as his ontological commitment exposes the excesses inherent in justice, and insofar as his ontological commitment will exceed every attempt of determining the form and shape of justice.[34]

The point of ascribing bi/sexuality to Christ is not to sexualize him, but rather to illuminate the strangeness of this God who demonstrates no boundaries for the commitments of his love nor regard for the law of any economy of exchange. Althaus-Reid can also call this fundamental trait of God God's "omnisexual kenosis," which is material and determinate while utterly unconcerned with living the "proper" story, the prescribed script, the assigned identity categories, or fixing a stable meaning to them.[35] As Althaus-Reid's use of the term bisexuality weaves together meanings of sexual orientation and non-binary or multigender identity, it traverses not only the separation between God and humanity but also between Christ's love and Christ's essence, "work" and "being." Similarly, Barth would have talked about the "humanity of God" as God's love for humanity, as God's ontological self-determination and God's passionate action for the human being. Indeed, God's ontological self-determination *is* God's passionate action for the human being: the election of Jesus Christ. The determinate reality of who this God is thus not only unites the twofold commitment into one but also identifies this commitment as one that is at once ontological, epistemological, and ethical.

Queer grace is thus found in God's *kenotic solidarity* that does not insist on sameness to direct itself toward an Other. Carefully distinguished from homo-solidarity in this sense, kenosis marks a commitment to the other that goes

---

34. Althaus-Reid, *Indecent Theology*, 157.
35. Althaus-Reid, *The Queer God*, 57.

beyond economies of reciprocity, similarity, or essence, whether as a condition or telos of communion and community. Instead, it gives itself up into what is unlike, overcoming the need and sense of such boundary in the creation of messy, fleshy solidarity. God's kenotic solidarity is just as excessive as God's stubborn faithfulness: beyond considerations of justice and merit, God insists on being-with the Other. Precisely what we lift up as love in sovereign freedom thus becomes in practice un/just, vulnerable, entangled, and queer in the concrete material conditions of fleshy existence of concrete geo-historical contexts. God's loving solidarity is as messy as it is kenotic—and messy *because* it is kenotic.

The un/just messiah Jesus is God's kenotic movement out of positions of mastery into enfleshed love, with its concomitant conditions of illegibility and vulnerability. The real lives of real people give ample testimony of the reality of a strange and curious "queer holiness" where lives are "lived in justice, even if outside the law."[36] "Queer holiness finds God, as a stranger at the gates of Hegemonic Theology"[37] and insists on the reality of the kingdom "among you" (Luke 17:21), not in some transcendent otherworldly realm, but in the otherwise realities that already exist in, with, and under the law. It insists that those loves that exceed the space and shape that society allots for them might be revelatory of divine kenotic love as well as knowing "more and . . . better about alternative projects for justice and peace."[38] Diversely enfleshed alternatives to dominant social orders "amongst loving expressions of relationships at the margins of the defined decent and proper in Christianity"[39] are material incarnations of holiness. The sexual stories Althaus-Reid tells defy and challenge colonial, imperial, and heterosexual logics as she finds God in the everyday lives of poor people, queer people, strangers and exiles, sex workers and sexual outcasts, where spaces are opened up for difference, encounter, and community beyond categories and rationales of whatever "decency" without indulging in romantic ideas. Such marginal alternatives embody the prophetic disruption of norms that might even conventionally be associated with sainthood but also queer it.[40]

For God as much as for human beings, reality can only be approached through incarnation. In incarnational, kenotic love, reality ("being real") and commitment ("becoming real") converge—in all ontological, epistemological, and ethical dimensions of such a statement. Faith—in its epistemological inflection as faithfulness to the revelatory excesses of reality—has already

36. Althaus-Reid, *The Queer God*, 169.
37. Althaus-Reid, *The Queer God*, 171.
38. Althaus-Reid, *The Queer God*, 171.
39. Althaus-Reid, *The Queer God*, 171.
40. Althaus-Reid, *The Queer God*, 160.

raised the question of adequate *care* for this reality in epistemological practice of solidarity with it. In faithfulness to the reality of God and the reality of people, the theologian is called to attend epistemologically to the shape of a reality that ontologically embodies a movement of kenotic solidarity.

As a form of theological realism that is likewise intent on "becoming real," Althaus-Reid suggests that the theologian, in testimonial correspondence to such divine bi- or omnisexuality, needs to assume "a critical bisexuality,"[41] which she envisions not as "a question of individual sexual identity, but of an epistemological identity"[42]—a double commitment to true humanity and true divinity, a twofold desire for heaven and earth, where one does not invalidate or threaten the other: both desires can only be fulfilled together, and the boundary cannot always be drawn neatly. Once more, Althaus-Reid's use of the term "bisexuality" oscillates between bisexual orientation (beyond "mono-loving,"[43] desire of both God and humanity) and bi-gender identity (as applied to Christ's two natures, divine and human) as well as the excess of dyadic orientations (homo- or heterosexual) and genders (beyond male and female) altogether. Critical bisexuality thus marks an epistemological stance that resists the imperative to "remain mono-faithful to [any] one heterosexual, or lesbian, or gay, or uncritically bi way of understanding."[44] Rather, it embraces a critical orientation of "giving space to the contradictory or different co-residing together,"[45] pointing to instability and fluidity of categories that "cannot be pinned down in a stable or fixed way,"[46] nor confined to a predetermined number or identity of commitments.

Linn Tonstad rightly points to Althaus-Reid's critical bisexuality as a logic of "both/and" rather than "either/or." It resists not only the binaries of dominant normativities but also the binary of normative/anti-normative thinking, or of reparative-vs.-paranoid reading. Tonstad suggests that such a critical bisexuality beyond anti-normativity marks not a retrieval after critique, but a form of "recursion" that "interdigitates" the two (somewhat, I hope, like I have interdigitated Barth's and Althaus-Reid's theological voices in this book).[47]

Indeed, such interdigitation might be what critical epistemology looks like when turned into method, just like Barth's *via dialectica* is essentially an interdigitation of the *via positiva* and *via negativa*. But in light of our investigation so far, I am not content with the back and forth that such a posture—whether

41. Althaus-Reid, *The Queer God*, 16.
42. Althaus-Reid, *The Queer God*, 15.
43. Althaus-Reid, *The Queer God*, 19.
44. Althaus-Reid, *The Queer God*, 19.
45. Althaus-Reid, *The Queer God*, 120.
46. Althaus-Reid, *The Queer God*, 16.
47. Linn Marie Tonstad, "Ambivalent Loves: Christian Theologies, Queer Theologies," *Literature and Theology* 31, no. 4 (2017): 472–89, 484.

conceptualized as dialectics or interdigitating—suggests. It is too reminiscent of the biphobic prejudice that would find in critical bisexuality merely a lack of commitment and identity. Instead, critical bisexuality comes from a primacy of grace that engenders both the normative and anti-normative conclusions, both gospel as the content of law and law as the form of the gospel. The twofold commandment—love of God and love of neighbor—is an ethical inflection of the two natures of Christ: an ontological rendition of incarnation that gives epistemological access to reality—and which retroactively calls into question its binary division in the first place. Which is why at the end of the day, Althaus-Reid's "omnisexual kenosis" might be the more appropriate inflection of the insight than the pointers to "critical bisexuality." Might such a critical bi- or kenotic omni-sexuality with its fierce, if multiple, ethical commitments in the midst of unredeemed reality be surprisingly reminiscent of Barth's Christocentrism as a theological stance, where God's humanity engenders our co-humanity, where the "one Word of God" articulates both gospel and law, where the law can become the form of the gospel, and where ultimately, a *tertius usus legis* rather than its abandonment "after" Christ becomes needful?

Not all is lost when hope (in epistemological progress) is lost. Faith and love remain.[48] Any epistemological project must be committed not only to saying something true about reality but also to become real in embodying the truth it discerned and to be ready to give up its idealities in kenotic solidarity with reality. God's excessive love, which is God's excessive nature, poured out kenotically, gives rise to multiple commitments for the theologian, as well, in practice always somewhat in tension. In defiance of hubris, the theologian is called to kenotically messy forms of epistemological *solidarity*, to change the conditions of theological production and to seek out collaborations that are not founded on sameness: not on identity or similarity, affinity or legibility, integration or coherence, nor on binary opposition in any of these terms, and to attend to the messy and unruly insights generated from experiences that it remains tempted to idealize. In defiance of sloth, theological realism demands incarnated, epistemological practices of solidarity as performance of divine and human friendship and love—a "staying with the trouble"[49] beyond merit, gain and success, and even beyond legibility and understanding. Rather than

---

48. This insight, of course, has been made by marginalized communities for a long time. Examples include Delores Williams' shift from a hermeneutic of liberation to a hermeneutic of survival, or more recently, Ta-Nahesi Coates, *Between the World and Me* (New York: Random House, 2015).

49. Donna Jeanne Haraway, *Staying with the Trouble: Making Kin in the Chthulucene* (Durham; London: Duke University Press, 2016).

aspiring to itself be "a form of soteriology",[50] a theology that heeds the reality principle engages in the humbler but no less needed task of "turning the sick man back and forth."[51] As a reflection of God's will to become real, it demands practices of kenotic solidarity that defies the sloth of giving up on human misery and human joy in resignation or refusal and instead lean into incarnate existence in all its messiness.

TRUTH'S INDECENCY (INDECENT HONESTY)

Any epistemological project must be committed to reality—and the deepest reality that theology comes from is that this world is "a world of both sin and grace."[52] The excessive positivity of revelation and its manifestation in glimpses of queer holiness has a critical, negative correlate. What is real imposes itself beyond or at the margins of the symbolic orders or calculations of exchange, disrupting them but also revealing them for what they are. At the margins and failures of our symbolic and political systems, where the real shows itself in joy and pain, the theologian's commitment to the excessive nature of reality translates into a commitment to resist reality as it finds it by telling its truth.

Queer grace is found in God's *revelatory unmasking* of the falsehood of idealities that render reality indecent, the falsehood of both mastery's hubris and despair's sloth as idols that are dead and death-dealing. God's honesty in subverting and unmasking is thus as indecent as it is revelatory—indecent *because* it reveals things for what they really are. "Honesty" is one of the few unambiguously positive categories in Althaus-Reid's writing (maybe apart from "consent". Even "excess" and "disruption" contain complications). Honesty stands in marked contrast to "decency": acknowledging the messiness of reality versus telling its cleaned-up versions. The term "decency" of course has explicit sexual valences, in which such cleaning-up of reality often asserts itself, but it is fundamentally not just about a moral, but about "an epistemological ceiling."[53] Decency is about the regulation of what can be said and thought by symbolic orders. Its sexual and political consequences go hand in hand: "Decent Christian women, unfortunately, make decent citizens too," while transformative action can only ensue through subversion and transgression:

---

50. Sobrino, *The Principle of Mercy*, 37.
51. Barth, "The Word of God as the Task of Theology," 175.
52. Sobrino, *The Principle of Mercy*, 6.
53. Althaus-Reid, *Indecent Theology*, 167.

"Indecency may be the last chance for a surplus of Christianity to transform political structures."[54]

The Barthian and the Liberation theologian will be tempted to leverage theological realism for prophetic critique: the reality of God resists the (un)reality of sin; the sovereignty of God necessitates resistance to the quasi-sovereign aspirations of political powers; the God of the oppressed (the poor, the marginalized, the queer) prompts critique of the dominant symbolic (economic, social, and epistemological) orders. Such prophetic critique is important and will remain necessary. But its antagonistic clarity lends itself to become yet another permutation of "T-theology" or falsehood. Indecent theology goes further in its doubting and in its "disrespect for the interpellative, normative forces of patriarchal theology."[55]

As drawn out in chapter 1, honesty becomes indecent because it attends to the obscenity of reality: not its clarity but its obscurity, its ambivalence, and its viscosity. This is why it commits to materiality, why it turns to everyday life as passing under the radar of idealistic constructions, and why sexual stories are such a primary site for its practice, because per/version and obscenity are exposed and exhibited rather than cleaned up. But none of these sites can be essentialized, idealized, either, or turned into methodological principles lest the supposed "authenticity" of the poor, of the quotidian life, or of sexual excess become romanticized and lose their traction of reality—thus Althaus-Reid's critique of Liberation Theology (which could easily extend to forms of Queer Theology today that simply celebrate sexual libertinism against sexual orders in the antagonistic—and thus idealistic—fashion of other Systematic and Liberation Theologies). The honesty of theological realism demands to neither idealistically pit God against a—material or ideological—reality from which people are to be liberated, *nor* to unequivocally identify God with it.

The reality of God and the real lives of real human beings defy the lie of mastery and prompt indecent revelations of both the beauty and the horror, the violence and tenderness, the banality and glory of things in all their ambivalent multiplicity, pluriformity, and unruliness. In defiance of falsehood, theological realism demands an *indecent honesty* that commits itself to more serious doubting, and to telling the truth of things as it finds it, not as they ought to be according to whichever (theo-)logic, including a queer one. The theological realist is thus called to engage in ongoing searching and yearning, to speak "indecently, queeringly clear"[56] in the midst of sanitized truths, to expose the obscenity of reality, in acts of epistemological deviance and epistemological

54. Althaus-Reid, *Indecent Theology*, 169–70.
55. Althaus-Reid, *Indecent Theology*, 95.
56. Althaus-Reid, *Indecent Theology*, 95.

transvestism beyond simple prophetic antagonism, to engage in ongoing searching and yearning rather than propose solutions, and to continue not only to see the unseen but also in doing so to remain "on the move, or on the run" while sporting a variety of biographical or disciplinary passports.[57]

A BETTER WAY?

The systematician might of course recognize in faithfulness to the margins and excesses as an epistemological way of attending to revelation, messy solidarity as an epistemological way of attending to incarnational kenosis, and indecent truth-telling as an epistemological variation of attending to the indecency of truth rather messed-up (messed-up because they are *realized*: inflected by life) counter-realities to Barth's threefold phenomenology of sin as hubris, sloth, and falsehood. As they defy sin—that which undermines trust, destroys the ability to love and be loved, and deprives of hope—excessive faithfulness to the margins, messy solidarity with unruly realities, and indecent honesty that resists symbolic interpellations as much as easy antagonisms, they might even be seen as riffs on Paul's threefold phenomenology of grace in faith, love, and hope: slightly more realistic versions of the *better way* that Paul invoked against the trust in diverse but competing human abilities in his congregation (1 Cor. 12:29–13:13).

Faith, love, and hope have often been conceptualized as theological "virtues." And some might seek relief from the impossibility of securing "good theology" by way of method by cultivating moral excellence in the habits and dispositions of the theologian instead. In contrast to method, virtue signals the absence of a determinate law and procedure that one could follow to achieve progress, and it places emphasis on practice rather than results, formation rather than telos. Virtue might thus at best convey an orientation toward a "good" that finds its purpose and exercise in iterative practice, rather than the achievement of a final state or even incremental progress, and the distinction of a sustained orientation toward a "better" without a clear progress in its pursuit but a cultivation of certain acts and habits for their own sake. Of course, the aspiration to moral excellence implicit in virtue, with its location of goodness in character, its classical valuation of moderation, its rather individualistic cultivation of perfectionism, and its a-material tendency, are quite alien to the general direction we have been pursuing in this study so far.

"To speak of faith, hope, and love," Christoph Chalamet writes, "implies speaking of God. More precisely, it means speaking of God's faithfulness,

57. Althaus-Reid, *Indecent Theology*, 82.

justice, and love that call forth and provoke, in many different ways, such a triadic response in human beings and in communities of faith."[58] In the first place, then, faith, hope, and love pertain to who God is. God's incarnational insistence queers God to the point of no return, and, more importantly, queers any binary division—not only the boundary between heaven and earth, divine and human but also the clear-cut distinction of sin and grace, virtue and vice, salvation and existence. The Un/Just Messiah is an irredeemably troubled and equivocal figure who has never ceased to disappoint our assumptions, scandalize our understanding, or mess with our categories. He does the same with faith, love, and hope. Faith, love, and hope are God's character, as becomes visible in the incarnation's excessive faithfulness to creation even against and beyond its resistance, in the incarnation's kenotic solidarity with creation, which does not regard sameness with God as something to be exploited, in the indecent honesty of the incarnation's revelation: scandalous, vulnerable, and disruptive.

Further, as God's character, faith, love, and hope are also essentially grace. God's gifts to the world, they are found in this world as inexplicable manifestations of grace, actually existent incarnations of grace that offer us concrete sites where something of God and God's hope for this world can be glimpsed and experienced. Thirdly, these manifestations of faith, love, and hope in the world are epistemologically salient: they constitute ways of being introduced to God. God allows Godself to be found in faith, love, and hope. They can become sites not just for discerning God's presence and God's work, but also for guiding the human response and correspondence to such grace. Faith, love, and hope, then, are also tasks, or rather, guiderails for any concrete response to God's call, as response in correspondence to it.

Rearticulating grace as divine faithfulness, kenosis, and revelation, with Barth and Althaus-Reid leads to "queer virtues" of stubborn excessiveness, messy solidarity, and indecent honesty. As craters and signposts of queer holiness, they are reflections and glimmers of divine grace in a world that to some extent remains surprised by their presence. These queer "virtues" might be traced in many areas of human existence; the one that concerns me here are their epistemological versions.

The Systematic Theologian in me is tempted to use this triptych as a blueprint to trace the shape of divine grace and our response or correspondence to them. The Queer Theologian in me scoffs at this desire, and insists that nothing protects such "virtues" from becoming romanticized into pure and clean characteristics ascribed to a speculative deity, and subsequently into sanitized

58. Christophe Chalamet, *A Most Excellent Way: An Essay on Faith, Hope, and Love* (Lanham: Lexington; Fortress, 2020), 16.

and idealized versions of Christian life (and epistemology). At the very least, they will be in ongoing need of being subjected to "the reality principle" and to be re-articulated with a higher degree of concreteness and materiality. They need to do justice to the determinate character of God (theological realism), the concrete shapes of the real lives of real people (material realism); taking as seriously the reality of grace to be found in both (salutological realism) and the persistent complicity in sin (hamartiological realism). Where they become real in commitment to actual creatures and in defiance of the powers of hubris, sloth, and falsehood, they become messy, excessive, indecent—in short: queer. The material reality check I want to use—without turning it into another methodology—is one that understands theology as a material practice of conceptual design as informed by faithfulness to sites of failure, excess, and marginality; kenotic solidarity with the messiness of real life in iterative critical and constructive feedback and feed-forward loops; and indecently honest appraisal of its own conditions of production, its affordances, and their uses. A first test case for such a vision, however, must be the analysis that generated it: reading method through the theological dialectic of law and grace.

Chapter 5

Before the law

AFTER METHOD, BEFORE THE LAW

A door is always a scene of instruction.
—*Sarah Ahmed*[1]

Method cannot save us. This statement is less a dismissal of method and more of a theological critique of its *use*—in the double sense of its purpose and its applications. There *is* a use of method *after* method, a use of method that is, in theological and hamartiological realism, committed to "becoming" real. In its critically bisexual orientation to the reality of God and the reality of the human being, it attends to revelatory excesses, dwells in messy solidarity, and practices indecent honesty in order to do *better*: redesigning theology in full consciousness that it will never be *good*.

Method cannot save us, but this does not mean that it cannot do anything for us. For starters, it can allow us to glean a more precise outline of our need for redemption without ever achieving it. As Barth says, "it simply leads *up to* the front of this door that can only be opened from the inside."[2] Subsequently, it can continue to accompany our endeavors to strive for relative peace under conditions of finitude and fallenness (*primus usus*), it can help us understand our own need for redemption (*secundus usus*), and it *can* (!) guide the pursuit of relatively *better* forms of theology *after* grace (*tertius usus*).

---

1. Sara Ahmed, *Complaint!* (Durham: Duke University Press, 2021), 228.
2. Barth, "The Word of God as the Task of Theology," 194.

127

Such a third use of method will, however, have to be applied first of all to its own diagnosis. What does it mean to invest in doing *better* while fully conscious of one's inability to do *good*, how can one understand that even diagnosing one's own condition will remain complicit in the very issues one denounces—and *at the same time* attempt to point to something *better*? This—to put it abstractly—is the question the present chapter tries to recursively apply to the work we have done so far.

To put it more concretely: Beyond the notions of sin and grace, informing the task and shape of theology, a theological conception of the law has been central to my framing of theological method. The old problem of justification surfaced in the attempt to redeem theology by way of method, noting the old consequences: a tightrope act between self-righteousness and despair, and concomitant otherization and ostracization of those who were not able to measure up to the standards of method (whichever method)—or, in turn, of those who lift up the law of method too high. And the old queer critique surfaced in the attempt to discipline theological scholarship by way of method, noting the old consequences of the random fixing of the dominant as the authoritative, otherizing or invisibilizing nonnormative experiences and lives both epistemically and socially. Lutheran mistrust against "works of law" and queer mistrust against normativity thus came together in a shared suspicion of method as "law." Their anti-legalistic sensitivities allowed me to bring doctrine and queer theory, Karl Barth and Marcella Althaus-Reid, Systematic Theology and Constructive Theology into conversation. A push-back against method's redemptive promise, and the dead-ends and violent effects into which it leads, has been the subtext of the book. A threefold use of the law "after grace" even structures its whole architecture.

But grace is messy, and it messes with those it touches. It leaves no one unchanged, not even theology's diagnosis of its own crisis, here framed along the lines of "Law." "Law" is, of course, not a neutral theological category, and theological anti-legalism has a notoriously problematic anti-Jewish ring. A highly specific and contextually embedded conceptual design with ecological sensibilities, practical commitments, and material ramifications in specific affordances and disaffordances, "Law" is a theological term that is particularly fraught with all the ambivalences in use or misuse, with histories of violent effects and exclusions, and with the hubris, sloth, and falsehood of "decency" as pinpointed by now extensively by the self-critiques of both Systematic and Constructive Theologies. Is this doctrine—with which in some sense the whole design of this proposal stands and falls—an irredeemable product of a fallen theological imagination? Can it be converted, transformed into something that might yet testify to grace? And if so, what possibilities of faithful redesign, repurposing, or recycling present themselves as we constructively reconceive the theological status of method as "law" in theological epistemology under its own third use? Theological conceptions of the "law" thus become our first case study for something like a method *after method*.

After method, we find ourselves "before the law," a scene famously described by Franz Kafka. In this chapter, Kafka's eponymous parable will serve as a lens for exploring and assessing the conceptual affordances and possible design failure of "the law," as well as its potential *use* in theology "after method." This is how the story goes:

> Before the Law stands a doorkeeper. A man from the country comes to this doorkeeper and requests admittance to the Law. But the door-keepers says that he can't grant him admittance now. The man thinks it over and then asks if he'll be allowed to enter later. "It's possible," says the doorkeeper, "but not now." . . . The doorkeeper gives him a stool and lets him sit down at the side of the door. He sits there for days and years. He asks time and again to be admitted, and wearies the doorkeeper with his entreaties. The doorkeeper often conducts brief interrogations, inquiring about his home and many other matters, but he asks such questions indifferently, as great men do, and in the end he always tells him he still can't admit him. The man, who has equipped himself well for his journey, uses everything, no matter how valuable, to bribe the doorkeeper. And the doorkeeper accepts everything, but as he does so he says, "I'm taking this just so you won't think you've neglected something." . . . Before he dies, everything he has experienced over the years coalesces in his mind into a single question he has never asked the doorkeeper. . . . "Everyone strives to reach the Law," says the man, "how does it happen, then, that in all these years no one but me has requested admittance." The door-keeper sees that the man is nearing his end, and in order to reach his failing hearing, he roars at him: "No one else could gain admittance here, because this entrance was meant solely for you. I'm going to go and shut it now."[3]

In Kafka's enigmatic parable, the law assumes the form of a physical space of inhospitable, or at least deeply ambivalent, design. Desiring access, a man spends all his energies, belongings, and ultimately his whole life attempting to be let in. But this permission is never granted by the doorkeeper, who also insinuates that he is only the first in a row of insurmountable barriers. If the story is a parable (as we will assume), its moral seems vexingly elusive. This elusiveness is further compounded by the story's central place in Kafka's unfinished novel *The Trial*, where Joseph K. and the priest who narrates the

3. Franz Kafka, *The Trial: A New Translation Based on the Restored Text*, tr. Breon Mitchell (New York: Schocken, 1999), 215–17.

parable embark on an—ultimately inconclusive—discussion over its meaning. Is it that, as maps onto Josef K.'s own frustration with an intractable bureaucratic system, the man has been deceived by the doorkeeper, and should have put no faith in his allegations? Is it that the man was subjected to a test that he failed by waiting acquiescently—ought he to have entered without permission? Or is it that the law in and of itself is not for entering, but for something else—but what? The exegetical back and forth in the novel only draws out the defeat further: it renders any unequivocal understanding performatively inviable in the multiplicity of partial interpretations.

Whether for Kafka "the law" references inscrutable legal bureaucracies or a theological conception remains open. In any case, it presents itself as a structure that is as overbearing as it is impenetrable. Inaccessible even to the best efforts, it engenders a deep sense of futility. The question arises—is this inaccessibility a *design failure* or is it *failure by design*? Is it a bug or a feature of "the law"? Does it rest on a misunderstanding, a miscommunication that might be remedied by way of *better* design—or is this failure precisely the intended outcome of the design? Playing with Kafka's enigmatic story, this chapter will explore a few possibilities of how to interpret method's failure theologically and theoretically, and what perspectives such readings might offer for the redesign of theological method *after method*.

GETTING IN, OR: LUTHERAN NORMAN DOORS?

Kafka's invitingly open, yet effectively inaccessible door might be a metaphor, but actual doors might have something to teach us about conceptual doors. In Don Norman's *The Design of Everyday Things,* "Norman doors" became a proverbial design failure in the quest for usability.[4] The term references the conflicting signals of an embedded functionality that leads to predictable "user error" and frustration: While the sign "push" correctly aligns with the affordance of the door to be pushed open, the form of the handle signals "pull" to the hand gripping it. Such conflicting signals will predictably lead to scenes where a user will exert ever more force to get into a building—to no avail. Their effort will be misled and frustrated by the resistance of the door.

In Kafka's parable, the door beckons the man in the story to enter it, and the man is aware that "the Law should be accessible." Yet the doorkeeper in front of the door sends the opposite signal, both by his presence and by verbal reinforcement. The man seeking access is left in limbo and confusion,

---

4. Don Norman, *The Design of Everyday Things: Revised and Expanded Edition* (New York: Basic, 2013).

commanded and forbidden at the same time to enter "the Law," pushing against it and being pushed back by it. Unable to resolve the conflicting signals into a course of action, he remains stuck in front of the door.

In Barth's reflections on theological method, as we have seen in chapter 3, the theologian is similarly stuck between the unresolvably conflicting signals of "must!" and "cannot!" We have traced the epistemological dilemma back to the Protestant doctrine of justification, where the law sends similarly conflicting signals. In its form as command, it prompts the user to exert herself and "push through." However, under the affordances of grace the invested effort will hit the user over the head as works-righteousness, and effectively obstruct the very access to grace that had been promised as divinely granted. According to the conflicted logic of this door, the attempt to obey and do the right thing does not lead to being admitted, rather, it leads straight to condemnation. Martin Luther's despair in pursuing perfection in a law that seemed to ever turn against him is well known. Similarly, in *The Word of God as the Task of Theology*, Barth despairs over the task to preach the word of God when any attempt to do so invariably oversteps the creaturely boundaries into which said word provides insight. Barth's dialectical non-resolution of "knowing both and giving God the glory" remains more ambiguous than Luther's famous break-through insight: "By grace alone! Not by works of law!"

Spelling out the doctrine of justification in long dogmatic treatises or in slogans like *sola gratia* and *sola fide* might then be likened to the impulse of a frustrated user to fix an instruction to the misleading door: "Step back, door opens automatically." Such instructions are intended to provide the much-needed clarification and avoid user error. But, as in the case of the Norman door, the added instruction does not correct the faulty design, it only heightens the performative contradiction. The intuitive impulse of the person in front of the law will still be to push harder and harder. Rather than afford relief and clarity, the explanatory sign will only increase the frustration and the feeling of inadequacy. Running against the door and being hit over the head by the design, the user feels all but mocked by a grace that proves ever more elusive the more one tries to pursue it.

In a "Norman door," the fault lies in the mismatch of the design's embedded functionality and its tactile signaling—but where would we locate the design flaw in the theology of the law? In Luther's case, it might lie in a misinterpretation of the biblical witness, especially Paul's understanding of law and grace as opposed, even mutually exclusive principles ("push"/"pull"). This Lutheran distinction has been plagued from the outset not only by the frailty of its ethical implications but also by the anti-Judaism embedded in its conceptual design. Even as Luther's famous text *On the Freedom of a Christian* conceptualizes a dialectical unity of freedom and obedience, its parts are constantly in danger of being mapped out dualistically.[5] Freedom will be identified with the inner person and the spiritual life, and obedience with the outer person and the political or ethical life. The same distinction gets mapped as one of gospel and law, of New and Old Testament, and can quickly turn into the distinction between the God of Jesus Christ and the God of Israel, the Christian faith and Judaism. This mushrooming dichotomy has been most fateful historically, and it is questionable whether it can be disentangled from the theological design: According to Luther's logic, all theological understanding hinges on getting the fundamental distinction of gospel and law right.[6]

Tellingly, Luther's own well-documented hateful tirades against "the Jews" embody the staunch anti-Judaism that the theological dichotomy suggests.[7] While some continue to search in Luther's theology for principles that would allow to frame his political stance as "against his better judgment,"[8] i.e., as a personal blemish independent of and even inconsistent with his theology, most interpreters today acknowledge Luther's anti-Judaism unapologetically.[9] But if we continue to follow the insights of design, as guided by our examination of this curious conceptual "door," design theory would invite us to look beyond the intentions of the designer, that is, beyond defending or indicting the man Luther, his convictions, articulations, actions, and their consistency. The design lens prompts us instead to focus on the affordances of Luther's theology of justification for anti-Jewish hate and violence, which should be unacceptable for ethical, political, and yes, theological reasons.

Recent studies uncover a direct line from Luther's theology to the manifest anti-Semitism of his heirs in the twentieth century, with its horrifying culmination in the Holocaust.[10] In light of the demonstrable affordances of Luther's law/gospel distinction for discriminatory, oppressive, and ultimately

5. Martin Luther, *The Freedom of a Christian, 1520: The Annotated Luther*, ed. Timothy J. Wengert (Paris: Fortress, 2016).

6. A sentiment he expressed often, captured in Luther's 1521 statement, "almost all Scripture and the understanding of all theology depends on the proper understanding of law and gospel." (WA 7.502,34–35).

7. A helpful compilation of Luther's writings on the Jews can be found in Martin Luther, *Martin Luther, the Bible, and the Jewish People: A Reader* (Minneapolis: Fortress, 2012).

8. Eric W. Gritsch, *Martin Luther's Anti-Semitism: Against His Better Judgment*, (Grand Rapids: Eerdmans, 2012).

9. Cf. e.g., Thomas Kaufmann, "Luther, Martin," in *Handbuch des Antisemitismus: Judenfeindschaft in Geschichte und Gegenwart*, ed. Wolfgang Benz, 2.2:501–6 (Berlin: De Gruyter, 2009); Thomas Kaufmann, *Luther's Jews: A Journey into Anti-Semitism* (Oxford; New York: Oxford University Press, 2017).

10. Cf. Peter von der Osten-Sacken, *Martin Luther und die Juden: Neu untersucht anhand von Anton Margarithas „Der gantz Jüdisch glaub" (1530/31)* (Stuttgart: Kohlhammer, 2002); Harry Oelke, ed. *Martin Luthers „Judenschriften": Die Rezeption im 19. und 20. Jahrhundert*, Arbeiten zur kirchlichen Zeitgeschichte B64 (Göttingen: Vandenhoeck & Ruprecht, 2016); Susannah Heschel, *The Aryan Jesus* (Princeton: Princeton University Press, 2010).

genocidal purposes, people have asked whether Luther's theology of justification is beyond redemption,[11] or inquired whether faithful redesigns of his
doctrine—heeding Adorno's new categorical imperative to "arrange [all]
thoughts and actions so that Auschwitz will not repeat itself, so that nothing
similar will happen"[12]—is possible and necessary.

Fortunately, theology does not stand and fall with a Lutheran distinction
of law and gospel. For several decades now, New Testament scholars have
posited that Luther's understanding was not simply a quite particular but ultimately an inaccurate interpretation of the biblical witness. The so-called New
Perspective on Paul, first articulated prominently by Krister Stendahl and E.
P. Sanders, revealed that the question that plagued Luther—"How might I
be saved?" or "How might I get *access* to grace?"—was neither the question of
Jewish law in the first place, nor the question to which Paul's reformulation of
it responded.[13] The New Perspective contextualized the New Testament writings to point out that the Jewish understanding of law was never about what
Luther denounced as works-righteousness, "earning salvation" by one's own
powers. In Jewish theology, the Torah was always seen as a particular kind of
grace, providing the picture of a life lived in the presence of God. Its purpose
as much descriptive as it is regulatory, its conversational nature dispels the
terrifying but false dualism of impeccability or reprobation and invites attention to the ways in which life both changes and stays the same in a theocentric
orientation. "The Law," then, might more adequately be compared to an
instrument of narrating and navigating imperfection than one of achieving
perfection; not a means of "getting in" but one that affords the means of "staying in" a space mapped out by grace.

Paul's theological redesign of Jewish theology, by extension, was not
about repudiating works-righteousness or works of law as such, but about
drawing out the communal vision of God's election (God's grace!). Paul's
critique, then, was less about changing the design than about increasing
its usability beyond the originally envisioned users, inviting further constituencies into adopting and inhabiting it. This does neither imply the
erasure of all differences nor an unmarked universalism, as is sometimes
maintained in less overtly anti-Jewish, but still implicitly supersessionist

11. Andreas Pangritz, *Theologie und Antisemitismus: Das Beispiel Martin Luthers* (Frankfurt /
Main: Lang, 2017).

12. Theodor W. Adorno, *Negative Dialectics*, tr. E. B. Ashton (Routledge; Taylor & Francis.
London, 2003), 365.

13. Cf., e.g. Krister Stendahl, "The Apostle Paul and the Introspective Conscience of the
West," *Harvard Theological Review* 56, no. 3 (1963): 199–215; Krister Stendahl, *Paul Among Jews
and Gentiles and Other Essays* (Philadelphia: Fortress, 1976); E. P. Sanders, *Paul and Palestinian
Judaism: A Comparison of Patterns of Religion* (Minneapolis: Fortress, 1977).

readings. Rather, it implies that Paul's Christ transforms the criteria of kinship to Israel for whom the house was built to be inhabited.[14]

Luther, puzzling over the design of the door, pondered whether it had been installed the wrong way around: Never intended to be forced open from the outside, this door had long been thrown wide open from within. But if neither the Torah to which Paul referred nor his own theological reformulation of the law in relation to the gospel were about "getting in" in the first place, and in both cases no dualistic distinction between law and grace could be drawn, then maybe the door never was a front door at all; maybe it had always been an internal door that allowed for the inhabitants to make good use of the space in different rooms. And maybe Paul the Jew's reinterpretation was neither a demolition of the house of Israel nor an abolition of space dividers altogether, but an accessibility update that allowed the same internal door to be operated by differently equipped users according to the gracious functionalities that had always been embedded in God's design.

In their rapid transformation of the instable Weimar Republic into the Third Reich's totalitarian regime, the Nazis rode the waves of a theological Luther revival, celebrated Luther as a national German hero, and declared the cultural superiority of a Christian "religion of love" over a Jewish "religion of law." In what would become his farewell address to Christians in Germany after his suspension from office,[15] Karl Barth formulated a theological counter-design against dichotomic conceptions of law and gospel with a one-sidedly negative understanding of the law. Leading with the ontological primacy of grace rather than the (assumed) chronological primacy of law, Barth deprives the law of its independent and oppositional character to grace and turns both into dimensions of the "one word of God in Jesus Christ," effectively collapsing the binary into a porous co-constitutive entanglement.

Barth's redesign taps into his Reformed heritage: While just as committed to the doctrine of justification as Lutherans,[16] Reformed appreciation of covenant theology, its insistence on the unity of "Old" and "New Testament"

14. Cf. for a critique of the non-ethnic and universalizing readings of Paul, Denise Kimber Buell and Caroline Johnson Hodge, "The Politics of Interpretation: The Rhetoric of Race and Ethnicity in Paul," *Journal of Biblical Literature* 123, no. 2 (2004): 235.

15. The historical circumstances were quite dramatic. After refusing to give an unqualified oath of allegiance to Adolf Hitler, Barth was suspended as university professor. As Barth was already prohibited from public speaking, Karl Immer, pastor of the Barmen-Gemarke church in which the famous *Barmen Theological Declaration* had been signed in 1934, read what would become Barth's unofficial farewell lecture, whereupon the Gestapo present escorted Barth across the Swiss border. Cf. the detailed reconstruction of events in the introduction to Karl Barth "Evangelium und Gesetz," ed. Lucius Kratzert and Peter Zocher, 55:172–220. GA. (Zürich: TVZ, 2021).

16. Cf. Dirk J Smit, "Paradigms of Radical Grace," in *On Reading Karl Barth in South Africa*, ed. Charles Villa-Vicencio (Grand Rapids: Eerdmans, 1988), who compellingly argues that

and its emphasis on election as the foundation of belonging to God's people rather than works of law had traditionally allowed Reformed theology a more nuanced appreciation of the law.[17] Barth, too, dismisses a dualistic treatment of law and gospel that devalues the law, while at the same time resisting the theological celebration of any law that is not an expression of God's enfleshed humanity and co-humanity in Christ. The good news always comes in and with a specific *form*—it cannot be had apart from it. Not an independent command or norm, this form is simply the shape the gospel takes when embodied: "the content of the Gospel also has a form, is not simply one more of God's works, but is precisely the work of God which makes room for the Gospel in our human sphere and room for us [human beings] in the sphere of the Gospel."[18]

Barth remains adamant that this dialectical relationship of gospel and law can never be directly, conclusively, and unequivocally identified with any particular form of life or theological method without once more running into the danger of self-justification. In theological method, too, there can be no L-law that can in and of itself have any validity, "there can never be claims and demands which would have legal validity from another source or in themselves: there can only be *witnesses*."[19] Rather than dismiss concerns about the *form* of the gospel, or even antagonize them as "law" in opposition to the gospel, discernment remains needed to identify contextually, locally, tentatively forms of witness to this gospel to best embody and even reveal it. Seeking for such corresponding witness remains demanded, commanded. Barth draws out the implications for the pursuit of ethically and politically adequate "necessary *form[s] of the Gospel*, whose content is grace,"[20] and we might extend this insight to the ongoing need for methodological forms that are adequate to the content of faith.

"The law," then, as a theological notion might not *have to be* a theological Norman door's occasion of failure and frustration, even as some of its theological conceptualizations have become one. Luther's biblical misinterpretation—which the design lens might illuminate as the attempt of forcing given materials into a form to which they did not lend themselves well—led to a

---

the doctrine of justification is not just a Lutheran doctrine but at the core of all Reformation theology, even radicalized by the Reformed.

17. Zwingli even suggested that "Torah," as a gift from God, ought to be translated as "gospel" rather than "law": Huldreich Zwingli, *Auslegen und Gründe der Schlussreden: 14. Juli 1523*, ed. Emil Egli and Georg Finsler, Huldreich Zwinglis sämtliche Werke Vol. 2. CR 89 (Leipzig: Heinsius, 1908), 2:232.

18. Karl Barth, "Gospel and Law," in *Community, State, and Church*, ed. David Haddorf, 71–100 (Eugene: Wipf & Stock, 2004), 81.

19. Barth, "Gospel and Law," 83.

20. Barth, "Gospel and Law," 80.

design failure: the construction of a door that slaps those who try to enter through it in the face, or, in the symbolism of Kafka's parable, lets the man spend his life in the futile attempt to be admitted. Even worse, this door did not resist but permitted and facilitated the violent, ultimately genocidal exclusion of the very inhabitants who had the theologically strongest and well-established claim to that space in the first place—the Jewish people. No amount of explanatory signs that spell out "grace" counteract the intuitive, haptic, material affordances.

While Reformed theologians were far from being immune to anti-Judaism, their theological designs did not afford as smooth a conflation of Judaism as a "religion of law" and Christianity as a "religion of grace" as has animated much Christian anti-Jewish hate.[21] Rather than project the distinction into interreligious, ethnic, and racialized divisions, they had long retained a theological appreciation of the law for Christian life, as most evident in the emphasis on the so-called third use. Operative in the sanctification of believers, i.e., "after" grace, this *usus in renatis* was thus also less easily misconstrued into an instrument of "getting in." In our quest for method, too, such a *tertius usus* allows navigating ever remaining imperfections while living into grace, pointing to the possibility of a non-redemptive use of the method outside of, or after, justification.

QUEER BINARIES, OR: STAYING OUT?

The Lutheran anti-law sentiment has a queer counterpart: anti-normativity. Their shared sensibilities grounded our contestation of theological method. If there is a need to critique Lutheran anti-law sensibility in favor of a less anti-Judaistic, more Reformed understanding of the law as the form of the gospel, are there similar needs for critical evaluation of queer theory's anti-normativity? Might the historically so fateful *Lutheran* design failure reveal issues in *queer* conceptual design?

To rehearse that "method cannot save us" will obviously only be preaching to the queer choir. As a matter of principle, queer theory sounds an important "anti-methodological impulse"[22] that can variously be cast as active refusal or less heroically, although sometimes just as romantically, as failure. After all, if "queer" is identified with anything theoretically, it is with anti-normativity: not just with disruption of and resistance against particular prevailing norms

21. Cf. the instructive comparative studies of Melanchthon, Zwingli, Bullinger, Bucer, and Calvin by Achim Detmers, *Reformation und Judentum* (Stuttgart: Kohlhammer, 2001).
22. Heather Love, "Queer Messes," *Women's Studies Quarterly* 44, no. 3/4 (2016): 345–49, 347.

and normative frameworks, but with the refusal of methodology as a disciplinary straightening device, instead opting for more creative paths of per/version and subversion. Queer, almost by definition, points toward the misfit, the outsider, the trickster, the vagabond—all those who fail to become legible to prevailing norms and regimes, whether intentionally or unintentionally, whether by their own volition or external forces. Queer also sounds a profoundly anti-disciplinary rallying cry of defying norms, categorizations, and discipline(s). Anything worthy of the name "method" might thus seem like capitulation to academic norms, and as compromising the critical stance and minoritarian ethics to which the epithet "queer" aspires.

But if method cannot save us, anti-normativity cannot save us either. The anti-normativity impetus has often been denounced as supposedly performatively self-defeating. But those who triumphalistically "uncover" normative commitments in queer theory fail to recognize that queer anti-normativity is not about a *principle* of anti-normativity, nor about finding a supposedly norm-free stance that can look down on the limitations of the normatively bound. Principled anti-normativity is as much a "straw queer" as a mutually exclusive view of law and gospel makes for a "straw Lutheran"—as if any queer thinker worth their salt would build their case on a binary distinction of normative and anti-normative.[23] Queer anti-normative sentiments emerge out of an existential and theoretical wrestling with the inherent and irreducible violence attending any project of normativity, including its own. In that sense, anti-normativity has never been the point of queer theory, even as it has often marked its interventive strategy, just like anti-law sentiments never were the point of the Reformers, even as they became the strategic consequence of their insistence on the primacy of grace (also understood not as a principle, but as a living reality). It is no self-contradiction that queer theory holds normative commitments, or that it works constructively rather than only deconstructively. Both its normative and anti-normative impulses emerge out of the same insight, just like the Reformers' insistence on both gospel and (anti-)law emerges out of the same insight.

23. Halberstam objects that queer theory never offered a simple normative-antinormative oppositionality, such a construction is "a straw queer, an Aunt Sally, a rag and bone target for any straight thinkers who want to score points in an academic marketplace of diminishing returns." Lisa Duggan's reminder is well taken, too, that no queer critique of anti-normativity can simply move "beyond" anti-normativity's critical impulses lest it become complacent, neoliberal, white. Cf. Jack Halberstam, "Straight Eye for the Queer Theorist: A Review of 'Queer Theory without Antinormativity,'" *Bully Bloggers*, September 15, 2022, https://bullybloggers.wordpress.com/2015/09/12/straight-eye-for-the-queer-theorist-a-review-of-queer-theory-without-antinormativity-by-jack-halberstam; Lisa Duggan, "Queer Complacency Without Empire," *Bully Bloggers*, September 22, 2015, https://bullybloggers.wordpress.com/2015/09/22/queer-complacency-without-empire.

If a critique of performative self-contradiction were to be leveled against queer theory, it would not be on the basis of its remaining normative commitments. It would be around the question whether anti-normativity effectively becomes "a practice of epistemic mastery,"[24] as Linn Tonstad cautions, which secures authority, potentially even domination, through hypercriticality and principled oppositionality. Queer theory's equivalent to the Lutheran "Norman door"—where pushing harder leads to self-defeat due to conflicting signals in the setup—might lie where anti-normativity becomes a "way to authorize itself via a series of apparently self-effacing, nonterritorial gestures that are always open to the future and hence not vulnerable to being ruled redundant in turn."[25] Where anti-normativity becomes normativity's binary opposition, we might thus sense a structural form of supersessionism emerging in queer theory that is as reductive of a complex reality as it is ethically and politically questionable.

Albeit not through the lens of its structural supersessionism, queer theorists and theologians have called into question the identification of "queerness" with "anti-normativity" on theoretical as well as ethical grounds. They have publicly distanced themselves from a "reflexive commitment to antinormativity"[26] that can quickly become a "disciplinary normativity of antinormativity."[27] Whole journal issues envision *Queer Theory without Anti-normativity*.[28]

Linn Tonstad challenges a principled anti-normative stance in queer theology by asking, "Does the more critical, suspicious, and paranoid queer theologian in fact *save* Christianity?"[29] I would like to assume that her language does not accidentally tap into the semantics of salvation, and that her critique of hypercriticality does not accidentally harness language of (self-)justification when she cautions the queer theologian that, "Our love for justice may also be our love for *our* justice."[30] Just like "grace" cannot be turned into a principle, lest it become "law," but can only be found time and again anew, so then anti-normativity should also not be turned into a principle. Where the gospel (including the gospel of critique) turns into a self-immunizing and self-affirming practice of mastery, it falls into forms of hybris and supersessionism that are theologically/theoretically questionable and engender terrifying consequences.

24. Tonstad, "Ambivalent Loves," 478.

25. Annamarie Jagose, "The Trouble with Antinormativity," *Differences* 26, no. 1 (2015): 26–47, 34.

26. Tonstad, "Ambivalent Loves," 473.

27. Tonstad, "Ambivalent Loves," 475.

28. Cf. *differences* 26.1 (2015), edited by Robyn Wiegman and Elizabeth A. Wilson.

29. Tonstad, "Ambivalent Loves," 482.

30. Tonstad, "Ambivalent Loves," 479.

A straightforward anti-normativity fails to appreciate how norms work: It would be naive to see them as inflexible and brittle overdeterminations that *every* living and breathing person subtly disrupts *and thus* subverts at the end of the day, as is sometimes claimed following Judith Butler's foundational study.[31] Instead, norms engender powerful and complex performativities whose imperfect and aspirational repetition is precisely what keeps the norm in place. Norms pertain to the productive rather than merely oppressive operations of power, as Foucault's work reminds us.[32] Norms are much more capacious, flexible, and generative than a common understanding of them suggests, are inclusive rather than exclusive, flexible rather than brittle. Deriving their relative stability from nonnormative/deviant performance, they are not simple instruments of exclusion, but force fields that generate subjectivity and afford means to navigate difference. The relationship between norms and freedom is as irreducible to a simple binary as the one between law and gospel.

This is not to downplay the real violence that can be perpetrated and perpetuated by normativity. Quite the contrary, it is to attend to it in a more nuanced and less (dare I say it?) binary way. Anti-normativity is neither a remedy nor an escape from the violence of normativity, in fact, it relies on the very mechanism of differentiation that is a distinct functionality of the *norm* itself. Just like the gospel/law binary opposition, the normativity/anti-normativity binary opposition might be a Norman door: conflicting signals that obscure how the mechanism of the door works and thus render it inoperable rather than making it operational.

Tonstad's call is highly welcome when she challenges queer theology and queer theory to think "harder about the consequences of its own reflexive commitment to antinormativity—not for the sake of repairing normativity, but in order to develop a wider theoretical vocabulary for analysing normativity's flexible operations and the many different positionalities on which it depends."[33] To go beyond anti-normativity is not a return to uncritical normativity, but an extension and radicalization of the same critique that grounds the anti-normative impulse. In theological terms, it is the reminder that faith, too, can become a "work," a better work, the best, the only work that works salvation—starting the whole works-righteousness spiral once more. The theologian might of course remember that the point of *sola fide* never was that faith itself saves, if by faith we mean an affect, conviction, or practice on the human

31. Judith Butler, *Gender Trouble: Feminism and the Subversion of Identity* (New York: Routledge, 1990).

32. Michel Foucault, *Discipline and Punish: The Birth of the Prison* (New York: Random House, 1977); Michel Foucault, *Power/Knowledge: Selected Interviews and Other Writings, 1972–1977* (New York: Pantheon, 1980).

33. Tonstad, "Ambivalent Loves," 484.

side of the *fides qua creditur.* Rather, it is the *object* of faith, the faith-independent reality of the *fides quae creditur,* that becomes salvific. Just like faith can turn into a work when reified into a self-sufficient principle rather than understood as a relation dependent on its object, so anti-normativity can quickly become a normative, self-authorizing stance when understood as a principle rather than as a material commitment to the reality that always exceeds whatever normative framework we offer, to that which is otherized and harmed by any prevailing normative framework, to the forms of life that never become livable, legible, grievable, salvageable, and redeemable. Just like faith is not first and foremost a critique of works, but only secondarily engenders one, thus a queer stance might not first and foremost be identified with anti-normativity, even as it might contextually become necessary to articulate it as such.

A different genealogy of "queer" might foreground its resistance to binary categorizations, including a resistance to the temptation of casting itself as *essentially distinct* from that which operates in methodological and disciplinary fashion. Methodologically, queer theory might very well leverage a "failure to adhere to stable classificatory systems or to be contained by disciplinary boundaries."[34] It might even aspire to disrupt and critique, scandalize and expose, perform contradictions as well as per/versions, for the purpose of revealing the productions of prevailing norms in their particularity as well as the exclusions that attend them. It might not cast such proceeding in terms of method but rather as intervention, or frame them more as an art than a science. But when it starts discerning in its stance maybe "not so much a method as (principled?) avoidance of method,"[35] something *like* a methodology *after* method, in a sustained critical practice, effectively comes into view. To pair the terms "queer" and "methodology" might be less of a contradiction than "a productive oxymoron."[36] Its distrustful stance vis-à-vis norms and its critiques of normativity's productivity has never prevented queer theory (or queer theology) from engaging in deliberate, intentional, and self-reflected ways, let alone understand its interventions as profoundly ethically driven— thus proceeding arguably both with a recognizable methodology as well as a distinctly normative impetus.

In the work of Marcella Althaus-Reid, for example, it is quite clear that her fervent, even radical criticism of prevailing ideological, theological, and material structures of cisheteronormativity, patriarchy, and colonialism does not emerge out of an abstract principle of negativity or anti-normativity, but

34. Jane Ward, "Dyke Methods: A Meditation on Queer Studies and the Gay Men Who Hate It," *Women's Studies Quarterly* 44, no. 3–4 (2016), 71.

35. Michael Warner, "Uncritical Reading," in *Polemic: Critical or Uncritical,* ed. Jane Gallop, 13–38 (New York; London: Routledge, 2004), 18.

36. Ward, "Dyke Methods," 71–72.

out of attention to real if fragmentary glimpses of grace, love, and community "lived in justice even if outside the law."[37] Neither does her queer positioning engender a refusal of all norms, in fact it develops a distinct, if not precisely systematizable ethos that calls for honesty, practices consent, opens up room for solidarity, and attends to excess.

As Barth casts the divine "yes" as overshadowing the attending "no," thus Althaus-Reid posits not ideology critique, but a truly material theology as her intention. Barth finds as the given and remaining starting point of theology not a principle like grace, but a person—the embodied, historical, and personal reality of grace in Jesus Christ: the "human being for others";[38] Althaus-Reid calls Jesus the "un/just Messiah"[39]—disrupting and subverting the functioning of any law according to which he might claim such a title, not replacing it with a different normative logic, while also just as clearly positively pointing to a justice beyond the law. Just as Barth maintains that *"methodus est arbitraria,"*[40] Althaus-Reid advocates a "poaching" of method.[41]

Might Althaus-Reid's postulation of "justice" in counter-distinction to the rigidity of a "law" be similar to Barth's insistence on the necessary "form" of the gospel? Both distinctions are as real as they are elusive, as necessary as they are dispossessive, both continually have to be discerned and practiced out of the positive yet undefinable reality of grace—for Barth to be found in the person of Jesus Christ, for Althaus-Reid arguably in more pluralistic, but still fiercely incarnational and messianic forms—yet can never be turned into a system or law of their own?

Queer thought, then, might have its own version of the "Lutheran" vs. "Reformed" distinction regarding the law—differences in emphasis and in pragmatics on the ground of generally shared insights. The theological issues discerned in the Lutheran design of "the law" might alert us to structural issues attending some versions of queer anti-normativity as well. At the same time, if we draw more strongly on the "Reformed" rather than the "Lutheran" sentiments in queer theory/theology, i.e. its commitment to deconstructing binary oppositions rather than its push-back against normativity, its scavenger uses of method rather than reducing itself to a principled and curiously "straight" anti-normativity, and its insistence on the actually existing (if elusive) reality of grace rather than its reduction to loops of ideology critique, we might gain further constructive insights into the theological design, as well as pointers for its potential redesign.

37. Althaus-Reid, *The Queer God*, 169.
38. Cf. Barth, *CD III.2*, sec. 45.1.
39. Althaus-Reid, *Indecent Theology*, 156.
40. Barth, *CD I.2*, 860; Barth, *CD IV.3*, 1961, 5.
41. Althaus-Reid, *Indecent Theology*, 112.

In this vein, we might extend the critique against "the law's" functionality of "getting in" also against its more recent redesign into an instrument of "staying in": In a queer analysis, it is less the direction of the movement that comes into question as the underlying division into insiders and outsiders in the first place. Queer anti-normativity would suggest that the desire to circulate freely within the law might be just as misdirected as the desire to gain access. Against both "getting in" and "staying in" logics, the deliberate option of "staying out" comes into view. Not just the logic of working one's own redemption, but also the logic of expanding the scope of election, redemption through inclusion, and the desire for it become questionable.[42]

FORCING FUNCTIONS, OR: INCOGNITO GRACE?

As we circle back to Kafka's door scene, we wonder, what else might the use of a door be? If "getting in" is not the primary purpose of this door, is it even so clear that the man in the story *fails*? Maybe we ought to understand his "staying out" not so much as a consuming and frustrating desire to gain admission, but as a strategic refusal to go away, or as a patient outmaneuvering of the law.[43] Rather than being a failed quest, Giorgio Agamben, for example, concludes that the man's persistence is ultimately a "complicated and patient strategy to have the door closed in order to interrupt the law's being in force."[44] For Agamben, the man in the story paradoxically *succeeds*, and ultimately prevails over this law. This reading admittedly resonates to some extent with Franz Kafka's own sentiment that "all human errors are impatience, a premature breaking off of a methodical approach."[45] But maybe

---

42. Cf. Tonstad, "The Limits of Inclusion," 2015.

43. There is a long tradition, especially among Jewish interpreters, to discuss Kafka's parable in relation to the "life lived in deferment" waiting for the messiah. Gerschom Scholem and Walter Benjamin have seen in it a mythical foundation of the law. Jacques Derrida has linked it to a justice that is always to come, *a-venir*, an out-of-reach event that "happens not to happen" without ceasing to require our response. Martin Buber has posited that the gate of the law leads "to the world of meaning," while Massimo Cacciari finds that the very openness of the door is what bans and immobilizes any attempt to gain entrance: Gershom Scholem, *The Messianic Idea in Judaism: And Other Essays on Jewish Spirituality* (New York: Schocken, 1995), 35; Walter Benjamin, "Letter to Gershom Scholem on Franz Kafka," in *Selected Writings, Volume 3: 1935–1938*, ed. Edmund Jephcott and Howard Eiland, tr. Edmund Jephcott, 322–29 (Cambridge: Cambridge University Press, 2002); Jacques Derrida, "Before the Law," in *Acts of Literature*, ed. Derek Attridge, 181–220 (New York: Routledge, 1991); Martin Buber, *Two Types of Faith* (Syracuse: Syracuse University Press, 2003); Massimo Cacciari, *Icone Della Legge* (Milan: Adelphi, 1985).

44. Agamben, "The Messiah and the Sovereign," 174.

45. Franz Kafka, *The Aphorisms of Franz Kafka*, ed. Reiner Stach (Princeton University Press, 2002), 4.

Agamben's anti-normative interpretation is all-too straight, and maybe Kafka is not the best interpreter of his own parable. Maybe there is failure in this parable, after all, but maybe it is not the failure to gain admission. And maybe there is victory in this parable, but maybe it is not a victory *over* the law.[46]

Eli Schonfeld finds in Kafka's story a different kind of redemption—unrecognized, yet nevertheless effective. Jewish interpreters of Kafka have tended to pick up on the characterization of the man in the parable as "a man from the countryside," the ignorant *'am ha'areṣ* whom the Talmud systematically contrasts with the learned *talmid chacham*, the wise pupil.[47] Kafka's characterization insinuates such an ignorance: The "man from the countryside" does not understand how to study the law and how to distinguish legalistic *Gesetz* from the life-giving teaching and guidance of *Torah*. If we are tempted to read the parable as a reproach and failure of such ignorance, Jewish interpreters point out that this ignorance is not held against the man. Rather than chiding one approach to the law as failure and elevating a different one as successful, the parable points to a particularly ingenious feature of the law's design to achieve its purpose regardless of user sensitivity or training.

Allowing access is neither the only nor the best thing a door can do under certain circumstances. Maybe Kafka's impenetrable door is no Norman door but what Don Norman called a "forcing function"—a physical constraint that, for safety reasons or to avoid certain forms of user error, locks a user in or out until they engage in the appropriate behavior.[48] Examples for forcing functions are the microwave that will not run unless the door is closed, the elevator door that will not close as long as someone is blocking the door frame, the car door that will not unlock unless the vehicle comes to a full stop, or the fire door that closes automatically to cut off the spread of danger from one part of the house to another. While forcing functions are annoying and even frustrating for the user who experience them as failure to proceed, they prevent unsafe consequences and accidents. Failure, in all its frustration, becomes a particular form of success: the successful avoidance of harm and tragedy that would occur due to users' lack of attention, knowledge, or strength.

What if the failure in the parable is not the failure to gain admission, but the mistaken assumption (which we identified as vulgarized versions of Lutheran and queer theology) that the law's purpose is to regulate access through fulfillment? The inaccessibility of the door is less dysfunctional than it seems if we recognize

---

46. For a compelling critique of Agamben in this vein see Vivian Liska, "'Before the Law Stands a Doorkeeper. To This Doorkeeper Comes a Man . . .': Kafka, Narrative, and the Law," *Naharaim* 6, no. 2 (2013): 175–94.

47. Eli Schonfeld, "*Am-ha'aretz*: The Law of the Singular. Kafka's Hidden Knowledge," in *Kafka and the Universal*, ed. Arthur Cools and Vivian Liska, 107–29 (Berlin: De Gruyter, 2016).

48. Norman, *The Design of Everyday Things*, 141–45.

in it not a test or a puzzle to be solved, but an ingenious architectural coup. Not a *design failure*, but a forcing function's *failure by design*, it induces the man to spend his life precisely as he did: before the law, in constant unwavering attention to it.

The despair of the countryside man in the parable is much like that of Paul's Lutheran interpreters, for whom, contrary to the Rabbinic tradition, the only sense in the law seems to be to enter into it and fulfill it.[49] Without condemning him for his ignorance (or even inferring that it is this ignorance that prevented him from accessing the law), Schonfeld insists that what the *talmid chacham* knows (and what distinguishes them from the *am-ha'aretz*) is precisely that "the idea of penetrating the law, of *fulfilling* the law, is a false desire."[50] The parable even resists the option of directly explaining his mistake to the ignorant person, which might only have insulted, paternalized him, or driven him to give up and leave. Instead, the law is designed such as to gently but effectively afford the means to turn even the ignorant man's persistent, misdirected desire into faithful observance: As he remains set on gaining access, the design uses that desire against him—for him. Forcing him into an (ignorant!) observance of the law's intention *not to be fulfilled*, it allows him to dwell in a space that is full of grace even as his desire is frustrated. It is in this position outside the gates of the law, and in ignorance of its true functioning, that we witness "the appearance, against all odds, of this law which is not a law, of this law which defies the concept itself of law along with all the dichotomies that accompany this concept . . . the appearance of *Lehre*."[51]

Far from being to no avail, the man's pursuit was paradoxically successful, not as the triumph over the law Agamben envisions, but in the law's provision for and accommodation of his misdirected desire. The apparent bug—the door that fails to afford access—might be a feature, or, as Schonfeld explains, not an apocalyptic messianism but "a messianism of patience," which might be "the only messianic attitude that does not lead to . . . an abolishment of Judaism."[52] The Law, Schonfeld notes, "is there only in order to be placed before it. Not in order to enter it, or to accomplish it."[53] But it takes a special kind of ignorance to dwell in that space. Through the grace of the law's patient design, Kafka's man of the countryside is able to *remain* in that space where Mark's rich young man walks away, disappointed by the impossibility of fulfillment (Mark 10:17–22, cf. chapter 3).

We might find that Kafka's ignorant man has much to do with the theologian who attempts by intensive and ever more methodical pursuits to gain

---

49. Schonfeld, "*Am-ha'aretz*," 123.
50. Schonfeld, "*Am-ha'aretz*," 123.
51. Schonfeld, "*Am-ha'aretz*," 127–28.
52. Schonfeld, "*Am-ha'aretz*," 124.
53. Schonfeld, "*Am-ha'aretz*," 124fn49.

access to divine mysteries, establish herself as an epistemological insider, or to master, solve, and achieve theology. Unrecognized in our frustration, "being kept out" might sometimes be less of an exclusion than a forcing function, affording grace by another means than by direct communication. Much like Althaus-Reid's un/just messianism, this messianism of patience resists legibility and recognition according to the prevailing categories of success and failure, yet also evades their disciplining force and creates the potentiality of dwelling in a space outside the law. The failure of recognition is even instrumental to the functioning of the mechanism. The inability of "entering" opens up a wide landscape of possibility.

QUEER FAILURE, OR: REORIENTATIONS

A similar paradox connection between failure and possibility has been the subject of queer theorizations. As Jack Halberstam points out in *The Queer Art of Failure*, "[f]ailure is something queers do and have always done exceptionally well."[54] While there is nothing that *essentially* ties queer identities to failure, queers often have extensive experience in the inability to "fulfill the law" or to pass muster by its doorkeepers. Queer people know the very real frustration, marginalization, and loss that attend such a position "outside the law." They are also aware that beyond the reach of the law lies not nothingness, but a wide landscape that affords various possibilities of inhabiting, and even opens up unexpected forms of freedom.

Halberstam posits, "Under certain circumstances failing, losing, forgetting, unmaking, undoing, unbecoming, not knowing may in fact offer more creative, more cooperative, more surprising ways of being in the world."[55] Failure is hopeful where it frees from the disciplinary effects, toxic positivity, and "cruel optimism"[56] that attend the scripts of success. Mocking the narrow and confining imaginaries of achievement, Halberstam quips, "Let's leave success and its achievement to the Republicans, to the corporate managers of the world, to the winners of reality TV shows, to married couples, to SUV drivers."[57] Resignifying queer difference from an inability to conform or measure up to societal standards to a resourcefulness, Halberstam thus challenges us to mine queer failure for its potentials, and develop its capacities for

---

54. Halberstam, *The Queer Art of Failure*, 3.
55. Halberstam, *The Queer Art of Failure*, 2–3.
56. Lauren Berlant, *Cruel Optimism* (Durham: Duke University Press, 2011).
57. Halberstam, *The Queer Art of Failure*, 12.

questioning, resistance, survival, and world-making into an art or even a "way of life"[58] that opens up unknown possibilities of being in the world.

A failure to "get it" might be an important ingredient in practices of freedom cultivated under the name of failure. Certain forms of ignorance work as an obliviousness toward the norms of success, allowing for their performative non-recognition. Halberstam quotes the animated children's movie *Chicken Run*, in which a hen named Babs, confronted with the revolutionary charge, "We either die free chickens, or we die trying," naively responds, "are those the only choices?"[59] The failure to "get" the dominant logics surprisingly opens up room for hitherto unenvisioned possibilities, options that might seem less heroic or less fulfilling, but at second glance might also ultimately be more livable, more communal, more hopeful than whatever is defined as "success." "Orthodoxy," Halberstam maintains, "is a luxury we cannot afford,"[60] partially because its price may be too high, but also because it is not an end in itself. Like theory, orthodoxy is always "a detour en route to something else."[61]

Survival even "requires a certain amount of forgetting, repressing, moving on."[62] Developed by Toni Morrison, Saidiya Hartman, and Jamaica Kincaid, this insight might also apply to the possibility of surviving theology's crushing and paralyzing dilemma of method. The ability to keep going requires disarming the desire "to be good," intellectually or morally pure, whether in fulfillment or radical negation, that we have earlier critiqued for theological reasons. Being oblivious to what might or might not constitute success, and forgetting as a loosening of one's own attachments to it is what affords freedom from its double bind. To push back against Barth: rather than in our *knowing* "both our 'must' and our 'cannot'," we might come closer to "giving God the glory" in our *forgetting* both.

Not all forgetting is subversive or liberative—Halberstam points succinctly to forms of white male ignorance that sustain patriarchal, colonial, hegemonic projects, and we have already encountered Marcella Althaus-Reid's critique of decency's carefully curated ignorance (cf. chapter 1). However, "forgetting, when directed at prevailing paradigms can become a tactic for resisting their rule,"[63] for stalling "the reproduction of the dominant,"[64] and for presenting a rupture "with the eternally self-generating present, a break with

58. Halberstam, *The Queer Art of Failure*, 186, riffing on Foucault.
59. Halberstam, *The Queer Art of Failure*, 145.
60. Halberstam, *The Queer Art of Failure*, 16.
61. Halberstam, *The Queer Art of Failure*, 16, citing Stuart Hall.
62. Halberstam, *The Queer Art of Failure*, 86.
63. Halberstam, *The Queer Art of Failure*, 77.
64. Halberstam, *The Queer Art of Failure*, 80.

a self-authorizing past, and an opportunity for a non-hetero-reproductive future."[65] Loosening our grip on the mastery of knowledge is a requirement for the freedom to learn something *new*.

Measures of grace may thus wait for us in failure. A certain illegibility of such grace by prevailing categories of success is its price. Where the desire "to fulfill the law" so easily leads to Luther's Norman door against which one can only lose, even and especially when one succeeds (say, in establishing one's intellectual, moral, or spiritual superiority), grace might even necessarily take the form of failure as a certain mode of ignorance. It might be the only thing that keeps queer critique from turning into another heroic, hubristic enterprise, a counter-law, just like a certain form of theological dispossession is necessary to prevent the gospel from turning into supersessionism. With reference to the complicated history of gay male cultures and fascism, Halberstam maintains that there is nothing inherent in queer being, practice, experience, or desire that guarantees any particularly liberative, progressive, or deconstructive political stance.[66] Just as in Schonfeld's reading of Kafka's parable, a particular form of ignorance is thus not only permissible but even instrumental in this functioning of grace, as when such ignorance enables forcing functions that protect us from at least some misdirected desires, and from the cost of the success and recognition for which we strive.

The call to embrace failure then does not imply romanticizing and heroizing nonnormative lives and their potential, but offers a sobering reminder of the complexities and complicities of all our lives and desires. Failure's ignorance becomes a way of un-knowing that opens up space for "alternative ways of knowing and being that are not unduly optimistic, but nor are they mired in nihilistic critical dead ends."[67] It allows for existence between the "two equally bleak alternatives"[68] of negativity/nihilism and positivity/dogmatism, it authorizes an interest in "conversation rather than mastery,"[69] it invites us to gain knowledge from unexpected places and toward yet-to-be-determined ends, it authorizes a refusal to commit to any one particular form of orthodoxy or orthopraxy and instead invites attention to the modes of survival and the quality of life engendered or inhibited by methodological adherences.

Halberstam also finds that "failure loves company": it reorients us toward collaboration, allows us to find community with "all those who lost before"

---

65. Halberstam, *The Queer Art of Failure*, 70.

66. Halberstam, chap. 5: "The Killer in Me Is the Killer in You": Homosexuality and Fascism, in *The Queer Art of Failure*, 147–172.

67. Halberstam, *The Queer Art of Failure*, 24.

68. Halberstam, *The Queer Art of Failure*, 120.

69. Halberstam, *The Queer Art of Failure*, 12.

us and who keep being denied access around us, it constitutes kinship beyond blood ties and even beyond species boundaries, and it allows for narration of multiple genealogies.[70] Such queer sociality does not necessarily come easy. In Kafka's parable, it is only at the end of his long life spent outside the gates of the law that the man starts pondering that he has not seen anyone else gain access or walk in. Maybe if there is a failure to be grieved in this story, it is the man's failure, for the longest time, to look around him and consider the possibility that he may not be alone. When he does, the first and only real change in his predicament happens: The doorkeeper closes the door for good. Maybe this closure, at last, gives the man permission to search for those who, like him, have been left out, and who populate the landscape around him. We do not learn about that. What we do learn, however, is that no one else has entered that door either. Even if Kafka's parable seems to remain in the individualizing mode of attempting to "get in," it also gives rise to the suspicion that the isolating pursuit puts one in larger company, and that the inside might, after all, be empty. In this way, as Schonfeld notes, the parable effectively "deactivates those classical dichotomies. Everything happens on the outside, and therefore the outside becomes the *locus* of meaning"[71] to which the reader is effectively redirected.

In her provocative text *Choosing the Margin as a Site of Radical Openness*, bell hooks acknowledges and names the suffering, pain, violence, and oppression in marginalization from the center—a different way of construing the inside/outside distinction. However, she refuses to see marginality as negativity, lack of attainment, or merely "a site of deprivation; in fact I was saying just the opposite, that it is also the site of radical possibility, a space of resistance,"[72] a space where survival depends on finding alternatives and building solidarity, and a space that becomes not only politically but also epistemologically generative. Already out of bounds of dominant ways of knowing, forced to see them "both from the outside in and from the inside out,"[73] marginality opens up the horizon to allow for "unlimited access to the pleasure and power of knowing, where transformation is possible."[74]

Maybe being denied access, being excluded, being kept out, and not getting it/in might also prompt a creative reorientation for the theologian. The inaccessible door of the law of method is highly successful in placing us on a wide open plane, before the law, outside the law, into solidarity with everyone else

---

70. Halberstam, *The Queer Art of Failure*, 121.

71. Schonfeld, "*Am-ha'aretz*," 124, n. 49.

72. bell hooks, "Choosing the Margin as a Space of Radical Openness," in *Yearning: Race, Gender, and Cultural Politics*, 145–53 (Boston: South End, 1990), 149.

73. hooks, "Choosing the Margin as a Space of Radical Openness," 149.

74. hooks, "Choosing the Margin as a Space of Radical Openness," 145.

who has never had or will never find "a door" to enter—"this door was only for you." Whatever our own social location and the specificities of exclusion and access, knowledge, and ignorance it affords, the impossibility of "achieving" theology by way of method invites us into a place of marginality that is not only imposed but also chosen for the unique perspective and solidarity it affords. In such marginality, we might even find ourselves in unsuspected company with those who never had a chance of "getting in" as well as with the One who chose to "go outside the camp."

In what remains of this book, I explore what happens when we allow theology to be reoriented and converted in such a way, and play with a looser use of method *after method* that riffs on queer virtues of excessive faithfulness, messy solidarity, and indecent honesty. As images from design studies—Norman doors, forcing functions, design failures, and redesign—have proven useful for a more realistic account of the work of theology that pays attention to its material conditions and effects and engages with epistemological "outsiders" in critical reassessment, I will continue to creatively draw from such an interdisciplinary, user-oriented framework—without postulating it as a new methodology.

PART III

How (not) to do better
(tertius usus legis)

Chapter 6

Cruising, or: The end of redemption and the beginning of ethics

REORIENTATIONS

> Let mutual affection continue. Do not neglect to show hospitality to strangers, for by doing that some have entertained angels without knowing it. Remember those who are in prison, as though you were in prison with them, those who are being tortured, as though you your-selves were being tortured. . . . Therefore Jesus also suffered outside the city gate in order to sanctify the people by his own blood. Let us then go to him outside the camp and bear the abuse he endured. For here we have no lasting city, but we are looking for the city that is to come.
>
> —*Hebrews 13:1–3; 12–14*

"Everything happens in the outside":[1] Schonfeld's distinctly Jewish interpreta-tion of Kafka's parable has interesting resonances not just with a more histori-cally accurate and theologically generative interpretation of Paul but also with another central New Testament text. With its rich tapestry of Hebrew Bible references and imagery that forms its "bone and marrow,"[2] the homily known as "The Epistle to the Hebrews" discusses at length the possibility for Chris-tians to *enter* into a "place of rest," only to conclude by prompting us to follow Jesus *outside*. Rather than promising access to a place of safety and belonging, it redirects the readers' desire: "Let us then go to him outside the camp and

---

1. Schonfeld, "*Am-ha'aretz*," 124fn49.
2. George Guthrie, "Hebrews' Use of the Old Testament: Recent Trends in Research," *Currents in Research: Biblical Studies* 1 (2003): 271–94, 272.

bear the abuse he endured. For here we have no lasting city, but we are looking for the city that is to come" (Heb. 13:12–14).

   This redirection might be experienced as disorienting and even frustrating.
No wonder that interpreters have often opted to define chapter 13 as a later
addition.[3] Current scholarship, however, stresses "the powerful rhetorical
character of the composition"[4] of the whole literary document as a homily:
Far from being incongruous with the main body, chapter 13 serves to bring
"the hearers to a direct engagement with the behaviors that are consistent
with the dispositions of faith, hope, and love that the author has consistently
encouraged in them."[5]

   Not incidentally, Hebrews has often been considered on par with Paul's
letter to the Romans, which for the Protestant tradition provided the main
materials for design and redesign of the doctrines of law and gospel, sin, and
atonement,[6] and which for Barth furnished "the great disruption" by the
divine "yes" and "no."[7] If in Romans, Paul solved the theological problem
of a division into inside and outside conceptually through a design for ingraft-
ing the gentiles into Israel's election, Hebrews' solution advances the converse
move: The movement of Christ outside the gates overcomes the division itself.
Rather than gaining an expansive interpretation of the law of grace by (potentially universal) inclusion as Romans does, Hebrews disrupts their neat distinction through God's kenosis. Rather than drawing the formerly excluded into
the space of kinship and covenant, God steps out.

   Hebrews reads Jesus' crucifixion—one of the homily's few references to
the historical Jesus, who was crucified outside of Jerusalem, at a distance to
the spaces of living and as a spectacle and warning to passersby—through the
lens of sacrificial offerings whose bones were burned outside of the camp. As
the Gospels flesh out, there Jesus also found himself in the company of other
crucified criminals, to whom he immediately extended the promise of grace.
What if we understood the turn of Christ—the reality of grace that has traditionally been interpreted as salvation, atonement, or redemption—to be *not*
the fulfillment of the law with the implicit or explicit supersessionist ramifications of such a notion? What if, in a slight but significant inversion, we conceptualized this turn instead as collapsing the distinction between inside and
outside—not drawing everyone into the covenant, but by God's own kenotic

   3. Cf. e.g. George Wesley Buchanan, *To the Hebrews* (Garden City: Doubleday, 1972), 267.
   4. Luke Timothy Johnson, *Hebrews: A Commentary*, New Testament Library (Louisville:
Westminster John Knox, 2006), 336.
   5. Johnson, *Hebrews*, 337.
   6. Cf. John Calvin. *John Calvin's Commentary on the Letter to the Hebrews*, tr. John Owen
(Louisville: GLH, 2020), 1: "No doubt the Epistle next in importance to that to the Romans is
this to the Hebrews."
   7. Barth, *Romans II*.

exit claiming this space outside the gates as one that is not devoid of grace, not removed from grace, but rather lived precariously and vulnerably, yet nonetheless "before the law"?

The law would then *function*, not by finding a worthy fulfillment in Christ, but by Christ's sacrifice of its fulfillment. The law, then, would not be about "getting in" or "keeping out," *nor* about "staying in." Instead, in its own enigmatic way, the law would be what ensures that everything happens "in the outside": self-emptying and self-*un*fulfilling, depriving the dividing line between inside and outside of significance and freely pouring out its grace.

"Queer theologians are the ones who consider to what excesses God takes God's love for humans, that is, which are God's transgressive desires and how we have sadly tamed or limited these villainies,"[8] Marcella Althaus-Reid notes, "This is the scandal of what T-Theology has carefully avoided: God amongst the Queer, and the Queer God present in Godself."[9] No wonder Hebrews 13 is a powerful subtext for much of her theology, as it describes God's own venture into the spaces of impurity and exclusion, vulgarity and vulnerability, excess and solidarity, as an omnisexual, nomadic, and promiscuous "love which crosses borders."[10] Althaus-Reid plays especially with intertextual resonances between Genesis 19—historically often read as a judgment on the (homosexually identified) "Sodomites"[11]—and Hebrews 13, to describe an act of hospitality that breaks down the common role distinctions: God, the divine host, kenotically becomes the stranger at the gate, outside the gate. In Hebrews, Christ's sacrifice *is* the sacrifice of the law, not its fulfillment, and hospitality to strangers is parenetically bound up with such kenosis. It is the category of sacrifice that brings together the Hebrew Bible and Christology rather than marking a supersessionist boundary between them.

This kenotic sacrifice of purity—of methodological, conceptual, ideological, theological, spiritual, material, and sexual purities—is not the end of ethics but its beginning. The whole homily is an exhortation to faith, hope, and love. It expands the understanding of worship to encompass "every aspect of

8. Althaus-Reid, *The Queer God*, 23.

9. Althaus-Reid, 33.

10. Althaus-Reid, 49. Beyond Althaus-Reid's adaptations, Hebrews 13 has become another key (sub)text for queer theology—not only in the reference to the God "outside the gates," but also with its emphatic command to hospitality.

11. The passage has since extensively discussed in LGBTQIA+ exegesis and reappropriated in queer readings, cf. especially Mark D. Jordan, *The Invention of Sodomy in Christian Theology* (Chicago: University of Chicago Press, 1998); Linn Marie Tonstad, "Everything Queer, Nothing Radical?" *Svensk Teologisk Kvartalskrift* 92, no. 3–4 (2016): 118–29; 2016; Kent L. Brintnall, "Who Weeps for the Sodomite?" in *Sexual Disorientations*, ed. Kent L. Brintnall, Joseph A. Marchal, and Stephen D. Moore, 145–60 (Fordham University Press, 2020); Brandy Daniels, "Is There No Gomorrah? Christian Ethics, Identity, and the Turn to Ecclesial Practices: What's the Difference?" *JSCE* 39, no. 2 (2019): 287–302.

public and private life"[12]—extending to the work of theology, as well, or even understanding all of life as the *doing* of theology in this way, beyond the possibility to secure it by way of whichever methodological paradigm.

The homily explicitly commands the reader to follow this move, to "go out" to Jesus "outside of the camp." Some scholars have read this as "a commitment to be the pilgrim people of God who leave behind the security of the familiar in order to respond to the call of God upon their lives."[13] Already Calvin stated that "we must go after him through exiles, flights, reproaches and all kinds of afflictions"[14] and encouraged his own refugee audience to, "whenever, therefore, we are driven from place to place,"[15] take comfort in the prospect of heaven rather than seeking earthly fulfillment, and contemporary interpreters have further drawn out the homily's potential for a theology of diasporic identity (re)construction.[16] Others have read the outside of the camp as "the public side . . . of the Christian faith,"[17] beyond the protection and safety of like-minded believers "confessing God's name in public, doing works of mercy, and sharing what we have with others."[18] "The place of rejection by the unbelieving world that despised him,"[19] this public is not only a place of exposition and exclusion, of suffering and reproach, it is also "the place of greatest impurity,"[20] an abandonment of the conceptual shelter any methodological camp provides.

"Going outside the gates" with Christ is thus not just to risk but to actively sacrifice the legibility, recognition, and justification that come with belonging to a "camp." Lingering on the outside, and staying "willfully unredeemed"[21] accentuates a susceptibility and even failure that Christians share with Christ, as it foregrounds the boundary-crossing solidarity of kenosis. What if instead of focusing our energies on the door, we let them be redirected to the open landscape? What if instead of seeking fulfillment and redemption for ourselves or policing the boundaries of inclusion or exclusion for others, we learned to

12. William L. Lane, John D. W. Watts, and Ralph P. Martin, *Hebrews 9–13, Volume 47B*, ed. David Allen Hubbard and Glenn W. Barker (Dallas: Word, 1991), 572.

13. Lane, Watts, and Martin, 574.

14. Calvin, *Calvin's Commentary on Hebrews*, 349.

15. Calvin, *Hebrews*, 350.

16. Cf. Jennifer T. Kaalund, *Reading Hebrews and 1 Peter with the African American Great Migration: Diaspora, Place, and Identity* (London: T&T Clark, 2019).

17. Thomas G. Long, *Hebrews: Interpretation: A Bible Commentary for Teaching and Preaching* (Louisville: Westminster John Knox, 1997), 144.

18. Long, *Hebrews*, 145.

19. Gareth Lee Cockerill, *The Epistle to the Hebrews*, New International Commentary on the New Testament (Grand Rapids: Eerdmans, 2012), 700.

20. Cockerill, *The Epistle to the Hebrews*, 700.

21. Karen Bray, *Grave Attending: A Political Theology for the Unredeemed* (New York: Fordham University Press, 2019), 4.

live "before the law" but "outside its gates," to dwell in, play in, and explore the landscape outside of it, making our transitory existence one committed to hospitality and care as much as to levity and solidarity with those who also find themselves inhabiting this space of marginality?

DWELLING, OR: EPISTEMIC NOMADISM

Grace cannot be turned into a method, but it has important meta-methodological ramifications. The takeaway from theology's ultimate impossibility is not that it is hopeless to do theology at all, but that such hope does not come from ourselves. As grace encounters us from the outside, the theologian finds herself existentially, ethically, and epistemologically oriented to the outside, as well: "In theology, the desire for exile is also a desire for revelation,"[22] as Althaus-Reid observes. Everything happens on the outside: that includes the encounter with the living God as well as the reorientation to our surroundings: not in fulfillment, but in transitory yet no less substantive forms of dwelling and wandering.

God pitching God's tent among mortals is the Hebrew Bible's metaphor for a mobile God leading God's people out of slavery, accompanying God's people through the wilderness, and being with God's people in exile. It is also the New Testament's language for the incarnation. John talks of the word as "dwelling," or maybe more accurately, "camping among us" (John 1:14). Revelation envisions God's tent not as fixing redemption but as God's way of meeting God's people where they are and making God's home among them (Rev. 21:3). Althaus-Reid points out that images of a divine nomadism speak to "Christ's high mobility" and the adaptability of God's love: its capacity to stay stubbornly faithful under changing and adverse circumstances rather than breaking. She draws out the endurance that comes with the apparent lack of stability or determinate shape of tents, which allows us to discover Christ in the instability and transience that marks our own processes of growth, and allows him to remain "a Christ of surprises."[23]

The language of tenting and dwelling stands in marked opposition to the search for redemption's closure. Althaus-Reid even calls them "two different economic orders,"[24] which are mutually exclusive. The nomadic orientation to the outside is a desire to follow human and divine bodies as they cross boundaries, and a readiness to cross "borders of thinking"[25] as necessary in

22. Althaus-Reid, *The Queer God*, 49.
23. Althaus-Reid, *Indecent Theology*, 120.
24. Althaus-Reid, *The Queer God*, 49.
25. Althaus-Reid, *The Queer God*, 50.

order to move along with them. A "nomadic movement of theology"[26] is warranted both in the shifting and unstable conditions of human lives as well as in the kenotic, boundary-crossing, boundary-dissolving nature of divine love, and the Queer theologian takes both as their starting point in reflection on the "love which crosses boundaries."[27]

Much like Althaus-Reid, Barth favors dynamic images for the pursuit of theology, images that imply the dynamic movement but also the faithfulness to the object whose movement one follows. Famously, Barth talked about the "bird in flight" to which the Christian can never do justice by fixing its image to any medium, but only by following its path,[28] or likens theology to a mountain hike, where one foot's movement has to be balanced out by the other one's, where even a moment's rest will result in falling down the narrow mountain ridge.[29] The hiker's interdigitation resembles a balancing-out of missteps in obedience to the terrain more than a method by which to secure himself. He can only keep moving precariously, propelling himself forward, falling forward, failing forward, without being able to land anywhere or to secure a stable standing position for himself, and even that can only be done in careful and realistic negotiation of the ground he covers. Walking is not only a metaphor for dialectic momentum, it also gestures toward a theological realism's need to attend to space and place, to trace and reflect its subject matter in dispossessive faithfulness.

"Walking is a powerful metaphor for doing theology,"[30] Althaus-Reid concurs. Her images of nomadism resonate profoundly with queer experiences of unbelonging, yet also of solidarity and commitment found in marginal existence. In her Argentinian context, the invocation of "walking" conjures not only a dynamic, unsettled-unsettling movement but also the sweat and clamor of protest marches in the street, where the *Madres de la Plaza de Mayo* keep the lament over (and search for!) their disappeared children alive even after they must long be dead, where those committed to social justice continue defying resignation and frustration with the tireless chant, "*Hay que seguir andando nomás* . . .*" ("It is necessary to keep on walking . . ."). This hymn by Carlos Saracini repeats a famous phrase by Bishop Enrique Angelelli, who was assassinated by the military for his social activism in the so-called Dirty War. "*Hay que seguir andando nomás* . . .*" might well be expressive of the "virtues" of stubborn faithfulness, kenotic solidarity, and an indecent honesty defiant of the ongoing, and insurmountable incertitude, disillusionment, and failure, as well as manifest

26. Althaus-Reid, *The Queer God*, 49.
27. Althaus-Reid, *The Queer God*, 49.
28. Barth, "The Christian in Society."
29. Barth, "The Word of God as the Task of Theology," 191.
30. Althaus-Reid, *The Queer God*, 73.

experience of violence and death. In such *"Hay que seguir andando no mas...,"* we might find theological realism's version of a *theologia viatorum*: not a dialectical resolution or *Aufhebung*, not a celebration of movement for movement's sake, but the necessary suspension in concrete motion by a commitment that is ethical as much as it is epistemological. Such movement does not gain its merit from the promise of a balance or determinate result, and it cannot afford to be oriented by an abstract horizon. It can only follow the bends of particular streets as it writes itself into their dirt.

As sketched out in chapter 4, an orientation to grace necessitates a theological realism as an "anti-docetic" and a-methodological commitment to *the real* over and against the ideal, to the former's messiness and unruliness over and against the latter's purity and sanity, to the former's inconspicuous and quotidian forms against the latter's grandiose and heroic aspirations, in the former's disruption of what we want to be, by what *remains*. It takes its cue from the reality of grace and attends to its determinate and surprising forms to provide concrete paths for testimonial correspondence. In hamartiological realism, it takes seriously the reality of sin in which the theologian, too, remains complicit, and which prompts her to anti-idealistically engage in apophatic or critical epistemic practices. In material realism, it takes into account how both grace and sin express themselves in the trajectories of real people. In incarnational realism, it does not content itself with the conceptualization of reality in language or thought, but embodies the anti-docetic commitment that conceptual work, too, must like God "become real" in its commitment to it in its concrete realities—realities both of grace and of pain, of holiness and of suffering. It faithfully attends to revelatory excesses, practices kenotic solidarity with the messes, and remains honest about the in/decent conditions and effects of theological production.

Sin might be a universal condition with many faces, but grace is always local. "God's unconditional grace and omnipotent mercy active in the person of Jesus Christ"[31] demands to be reflected differently in concrete situations. Barth will talk about parables of the kingdom, about sign-posts and likenesses and reflections, will invoke the Holy Spirit as the subject of any such true reflections, and will talk about Scripture as guidance for discernment of the concrete command in a concrete situation. Such talk remains rather vague while formulated abstractly, and it remains precarious and subject to revision in (every!) concretion. But when pressed concretely by a particular situation, Barth did not hesitate to take a decisive stance as to what the concrete command of God would be. Did he always discern rightly? Of course not. Did he sometimes read his own prejudices and preferences into the command of

---

31. Smit, "Paradigms of Radical Grace," 40.

God? Most likely.[32] Does that mean that such discernment is better left un-undertaken? By no means.

"The fact that all our actions are sinful does not mean that some actions are not more adequate analogies of God's grace and mercy than others."[33] Just because we cannot get it right does not mean that we cannot do better, and that there are not concrete tasks with which we are entrusted in our respective, local, positions. Concrete, material analysis in exploration of the terrain and concrete, reflective ecological fitting will have to be conducted in encounter and engagement with concrete context, time and again. There is no general outline that can be applied to all situations. If the preoccupation with self-justification as a means of redemption has become unnecessary and therefore impossible, this also means that no singular *way* of doing things (in ethics or in method) can be unequivocally elevated as "the way." Any witness to grace, any enfleshment of queer holiness will remain precarious and unredeemable in principle, and the pressing questions of what to do and how to do it can neither be resolved universally nor definitively, let alone abstractly.

Overcoming both the temptation to strive for unequivocal progress and the temptation to strive for an unreachable critical distance, the theologian is invited to discern his own local complicities as well as local possibilities to inhabit and adapt to the terrain, striving to do

> "a little better . . . , avoid at least some of his previous mistakes, renounce at least some of the rigid or dissolute practices in which he has hitherto lived, give up at least some of the follies and wickednesses which have hitherto sprung unchecked from the sources of his deep unwisdom, compensate for at least some of the harm he has done and take some intelligent counter-action."[34]

The discernment of such a relative *better* is always indexical to where theology finds itself at any given moment, it is always a conversion in light of the specific shapes of "bad theology" and the specific ecological requirements of particular contexts at hand. There is no guarantee that such discernment—now guided by a pluriformity of approaches, by Scripture or experience, by tradition or strategy—will come to the right conclusions. Realistically, we will find material effects of epistemological sin in all our theological work, in whichever epistemic ecology. Any *better*—more self-reflected—way of doing theology would take this into account: By never identifying any of our ways of doing theology too closely with the truth of God for one, and by devising an

32. Cf. Smit, "Paradigms of Radical Grace," 42.

33. Smit, "Paradigms of Radical Grace," 43.

34. Karl Barth, *Church Dogmatics III.4: The Doctrine of Creation*, ed. Geoffrey W. Bromiley and Thomas F. Torrance (Edinburgh: T&T Clark, 1961), 238.

analytic apparatus to discern how our particular way of doing theology at any given time *always also* twists the truth and becomes harmful.

Better ways of doing theology will continue to seek God outside the gates even of its currently cherished approach, not as its prized possession. No round of critique, no temporary deployment of method, no contextual insight will have the last or only word. No trail map should be absolutized into a road to the kingdom. When we fail to understand, say, the biblical canon as a *critical* mode of *navigating* a distinct epistemological vulnerability and turn it into a principle, we fall into the trap of fundamentalism. Similar dangers loom when we fail to understand Systematic or Constructive methodologies as *critical* modes of navigating distinct epistemological vulnerabilities. They are not *the* form of theology; they are tools designed to facilitate transitory existence in by and large inhospitable landscapes. Rather than seeking redemption in (whatever) method, theology is called to engage in a nomadic movement as it follows bodies divine and human, navigating this space before the law outside its gates, finding resources and community in unexpected places. Living out in the open—transient, unsheltered, and at risk—allows for a versatile following of currents and desires, attentive exploration of the features of the landscape, and honest encounter with co-dwellers in mutual hospitality.

"*Hay que seguir andando nomás . . .*" is then a cry of perseverance, realism between exhaustion and renewal. No methodological fix and no new insight will bring an end to such laborious, ongoing orientation toward the *better,* nor will its practice cease to rely on the same instruments and processes it has hitherto employed.

CARING, OR: METHOD, UNREDEEMED

In his own despair over the impossibility of achieving the task of theology by way of whichever method, Karl Barth cries out,

> "Every possible variation . . . has long since been tried out and tested. Do these things really amount to anything more than just a turning of the sick man in his bed from one side to the other for a little diversion? . . . At any rate, we cannot hope that a change of method or orientation, unavoidable though such changes always are, will free us from our plight."[35]

The self-chosen image of turning the sick man back and forth inadvertently illustrates both the hubris and the sloth of the despairing theologian: He

35. Barth, "The Word of God as the Task of Theology," 175.

remains convinced that his work ought to be that of healing—of saving!—the
patient (who is also theology itself, of course) from their affliction—while in
the same breadth dismissing and thus presumably also practically neglecting
the real material labor that is required of him: the work of care to alleviate
the person's pain and suffering, the practice of attention to safeguard their
dignity, to keep their life livable and make their death grievable. In the reality
of the health care setting from which the image is chosen, it would be absurd
to frame the work of turning the sick patient back and forth as "doing nothing" or as a hopeless pursuit. It might be tiresome and exhausting labor, and it
might not in and of itself bring healing, but any process of the survival that we
call life requires such intensive practices of care in order to carry on, as well as
to stave off secondary infections, bed sores, and other duress in the meantime.

Barth seems to miss that implication, even as, rather than calling for a
change in practice (which change in practice, after all, should save theology?),
he calls for a change in self-awareness after which not a totally new and different life awaits, but the need to . . . "persevere."[36] It is the change in orientation—the conversion—that allows the theologian to now go about their
business, even as from the outside, things seem relatively unchanged. Not
the orientation to success, but the commitment to the required care is what
prompts the ongoing labor of the theologian. The examples Barth invokes are
remarkably material: "A mother cannot walk away from her children and the
shoemaker cannot walk away from his block, and we cannot be convinced
that the dialectic of the children's nursery is any less effective than the dialectic of our theological study halls."[37] Barth's own perseverance is marked by
a quasi-dialectical oscillation between position and negation while anchoring
himself in christological realism, and Althaus-Reid invests in a critical bisexuality as she seeks for more creative per/versions of the themes of theology.
Beyond both their interdigitations, I want to linger with the image of the sick
man and ask, might method, too, be converted from a tool for (self-)redemption
into an instrument of *care*?

Whatever the task of theology is, it is certainly not to dwell in its own misery. Barth plays with the thought of giving up, invoking similar images of
hopelessness and even suicide that we found in Edelman and De la Torre,
only to come to the opposite conclusion: "Should we hang up our hats and
become happy, like other people? But people are not happy. . . . Giving up
theology makes as little sense as taking of one's life—nothing will come of it,
and nothing will change by doing so."[38] Giving up theology neither avoids

36. Barth, "The Word of God as the Task of Theology," 195.
37. Barth, "The Word of God as the Task of Theology," 195.
38. Barth, "The Word of God as the Task of Theology," 195.

hubris (there may be a special kind of *hubris* in wanting to distance oneself from the inextricable messiness of the work), nor *sloth* (there may be a special kind of sloth in scoffing at the unredeeming "care work" required even in theological epistemology: attending in faithfulness, solidarity, and honesty to the persistent reality of God and the persistent unhappiness of people), and most importantly, it is a form of theological *falsehood* as it denies and occludes the real reality of grace that we find in, with, and under failure and impossibility.

If justification by grace through faith is a central insight of the Protestant Reformation,[39] its articulation of the gospel, the divine "yes" whose demanding ramifications extend to all of Christian existence, then it is the irony in the history of Protestantism that it has failed to take grace seriously enough. With regard to its own pursuit, it has stayed in a mode of despair that keeps generating "false alternatives" and binary divisions.[40] A queer theology that moves beyond negativity and instead finds grace and holiness in "unlikely" places can remind Protestant theology of its departure from sovereign grace. Theological realism refuses to abstract into immortality-or-euthanasia as the only options imaginable for the sick patient, and attends instead to that stretch of territory in between. It might not be all that narrow a mountain ridge, after all; indeed, it might simply be the cobblestone grace that most of us call life.

What happens after revelation? After the revelation of one's own failure, as well as after the revelation that this failure is not all there is, that there is instead a wide-open landscape around one? Committed to the new life afforded by grace, the Reformers developed a *tertius uses legis* over an idealistic antinomianism. Committed to an ethics outside of the law, queer theorists point to the existence of otherwise possibilities in, with, and under failure over an all-too-simple anti-normativity. Running up against the Norman doors of a theological method-turned-into-"Law," we might find ourselves reoriented by their design rather than trying to fix it. The fact that method (or anti-method) cannot save us is only an issue as long as we arrogate to ourselves the work of saving. Once we "give up" (not hope, not labor, but) this false aspiration, a much more relaxed yet no less demanding stance toward the use of method is possible: It becomes relativized to a penultimate status, and disciplinary conflicts over method can safely be treated as theological *adiaphora* in a spirit of freedom. This opens the way to a pragmatic "*Methodus est arbitraria*. In each age and by each responsible theologian the best definitions, combinations, and conclusions must always be sought and found afresh in dogmatics with a

---

39. Smit, "Paradigms of Radical Grace."

40. Smit names those between orthodoxy and orthopraxy, Reformed Faith and Liberation Theology, Paul and Jesus; we might add: Systematic and Constructive Theology, dogma and critique, positivity and refusal, hubris and sloth, cf. Smit, 36.

continually new desire for obedience."[41] At the same time, none of the ambivalences in which the theologian finds herself are eradicated, nor are any of the epistemological, ethical, and political stakes lowered.

Grace does not relieve us of work—it sets us to work. What is true in ethics also holds for theological epistemology. The fear that sovereign grace makes ethics impossible—an accusation that has been leveled both against Barth's and Althaus-Reid's theologies—rests on a transactional understanding of ethics: that people have to be frightened and coerced, or at least coaxed by a cost-benefit calculus, into doing hard and difficult things. Those who seek to preserve ethics by denying grace might even have the more pessimistic anthropology than those who insist that the human being does not have to, thus will not, and thus cannot, earn their salvation. If the Heidelberg Catechism asks, "But doesn't this teaching make people indifferent and wicked?", it also immediately rejoins, "it is impossible for those grafted into Christ through true faith not to produce fruits of gratitude."[42] Similarly, Karl Barth reckons not just with the possibility but with the actuality of such witness despite its apparent "impossibility," and Marcella Althaus-Reid always already comes from the experience of "queer holiness" despite its unredeemed (and unredeemable) existence outside of the law. It is when the preoccupation with self-justification has fallen away that true freedom *for* an ethical life opens up, one that does not depend on a calculus of anticipated reward or punishment. It is when achieving "the good" is foreclosed that the pursuit of the better becomes necessary and possible. The epistemological consequence of radical grace is not that theology is impossible and meaningless, but that a different way of theology is now, and only now, possible: a radically de-economized way of doing theology.

Method, then, does not pertain to the locus of soteriology, but to the ongoing discernment of ethics. And here, it makes all the difference. "God does not need your good works, but your neighbor does," is a phrase often used to summarize Luther's view of the matter.[43] Whether God does or does not need better theology, we certainly do. Theology continues, it perseveres, not as a work that could ever be achieved, but as the labor of love: caring about and attending to the reality of God and the reality of people around it. It is gratitude, not condition, it responds to rather than preparing for the experience of grace.

---

41. Barth, *CD IV.3*, 5.

42. Office of the General Assembly, ed. Heidelberg Catechism, in *Book of Confessions: The Constitution of the Presbyterian Church (U.S.A.)*, 27–74 (Louisville, KY: Office of the General Assembly, Presbyterian Church [U.S.A.], 2014), Q64.

43. As referenced by Wingren, *Luther on Vocation*, 10.

"People are not happy . . ." Relieved from self-preoccupation, the theologian is challenged to look around themself and get to work. Doing theology (well) might be impossible, but that takes nothing away from its necessity. If the hubris of achieving theology is forbidden to us, then so is the sloth of resignation and hopelessness. As Eugene Rogers aptly puts it,

> "your search will misguide you, if you imagine 'strategies' and theology to be at odds. There is no 'strategy' apart from better theology. There is no better theology—and thus no strategy   apart from better exegesis, better Christology, better use of the liturgy, better recovery of patristic and medieval resources, and so on. . . ."[44]

The reality of God and the reality of the human being persist—and insist. They demand to be accounted for, and done justice to, intellectually and theoretically. In addition, God-*talk* always already exists and is always already at work in the worlds we inhabit, shaping realities and counter-realities, creating dissonances and issues. There can be no escape from (bad) theology, because (bad) theology is *always already here*. "Giving up" theology would simply mean to leave the current state of God-talk unchecked, in our image: leaving the "sick man" unattended and uncared for. We need theological reflection to better understand the ways in which the theologies we always already encounter at work are "bad," and we need theological engagement as a small effort to redesign them in slightly better ways. We need both to attend to the mundane and very material inflections of such plight, and to its laborious, iterative, and persistent practice rather than its teleological aspiration. This labor lacks the grandiose gestures of either heroic certainty or heroic refusal, attainable truth or achievable justice, it is much more unexceptional, but no less pressing. "Staying with the trouble"[45] is no less demanding than radical negation; it might not be any more rewarding in the ambivalence of its results, yet it remains an obligation for those convicted by stubborn faithfulness, messy solidarity, and indecent honesty. Practices of co-presence, attention, and care are better guidelines for theology's pursuit than orientations to fulfillment, perfection, and solution.

What if instead of despairing over the impossibility of "fulfilling the law," we allowed that failure to reorient (that is, convert) us, and invested in its use without staking our salvation on it? What if we gave up the aspiration of *saving* theology or *justifying* its endeavor, and instead (at the risk of sounding naive and pious), we sought for ways of *using* it that furthered love of God and love of

---

44. Eugene Rogers, "Doctrine and Sexuality," in *The Oxford Handbook of Theology, Sexuality, and Gender*, ed. Adrian Thatcher, 53–66 (Oxford: Oxford University Press, 2015), 53.

45. Donna Jeanne Haraway, *Staying with the Trouble: Making Kin in the Chthulucene*, (Durham; London: Duke University Press, 2016).

neighbor? After method, we thus find ourselves once more: before method, or more precisely: trying to spell out its *tertius usus legis* along the lines of itinerant dwelling with and laborious caring for.

CHILD'S PLAY, OR: GROWING SIDEWAYS

> Every thing else is child's play in comparison.
> —*Karl Barth*[46]

> There are ways of growing that are not growing up.
> —*Kathryn Stockton*[47]

> Whoever does not receive the kingdom of God as a little child will never enter it.
>
> —*Mark 10:15*

A growing unease may ask, but doesn't the de-teleologizing reorientation to the "outside" in nomadic dwelling and the endlessness of any practice of care make our push for a "better" theology altogether questionable? The sacrifice of the aspiration to achievement, legibility, and fulfillment and the commitment to itinerant perseverance seems to abandon any positive identification of the "better" or measurability of advance toward such goal, whether defined epistemologically or ethically. If we do not want to outright maintain that a desire for "better theology" is just as contradictory, just as misdirected as the desire for self-justification, what then does "better" mean once we lose the aspiration to reach or approach a goal? Is insight also subject to a radically actualistic eschatology, all events and glimmers with no way of sustaining and growing knowledge? How do we conceptualize the gain of theological knowledge *otherwise*?

If doctrine has long criticized ethical and political aspirations of historical realization of God's reign, queer theorization has pointed to the costs of investments in notions of progress and success with regard to epistemology. Their temporalities serve as straightening devices that curate certain ideas as ideals, validate advancement toward them, and pathologize all other paths as perversion, inversion, regression, reversion, and diversion (as has long been done in describing the deviation of queer people from "straight" cisheteronormativity). The teleological determination of progress fixes an idea of the truth

---

46. Barth, "The Word of God as the Task of Theology," 177.
47. Kathryn Bond Stockton, *The Queer Child, or Growing Sideways in the Twentieth Century* (Duke University Press, 2009), 11.

and measures progress by getting successively closer to it. But from which "God's eye point of view" would we be able to identify the position of this truth and measure our distance to it? Queer insights rightly call such an aspiration into question as ideology, and in theological language we would once more use the term hubris.

Rather than a teleological determination, we might conceive of an indexical appraisal of epistemological gain: its comparative relation to a respective "here." This is not so much to sacrifice objectivity for "mere" subjectivity, it is to use parameters of assessment that are accessible to the observer, thus affording relatively more rather than less objectivity, if neither universal nor comprehensive. It is in this spirit that I have recurrently spoken of "better theology": theological conceptual design as localized and material problem-solving, a comparatively "better than" *this* particular articulation of insight or *this* particular effect of bad theology as discerned out of particular perspectival vision. I have playfully detemporalized epistemological metaphors, spatializing them instead in order to reorient (another spatial metaphor) our thinking about thinking.

Spatial orientation is not just a metaphor in epistemology—it marks the perspectivity that attends embodied perception as such, and on which our sensory engagement with any environment depends. In embodied perception as much as in epistemology at large, what is designated as "forward" depends significantly on a person's orientation, and, if we want to retain temporal framings, on their hindsight. Spatial rather than temporal indexicality might help to envision at least a multiplicity of dimensions along which such comparative value might be measured against the illusion of unilateral progression toward which temporal metaphors of "better" tend. But forward may not be the only way to go.

There may be other ways to conceptualize growth, epistemological one, beyond its teleological *or* indexical determination: "There are ways of growing that are not growing up," writes Kathryn Stockton.[48] Against straight, linear, and "vertical" rationales of progress, redemption, and fulfillment of a preconceived ideal state, Stockton suggests that "growth" might be just as much "a matter of extension, vigor, and volume," of "connection and extension" rather than merely one of "verticality," "full stature (or reproduction)."[49] Stockton invokes the image of *The Queer Child* and its "sideways growth" to conceptualize such other forms of gains. Stockton's shift in assessing growth, development, progress, and gain from verticality to laterality and from temporal to spatial accretion allows a vision of epistemological gain beyond the frustrations and

48. Stockton, *The Queer Child*, 11.
49. Stockton, *The Queer Child*, 11.

coercions that attend categories of unambiguous, unilateral, and universal progress.

In *The Word of God as the Task of Theology,* Barth's formulation of the theologian's ends in a revealing image: "As theologians, we must speak of God. But we are humans and as such cannot speak of God. We ought to do both, to know the 'must' and the 'cannot,' and precisely in this way give God the glory," says Barth and adds, almost with a sigh, "This is our plight. Everything else is child's play in comparison."[50] In his frustration, he projects a romanticized idyll of simple, easy "play" in opposition to the grave and arduous task of theology, insisting that whatever theology is, it can never be *that.* But precisely this affective appraisal betrays the theologian who is still stuck in front of what he assumes to be a Norman door, the theologian who has not allowed himself to be reoriented by grace. The later Barth will insist that "The theologian who labors without joy is not a theologian at all. Sulky faces, morose thoughts and boring ways of speaking are intolerable in this field."[51] One might be reminded of Nietzsche's famous aphorism, "Better songs would they have to sing, for me to believe in their Savior: more redeemed would his disciples have to appear!"[52]

What then, if instead of "everything *else*" being child's play, that characterization might suit the work of theology, as well? What if "giving God the glory" hinges on renouncing the Promethean attitude toward the task and following the invitation to a posture of gratuitous, self-sufficient, exploratory, and creative, "child's play" in the midst of landscapes marked by catastrophe? Could it be that to take grace more seriously than sin would necessitate to hold even one's insurmountable sin and complicity with levity, and in gratitude lean into the space that the gospel opens up, cruising it, dwelling and playing in it?

Jesus' exhortation in the so-called Children's Gospel that "whoever does not receive the kingdom of God as a little child will not enter it" (Mark 10:15) might easily function as an invitation to methodological playfulness. But the story does not explicate what childlikeness consists in. As historically sensitized scholarship cautions, "We must dismiss from our minds any attempt to romanticise the child for this would have been foreign to the ancient world."[53] Imaginations of children as innocent and/or precious, or assumptions about

---

50. Barth, "The Word of God as the Task of Theology," 177, slightly revised translation.

51. Barth, *CD II.1,* 656.

52. Friedrich Nietzsche, *Thus Spake Zarathustra,* tr. Thomas Common (Standard Ebooks, 2021), 106, translation adapted.

53. Ernest Best, *Following Jesus: Discipleship in the Gospel of Mark,* Journal for the Study of the New Testament 4 (Sheffield: JSOT Press, 1981), 108. For a summary of scholarly interpretations of "childlikeness" in this passage, see Dan Otto Via, *The Ethics of Mark's Gospel–in the Middle of Time* (Philadelphia: Fortress, 1985), 129.

the humility and trustfulness, obedience and simple faith of the child might speak to "our present day but not the first century."[54] Does it even speak to our present day? This figure of the child, innocent because it is shielded from sex and other pleasures of adult life, and priceless because it is shielded from the exigencies of labor economies, crime, violence and other hardships of adult life, might be a white, middle-class prop for consumerism and conservative politics. Marcella Althaus-Reid reminds us that the unblemished and desexualized, dependent and obedient child is a figure that has little to do with those who grow up in poverty. Themselves "children of children," "the children of the poor circulate around circles of promiscuity and loneliness and they hear and see many things: they know the names of the men to whose rooms they should never go because older girls or boys have told them not to do so; or the price some may ask you to pay for a gift of some sweets."[55] The romanticized figure of "the innocent Child" queers actually existent children beyond recognition into precocious, indecent, premature, and suspicious beings who will be criminalized, blamed, and punished for their failure to embody proper "childlikeness."

Particular inflections of sociality, ignorance, and interdependence might be at play in children's lives, but the existential "dependence" so often attributed to children with religious verve is no Schleiermacherian ultimate feeling. Far from romanticism's self-consciousness, the dependence that characterizes children, and that is easily idealized into notions of trustfulness, obedience, and humility, attends physical weakness as well as legal and economic precarity. This even holds true today for those children who do not hold the "priceless" status of a privileged class in many parts of the world. It was even truer in the ancient world. More historically conscientious scholarship on Mark's "children's gospel" will remind us that "The point is probably not so much the unquestioning trust that children display, but the fact that they had no social status. . . . The kingdom belongs to the likes of children, just as it also belongs to the likes of the poor."[56] Jesus' embrace of the children—who "religiously . . . were nonentities, disqualified from participation"[57]—is part of his broader embrace of the marginalized, those excluded by the standards of society.

Mark's composition locates the child of 10:13–16 in careful juxtaposition to the rich young man of 10:17–22 whom we already encountered in chapter 3. The two stories illuminate one another: What the child lacks, and this is what

54. Robert H Stein, *Mark*, Baker Exegetical Commentary on the New Testament (Grand Rapids: Baker, 2008), 463.

55. Althaus-Reid, *Indecent Theology*, 136–37.

56. Richard Bauckham, *Jesus: A Very Short Introduction* (Oxford: Oxford University Press, 2011), 77.

57. Boring, *Mark*, 289.

makes it the model for discipleship, is precisely the power of the rich man to make things happen.[58] In Mark, the children's gospel then forms an analogy to the beatitudes in Luke and Matthew, sketching not so much the contours of a new, if inverted, social hierarchy, but of *God's* outside-going orientation that favors the poor, hungry, destitute, and marginalized.[59] There is no essential quality that elevates the child into a model of discipleship; Jesus' kenotic orientation "outside the gates" does.

Queer theory, too, reminds us not to romanticize the child as we explore the possibilities that child's play opens up for a theological reorientation of epistemological value. Its child is a remarkably ambivalent figure. Where Lee Edelman denounced "the Child" as a figure that is innocent, desexualized, fragile, and in need of protection, a projective and idealized figure of reproductive futurism with its relentless exclusion of queer existence (cf. chapter 3), others insists that, on the contrary, the child figures a very similar priceless worthlessness,[60] and a similar temporality of delay and deferral,[61] as the figure of "the Queer" to which Edelman *opposes* it.

Like the queer, the figure of the child is strangely suspended from the unidirectional progress of time toward the future and from the literal and figurative economies of (re)production. Children exist in an obscure laterality to the adult world, they inhabit their own temporalities and point any direction but "forward." Relegated to a detemporalized space of deferred development, they are marked by a status of "not yet," outside of sexual reproduction as well as of monetized values of exchange, even so erotiziced and fetishized by consumerism and capital. Children are remarkably queer, and like queers, their paths, desires, and futures are not always straight. They move sideways: lingering, repeating, deferring, and delaying. They have sideways motives that remain obscure and illegible and which are often uncomfortably sexual or criminal to adult sensibilities. They form sideways relations to adults, other children, nonhuman animals, and inanimate objects. And they even develop sideways futures, futures that are not pursued according to straight logics. Even their assumed growth and development (into "queer" or "straight" figures, among other things) will be diagnosed backwards at best. In the meantime, Stockton claims, children live their lives horizontally more than vertically, growing sideways instead of growing up. As a figure that resists the pull of normative

58. Cf. Black, *Mark*, 227. For similar conclusions, cf. Adela Yarbro Collins and Harold W. Attridge, *Mark: A Commentary*, Hermeneia: A Critical and Historical Commentary on the Bible (Minneapolis: Fortress, 2007), 471; Boring, *Mark*, 289–97.

59. Cf. Collins and Attridge, *Mark*, 472.

60. Cf. Viviana A. Rotman Zelizer, *Pricing the Priceless Child: The Changing Social Value of Children* (New York: Basic Books, 1985).

61. Cf. Philippe Ariès, *Centuries of Childhood: A Social History of Family Life* (New York: Knopf; Random House, 1962).

temporalities, whether in supposedly blissful ignorance of them or in painful failure to succeed according to adult logics, queer sociality has thus (re-)discovered and celebrated the child who is always already queered (economically, sexually, racially, and in a variety of other dimensions) to resist violent and normalizing visions of progress, development, success, and fulfillment.

In Halberstam's theorizations of failure, the "childish" comes into view as a site of unbelonging, real and perceived inabilities to measure up to "adult" norms, and naive or cultivated ignorance toward what counts as success and how to attain it. Childish existence thus opens up spaces beyond straight logics and temporalities and often allows for more creative and more collaborative ways of being in the world. Drawing out such lines, "child's play" then constitutes a subversive and subverting practice of imagining and inhabiting other worlds beyond questions of viability and success. The "silly archives" of animated children's films that Halberstam studies in particular teach us to "work together, revel in difference, fight exploitation, decode ideology, invest in resistance."[62]

There is a famous anecdote from World War One, according to which a German military post telegraphed to the Austrian allies, "The situation is serious but not catastrophic." To which the Austrian post allegedly replied, "Here, the situation is catastrophic, but not serious." Advocates of political as much as epistemological hope or hopelessness equally reduce the range of movement, either attempting to bring "forward" or "upward" movement about or swimming against its stream. But there are alternatives to taking the catastrophes of method too seriously, and the figure of the child, beyond its many problematic romanticizations, points to one such possibility: that of resisting the pull of seriousness, decency, responsibility that can envision only upward and forward movement, and instead dwelling in a mode of playful, non-ultimate, non-teleological engagement that opens up surprising sideways connections, insights, and thickenings.

As Stockton's vegetative, floral imagery connects organically to the ecological fitting described in chapter 2, it might encourage us to envision "sideways" uses of method, too, and "sideways" ways to conceptualize epistemic "growth." Greek *methodos* literally means: a way around, beyond, besides, or an after-way. Method thus might be thought of more as a detour than as a direct pursuit of a goal. Lingering and repetition rather than linear succession mark its methodological path. As it proceeds, it does not necessarily progress; its movement may be more one of exploration than of advance, or stuck in recurring loops, and the growth of insight associated with it might be construed "horizontally" in terms of accumulation and thickening more than

62. Halberstam, *The Queer Art of Failure*, 21.

in terms of "vertically" ascending and leaving behind. Theological work, too, might then be a work of accumulating perspectives, of making more or new connections, of extending the range of our movement or the repertoire of our tools to engage the environment, of growing "sideways" rather than getting closer to a preconceived goal along a charted path.

Resonances between the images invoked in this chapter—that of nomadic movement as a mode of dwelling in the reorientation to the outside, that of caring as ongoing theological labor out of commitment to divine and human bodies, and that of playing as a queering mode of engagement that promises surprising sideways gains—prompt me to finally postulate theological engagement of method *after method* as a form of epistemological "cruising." Cruising captures and combines traits explored in these previous sections into a thicker, more realistic version of the Reformers' *tertius usus legis*.

CRUISING, OR: EPISTEMIC PROMISCUITY

> Methodus est arbitraria.
> —*Karl Barth*[63]

> . . . a per/version, that is, deliberately taking what is considered as the wrong way in the Metà-ódos or methodological road.
> —*Marcella Althaus-Reid*[64]

> The mode of "cruising" for which this book calls is not only or even primarily "cruising for sex." I do see an unlimited potentiality in actual queer sex, but books of criticism that simply glamorize the ontology of gay male cruising are more often than not simply boring . . . [A]ffective and cognitive maps of the world that a critically queer utopianism can create, maps that do include utopia, need to be attended to in a fashion that indeed resembles a kind of politicized cruising.
> —*José Muñoz*[65]

In the riveting opening passage of his *Cruising Utopia,* José Muñoz envisions the restless, searching, and yearning movement of queer cruising in language ripe with theological overtones:

> Queerness is a longing that propels us onward, beyond romances of the negative and toiling in the present. Queerness is that thing that

---

63. Barth, *CD I.2*, 860, Barth, *CD IV.3*, 5.
64. Althaus-Reid, *Indecent Theology*, 8.
65. Muñoz, *Cruising Utopia*, 18.

lets us feel that this world is not enough, that indeed something is missing. . . . Queerness is essentially about the rejection of the here and now and an insistence on potentiality or concrete possibility for another world.[66]

In such an eschatological fervor, grief and loss as well as glimpses of grace keep pointing us to a future horizon. But not settling for "what is" never allows theological realism to dive into an abstract utopian imagination. The secret is, as Muñoz knows from the great Ernst Bloch, to attend to the concrete utopias that the ephemeral and the quotidian gesture toward, and to cultivate concrete imaginations, always in critical conversation with the realities that will necessarily disappoint our hopes, but that are also contradicted by our utopias in their unquenchable urge to become real.

Living in the gritty wrestling of a theologically realistic "already-and-not-yet," a queer use of method looks like a "scavenger methodology that uses different methods to collect and produce information on subjects who have been deliberately or accidentally excluded from traditional studies in human behavior."[67] The metaphor of cruising might provide a queer reinterpretation for a *tertius usus legis* of theological method: not trusting (any) method to afford salvation, but on the assumption that salvation must be found otherwise—by alien, queer grace, which often closely resembles unredemption—it envisions a making-use of the law of method according to "a dual mandate. . . . To outline the conditions of queer worldmaking and to clarify, but not overdetermine, the conditions that 'make life livable.'"[68]

Cruising refers to a style of travel and movement that is characterized by a certain purposeful undirectedness and exploratory, transitory openness. Cruising is what children do when they start to move around, stabilizing and propelling themselves onward by grabbing onto rails, pieces of furniture, and walls, before walking self-sufficiently. "Just cruising" is a form of navigating urban landscapes. Riding around the blocks of the city, often along a habitual course, exploration without the *telos* of a well-defined intention or destination, it is performative, but also familiarizing: cruising is not only an existential mode of connecting to the landscape, cruising is the name of a knowledge gained by way of inhabitation, exploration, navigation. Finally, cruising invokes a gay culture of looking for casual sex partners, an intense form of interest in connection, being turned on by and finding pleasure with

---

66. Muñoz, *Cruising Utopia*, 1.

67. Jack Halberstam, *Female Masculinity* (Duke: Duke University Press, 1998), 13.

68. Amin Ghaziani and Matt Brim, "Queer Methods: Four Provocations for an Emerging Field," in *Imagining Queer Methods*, ed. Amin Ghaziani and Matt Brim, 3–27 (New York: New York University Press, 2019), 7.

strangers in momentary engagement. Its often name- or even faceless nature does not preclude encounter and care, as a form of knowledge that is intimate even as it is noncommittal. Cruising might also be conceived as a theological mode of engagement, navigating the landscape outside the gates of the law, in search for the other, in search of a livable past and present, haunted by what is lost even as it is continually "looking for the city that is to come" (Heb. 13:14). Cruising method, theology might make *use* of all kinds of different conceptual frameworks and methodological paradigms, while at the same time remaining a productive rather than reductive process, a "self-directed, open-ended and radical practice of looking that prioritizes pleasure and connectedness."[69]

Cruising is deeply a-romantic, in several inflections of the term. Many will find it unsanitary, gross. It is, however, excruciatingly honest and highly attentive. Even as it is disinterested in long-term commitment or compatibility, cruising is not devoid of ethics. Cruising develops distinct codes of signaling needs, of reading the landscape's dangers and opportunities, of scavenging opportunities between failure and oppression, of finding and fashioning glimmers of hope in the ruins, of offering hospitality and of providing mutual care to ensure that the fleeting encounter is a site of consent and pleasure for all involved. Tim Dean even suggests that cruising may point us toward modes of existence that are marked by radical hospitality, ultimate intimacy, and openness to the world.[70] Leo Bersani proposes that cruising's "deliberate avoidance of relationships might be crucial in initiating, or at least clearing the ground for, a new relationality."[71] It is a practice in which the "self," as represented by all markers of identity and particularity, is mostly left behind in favor of a "naked (in more than one sense) perception of otherness."[72] It can thus become a "training in impersonal intimacy"[73] where subjects do not have to establish or prove their dignity—as we might say theologically: it moves beyond justification.

Perhaps surprisingly for the sentiments of decency, then, cruising seems to resonate with the order of grace. Bersani suggests that it might "help us to at least glimpse the possibility of dismissing moral worthiness itself, of constructing human subjects whom such moral categories would fail to 'cover.'"[74] Bersani envisions a "metaphysical sociability" in which the self-subtractions and disinvestments that attend cruising open up "a new ethics . . . an ecological

---

69. Fiona Anderson, "Cruising as Method and Its Limits," *LUX*, August 23, 2017, https://lux.org.uk/cruising-method-limits-fiona-anderson/, 2017.

70. Tim Dean, *Unlimited Intimacy: Reflections on the Subculture of Barebacking* (Chicago; London: University of Chicago Press, 2009).

71. Leo Bersani, "Sociability and Cruising," *Umbr(a): A Journal of the Unconscious* no. 1 (2002), 20.

72. Bersani, "Sociability and Cruising," 21.

73. Bersani, "Sociability and Cruising," 21.

74. Bersani, "Sociability and Cruising," 20–21.

ethics, one in which the subject, having willed its own lessness, can live less invasively in the world [. . . where] it should then seem not only imperative but natural to treat the outside as we would a home."[75]

I am of course not the first to draw on the notion of cruising to conceptualize method *otherwise*, or, as I have been calling it here, *after* method. The searching, exploratory, and open-ended mode of cruising has been credited with "inbuilt potential for diversion, irregular connections and disorderly encounters," celebrated for its resistance to the projection of a predetermined outcome and potential of "*not* finding what you are looking for and being open to 'something you never knew you wanted, or even knew existed.'"[76] Such disorientation rather than epistemological determinism may be the precondition of what we call learning.

Cruising method suggests a mode of *epistemic promiscuity*, engaging with and moving through a variety of hermeneutical circles as drawn by different epistemic paradigms without committing to any of them in a principled or even temporally sustained way. It refuses the need for absolute disciplinary coherence, might draw on eclectic (or even "silly") archives, interweave multiple genealogies, or bring together methods that are typically cast as being at odds. If Schleiermacher's classic conception of the hermeneutic circle expanded our understanding in a rotation from text to context and vice versa, we might envision Systematic Theology's circle to move from part to whole and vice versa or Constructive Theology's from context to commitment and vice versa. Cruising their distinct hermeneutical circles might traverse these different motions without settling on any of them, taking what pleasure as well as knowledge they have to offer, playfully amplifying resonances with one another while freeing the other from the expectation to be or become the comprehensive fulfillment of all our desires and needs, and vice versa.

The reader might recognize that this is what I have been doing throughout this book in my double engagement with Systematic (Reformed) Theology and Constructive (Queer) Theology. The fact that these different theological approaches have engaged in open hostilities in the past (and ongoing), that they might not be long-term or comprehensively compatible, that they might outright contradict one another, and that many of their sensibilities are at odds with one another has not prevented me from engaging with both of them in attentiveness to both their respective requirements, but without taking them so serious as to prevent me from playing with them, or to add side conversations with design theory to enhance the experience. While such promiscuous engagement will fail to measure up to the exclusive disciplinary

75. Bersani, "Sociability and Cruising," 22.
76. Simon Ofield-Kerr, "Cruising the Archive," *Journal of Visual Culture* 4, no. 3 (2005), 357.

standards of any single epistemic paradigm, it also affords more "generative models of failure that do not posit two equally bleak alternatives."[77] As I have throughout attempted to augment the generativity of the encounter, interested in "conversation rather than mastery,"[78] it is my hope that the enticement of generativity, if not necessarily comprehensive satisfaction, will be experienced by the readers of this book as well. Have I done Systematic or Constructive Theology an injustice in my promiscuous engagement of them? Have I gone beyond Barth and Althaus-Reid's consent in my exploration, or might I have allowed them, too, to find surprising pleasures in the unfolding encounter? Is such promiscuous methodology sustainable into the long-term relationship of a master-paradigm that encompasses both? Probably not, but was that ever the aspiration? I for one have learned much in the encounter. Not only have I produced a host of playful resonances that might not otherwise have occurred, it has also been an immensely pleasurable experience.

Cruising allows us to envision ways of *using* method that recognize their penultimate, transitory, and yes, instrumental status while fiercely committed to an ethics of consent and care. Cruising denotes a mode of dwelling in, inhabiting, and navigating methodological paradigms with intense interest in what they might produce. It comes with clear codes that guide the search for a fitting partner, but without a requirement for comprehensive compatibility or long-term commitment; with an appreciation of grace encountered without staking one's salvation on it. Cruising divests from apologetics as well as from ultimate fulfillment without giving up the pursuit of moments of truth, encounter, and yes: pleasure. Cruising opens up a distinctly social epistemology with significant tolerance for abiding differences, navigating risks and pleasures together, committing to care at the site of engagement, while remaining nomadic, always propelled onward (and outward) in pursuit of "better theology."

In the search for partners in sex or in method, not all pleasures will be found in any one encounter. Freeing one another from this expectation takes off pressure and allows for a more honest appraisal of what any candidate has to offer. Any hermeneutic comes with its own hermetic, and every methodology's offerings are attended by particular limitations and exclusions. If Schleiermacher envisioned hermeneutical motion to result in an upward or outward spiral of ever-increasing understanding, we might be more cautious. Regardless of whether we follow Thomas Kuhn or Paul Feyerabend, we will expect that paradigm shifts do not only result in the increasing accretion but also in the demolition of knowledge, just like engagement with different partners

---

77. Halberstam, *The Queer Art of Failure*, 120.
78. Halberstam, *The Queer Art of Failure*, 12.

do not linearly build on one another or expand pleasure incrementally. A cruising of hermeneutical circles, in temporary engagement with different epistemes and methodologies, does not result in an expanded, larger, comprehensive hermeneutical circle of circles, or a meta-method of combining epistemes wholistically. Instead, we gain the possibility of journeying through the insights and criteria available by the standards of different available paradigms, an invitation to explore and inhabit them temporarily, make use of all of them in a casual engagement that takes one-self less seriously, does not ultimately commit to one specific method or thinks that everything will depend on its pure execution and exclusive application.

The capaciousness of cruising not only allows theology to find insight in unexpected places and from unexpected partners but also to make use of materials from sites that would be inhospitable as a more permanent abode. As queers know all too well, tactical forms of transience and noncommittal engagement can be deployed "to cruise places occupied by normative straightness"[79] and to "engage with the past without being destroyed by it."[80] Theology, too, has much to learn from epistemic projects that seem alien to it or with whom past encounters have resulted in hostility and harm. Cruising affords theology ways to engage with paradigms and methodologies, insights and interlocutors that might not be long-term compatible, and that it itself might, for better or worse reasons, deem unsavory or problematic.

Continuing tensions and abiding incompatibilities do not have to be a source of frustration; methodological imperfection and failure prompt us once again to take our insights less seriously and be readier to rethink our approach and practice. Even as preferences coalesce into orientations and codes to signal them might be established, it will be a matter of judgment which epistemic paradigms to engage on which occasion. It cannot be determined ahead of time which will yield the "best" results or what that would even mean. Everything needs to be negotiated. As one chooses the starting points that present themselves as most promising in an epistemic ecology, trial and error of what "works," what turns out to be comparatively "better" whether in anticipation or hindsight, and what becomes problematic according to new perspectival insights will continue.

To be clear: Not every method will be compatible with the needs and desires of theology. And where we open ourselves to encounter, there is no guarantee that the experience will be hospitable. Sometimes, when you screw with method, you get screwed by method. Of the partners that do offer

79. Cindy Patton and Benigno Sánchez-Eppler, eds., *Queer Diasporas* (Durham: Duke University Press, 2000), 14.

80. Heather Love, *Feeling Backward: Loss and the Politics of Queer History* (Cambridge: Harvard University Press, 2009), 1.

connection and insight, some will remain in tension or even outright contradiction with one another and with what theology seeks. While cruising will
expand the range of experience, it would also be foolish to think that accumulation of human efforts would escape sin any more than its finest exemplars
individually.

Inhabiting or cruising different methodological paradigms promiscuously and playfully, developing practices of care and attention, questions of
use come into view. Is the encounter merely instrumental, self-gratifying? If
it is not an end in itself, what is the right use of method—greater intimacy,
heightened pleasures, finding truth? Use has an ambivalent reputation in a
theological imaginary that enforces a binary distinction between divine and
all-too-human pleasures, which it intends to segregate along an *uti/frui-*
distinction. But what if we took use more seriously as a category of theological epistemology, investigating not only how we make use of method but also
taking into account the uses to which our theological designs lend themselves?
The next chapter explores these questions through a string of case studies, and
it does so in loose conversation with yet another promiscuous partner who has
occasionally been looped into the play so far: design theory.

Chapter 7

Using, or: The affordances of doctrine

THE TRUTH OF A BLADE[1]

In days to come
. . . .
Many peoples shall come and say,
 "Come, let us go up to the mountain of the LORD,
    to the house of the God of Jacob,
that he may teach us his ways
    and that we may walk in his paths."
For out of Zion shall go forth instruction
    and the word of the LORD from Jerusalem.
He shall judge between the nations
    and shall arbitrate for many peoples;
they shall beat their swords into plowshares
    and their spears into pruning hooks;
nation shall not lift up sword against nation;
    neither shall they learn war any more.
                              —*Isaiah 2:2–4*

Imagine you found a piece of metal. As you turn it in your hands, your fingers intuitively circle around to grip it. As you explore its sharp edge, your mind immediately frames the object as a blade.

---

1. The following section builds on a reflection I have previously published as "Swords to Plowshares: On Doing Election," *Stellenbosch Theological Journal* 8, no. 1 (2022): 1–14.

What you imagine that you could do with it will depend on a couple of different things. It will partially depend on the characteristics of the blade. The blade will communicate to you to some extent what it is *for*. Is its tip pointed or rounded? Does it have an edge or is it serrated? Does it have a handle or is it set into a moldboard? These things will prompt you to wield it with one or two hands, or to devise some sort of apparatus instead; and they will let you know whether the object is more effectively used for puncturing, for chopping, or for sawing.

What you imagine you could do with it will in another part depend on the characteristics of you, the agent: your experience and skills (hunting, farming, cooking, surgery?), your capabilities (what size, shape, strength have your hands? are you ambidextrous?), your needs (are you under attack, looking for a weapon to defend yourself right now? or are you hungry, rummaging through the drawer in search of something that will help you pry open a can of soup?), and not least of all: your imagination: "To one with a hammer, everything looks like a nail."

Imagine you found a blade in your tradition. "The word of God," the letter to the Hebrews claims, "is living and active, sharper than any two-edged sword, piercing until it divides soul from spirit, joints from marrow; it is able to judge the thoughts and intentions of the heart" (Heb. 4:12). The word of God is *as sharp as* a sword—but does that necessarily make it a *sword*? Just like in the case of a physical blade, what this metaphorical blade lends itself *to*— piercing or slicing, cutting or separating—will depend on the characteristics of this word itself *as well as* on the subject engaged by it, and on the relationship between them. Even as the letter to the Hebrews frames the word of God as an instrument of judgment, the passage leads with an interest in life. And so many of Jesus's own words draw on images of agrarian life much more than war. Think of the parables of the sower, the mustard seed, the weeds, the treasure buried in the field, and so on.

It might be worth pondering whether the sharpness and activity, the "liveness" and edge that is a characteristic of this "object," the word of God, may be closer to that of a plowshare than that of a sword. Both are instruments with sharp blades, both intervene in their environment, breaking things apart and breaking them open. Their affordances are remarkably similar, and while they cannot simply be used interchangeably, they can be transformed into one another with relative ease. The eschatological vision in Isaiah 2:3–4, Micah 4:2–3, and Zechariah 8 envisions how blades found in our traditions might be transformed, and how their affordances might be put to constructive use in a peaceful kingdom rather than the destruction of war. Even as judgment is part of such prophetic vision, the instrument of transformation is not a sword, and even instruments for killing are transformed into instruments of life: swords to plowshares.

Of course, we also find the tragic and ironic inversion of this vision from the book of Joel. In the face of an overpowering threat, Joel decides to put the

manifest and eschatological plowshares he finds in his own tradition to a different use: "Beat your plowshares into swords, and your pruning hooks into spears;
let the weakling say, 'I am a warrior'" (Joel 3:10). Such is the work of despair
that transforms every conceivable implement into instruments of war and death
in order to achieve judgment upon Israel's oppressors. The language is harsh
and the vision is grim. But even here, God's punishment on Israel's enemies is
invoked in hope of a divine intervention that would "effect the total renewal of
Jerusalem" such that the "earlier prophecy will come to fulfillment."[2]

What is the truth of a blade? You could stick it on a handle and use it as a
sword. Or you could stick it on a moldboard and use it as a plowshare. Which
is the adequate option? And how do we know? You could contemplate the
object itself for a long time trying to discern the truth of the blade. But at the
end of the day, such truth cannot be found apart from its use. Its use *matters*—
it matters because it makes a difference how a thing is used, and it matters
because the use *transforms* what the object means and signifies, does and stands
for, and ultimately *is*. The blade's *being* consists in its possible use by an agent.
Whether this blade *is* a sword or a plowshare depends not solely on the innate
qualities of the object, but on its relationship to the agent wielding it, and on
the actual use to which it is put in a given environment.

Now imagine you found a doctrine. You turn it in your hands. What you
imagine you might do with it will depend on a couple of things. The characteristics of the object, for one. Your own capabilities, skills, needs, and
imagination, conditioned by your experiences and context, for another. This
doctrine's affordances—its most likely and consistent uses—pertain to the
relationship between both, the object and the agent, in the environment. To
what uses might we put theology? One of cutting or one of plowing? One of
judgment or one of comfort? One of separation or one of grace? The proof of
the pudding is in the eating, the proof of the sword is in the cutting, and the
proof of the plowshare is in the plowing. What would be the proof of theology?

EPISTEMOLOGICAL MISFITTING:
LEARNING FROM DESIGN FAILURES

Those who are not quite at home—in a body, a discipline, a world—
have much to teach us about how things are built.

—*Sara Ahmed*[3]

---

2. Hans Walter Wolff, *Joel and Amos: A Commentary on the Books of the Prophets Joel and Amos*,
Hermeneia (Philadelphia: Fortress, 1977), 85.

3. Sara Ahmed, *What's the Use? On the Uses of Use* (Durham; London: Duke University Press,
2019), 19.

Design is the purposeful process of fitting a form to an environment, in partial control and partial dependence on both ends.[4] Better design, then—
whether of a house, a blade, or a doctrine—is form that is well-fitted to its
environment and to its purpose, and that constructively and creatively draws
out the potentials of its material toward given ends. Better design is one where
the capabilities and requirements of the user align with the properties of the
designed object to facilitate a desired outcome. In sum, better design is all
about affordances and their communication.[5]

> The affordances of the environment are what it offers the animal,
> what it provides or furnishes, either for good or ill. The verb to afford
> is found in the dictionary, the noun affordance is not. I have made it
> up. I mean by it something that refers to both the environment and
> the animal in a way that no existing term does. It implies the comple-
> mentarity of the animal and the environment.[6]

Gibson's term "affordances" was first coined in his ecological approach to
perception, but it resonates effortlessly with the field of architectural design:
Just as natural habitats and environments have affordances, so do built environments. In natural habitats, affordances develop in intricate co-evolutive
processes between multiple interacting agents and shaping forces. In architectural design, they are typically projected by a designer and/or discovered
by inhabitants or users. In both cases, affordances can neither be determined
unilaterally nor ahead of their actual use. They are relational, and thus often
multiple: A branch affords sitting for a bird, but not for a bear. The same
branch affords eating for the bear, but not for the bird. The branch's value for
either animal lies in its use—but it seems unnecessarily reductive to objectively
decide what its "proper" use ought to be. Different interacting agents may
discover and make use of different affordances.

Affordances in the built environment, too, are negotiated between the
designed structures and the inhabitants, visitors, and other users. As in natural
ecologies, thus in design, affordances do not describe self-contained properties of the object or environment, nor of the interacting agent. Rather, they
describe "a relationship between the properties of an object and the capabilities of the agent that determine just how the object could possibly be used."[7]

4. Cf. Christopher Alexander, *The Timeless Way of Building* (New York: Oxford University
Press, 1979).
5. For a brief history, see Jenny L. Davis, *How Artifacts Afford: The Power and Politics of Everyday
Things* (Cambridge: MIT, 2020), 25–43.
6. James J. Gibson, *The Ecological Approach to Visual Perception* (Dallas; London: Houghton
Mifflin, 1979), 127.
7. Norman, *The Design of Everyday Things*, 11.

The wall is for dividing spaces, the door is for entering, the chair is for sitting—the "forness" of these objects is relationally negotiated between user need and designer intention to accommodate these needs.

In its relational definition, the notion of affordances allows us to consider at the same time objective and subjective properties, physical and cognitive properties, facts and behavior. It pluralizes the consideration of uses and effects beyond the designer's intentions or even possibilities of anticipation. Affordances cannot be unilaterally determined by design—they depend on the capacities, needs, and imagination of the user, on the qualities of the object, and on the intentions, capabilities, and strategies of the designer. They may be projected by the designer, but those who use the object (or fail trying) also discover unintended affordances and disaffordances along the way.

Gibson points out that the theory of affordances marks "a radical departure from existing theories of value and meaning."[8] The way an object is used and what meaning it acquires in the world is not accidental or secondary to its design, but is what constitutes it. By virtue of its design, the object is not a piece of metal, but a sword or a plowshare; not a piece of fabric, but a blanket or a flag; not just ink on a page, but a certificate or a hymnal. The object registers in terms of what it allows one to do, is always already perceived as being "value-rich" rather than "value-free." Design choices are never neutral; they always *do* something or other. They facilitate certain kinds of use more than others, make some course of actions more plausible than others, enable some bodies more than others. As "that which mediates between features and outcomes,"[9] the notion of affordances allows us to conceptualize potential use in degrees rather than binaries, as well as to differentiate different intensities of influence. As they rely on the interpretation, agency, and capabilities of the user, affordances never altogether determine particular courses of action. Rather, affordances *suggest* certain uses over others, they "push, pull, enable, and constrain."[10] As the perceived action possibilities of an object in an ecology, affordances make up the implicit pedagogy of the designed object. They are a form of communication by way of design. As "[a]ny substance, any surface, any layout has some affordance for benefit or injury to someone,"[11] design becomes not only concerned with meaning but also with interpretation, and not only with pedagogy but also with ethics.

The notion of affordances prompts us to reframe our evaluation of designed objects from intention to actual effects, from conceptual responsibility to conceptual accountability, and from the intentions of the designer to the

8. Gibson, *The Ecological Approach to Visual Perception*, 140.
9. Davis, *How Artifacts Afford*, 42.
10. Davis, *How Artifacts Afford*, 6.
11. Gibson, *The Ecological Approach to Visual Perception*, 140.

experience of the user. It can be a powerful analytical tool, "demarcating the conditions under which technical systems *request, demand, encourage, discourage, refuse* and *allow*" certain uses over others, but also a critical tool that "lays the groundwork for intentional (re)design."[12]

As Don Norman translated the concept of affordances from the study of ecological perception to that of object design, thus queer literary theorist Eve Kosovsky Sedgwick has translated them to apply to conceptual entities—literary texts, ideological scripts, and social formations.[13] Sedgwick famously described the distinct epistemological affordances of "the closet"—a physical space lending its properties to a conceptual metaphor that denotes an epistemic ecology.[14] Sedgwick would go on to analyze patriarchy as "a web of valences and significations that, while deeply tendentious, can historically through its articulations and divisions offer both material and ideological affordances to women as well as men."[15] It is only consistent if a recent study has in turn recursively applied the notion of affordances to Sedgwick's own work: designed by the author, it now exists as an objective structure that "manifests spaces of composition for readers to inhabit and make use of."[16]

Like architectural structures, textual and conceptual structures can be inhabited and employed in different ways between builder intentions and user capabilities. Like other designed objects, texts and concepts supply embedded values and implicit pedagogies. They allow for certain uses more than others, present different functionalities to different kinds of users, although they can never unilaterally dictate their interpretations and applications. Like social formations and literary texts, thus theological ideas' and texts' meaning and value are negotiated in what uses they afford to potential and actual users, and agents can perceive, engage, and navigate them in different ways.

What happens if we put the design lens to *use* in theological reflection? Examining the affordances of theological notions through insights from design theory might allow us not only to better appreciate the *work* conceptual design is doing. Doing so might also allow us to diagnose ways in which theology can go *wrong*. Affordances are typically invisible—as long as they work, or as long as they work as intended. The power of affordances is that they make the use of an object seem natural and self-evident. A well-designed object minimizes

---

12. Davis, *How Artifacts Afford*, 20, italics in original.

13. I am indebted to Mark Jordan for this connection.

14. Eve Kosofsky Sedgwick, *Epistemology of the Closet* (Berkeley: University of California Press, 1990), 37.

15. Eve Kosofsky Sedgwick, *Between Men: English Literature and Male Homosocial Desire, Thirtieth Anniversary Edition* (New York: Columbia University Press, 2015), 141.

16. Tina Meyerhoff, "Affordances in the Work of Eve Kosofksy Sedgwick: Pedagogies of Writing, Reading, and Making," PhD thesis (City University of New York, 2019), 29.

the cognitive load for the user.[17] The object simply functions without us having to consciously engage and deliberate about how to use it, without having to know the intentions of the designer, without having to understand the philosophy or aesthetic theory behind it to know how to use it. That is, *if* the design "works."

Don Norman conceptualized affordances in the context of design *failures* (his famous "Norman doors," which we have already encountered in chapter 5). Design is a process of communication, and there are a variety of ways in which communication can go wrong. As affordances describe a relationship between functions of a designed object, and needs and capabilities of the user, a built or conceptual environment's design hinges on a multiplicity of factors. Affordances often become the site where design failures are discovered and addressed, as their relational quality helps diagnose misalignments between designers and users, vision and practical requirements, intended and factual uses, intended and factual users. As in designed artifacts, the affordances of textual and conceptual artifacts become crucial sites of negotiation, evaluation, and meaning—both positively and critically. We might ask: Where are the "Norman doors" of theology, which doctrinal "bugs" turn out to be features, and which failed affordances might yet be transformed into sites of insight and change?

What if, say, the functionality of an object exists but is not communicated well, and thus not discovered by the potential user? The already mentioned "Norman doors" diagnose a very particular failure of design. The functionality of the door to open is fully there, and the user is fully capable of operating it. However, Norman observed different people regularly making the same "mistakes" in the same environment of objects, either by failing to perceive the existent affordance altogether or by failing to discern correctly how they could interact with the functionality of the object. A sign on the door might explicitly read "push," but as long as the shape of the handles afford grasping and pulling, they will communicate to the average user—long before we consciously read the sign—that the door *is* for pulling. The failure lies not in the affordance, but in its communication, in the design's conflicting *signaling*, which obstructs its discovery and operation by the user.

Design is effective when the way users intuitively interact with the artifact is conducive to the desired results. Where that does not happen, thus Don Norman's conclusion, we ought to speak of design failure rather than user error. Regardless of the designer's intentions, if the created object does not effectively communicate how it can best be used, we ought to hold the

---

17. Cf. Steve Krug, *Don't Make Me Think, Revisited: A Common Sense Approach to Web Usability* (Berkeley: New Riders, 2014).

designer rather than the user accountable. Of course, designers cannot possibly anticipate all the different forces of the environment that will act upon their designed form, or entirely foresee how their artifacts will shape and condition, enable and disable, users in the future. But better designers will spend much time in observation, take into account how people move physically and "tick" psychologically. They will take care to align material properties and communication, signaling and actual functionality of their artifact: A handle will subtly communicate "pull" to the hand gripping it, a plate will subtly communicate "push" to the hand touching it, thus reducing the cognitive load for the user. And they will be dedicating themselves to critical and creative reflection about the subtle clues their design sends or fails to send, willing to go back and revise as needed. Better designers will devise structures that allow for early, regular, and critical feedback on key characteristics, and implement modifications in light of them.

A different kind of design failure obtains when the working of the affordance depends on certain assumptions about the user, effectively excluding those from use who do not fit those expectations. As every act of communication, design is directed to someone. You can be addressed by a design, and the design will tell you something about the intended user. It will enable people with certain characteristics to use it while denying access to and disabling others.[18] If the door is too heavy to be pushed open by an elderly person, if the photoelectric sensor is placed at a height where a person in a wheelchair will not trigger the opening mechanism, if the facial recognition software is unable to discern features in darker complexions, or if the width of the door frame does not allow a stroller to pass through, then the door, not affording passage to certain groups, effectively discriminates against them.

Communications scholar Sasha Costanza-Chock calls such design failures "disaffordances." Disaffordances occur, as Don Norman observed, when designers abstractly design for idealized human beings, where designers do not sufficiently account for variations in user features and design for standardized beings, or implicitly assume that users will be "just like them" in some crucial feature or capability. The user might be envisioned as the "average man," a standardization replete with racialized, class, and gendered effects.[19] Explicit standards or implicit assumptions effectively discriminate against or even altogether exclude users who are further away from the societal norm or different from the designer's implicit expectations.

18. Cf. Aimi Hamraie, *Building Access: Universal Design and the Politics of Disability* (Minneapolis: University of Minnesota Press, 2017).

19. Cf. Hamraie, ch.1 and ch. 2 on the invention of the "average man" as a template for industrial design and its effects on the standardization of bodies.

Like architectural designs, conceptual designs, too, can disafford access. Like architectural designs, conceptual designs can be based on idealized human beings, standardized images of the human, or intentionally or unintentionally project the designer's own characteristics into supposedly universally usable shapes. Feminist theologians have long pointed out that masculine language for God—whether resting on inadvertent projection or intentional idealization—reproduces the sexism of patriarchal societies theologically, effectively excludes experiences by people of other genders as source of theological reflection, and, in many traditions, has denied women access to ministerial vocations and positions of authority. Similarly, conceptions of the *imago Dei* that elevate certain forms of reason and rationality have been called out as excluding those from humanity who do not embody the same standards of reason—whether because of a disability, or because they have been racialized or gendered as "irrational." While such conceptual designs have often been criticized on the basis of their discriminatory effects, and rightly so, affordance theory allows us to analyze them more particularly as disaffordances by design—affording access and use of conceptual objects to some, while denying access and use to others.

As in the signaling failure recognized in Norman doors, one would hope that user feedback on disaffordances would prompt redesign. In both material and conceptual designs, disaffordances are not necessarily intentional in their excluding effects, nor is that the most important question. Disaffordances are complex sites of epistemological and political negotiation. Distinguishing affordances from disaffordances is not always straightforward or unambiguous. Lacks in accessibility may be trade-offs of central functionalities. For example, security doors are heavy for a reason: they intentionally make access more difficult. A parallel in theological conceptual design might be notions of the *imago Dei*—the conception affords infinite worth to human beings at exclusion of nonhuman creatures from theological consideration. Is the exclusion (with downstream theological effects for animal rights and ecological brutality) desired, intended, is it a necessary trade-off, and who decides which conceptual affordances and disaffordances count? The *imago Dei* design also runs on recognition software that has been developed and trained on the basis of specific groups of humans and has shown to be unreliable in equally picking out those of others. Are the resultant standardizations (and concomitant exclusions) of the human bug or feature, and who gets to decide?

Disaffordances may also be due to practical trade-offs between standardization and customization, between "universal" and individual design. Economies of scale require efficiency rather than the consideration of every possible case. In material design, standardizing the width of a door frame or the height of a kitchen counter is cost-efficient for production, installation, and maintenance, and it serves the vast majority of the population well as well as minimizing the negotiation that goes into everyday navigation, change in scenery, or repairs. It would not only be wildly inefficient to custom design every door and kitchen, it would also lead to more accidents and potentially, to larger-scale disaffordances. Defending the theological design of *imago Dei*, the theologian might offer that losing any conceptual distinction between the human and the nonhuman comes with its own losses, and that defining humanity by way of reason or spirituality rightly identifies capacities that *in most scenarios* accurately pick out humans from nonhuman creatures.

Both in material and in conceptual design, then, disaffordances are the cost of doing business, but the cost is rarely equally distributed. It reflects existing values and assumptions, reproduces and amplifies them in the material and conceptual designs we use. Costanza-Chock thus calls disaffordances "the most visible instances of a generalized and pervasive process by which existing technology design processes systematically reproduce (and are reproduced by) the matrix of domination."[20] They challenge us to recognize in them forms of "hard-coded Eurocentricity"[21] and treat them as the micro-aggressions they produce. How do we adjudicate different users' needs and capabilities with one another, and with other requirements in design processes? Who is enabled and disabled by design? Questions of justice and the values imbedded in our design emerge.

Design's poles of standardization and customization in navigating such questions might map onto different sets of commitments in theology, too. Standardization means designing for the "typical" (or preferred?) use case and the "average" (or dominant?) user, maximizing the cost-benefit ratio but excluding and invisibilizing users and uses who do not fit the "standard" (or normalized?) version of humanity. Customization diversifies design for a broader variety of use cases and user characteristics but is less universally applicable, and less "efficient" in terms of production and resources. The former might resemble the design principles in Systematic Theologies with its aspired universal applicability and neutrality toward differences in users and scenarios. The latter might resemble the design principles in Contextual Theologies with their attention to particularities in users and context. The different characteristics reflect values and choices that in practice will conflict to a certain degree. But, in material design as in theology, we might also lean into the creative potential of "failing to get it" sketched in chapter 5 and ask, "are these the only choices"?

20. Sasha Costanza-Chock, *Design Justice: Community-Led Practices to Build the Worlds We Need* (Cambridge: MIT, 2020), 46.
21. Costanza-Chock, *Design Justice*, 49.

In design theory, proponents of so-called *Universal Design* have long advocated for strategies beyond both standardization and customization in order to maximize the diversity of human experience and capabilities that any given design could accommodate. The notion was coined in 1985 by Ronald Mace and gained great popularity. Originating in disability activism, Universal Design was developed to make the built environment more usable, inhabitable, and visitable for disabled people. But rather than advocating for designed customized to disabled users, it simply advertised its principles as *better* for *everyone*: requiring less dexterity, mobility, and overall physical effort to navigate for a variety of body shapes, sizes, and capabilities.

> In the end there was nothing "special" or "handicapped" about [Universal Design]. This kitchen was merely made to work with the real people who lived there. Its universality came not from abstract specifications but from the lives of real people, creating spaces for their daily lives. No detailing or style or luxury could possibly be more precious than this simple quality. Universal design is perhaps just an overly clinical name for something we think we know but perhaps we don't—good design.[22]

Contrary to the possible interpretations of the name, Universal Design is not a hubristic or universalist claim about an obtainable quality or a strategy to achieve it. Its universality remains always elusive and aspirational. Mace explained,

> I have never seen a building or facility I would say is universally usable. I don't know that it's possible to create one. I'm not sure it's possible to create anything that's universally usable. It's not that there's a weakness in the term. We use that term because it's the most descriptive of what the *goal* is, something people can live with and afford.[23]

22. Cf. John Hockenberry, "Design Is Universal," Metropolis Magazine, December 2004 cited by Hamraie, *Building Access*, 7. While this perception itself has contributed greatly to its success, it is sometimes also charged with invisibilizing disabled people or concerns with its emphasis on marketability and usability by "everyone." Critical disability scholar Aimi Hamraie gives an extensive historical account and critical appreciation of Universal Design's epistemology and its valuation of disabled users' experience without claiming that everyone is disabled. In particularly nifty fashion, Hamraie demonstrates how on a meta-level, the concept of Universal Design itself is a design experiment, adapting in response to user response—an inadvertent case study for the idea of conceptual design that we want to develop here! Cf. Hamraie, *Building Access*, especially chap. 6.

23. Ronald Mace, "A Perspective on Universal Design," in *Designing for the 21st Century: An International Conference on Universal Design*, ed. Jan Reagan (Hofstra University, Hempstead, New York, 1998).

Theology has a long tradition of aiming at universal truths, but also counts on strong sensibilities for the theological, ethical, and political issues that attend human tendencies of projecting their own experience as universal. As in so-called Universal Design the aspirational universality of theology might function as a critical horizon that sustains the need for further examination as to the accommodation of diverse experiences, rather than the aspiration to positively come up with conceptual designs that fit everyone equally. In design as in theology, there are important limits to inclusion, not only practical limits as signaled by efficiency and feasibility but also the structural conditions of the logics of recognition, legibility, and normalization.[24] Given language's and image's conceptual determinations and differences in the intended and actual users of theological notions, we might ask—with Barth, no less—whether a universal design of theology is "necessary" or even "desirable."[25] As in design, so in theology, solutions *fitted* to different needs, different contexts and epistemic ecologies might be more adequate to the communicative and practical ends of theology—its witness. Of course, if in design questions of scale are important at a production and cost level, so they remain important in theology for epistemic reasons: "To each one their own theology" seems as unsatisfying, as one generic theology that affords the same uses in all conditions seems implausible.

Pushes for *Universal Design* have more recently been theoretically surpassed by calls for *Design Justice*. The emphasis on justice attends to the limits of inclusion practically and strategically. Rather than attempting to inclusively design "for all" at the same time, it makes transparent that designers have to make a conscious decision about *which* (i.e., *whose*) experiences to privilege at any given time—and draws the conclusion that the ethical choice is always the one that redresses the dominant dynamics and privileges marginalized experiences. In theological design, something similar has arguably been promoted in Liberation Theology's "preferential option for the poor," which insists that if theology proclaims good news for the whole world, its proclamation needs to extend to the depths of inhumanity. In order to achieve that, a supposedly universal "standard" form is not enough, nor is impartial neutrality. Rather, a radical commitment is demanded to center and prioritize those who have been considered "non-persons" by the prevailing systems.[26] In its confrontation of the structures of sin in the world, the universality of God's love entails and requires a strategic predilection toward the least. In its testimony to this God's love, should not theological design, too, entail and require a strategic

---

24. Cf. Tonstad, "The Limits of Inclusion," 2015.

25. Cf. Barth's famous push-back in, "Wünschbarkeit und Möglichkeit eines allgemeinen Reformierten Glaubensbekenntnisses. 1925."

26. Gutiérrez, *A Theology of Liberation*.

predilection toward the marginalized and excluded, and thus a strategic undoing of conceptual disaffordances?

KISS ME ON THE GAY ANTI-HOMELESS
BENCH, OR: ATONING THE ATONEMENT

Sometimes a design flaw is obviously a design flaw. Sometimes an exclusion is intentional—a feature of the design. Sometimes, however, it is an open question whether a given affordance or disaffordance is "a bug or a feature"—to speak in the idiom of software design. The response might depend on the needs, assumptions, intentions, and values of those conducting the assessment. The Gospel of Mark tells us a story of a paralytic whose four friends, breaking through a roof to get him to Jesus, overcome physical access issues in the built environment (Mark 2:1–12). In the story, the design of the house was not flawed. Its built structure afforded protection for a gathering of people against the elements. Even as it may not have intentionally excluded the paralytic man in particular, as a whole, the limitation of access to the space it afforded was quite deliberate. The house did not fail to afford its functionality to the intended users nor did it send mismatching signals about its possible use. The four friends did not encounter a design failure—they *disagreed* with a design that was working as intended.

Queer theorist Sarah Ahmed notes the self-reinforcing structure of disaffordances: "the system is working by stopping those who are trying to transform the system. This means that *to transform a system we have to stop it from working.*"[27] The four friends recognized that the social and architectural design would disafford them access, and that the only way to attain access for their friend was to disrupt the built structures from doing the work they were supposed to do. They thus actively disregarded (and disbanded) the intended use, literally breaking the design in favor of one that would afford access to their friend. The crowd, therefore, was also not wrong in their judgment of their actions as blasphemous—it rightly recognized the violation of the original design.

Who gets to decide, when push comes to shove, what uses a design *ought* to afford, whose needs *count*, and what constitutes *fair* use? And would we by and large privilege the designer or the users' (and, which users'?) interpretation in such discernment?

Consider the design of a bench, produced for a public space, such as a park, or maybe in front of a church. The bench sends very clear signals about its affordances. As you walk through the park, the first thing you would notice are

27. Ahmed, *What's the Use*, 212.

the blazing colors of the paint, coating the wooden beam in the hues of the rainbow. A bench issues an invitation, and what might express an invitation to do so better than the colorful stripes of Noah's ark, a symbol of life, gay pride, and LGBTQIA+ advocacy that functionally exclaims, "All are welcome."

But *are* all welcome on this bench? At second glance, another design feature comes into view: the bars that break up the bench's surface. While the bench affords sitting, it disaffords lying down for all but the smallest human body shapes. While the bench makes it easy to sit here and look over the park, it makes it virtually impossible to sleep on it. Whoever designed the bench might not have perceived its two messages as contradictory. Maybe they explicitly envisioned a nice gay couple kissing on this bench even as they were equally explicitly commissioned to prevent use by the homeless population.

The irony, of course, is that these are not disjunct groups: The homeless person excluded by design may very well be queer. Recent studies find that a disproportionate number of youth experiencing homelessness identify as LGB (around 30% as compared to around 3.5% of the general population, i.e., homeless youth are 8x more likely to be queer than their housed peers), or as trans/genderqueer (around 4% as compared to 0.3% of the general population, i.e., homeless youth are 13.5x more likely to be trans/genderqueer than their peers). Gender minorities (trans*, nonbinary, genderqueer people) are almost 6x as likely as the general population to have had recent experiences with homelessness, while sexual minorities (LGB people) are still twice as likely as the general population to have recent experiences with homelessness. 16.9% of sexual minorities have experienced homelessness at some point in their lives, as opposed to 6.2% in the general population—almost 3x as likely.[28] The rejection of many queer people by their family is compounded by the harassment and abuse they experience in many homeless shelters. Intersectional factors like race, class, drug use, and sex work further exacerbate these effects. What message is this bench sending to the queer or transgender homeless youth? Hardly one of welcome. If this is not a design flaw but the intended effect, then it is highly cynical to clothe this message in the colors of the rainbow.

Which affordances and disaffordances are perceived and available might change, we have said, due to their relational nature. A door may afford opening only to people of a specific height or physical strength, maybe even intentionally, to afford certain forms of security. A bench might afford support for those who are seeking a romantic scene for kissing, but not for those who

---

28. Bianca D. M. Wilson et al., "Homelessness among LGBT Adults in the US," UCLA School of Law, Williams Institute (2020). While no reliable numbers are available for lifetime homelessness experiences of trans people, they might even be higher still.

sorely need a place for the night. Disability and crip studies have coined the term "misfits" to highlight that it is not certain bodies who fail to conform to the designed environment; "misfits" are produced by the design when it "does not sustain the shape and function of the body that enters it."[29]

Exclusion is not only a social and political fact, it is also an epistemological one. Not needing to understand an affordance is a privilege. In turn, people for whom a design *does not work* typically have greater insight into how an object *factually* works than those to whom it seems natural. "Ask an architect about their work, and you may learn more about the style, form, materials, structure, and cost of a building than the bodies or minds meant to inhabit it. Examine any doorway, window, toilet, chair, or desk in that building, however, and you will find the outline of the body meant to use it,"[30] Aimi Hamraie notes. Ask, in turn, a body excluded by the design, and they will be able to tell you about both the kinds of uses the design affords as well as of its particular disaffordances that remain invisible to those privileged by it.[31]

The homeless person knows more about this bench then someone who just rested on it on a walk. They notice not only the affordances that remain invisible to the intended users but also the particular disaffordances for unintended users. If you have never experienced homelessness, the conflicting signals of the bench might not even have registered—simply because, *for you* there was no conflicting message, no disaffordance. If you are able to use a design without needing to understand it, it most likely was designed with you or someone *like* you in mind, not only serving your practical need but even alleviating your cognitive load in doing so. In the case of our bench, it is quite conceivable (although not necessary) that the designer is a queer person, but it is unlikely that they have ever experienced homelessness.

Knowledge and access are interwoven: Disaffordances actively disable certain users, rendering them effectively less competent to use the design. Being disafforded access affords its own unique kind of knowledge of how an affordance works. Knowing how an affordance works or does not work allows one to create different kinds of affordances for access: enables creative redesign. In practices that Hamraie calls "knowing-making," those disabled by a design become "lead users" who innovate solutions for the design problems they encounter in their built environments. Epistemic activism might both guide

29. Rosemarie Garland-Thomson, "The Story of My Work: How I Became Disabled," *Disability Studies Quarterly* 34, no. 2 (2014), cf. also Rosemarie Garland-Thomson, "Misfits: A Feminist Materialist Disability Concept," *Hypatia* 26, no. 3 (2011): 591–609.

30. Hamraie, *Building Access*, 19.

31. Such epistemic privilege of the otherwise underprivileged or marginalized is one of the major insights from Feminist Standpoint Epistemology. Cf. Patricia Hill Collins, "Learning from the Outsider Within"; Collins, *Intersectionality as Critical Social Theory* (Durham: Duke University Press, 2019).

the pursuit of justice and the pursuit of better knowledge at the same time, challenging not only "the built arrangements of segregated spaces, but also the structures of knowledge production itself."[32]

As in design so in theology, the imagined users often look much like the designer. This is not altogether surprising. But it brings to the fore the crucial epistemological importance of misfits to reveal the ways in which theological designs, too, *work* (or not). It is the design that enables or disables different users in different ways, but only when diverse bodies start using a design does this become explicit. Designers should not balk at what to them might appear a disruption or misunderstanding of their work, but welcome it as critical feed-back to improve it. Unaddressed users and unintended uses are irreplaceable sources of insight and critical partners in redesign processes. As Sarah Ahmed says, "Those who are not quite at home—in a body, a discipline, a world— have much to teach us about how things are built."[33] As in design so in theology we might imagine a world where "the blame for the misfit is placed upon the environment and it is subsequently changed."[34]

There are many rainbow-painted anti-homeless benches in theology, many cases where the practical effect of the design belies its stated message, where the intention and the actual use tell two different stories, and where this only becomes apparent when we complicate our analysis of affordances by intersectional difference. I, for one, want to read such cases as design failures inviting creative redesign, rather than as cynicism. Doing theology through a design lens would make such conflicts legible and addressable in a different way. Let us consider a by-now classical example of Constructive-theological critique of Systematic Theology, Womanist contentions against atonement theology.

Theologies of the atonement articulate that Christ's suffering revealed God's love and faithfulness and became redemptive in reconciling humankind with God. The atonement thus marks God's victory over death and sin, which prove furthermore unable to separate humankind from God's love. Some interpretations cast atonement in the logic of a penal substitutionary model. According to John Calvin, Christ was "put in place of evildoers as surety and pledge—submitting himself even as the accused—to bear and suffer all the punishments that they ought to have sustained."[35] Like many other interpreters, Calvin highlights a double substitution, a redemptive switching of places:

---

32. Hamraie, *Building Access*, 10.

33. Ahmed, *What's the Use*, 19.

34. Edward Steinfeld, "Barrier Free Access in the Man-Made Environment: A Review of Current Literature. Interim Report," (Syracuse University, NY School of Architecture: Department of Housing and Urban Development, Washington DC, Office of Policy Development and Research, October 1975), 14.

35. Calvin, *Institutes*, II:16, 10.

"Death held us captive under its yoke; Christ, in our stead, gave himself over to its power to deliver us from it."[36] Atonement theology maintains that Christ suffered *for us* at the cross, in the double sense of "in our stead" and "for our benefit."

As the homeless queer kid might scoff at the bench and point out that its "all are welcome" obviously did not include them, so some Womanist theologians have scoffed at the doctrine of atonement and pointed out that the "in our stead" surely did not translate into "for our benefit" for them. Delores Williams famously draws out how notions of substitution and vicarious suffering have not only *not* alleviated Black women's plight but even further reinforced their vicarious suffering in diverse roles of substitution, both under slavery and after it.[37] Neither the traditional comfort promised by the doctrine of atonement, nor Black theology's insistence that redemptive suffering would be liberative[38] was found to match Black women's lived *experience* of atonement theology.

Of course, one might argue that the doctrine was never benevolently designed, but served to justify submission and even suffering all along—think of the histories of monasticism and martyrdom, for example. But let us jettison such suspicions in favor of a more charitable reading. We might then maintain, with leading proponents of the Reformed tradition, that atonement is "full of wonderful consolation,"[39] as it presents the sacrifice to end all sacrifices (Heb. 10); that it reveals our "filial relation to God,"[40] and that it is ultimately "about the initiative and aims of God's love."[41] The doctrine, we would find, is about comfort, about the limitation of punishment, about the limitation of suffering, and about the liberation of the believer from the physical and emotional burden of such a conception. This doctrine is supposed to be a door, not a wall; a bench that affords resting to *all*, including disenfranchised populations.

Delores Williams' critique thus points out a particular disaffordance of the doctrine: The doctrine meets bodies and experiences whom, it turns out, it

---

36. Calvin, *Institutes*, II:16, 7.

37. Williams, *Sisters in the Wilderness*.

38. From Martin Luther King, Jr., to Cecil Wayne Cone, *The Identity Crisis in Black Theology* (Nashville: Barbour, 2003); J. Deotis Roberts, *Liberation and Reconciliation: A Black Theology* (Maryknoll: Orbis, 1994); James H. Cone, *A Black Theology of Liberation*, 40th Anniversary edition (Maryknoll: Orbis, 2010).

39. Calvin, *Institutes*, II:16, 10.

40. John McLeod Campbell, *The Nature of the Atonement and Its Relation to Remission of Sins and Eternal Life* (Cambridge: Macmillan, 1856), 185.

41. Martha Schull Gilliss, "Resurrecting the Atonement," in *Feminist and Womanist Essays in Reformed Dogmatics*, ed. Amy Plantinga Pauw and Serene Jones, 125–39, Columbia Series in Reformed Theology (Louisville: Westminster John Knox, 2006), 126.

was not designed to accommodate, and whom it thus "misfits." On behalf of Black women, Williams reports, actually, this doctrine does not afford me the promised functionality of love, comfort, consolation, end to vicarious suffering, end to self-sacrifice. This door does not afford me access; this bench is not welcoming me; this tree of life once more turns into a cross that I have to bear. Rather than offering hope, life, and freedom from the powers of sin, this cross has only glorified suffering: Black women's coerced as well as voluntary surrogacy, and the abuse that has attended it, have been justified and legitimated by it. Rather than offering liberation and emancipation, this cross has only reinforced "violence, victimization and undeserved suffering."[42]

Williams' critique of atonement theology can thus be considered an apt exemplification of epistemic "misfitting": It is more and something different than a bug report of a design failure. It reveals systemic discriminatory effects of a design that obtain because the design was modeled after a specific, and implicit shape of human existence. Not only has it neglected nonnormative bodies and experiences, it also has actively disafforded them access in a way that has perpetuated the discrimination and violence they already experience from society at large.

Ethics and work for justice cannot focus merely on the application of theological notions, but on the epistemology and politics written into their design. Williams' uncovering of the disaffordances of atonement theology immediately points us to the conditions of its knowledge production: The doctrine's historical designers and intended users as well as its limitations are cast into sharp relief, and we gain insight into how a change in the production of theological knowledge might result in quite different doctrinal designs.[43] Indeed, as lead users become designers, Womanist theologians have designed their own christological solutions that afford the comfort and abundance of life asserted in Jesus Christ that they failed to find in the cross. Delores Williams herself calls into question "whether the image of a surrogate-God has salvific power for black women or whether this image supports and reinforces the exploitation that has accompanied their experience with surrogacy."[44] Her redesign, informed by biblical scholarship and sociology, foregrounds the life of Jesus and his ministry of healing rather than his death. It advocates a hermeneutic of survival and quality of life as a more realistic as well as exegetically more accurate vision for the flourishing of Black women intended by God than the exodus narrative of liberation or redemptive suffering advocated by Black (male) theologians or feminists.

---

42. Williams, *Sisters in the Wilderness*, 217.
43. Cf. "The aim of theological and economic reflection should not be a new system of distribution, but a different system of production" (Althaus-Reid, "Outing Theology," 148).
44. Williams, *Sisters in the Wilderness*, 179.

Other Womanist theologians, sharing Williams' diagnosis, developed different christological redesigns. Jacquelyn Grant defended a high Christology in which "Christ is a black woman," the divine co-sufferer with the plight of the most oppressed.[45] Taking into account the comprehensive testimony about Jesus, Kelly Brown Douglas insisted that God is as Christ does, but that the cross ought not to be read apart from the rest of the story: through the incarnation, ministry, death, and resurrection of Jesus, God lives and struggles in solidarity with society's victims and promises them new life, too.[46] JoAnne Marie Terrell, further, points out that despite the problems that Williams names around surrogacy, Black women have historically found salvation and meaning in Jesus' tragic and unjust death at the cross, which afforded them a transformative self-understanding as "sacramental witnesses." Rather than reducing them to suffering and victimization, Jesus' cross has thus empowered them to be agents and mediators of God's love for them and for the world as "victims-become-victors."[47]

My interest here lies not in promoting any particular version of such christological redesign. My interest lies in elucidating to my fellow Systematic Theologians that dismissing Womanist critiques of atonement as heretical or even ignorant of the doctrinal exigencies ("Let's hand them a manual!") misses the mark. Their "misfitting" of atonement theologies reveals a similar design incongruence with intersectionally discriminatory effects as we have seen them in the queer anti-homeless bench; their adaptations are no "user error," but point to a *design failure.* Womanist counter-proposals, in turn, are by no means iconoclastic, they insist rather faithfully on the promised *beneficia Christi*: redemption, consolation, and reconciliation; life, hope, and flourishing as discerned in mediating the biblical witness and the faith of the church. Womanist redesigns of Christology might thus be understood as conceptual versions of Hamraie's "knowing-making,"[48] constructive curb-cutting of a doctrine until it affords the promised functionality in relation to these unanticipated users. In this sense, Womanist Christologies that draw on Jesus' ministerial vision rather than his suffering and death, that put his cross into the larger context of his life, or that emphasize the sacramentality of his death can be understood as "user-led innovation,"[49] where users faithfully stick with the original prod-

45. Jacquelyn Grant, *White Women's Christ and Black Women's Jesus: Feminist Christology and Womanist Response*, American Academy of Religion Academy Series 64 (Atlanta: Scholars Press, 1989).

46. Kelly Brown Douglas, *The Black Christ* (Maryknoll: Orbis, 1994).

47. JoAnne Marie Terrell, *Power in the Blood? The Cross in the African American Experience* (Maryknoll: Orbis, 1998), 34.

48. Hamraie, *Building Access*, 68.

49. Eric Von Hippel, "Lead Users: A Source of Novel Product Concepts," *Management Science* 32, no. 7 (1986): 791–805.

uct but, knowing their own needs better than the "professional" designers do, adapt and tweak it further to meet them more precisely.

More in general, the debate around atonement reveals theology's inherent need for critical feedback from "outsiders" and "misfits"—those who historically have been excluded from its production, those whom our traditional designs did not take into account and whose bodies and lives we fail by it, those who find no use in it, and those who are all but disabled by it. Theological "misfits" reveal previously invisible limits or even failures of the theological designs we inhabit. As bug reports, they invite us theologians (especially of the Systematic variety) to go back to the drawing board and redesign our theological notions. As user-led innovations, they even offer us solutions that honor the materials they work with while reshaping them to address their particular requirements.

Theological designers would do well to listen to those who tell us about the uses our designs afford or fail to afford. As in architectural, so in conceptual design, "Those who are not quite at home—in a body, a discipline, a world—have much to teach us about how things are built."[50] Ideally, we would develop structurally maintained practices and recursive publics to facilitate such reports rather than penalize them. Theological misfits and queer misappropriations might even gesture toward otherwise possibilities that are less heterodox than they are eschatological.

QUEER USE

Queer-feminist theorist Sarah Ahmed has coined the term "queer use" for the fact that "things can be used in ways other than for which they were intended or by those other than for whom they were intended."[51] The designer might see in queer use a failure of design: that the design did not sufficiently convey how it was supposed to be used *properly*, that it was inefficiently designed so that the user adapted and repurposed it, or that it simply unintendedly lent itself to unforeseen creative reappropriations. Sometimes queer use might be an active refusal or a resistance to the dominant or just the intended uses of a design. It can be a form of subversion, of poaching, a form of "occupying" design and opening it up to otherwise possibilities. Sometimes, queer use simply *happens*, apart from any grand aspirations or intentional subversions, as when birds nest in a mailbox.

50. Ahmed, *What's the Use*, 19.
51. Ahmed, *What's the Use*, 199.

Queer use is more than an adjective for a particular kind of use. Rather, the range of factual uses points to the queerness of use as such: its ambiguity, its unforeseeable turns, and its open futures. Queer use is what *queers* use as it "make[s] use strange": It marks use as a site of ongoing epistemic negotiation and material transformation.[52] Queer use might even be strategically employed in a form of epistemic activism, "to make use audible, to listen to use, to bring to the front what ordinarily recedes into the background."[53]

Queer use thus has a revelatory function in making implicit assumptions of design explicit, its incongruities, its effects, and its potentialities—what could have been and what might yet be. Queer use also has a transformative function: the alternative uses it generates intervene in the epistemic and material order of things, they open up new and different possibilities for interacting agents, and change the nature of the designed object as well as its environment. Queer use does not succumb to the naiveté of accepting things as they are as good, or even "fixable," nor does it give in to the heroic temptation of refusal. Instead, it offers an "ethics of finitude,"[54] much more messy, much less clear-cut, yet fervently committed to "use the tools available"[55] even where no complete dismantling is in sight, instead preserving the marks and injuries they leave.

Ahmed's notion of queer use draws on design logics in engaging built environments, structures, and objects. It can also be applied to conceptual design. Ahmed reflects, "To recycle or reuse a word is to reorient one's relation to a scene that holds its place, as memory, as container, however leaky."[56] Conditioned by the past, but not confined to it, open to a future, but never starting from scratch, to queer use means to "*recover* a potential from materials that have been left behind, all the things you can do with paper if you do not follow instructions."[57] When applied to conceptual objects, queer use resonates with reading strategies that have been offered in queer hermeneutics. Queer use queers them, too.

Eve Kosovsky Sedgwick famously distinguished between paranoid and reparative reading strategies. With the provocative subtitle, *You're So Paranoid, You Probably Think This Introduction Is about You*,[58] Sedgwick described such readings as paranoid, which, based on a hermeneutics of suspicion, are primarily defensive, expose all ugly truths, and do not experience any bad

52. Ahmed, *What's the Use*, 198.
53. Ahmed, *What's the Use*, 198.
54. Ahmed, *What's the Use*, 226.
55. Ahmed, *What's the Use*, 17.
56. Ahmed, *What's the Use*, 198.
57. Ahmed, *What's the Use*, 208, italics in original.
58. Eve Kosofsky Sedgwick, "Paranoid Reading and Reparative Reading; or: You're So Paranoid, You Probably Think This Introduction Is about You," in *Novel Gazing: Queer Readings in Fiction*, ed. Eve Kosofsky Sedgwick, 1–39 (Durham: Duke University Press, 1997).

surprises, because they have already expected the worst. In turn, reparative readings are those that are "on the side of multiplicity, surprise, rich divergence, consolation, creativity, and love."[59] Paranoia is often perceived—or self-stylized—as the more critical, more sophisticated mode of engagement, especially in a world that has been less than welcoming in the past. But, Sedgwick prompts us to wonder, is paranoia's hypercritical negativity not a defensive reflex that ultimately confines the engaging subject to a repetition of the negation it experienced? While paranoid readings are good at "anticipating trouble, explaining negative attachment, ordering information," they are also mimetic, reproducing what they anticipate, and they are notoriously bad at "imputing positive motives for desires to ameliorate, to rebuild, tending to discount these either as naivety or delusion."[60] As *warranted* as paranoia might thus be, we might also ask, is it *desirable*? Could there be other, more capacious possibilities—not as accurately accounting for the world as it is, but as opening it up to what it might yet become? Heather Love notes that, "For groups constituted by historical injury, the challenge is to engage with the past without being destroyed by it."[61]

Queer-feminist thinkers have argued reparative readings might be *more* critical than paranoid ones: Reparative readings reject the logic of pure beginnings as well as that of the strong and detached subject position, and instead display creativity as well as faithfulness in the face of the messy entanglements of human history. "No less acute than the paranoid position, no less realistic, no less attached to a project of survival, and neither less nor more delusional or fantasmatic, [reparative reading strategies] succeed in extracting sustenance from the objects of a culture—even of a culture whose avowed desire has often been not to sustain them."[62] Queer theologian Susannah Cornwall has argued for understanding the reparative strategy as a distinctly eschatological reading—as it opts for a better future, it also practices "sociability with the dead."[63] Reparative readings do not condone any of the harm done, nor do they strive to redeem what has been. We might better understand them, with a nod to Genesis 32:26, as wrestling with their inherited materials until they yield a blessing.

---

59. Heather Love, "Truth and Consequences: On Paranoid Reading and Reparative Reading," *Criticism* 52, no. 2 (2010): 235–41, 237.

60. Susannah Cornwall, "'Something There Is That Doesn't Love a Wall': Queer Theologies and Reparative Readings," *Theology & Sexuality* 21, no. 1 (2015): 20–35, 21.

61. Love, *Feeling Backward*, 1.

62. Sedgwick, "Paranoid Reading," 35.

63. Cornwall, "Something There Is That Doesn't Love a Wall," 27.

Many scholars suggest that both strategies should be practiced alongside one another, or that a "third" is needed.[64] In queer theory and theology, a certain "reparative turn" has, if not replaced the paranoid strategies of queer anti-normativity and antisociality, then complemented and to some extent decentered them in "the work of love."[65] These reading strategies' affective relationship retains connections to the imagined or real authors and contexts of the studied texts. In queer use, designers recede even more into the background behind the objects of engagement than in textual study. In the material and conceptual design cases studied in this chapter, the criteria for redesign were found in matching design functionality and user need more adequately. In that sense, they were deeply reparative projects. Yet redesign goes far beyond reparation and restoration, without being constricted to paranoid interpretation.

Ahmed's "queer use," applied to hermeneutics, could provide just such a third strategy—not only of reading but also of use; not only for object design but also for the conceptual design of theology. Where paranoia and reparation filter into hermeneutics from psychoanalysis and enter theory as seemingly opposed styles, "queer use" as a material reading strategy, a hermeneutic of use, appropriation, and redesign might offer a way to blur the false binary of paranoid and reparative modes of engagement.

Rather than moving from a mode of paranoid critique to reparative redemption of given materials, queer use's conceptual *repurposing* (the reuse of the same object toward a different purpose) and *recycling* (the material transformation of its material toward a different purpose) include critical and redemptive moves, but neither is the exclusive or even motivating factor. Queer use does not spare the designer's intention its hermeneutics of suspicion. Its faithfulness is not to them. It lies squarely with the future, even as it continues working with given environments and materials, without committing to their historical uses or their original purpose. Queer use's creativity lies in its eschatological imagination that offers critique without disengaging and salvages without redeeming as it directs materials toward new and "better" ends, without restoring their intent or disambiguating their meaning.

In the utopian vision of queer use, swords can become plowshares. Doctrines that have been weaponized can become instruments of critique as well as redemption, or something beyond them entirely. Feminist and queer

64. Cf., e.g., Love, "Truth and Consequences"; Cornwall, "Something There Is That Doesn't Love a Wall."
65. Deborah P. Britzman, "Theory Kindergarten," in *Regarding Sedgwick: Essays on Queer Culture and Critical Theory*, ed. Stephen M. Barber and David L. Clark, 121–42 (New York: Routledge, 2002), 123.

reappropriations of the doctrine of sin might constitute such an example of queer use in its creative repurposing and non-redemptive salvaging.

SWORDS TO PLOWSHARES, OR:
SALVAGING BEYOND REDEMPTION

Imagine you found a blade, we said. Now, think of the doctrine of sin as such a blade.

Like a blade, the doctrine of sin affords cutting. But cutting is an activity that can serve a variety of different, and seemingly contradictory uses: It could fulfill a function in the battlefield or in the corn field, in the kitchen or in the hospital. The meaning of the doctrine lies not only in the functionality of this blade but also in the end toward which it is used. The blade of sin can be used as an instrument of warfare: of boundary drawing, condemnation, and exclusion. It can also be used as a surgical instrument: one of critique that, oriented toward excision could become an instrument of healing and hope. In sum, the doctrine of sin can be used as an instrument of judgment or as an instrument of grace.

Historically, it has often been employed to demarcate the boundaries of orthodox faith or orthoprax conduct. In this vein, "sin" has been wielded by dominant groups against those framed as deviant and abnormal, or against those who threatened the inherited power distribution. Even so, the blade of sin has creatively been repurposed in the opposite direction. Appropriating the blade that had once been wielded against them, people have turned the same instrument into a scathing indictment of their oppressors.

In such a turn-table maneuver, second wave feminists noted that wielded by men, the doctrine of sin's affordances reinforced the subjugation of women under patriarchy: it lent itself to condemning women's emancipation and political self-assertion as pride and hubris.[66] In her paradigm-shifting essay, *The Human Situation: A Feminine View*, Valerie Saiving did something that we might adequately capture only through a design lens: rather than debating whether sin was rightly defined, or whether the feminist movement was rightly identified as falling under this verdict, Saiving brought the *affordances* of the doctrine to attention in their relational constitution by the engaging agent.

The doctrine of sin, she confirmed, possessed the traditionally ascribed capacity for "identification with pride, will-to-power, exploitation, self-assertiveness, and the treatment of others as objects rather than persons," and it

---

66. Valerie Saiving, "The Human Situation: A Feminine View," *The Journal of Religion* 40, no. 2 (1960): 100–112.

subsequently conceptualized redemption not incorrectly as the countermotion to such sin, "restoring to man what he fundamentally lacks (namely, sacrificial love, the I-Thou relationship, the primacy of the personal, and, ultimately, peace.)"[67] However, Saiving's critique uncovered that such traditional uses were not object-inherent qualities, but instead depended on the relationship between the doctrinal object and its—historically predominantly male—users.

The same instrument, Saiving found, when applied to the experience of women instead of men, ought to be able to pick out quite different phenomena as sinful, namely an "underdevelopment or negation of self" rather than its self-aggrandizement.[68] The lens of affordances elucidates that such a different outcome is quite germane to the same object's functionality in relation to user characteristics. In light of the different uses the same doctrine might yet afford to different users, Saiving thus urged for a conceptual distinction between "Masculine" and "Feminine Sin." In sum, Saiving shifted the analysis of the doctrine from its meaning to its affordances in interaction with diverse users.

Other feminist theologians like Rosemary Radford Ruether and Mary McClintock Fulkerson went a step further in wielding the doctrinal blade against the tradition from which they inherited it: Rather than merely showing that the blade was capable of cutting different things, they demonstrated that it could be wielded to defeat the very powers that had fashioned it. In particular, they used the conceptual grammar of sin to denounce patriarchy itself as committing the sin of self-aggrandizement and idolatry,[69] diagnosed sexism as "distorted relationality,"[70] or even as "original sin" contrary to God's plan.[71] Given this usefulness for core feminist concerns, some went so far as to claim that "no single topic in Christian theology has more resonance with feminist theory than the much disdained topic of sin."[72] Rachel Baard succinctly sums up the edge of such critique in the observation, "much of classical sin-talk is so destructive in the lives of women that it becomes sinful itself."[73]

---

67. Saiving, "The Human Situation: A Feminine View," 107.

68. Saiving, "The Human Situation: A Feminine View," 109.

69. In this inflection, sin was even used by "radical" post-theological and gender essentialist feminists like Mary Daly, *Beyond God the Father: Toward a Philosophy of Women's Liberation* (Boston: Beacon Press, 1973).

70. Rosemary Radford Ruether, *Sexism and God-talk: Toward a Feminist Theology* (Boston: Beacon, 1983), 174.

71. Mary McClintock Fulkerson, "Sexism as Original Sin: Developing a Theacentric Discourse," *Journal of the American Academy of Religion* 59, no. 4 (1991): 653–75.

72. Serene Jones, *Feminist Theory and Christian Theology: Cartographies of Grace*, Guides to Theological Inquiry (Minneapolis: Fortress, 2000), 96.

73. Rachel Sophia Baard, *Sexism and Sin-Talk: Feminist Conversations on the Human Condition* (Louisville: Westminster John Knox, 2019), 110.

Baard explicitly conceptualizes the question as one of the use and "practical effects"[74] of doctrine—while still framing such use and function lin-
guistically, namely as rhetorics: "Classical sin-talk has often functioned as a
rhetoric of death for women, and therefore any suggestions for emancipatory
sin-talk would aim at developing sin-talk that denounces death and death-
dealing rhetoric, prompting sin-talk that is life-giving rhetoric aimed at human
flourishing."[75] Baard notes that feminist theologians "'speak' a traditional
language but say something new with it because they speak from a different
place,"[76] thus making "rhetorical *use* of the concept in arguing against it."[77]
By resorting to the same language of sin in denouncing the doctrine's effects,
we might say that feminist theologians effectively snatched the blade out of
the hand of the male-stream tradition and, leaving its material/grammatical
structure and functionality intact, effectively turned the same blade against the
former oppressors.

Both moves—the shift from meaning to affordances as well as critical reappropriations of a design against its earlier uses—have also been made by queer
theologians. They have argued that the doctrine of sin "exposes homophobic
ideologies as sinful, and explains how sinful discourses shape us."[78] Queer
theologians, too, have subsequently endeavored to use the same object toward
a different purpose, whether minimally described as "crafting a doctrine
that does not reinforce homophobia," or more ambitiously hoping that their
appropriation might "invigorate inherited doctrines and extend welcome and
reconciliation to all."[79] While often starting with a hermeneutics of suspicion,
such projects have thus effectively moved from the paranoia of ideology critique to the reparative endeavor of using the same doctrine to open up possibilities for flourishing instead of extending its death-dealing nature.

Other queer theologians have gone even further in conceptual repurposing.
In their queer use of the doctrine, they have called into question its ascribed
use as such and critically interrogated the theological usefulness of such use.
Linn Tonstad notes, "Our problem as homosexuals is not primarily that we,
in particular, have been placed on the side of the sinful, threatening order. It
is the distinction between the good and the bad to begin with, the virtuous and
the filthy, the deserving and the undeserving."[80] Beyond wielding the same

74. Baard, *Sexism and Sin-Talk*, 19.
75. Baard, *Sexism and Sin-Talk*, 11.
76. Baard, *Sexism and Sin-Talk*, 111.
77. Baard, *Sexism and Sin-Talk*, 119, my italics.
78. Mary E. Lowe, "Sin from a Queer, Lutheran Perspective," in *Transformative Lutheran
Theologies: Feminist, Womanist, and Mujerista Perspectives*, ed. Mary Streufert, 71–86 (Minneapolis:
Fortress, 2010), 85.
79. Lowe, "Sin from a Queer, Lutheran Perspective," 85.
80. Tonstad, "Everything Queer," 2016, 129.

instrument either toward the same ends by different users, or toward different ends by the same users, we might say that such a critique instead makes the traditional use of the doctrine visible—insofar as use is a function of usefulness for some party against another—and disavows such use altogether. The question is not, according to Tonstad, *against whom* the blade of sin ought to be used so as to be used *rightly*, but *whether* it ought to be used as a knife—for separating and cutting—in the first place.

As Ahmed asks, "What's the use (of use)?," Tonstad resists the temptation to simply deflect the blade, as well as the temptation to use the same blade to fight back. Rather than apologetically arguing that homosexuals are not sinners, and instead of accusing homophobes of being the "real" sinners, Tonstad challenges us to embrace the pronouncement of sinfulness, while at the same time taking away its dividing edge by extending it to humanity at large. Drawing on Geoffrey Rees' *Romance of Innocent Sexuality*,[81] Tonstad's queer use of sin refuses to make use of the affordance of the blade to divide, or to conceptually distinguish between good and bad subjects. Using sin to otherize an other, whether the deviant "other" or the dominant "other," invariably serves the purpose of seeking individual self-righteousness and thus only offers variations on the same theologically questionable pattern with the same harmful effects. Instead, Tonstad's queer use of sin cultivates the ground for a shared life by using the doctrine to put everyone on a level playing field. In a gesture reminiscent of Barth's common humanity "grounded upon a negative,"[82] Tonstad's culminating plea is thus the refusal to be redeemed on the back of a thus excluded "other," and the insistence on messy solidarity instead of judgment: "So let us place ourselves with the filthy, undeserving, sinners; let us stay with the Sodomites."[83] Instead of turning the blade of sin back against the oppressor, we might say, she opts for turning it into a plowshare.

In this particular repurposing, a queer use of sin is curiously both more orthodox and more radical at the same time: It is surprisingly more faithful to the material doctrine than common versions of LGB advocacy, and in this sense, reparative. It retrieves Augustine's deep sense that the alienation and division he struggled with spoke to something in the human condition at large, and revives Calvin's conviction that total depravity is a comforting idea that binds us together in God's grace rather than separating people by the degrees of their righteousness. At the same time, queer theology's queer use of sin is not only paranoid of the doctrine's original intentions or historical uses but also of the *use* of simply reappropriating it. Tonstad claims that she exercises

---

81. Geoffrey Rees, *The Romance of Innocent Sexuality* (Eugene: Cascade, 2010).
82. Barth, *Romans II*, 1968, 101., cf. chapter 3.
83. Tonstad, "Everything Queer," 129.

judgment "not only of whether to retrieve Christian traditions, but of which Christian traditions we are retrieving."[84] But in my reading, her question is not so much about "which," either, as it is about "how" and "to what ends." It opens up the range of inflections in Ahmed's question "What's the use?" At the end, it is not about *whether* we work with the past we have inherited, or *which part* of this past we work with, but toward *which future* we use it—a discernment that is distinctly theological in nature, more precisely: eschatological.

The word of God may be a double-edged blade, and the doctrine of sin has certainly been used as a weapon in the past. But maybe, just maybe, this blade could be put to use as a plowshare rather than as a sword. Where tradition has leveraged affordances of the grace of God as swords against queer others, we might exploit the same affordances to turn them into plowshares once more: instruments for the hard work of community, kingdom-building, and peace, rather than instruments of enmity and war, instruments of life and growth and flourishing rather than instruments of death and destruction and devastation. Such uses as open up room for grace and communal redemption in, through, and under a universal judgment might more adequately testify to a God who does the same. After all, the prophet paints an eschatological vision in which "nation shall not lift up sword against nation, neither shall they learn war any more." (Isa. 2:4 / Mic. 4:3)

The doctrine of sin is only one of the blades we might find in tradition. What other theological concepts and loci might yet be creatively repurposed from instruments of war into instruments of *shalom* to better testify to God's own creative redesign in history? The Lordship of Christ, the Fatherhood of God, the *imago Dei*, or the doctrine of election come to mind, to name but a few.[85] We might ask whether all materials of tradition are salvageable. Maybe some have to be put to rest for the abuse they give rise to. But if we believe the eschatological promise that God will make all things new, we might push to expand potential uses beyond what paranoia projects and to the most capacious reimaginations we find ourselves and our doctrinal affordances capable of.

After all, God's own ongoing work with creation might well be understood along the lines of creative and transformative redesign. Creative repurposing of given materials to open up new possibilities seems to be at the heart of how the Holy Spirit works. What kind of *use* does the resurrection make of the cross? It exposes its death dealing nature without becoming stuck in paranoia. It neither undoes the harm that the cross has done, nor does it simply cast it into a new light in hindsight, revealing the life that was hidden under death

---

84. Tonstad, "Everything Queer,"123.
85. I have recently undertaken this latter analysis in Reichel, "Swords to Plowshares."

all along. No, the cross—an artifact designed with great ingenuity not just for killing, but for public, drawn-out, and spectacular forms of corporeal torture, is transfigured into a tree of life. The resurrection of Christ substantially transforms the cross, not by repairing its past, but by opening it up to a different future, generating life-giving affordances out of death and hope out of despair. If an instrument of torture can become a source of hope, what materials should ever be abandoned as hopeless cases? The cross become tree of life promises the possibility of God's redesign of all of creation for the purposes of God. Creative redesign might even be a vision for eschatological transformation of creation. Lisanne Teuchert has proposed to think of Christian eschatology in terms of creation's "transfinalization" and "transignification." This language, taken from a eucharistic theology's redesign of the doctrine of transubstantiation toward a more relational ontology, might fit well with the relational ontology of design theory.[86]

Architect and theologian Murray Rae suggests that a design-redesign model of "transforming the world through adaptation and renewal"[87] is a more apt description of Christian eschatology than the one-sided options of annihilation or restoration. Rae takes the not just metaphorical, but very material rebuilding of decayed and fallen Rome as a material case study for such a "transformative eschatology": The repurposing of military structures for ecclesial use, the reuse of old idioms toward new ends, and the appropriation of secular and "pagan" buildings for ecclesial purposes might be signs and parables for God's active redesign of the material world toward redemptive ends. Just as such architectural transformation draws on the inherent ambivalence of human artifacts to press from them witnesses to the salvific purposes of God, Rae envisions eschatology, too, to be more of a "conversion" of lived history than either its destruction or its resetting to some projected initial state.[88] Christian eschatology, with its dialectic of continuity and discontinuity to the created world and its history, bears strong similarity to the third way between paranoid and reparative readings that queer use suggests. We might thus think of grace as God's creative salvaging from the rubble, a divine repurposing to new ends that promises a different world, both in its process and in its effect.

---

86. Lisanne Teuchert, *Gottes transformatives Handeln: Eschatologische Perspektivierung der Vorsehungslehre bei Romano Guardini, Christian Link und dem „Open theism"* (Göttingen: Vandenhoeck & Ruprecht, 2018), 224. Teuchert's transfinalization remains vexingly close to transsignification. Applying her concept in a design context for the material repurposing of doctrinal concepts allows us to shift it further from retroactive reinterpretation to material transformation by way of conceptual re-application.

87. Thus the subtitle of the book, Murray Rae, *Architecture and Theology: The Art of Place* (Waco: Baylor University Press, 2017).

88. Rae, *Architecture and Theology*, 87.

Is it so surprising that Ahmed's description of a queer use also sounds almost eschatological? She emphasizes how queer use does not "get used to" the logics of dominant systems and refuses to work "with" them in the sense of affirming their logics, intentions, and historical effects. But neither is queer use simply destructive or a way of opting out:

> If I have considered queer use as how we dismantle a world that has been built to accommodate only some, we can also think of queer use as a building project. We might aim not to build more secure institutions, using the well-used paths, but to build from the needs of those who are not enabled by following those routes. Such spaces might be understood as shelters: places to go for nourishment so that we can return to do the hard work of dismantling what has become built into a system.[89]

Resisting the binary options of eschatology as annihilation or restoration, queer use slices out a creative and constructive edge. Working with and against the grain of the world at the same time, queer use is decidedly agnostic toward designer intent and committed to constructive salvaging, "making a way out of no way" in ways that are astoundingly resonant with eschatological transformations. It carries the dual valence of epistemological and ontological transformation, when objects and structures that are designed to quite specific uses are directed to new purposes, changing their meaning and their value radically. And not least, queer use lingers in the same kind of ontological precarity and utopian promise as the eschatological "already and not yet."

The cross become tree of life, the bread and wine become flesh and blood of Christ in the eucharistic sacrament, the bodies of human beings becoming body of Christ—one might argue that these epistemically as well as ontologically transformative divine redesigns suggest something like a material history of queer use in God's own path; and theology has conceptualized these transformations under different doctrinal loci. Attention to these divine as well as historical redesigns might invite the theologian to understand doctrinal reworking not as a betrayal of the tradition, but as part of their priestly office in pointing to God's transformative redesign of the world.

89. Ahmed, *What's the Use*, 221–22.

Chapter 8

Building, or: The Truth of a House

CONSTRUCTIVE FAITH

When he returned to Capernaum after some days, it was reported that he was in the house. So many gathered around that there was no longer room for them, not even in front of the door; and he was speaking the word to them. Then some of them came, bringing to him a paralyzed man, carried by four of them. And when they could not bring him to Jesus because of the crowd, they removed the roof above him; and after having dug through it, they let down the mat on which the paralytic lay. When Jesus saw their faith, he said to the paralytic, "Child, your sins are forgiven." Now some of the scribes were sitting there, questioning in their hearts, "Why does this fellow speak in this way? It is blasphemy! Who can forgive sins but God alone?" At once Jesus perceived in his spirit that they were discussing these questions among themselves; and he said to them, "Why do you raise such questions in your hearts? Which is easier, to say to the paralytic, 'Your sins are forgiven,' or to say, 'Stand up and take your mat and walk'? But so that you may know that the Son of Man has authority on earth to forgive sins"—he said to the paralytic—"I say to you, stand up, take your mat and go to your home." And he stood up, and immediately took the mat and went out before all of them; so that they were all amazed and glorified God, saying, "We have never seen anything like this!"

—Mark 2:1–12[1]

1. Translation adapted from NRSVue.

Queer use, we said with Sarah Ahmed, points to the queerness of use. The same applies to queer virtue. It does not point to particular virtue of queer people (who are by and large as virtuous or non-virtuous as anyone else), it points to the queerness of faith, love, and hope. On the ground, they may not always look pious. They may look quite out of place, they may *take* things out of place and rearrange them drastically, irreverently. Excessive commitment, messy solidarity, and indecent honesty have the tendency to make unorthodox interventions that also call into question what is otherwise celebrated as virtuous. Mark 2 tells such a story of out-of-place faith that queers what passes as virtuous and lets something like virtue appear in disruption.

In Mark's Gospel, Jesus' christological status is not established by way of birth narratives, but by his public ministry of healing.[2] Jesus' early public ministry culminates in 2:1–12, before his activity shifts to discipling and teaching. The readers would thus expect an account of miraculous healing to happen here. And indeed, the story is often titled as "the healing of a paralytic" person; but the actual healing happens oddly on the side. The story is also quite explicitly about the forgiveness of sins; however, we do not learn anything about the person's past conduct. And then, the story is also effectively about disablement and enablement by built environments and social relations; but these dynamics are not explicated in the story's conversations. Reading it instead as a story primarily about the queer virtues of faith, love, and hope, in the excessive commitment, messy solidarity, and indecent honesty sketched earlier (cf. chapter 4), makes these intertwined layers of meaning fall into place slightly differently.

In the Gospel of Mark, people are often pronounced as healed by faith or saved by faith, and this story resonates with that pattern. But what does faith mean here? And *whose* faith are we talking about? The paralytic man utters no confession nor does he pledge any conversion. We do not even know whether it was his express wish to be brought to Jesus. The faith that matters in this story is neither a matter of statements of belief, of which we hear none, nor of individual convictions, of which we learn nothing. The faith that matters in this scene is the lived, communal solidarity on behalf of an excluded friend, an irreverent solidarity that actively redesigns the built environment to bring reality into conformity with their commitment. What figures as faith in this story are the actions of the four friends[3] who not only physically haul their

---

2. Cf. Gerd Theissen, *The Miracle Stories of the Early Christian Tradition* (Edinburgh: T&T Clark, 1983), esp. 21–22.

3. Anna Rebecca Solevåg, *Negotiating the Disabled Body: Representations of Disability in Early Christian Texts* (Atlanta: Society of Biblical Literature, 2018), 38, questions the ableist tendency to assume disabled people poor and helpless. The paralytic in the story might be affluent and bold: owning a home and commanding four carriers who might be slaves or family members

friend to Jesus but also use creative imagination and brute force to overcome the physical obstacles standing between their friend and Jesus. Of these physical obstacles, his bodily impairment is not even the most salient: social crowds and built structures stand in their way, barring him from access to grace.

Beyond the fact that this faith is communal and articulates itself in action, it is also remarkably not primarily a faith *in* Christ. It is first of all a commitment *to their friend* that, when it exceeds what the environment offers, reshapes the world to do justice to the reality of his condition and the reality of his need. Surely, the shape of this commitment entails a trust in Jesus, a trust that getting their friend to Jesus will help him. But this trust is neither a merely cognitive or affective state, neither a conviction nor a passive waiting. It is not an acceptance of things as they are, but actively, and quite indecently unsettles them to overcome the very real obstacles that separate their friend from Jesus. Thirdly and crucially, then, it is a faith that literally *matters*: It intervenes materially, it moves if not mountains or hearts, then built environments to get their friend to Jesus.

If the effects of sin manifest in alienation and separation, the man is indeed saved by (their) faith: It is the excessiveness of their commitment that overcomes his exclusion and isolation. Making true what it takes as true, this faith redesigns the physical space in such a way that the paralyzed man is able to be there with them, and with Jesus, not only despite his condition but also in and with his condition. The physical environment is redesigned to do justice to his lived reality as part of this community of friends. In an act of what we might call truly *material* theology, faith quite literally de- and re-constructs barriers in order to, by redesign, effect the *adequatio ad rem* of the architecture that had relegated their friend to an excluded position outside the gates, to the grace they found to be a reality in Jesus.

This faith is as utopian as it is pragmatic. It insists not just on the possibility but the necessity of a different reality and gets its hands dirty. It makes the seemingly impossible true by getting real. The paralytic is not afforded a space in some corner of their community; the friends transform the community into one that can be visited by their paralytic friend. His separation is healed by their material redesign of the space, rather than by a normalization of bodies. Healing is the active faith that redesigns structures—physical and conceptual—to correspond to the reality of faith.

---

rather than friends. Regardless of his social status, however, the four carriers are credited with the activity and with the faith that animates it. They also seem to emerge from the crowd at large rather than to be with the paralytic against the crowd ("some of them brought a man to him, carried by four of them"). I thus chose to read the four as manifesting reconstructive faith rather than merely executing a command.

The story reports that when Jesus saw their faith, he pronounced: "Your sins are forgiven." The curious change of subject—from *their* faith to *his* sins— might be less suggestive of an active response to their actions, by which Jesus would have graciously rewarded the faith they put in him. Instead, the statement might be read as a performative affirmation, witnessing to what the faithful commitment to their friend has already achieved: "(I see and am able to confirm that) Your sins are forgiven!" Blasphemous indeed! Who can forgive sins if not God alone? (What even makes us so sure that the crowd was indicting Jesus's statement and not the actions of the four friends he acknowledges in it?) If Jesus subsequently instructs the formerly paralyzed man to get up and walk, it seems to be serving more pedagogic than rehabilitative purposes: to demonstrate to the irritated crowd not just the legitimacy but the effectiveness of the healing that has already taken place.

Exegetes and scholars of disability will have more to say about these interpretations and their validity. But I want to take the story as an opportunity to ask: What if the active redesign that we see communal faith do in this scene could also be a model for understanding the work of theology? What if we subjected our theological concepts to the same kind of critical scrutiny to which the friends in this story subject the built environment—inquiring faithfully about the access they provide or obstruct to grace, ready to commit the blasphemy of taking them apart and redesigning them until they afford such access? What if, in true Althaus-Reidian (or Barthian?) "indecency," faithfulness requires a "break, not with the impiety, but with the *piety*"[4] of what we have inherited? What if we understood theology to be an exercise in design and redesign in excessive commitment to reality, in stubborn solidarity with it, and indecent honesty about it? Grace truly might be that demanding.

THEOLOGY AS CONCEPTUAL DESIGN?

In Mark's account, the redesign engendered out of the excessive commitment of faith is a literal, material one. In the previous chapters, I have already started playing with notions from design theory, applying them to the conceptual work of theology. In this chapter, I explicitly lay out a case for thinking of theology as conceptual design, and what such a lens might offer us. After all, the root metaphors of Systematic Theology and Constructive Theology already inhabit the semantic space of construction and of system-building; they stem from the imaginary of architectural design. Systematic Theology actively constructs the conceptual systems through which it renders received

4. Karl Barth, "The Word of God as the Task of Theology," 183.

faith-claims coherent. Constructive Theology even more explicitly recognizes its work as one of, well, construction. Taking the design images at work in both frameworks seriously might help us to recognize that far from relativist constructivism, the ethical and epistemic move here is one of critical attention to the conditions and requirements of construction as well as to the operative effect of conceptual systems. If Systematic Theology is not free of constructive activity, Constructive Theology, in turn, is not free of coherence nor of norms, but proceeds rather systematically in its epistemological self-reflection, its principled examination of latent power structures, and its fierce ethical commitments.

When we think of design, the drawing and building in architecture comes to mind, as do the activities of mass production and marketing of objects for consumption, as well as engineering technologies from the factory line to today's information and communication technologies. Along with the arts, all of these "applied" fields have developed their own professions as well as theorizations ever since the Industrial Revolution turned design into a matter of scale and efficiency. But architectural structures, industrial design, software, and media products are by no means the only things that are subject to design processes.

"All men [sic!] are designers. All that we do, almost all the time, is design, for design is basic to all human activity,"[5] Victor Papanek famously opens *Design for the Real World*, and introductions to design theory have ever since lead with statements like "design is everywhere."[6] Design is the structuring and reshaping of given materials for an intended purpose, discovering and attending to material, agential, contextual, and ecological possibilities and constraints in the process. Design creates patterns that allow, invite, discourage, or prevent particular uses, uses that make objects accessible or inaccessible, helpful or harmful in particular situations and to particular users. In this sense, ideas and concepts are just as much designed artifacts as material objects: They are crafted with specific intentions and purposes, making use of existent materials and attending to their constraints, and responding to contextually articulated needs and requirements, or fit.

Have not great theological works often been likened to cathedrals? The architectural image combines references to Systematic Theology's impressive logic, stunning aesthetics, and practical religious purpose. Systems develop knowledge architectonically, with principles that have as much regard for beauty as they have for truth, as much regard for function as they have for form. The architectonic imagery at work in Systematic Theology bridges cognitive

5. Victor J. Papanek, *Design for the Real World: Human Ecology and Social Change. With an Introduction by R. Buckminster Fuller* (Toronto; New York; London: Bantam, 1973), 23.
6. Hazel Clark and David Brody eds, *Design Studies: A Reader* (Oxford; New York: Berg, 2009), 1.

criteria to an orientation by and to the religious life of a faith community—as Barth emphasized, theology is "a function of the church."[7] The mathematical precision and design acumen that go into the building of a cathedral are not self-sufficient rational principles. They serve a purpose: reflecting in the perfection of the structure the glory of God, as well as practically orienting Christian life, directing believers to worship.

Of course, Systematic Theology might understand its architectonic imagery as a metaphor. After all, design is traditionally oriented toward the realization of physical forms, while theology works primarily on intellectual or cognitive formations. Yet, the divide between physical and cognitive forms is not as neat and clear-cut as it would seem, and besides, there is precedent to think about one in terms of the other. Nicholas Rescher's account of cognitive systematization (see chapter 2) already suggested that the systematic approach is "a 'design for knowing,' and [that] system building is preeminently a problem of rational design."[8] Even Thomas Aquinas insinuated that the term "architect" might be applied to the philosopher or knowledge worker: the term designates someone who knows how things should be ordered and arranged. Thus, the master arts that rule other arts are also rightly called architectonic. Drawing on Paul's self-description "as a wise architect, I have laid the foundation" (1 Cor. 3:10), Aquinas implicitly positions Christ as the wise man whose rules govern the architectural design of subordinate artisans.[9] It may thus not be accidental if theological system-building has always been "amphibious," crossing between cognitive and material realms, as Rescher described it;[10] it might only be drawing out the implicit theo-logic according to which divine knowledge organizes the material order of the universe.

Cognitive systematization not only forms ideas; it also shapes and is shaped by the spaces we inhabit, the way we build relationships, and how we order movement and exchange. Constructive Theologies like Marcella Althaus-Reid's have long paid attention to how the apparent disjunction of intellectual/spiritual and material/physical worlds is itself part of the self-concealment of how systems work. With the increasing development of informational and computational systems design, the boundaries between metaphoric and literal use have become even more porous, and beyond the constructive aspect of design its ethical as well as epistemological dimensions are increasingly coming to the fore.

Systematic Theology's long-standing epistemic cue giver, philosophy, has itself started reconceptualizing its work as one of design. Philosophers have

---

7. Barth, *CD I.1*, 1.

8. Rescher, *Cognitive Systematization*, 14.

9. Thomas Aquinas, *Summa Contra Gentiles: Book One: God*, ed. Anton C. Pegis FRSC (Notre Dame: University of Notre Dame Press, 1975), I.1 (p. 59–60).

10. Rescher, *Cognitive Systematization*, 14.

long inquired into the not merely epistemic but material work that concepts *do*, especially where they have attended in their analysis to categories of gender, race, and ability.[11] The notion of *conceptual engineering* has recently created a significant buzz in the analytic philosophical community, in the attempt to devise strategies for the implementation, evaluation, and redesign of philosophy's conceptual repertoires.[12] Drawing on the logics of information systems, Luciano Floridi has recently advocated for replacing an understanding of philosophy as observation and propositional representation of reality with one of *conceptual design*.[13]

Philosophy, after all, has to grapple almost as much as theology with the impossibility of demonstrating its truth-claims by way of correspondence to external realities. Floridi invites the field to recognize that, "Philosophical questions are ultimate but not absolute questions, which are not answerable empirically or mathematically, but are open to informed and rational disagreement. The best way to address them is by developing philosophy as conceptual design, and this requires its own logic."[14]

By conceptual design, Floridi envisions a kind of "semantic information modeling" that is "consistent with creative forms of reasoning, with the identification and exploitation of constraints and affordances, and hence the satisfaction of requirements."[15] In terms of such requirements, Floridi does not dismiss or replace earlier cognitive standards, but complements them and shifts their emphasis. Existent standards are mostly concerned with two temporal extensions: a system's past (its conditions of possibility) and a system's present (its conditions of in/stability). The design lens brings into view the

11. Cf., e.g., Sally Haslanger, "Gender and Race: (What) Are They? (What) Do We Want Them To Be?" *Noûs* 34, no. 1 (March 2000): 31–55.

12. Cf. e.g., David J. Chalmers, "What Is Conceptual Engineering and What Should It Be?" *Inquiry* (2020): 1–18; Herman Cappelen, *Fixing Language: An Essay on Conceptual Engineering* (Oxford; New York: Oxford University Press, 2018); as well as special issues of *Inquiry* 63 (2020) and 64 (2021).

13. See esp. Luciano Floridi, "The Logic of Design as a Conceptual Logic of Information," *Minds and Machines* 27, no. 3 (2017): 495–519; "What a Maker's Knowledge Could Be," *Synthese* 195, no. 1 (2018): 465–81; *The Logic of Information: A Theory of Philosophy as Conceptual Design* (Oxford: Oxford University Press, 2019).

14. Floridi, *The Logic of Information*, 205.

15. Floridi, 195. Modeling as an epistemological practice has been applied to theology by Benedikt Friedrich. Modeling techniques facilitate exploration, optimization, verification, communication, and definition of (theological) concepts. While necessarily reductionistic and incomplete compared to reality, models allow the (conceptual) designer to heuristically isolate specific aspects of an issue or a structure to study not only their coherence but also the specific path dependencies closely, testing them intellectually as well as materially. Cf. Benedikt Friedrich, *Modelle der Erlösung: Eschatologische Denkformen im Anschluss an die Theologie Karl Barths*, Theologische Anstöße (Göttingen: Vandenhoeck & Ruprecht, 2023).

possibility for and necessity of standards extending to a conceptual system's future: its conditions of feasibility and use.[16]

Understanding philosophy as conceptual design is neither anti-constructive nor anti-systematic and by no means relativistic or anti-rational. Rather, it recognizes that construction requires coherence, but that systematicity is *not enough*. Floridi notes, "the essence of philosophy is not logic, but design. Logic is only a second-best compromise, in the absence of design."[17] In that sense, we might say that design *better* responds to the particularities of the discipline's requirements than either cognitive systematization or critical constructivism alone. A similar case could be made in theology—and, due to the inherently incarnational and communicative particularities of theology, maybe even more so than in philosophy.

We are used to thinking of theology as a truth-seeking endeavor, but what if we instead saw it as an architectonic task of conceptually designing imaginaries for people to inhabit, or the task of fitting ideas to theological uses? Systematic Theology already understands itself as ordering given materials into coherent and cohesive cognitive structures. And Constructive Theology thinks about this ordering in terms of its material effects, working intentionally toward desired outcomes and making the way users interact with the conceptual objects it crafts an intrinsic part of theology's responsibility and accountability. Both Systematic and Constructive Theology are de facto already engaged in conceptual design. Explicitly reflecting on them as such might help us understand their differences as foregrounding different aspects of the same metaphor. It might allow us to go constructively beyond Systematic Theology and systematically beyond Constructive Theology. Understanding theology as design would entail the constructive ordering and structuring of theological concepts. It would take into account not only internal architectural structuring by cognitive criteria of cohesion and coherence but also the practical effects and uses of doctrine, its affordances and materialized ethics, and necessitate the development of nimbler practices of feedback and redesign.

Raised both by the biblical story at the beginning of the chapter and by the "building" imaginary at work in the names of "Systematic" and "Constructive" theology, the image of the house aptly conveys strengths of design theory, conducive to doing theology *better* without insinuating that it is the best, the perfect, or the only possibility to pursue. Design will not *save* theology, either, but the shared investment in doing *better* under and despite ongoing conditions of finitude and complexity, imperfection and uncertainty, remedial

---

16. Floridi, *The Logic of Information*, 204, sees "past" conditions as modelled by a Kantian transcendental logic, "present" conditions by a Hegelian dialectical logic.

17. Floridi, *The Logic of Information*, 205.

pragmatism and eschatological openness, might open up instructive resonances between these two fields.

THE PROMISE OF DESIGN

There can be no right life in the wrong one.
—*Theodor Adorno*[18]

In my father's house, there are many dwelling places.
—*John 14:2*

Shift or Expansion of Criteria

The design lens first of all effects a considerable expansion as well as a shift
in the criteria of theological work. Paul Feyerabend postulates, "scientists are
like architects who build buildings of different sizes and different shapes and
who can be judged only *after* the event, i.e., only after they have finished their
structure. It may stand up, it may fall down—nobody knows."[19] There is some
truth to this insight: Like architectural design, theological design will not be
able to consider all variables in advance and will partially have to proceed in
trial and error. However, against Feyerabend's nonchalant portrayal, many
potential causes for collapse can obviously be discerned (and taken into consideration) well in advance. In addition, *better* theology will not ignore this condition and develop loops for evaluation, feedback, and redesign of its design.

If theology indeed builds *a house* of sorts—a symbolic and intellectual habitat
in which people can dwell, which orients their lives and shapes their perspectives, movement, and relationships—and if theological concepts are indeed
objects with which we live and which we use and wield in specific ways, then we
ought to think of their design in terms of what practices, acts, movements, and
postures they enable and facilitate, obstruct or impede, encourage or habitual-
ize. Their meaning is not only in their referential value but also in their use.[20]
Rather than do away with criteria for theological truth-claims, the design lens
expands the range of criteria that come into view. And even the complication of

---

18. Adorno and Jephcott, *Minima Moralia*, 42, translation adapted.

19. Feyerabend, *Against Method*, xx.

20. Such a conception of meaning has more generally been proposed in Wittgenstein's
philosophy of language. Arguing that "the meaning of a word is its use in the language,"
it pragmatically bridges questions of truth and use. Cf. Ludwig Wittgenstein, *Philosophical
Investigations* (Oxford: Blackwell, 1953), 43. My proposal goes in a slightly different direction as I
am less interested in discursive use to describe the meaning of terms than in the assessment and
critique of its uses.

conclusive evaluation may, after all, not be a disadvantage. It might indeed be a matter of greater intellectual honesty and transparency.

So, what is the truth of a house—a material or a conceptual habitat—and how do we establish it? Lest the question seem nonsensical or concerned with its factual existence, we might ask not *if* the house is true, but *true to what?* That houses can be designed quite differently should not detract from the fact that the quality of their design can be assessed. But rather than one single conclusive criterion, a range of criteria will have to be weighed. Some will be universal, others highly contextual; some quite pragmatic, others rather utopian. Some will have to be considered in advance, others will only come into view retrospectively.

Obviously, coherence will remain a basic requirement in architectural design, for both aesthetic and pragmatic reasons. In physical as in conceptual structures, if there is not enough coherence and cohesion between the different parts, everything collapses. There are also external realities that pose near-universal requirements for which any built structure will have to account. In the case of material architecture, such near-universal requirements might be articulated by the laws of statics or the constant of gravity. In the case of conceptual architecture, similar constants will be articulated in the form of logical requirements. In either case, *better* design will be systematic, coherent, and corresponding to external realities, just like inherited truth theories demanded all along.

At the same time, accountability to laws of physics, mathematics, or logics becomes a minimal requirement, not by any means sufficient as a standard for *good* design. And establishing a design's one-to-one correspondence to an ideal object or perfect internal coherence and consistency becomes less pertinent than its adequacy regarding aesthetic, pragmatic, and ethical requirements.

Questions of a design's projected purpose and its actual use come into play. Not all houses—physical or conceptual—look the same, and for good reasons: Difference is not only an expression of aesthetic variation but also of attunement to further requirements. When planning a physical house, we would ask questions like, what is the house *for?* A communal gathering place will have a different outline than a family home. What materials are available for building it, and what possibilities and limitations do we inherit from them? Whether working in marble or pine, not every structure is feasible. What geological requirements have to be taken into account, what cultural and legal ones? A prudent architect will not build on sandy ground, as the bible reminds us. From what does the house provide shelter and protection? To what kinds of bodies does it provide access, and who and what does it keep out? How will it structure the lives of the people who dwell in it? How will it inform their routines, their emotions, their interactions? What kind of movement, rest, and interaction does it allow? All of these questions will have parallels in conceptual design, including theological design.

For both physical and conceptual structures, such questions clarify that a constitutive contextuality of requirements, as well as a wide range of possibilities to respond even to the same set of requirements, do not result in the abandonment of criteria by any means; if anything, they result in higher degrees of complexity in assessment. While it might seem impossible to affirm "the truth" of a house, and misguided to aspire and build the one perfect house, it is arguably quite possible to establish the *falsehood* of a house, and even on a variety of different counts. For a physical house, we might ask: Which ecological, material, and cultural requirements does the house fail to honor? How does the actual use of the house betray its lofty ideal? Where does the architectural design not *do its job* properly? But also: What might be wrong about the ways in which it *does* do its job properly? Which forms of relating, living, and moving does the design render natural, unquestionable, and invisible? Which does it impede? To whom does it afford access and shelter, whom does it exclude, imprison, or expose? How do we evaluate the dynamics the designed environment engenders? All of these questions will have parallels in conceptual design, including theological design, as well.

In Mark's narrative, the four friends found the house inadequate to the reality of their friend as well as to the reality of grace that demanded its ability to be accessible and to be visited. Their irreverent disregard for the current material form of the house, their deconstruction and redesign, was an indictment of its falsehood in the equally pragmatic and utopian impetus to conform the built structure to these realities, to overcome its actively falsifying obstruction of the truth, to make the house a place that would enable the experience of grace, community, and healing. In that sense, these friends' "blasphemy" overcame the "falsehood" of theology's conceptual designs that the "orthodoxy" of Job's friends did not.

Such faithful irreverence is not without precedence. Throughout the biblical corpus, built structures are designed to facilitate God's presence in the midst of God's people, and they undergo frequent reevaluation and redesign—from portable tabernacle (which could accompany God's wandering people through the wilderness, but was also at risk and could be captured by enemies), to singular temple (which afforded stability, facilitated "proper" glory and worship, while highly regulated thresholds of access both barred and protected people from direct encounter with God), to incarnated presence in the body of Jesus Christ (which afforded much more intimate ways of relating, co-presence and encounter, while also proving much more vulnerable to violence and death). These examples insinuate the need for a theological analysis of architecture. They also suggest the potential of architectural images to illustrate theological notions materially.[21]

21. For studies in such interdisciplinary interpretation, see Rae, *Architecture and Theology*.

But beyond the possibilities of physical design to express or inform theological insight, what concerns us here is to understand the very work of theology as conceptual design. Arguably, this is the theological contention we see Constructive Theology raising against Systematic Theology, drawing out the ways in which its conceptual designs point people effectively *away* from the theological truths it purports to reflect, is only inhabitable by some, and quite inaccessible for others, and might even actively prevent the Spirit from blowing. Can we reevaluate and redesign theological concepts and doctrines in similar ways as the four friends in the parable evaluated and redesigned the built environment, in similar ways as different built environments for the presence of God are reevaluated and redesigned in Scripture?

Nicholas Rescher points out that a system's assessment cannot be separated from its use, and that assessment criteria regarding the "intellectual consistency" of cognitive systematization need to be complemented by feedback loops regarding their "pragmatic efficacy." While both critical criteria are indispensable, according to Rescher it is the latter that should be the "final arbiter of adequacy."[22] We might say that in conceptual design, a system is justifiable most centrally by its use—and less by the intentions of its designers or the principles according to which they planned it.

Viewed through the design lens, considerations like ecological fitting, user-orientation, and the uses to which designs are put reveal themselves to be far from epistemic relativism or market-driven commodification of faith. Instead, they manifest the faithful—if on the face of things somewhat blasphemous—commitment that the *work* that theological ideas *do* and how they bear on "the real world" needs to be adequate to the truth they bear witness to, as well. What does our theology *do* in the lives of people? What uses does it afford? Whom does it enable to do what? What kinds of interactions does it engender? How does it shape our relationships to self, other, world, and God? How does it direct our actions and behaviors? And so on. The uses they afford establish what meaning theological notions have, what insights they correspond to, what truth they reflect.

As we examine individual theological notions as artifacts, we are also challenged to think more generally about the purpose of theology as a discipline, a practice, and an ecology. What effects in the lives of people and communities should it engender? What is it that the conceptual objects (notions, doctrines, loci) it designs are meant to communicate? What actions and behaviors, perceptions and habits should it facilitate or constrain? What uses of theology are *better* than others, and can we develop methodological standards and procedures to discern between theologically more and theologically less adequate

22. Rescher, *Cognitive Systematization*, 102–3.

uses? And lest some would be tempted to dismiss such questions as "merely" ethical or pastoral, let me put them in unmistakably *theo*logical terms: What do the uses afforded by theology say about who God is, about the reality of the human being *coram deo*, and about what right relationship between God, world, other, and self would look like? What practical uses of theology would best *reflect* and witness to who we claim God to be?

In short, the uses theological notions afford are an irreducible part of their *adequatio ad rem*. *Adequatio* denotes then not so much the technical correspondence of bygone theories of truth as it aims at conceptual concordance with material realities and real-life effects in what we might name theologically as a *testimonial correspondence*: Do our theology's effects correspond to its words, and does such correspondence in turn reflect that of which theology speaks? The witness does not need to become identical with what it witnesses to—in fact, it needs to remain recognizable in its non-identity—but the witness has to point to and adequately *reflect* that to which it witnesses. Barth was fond of illustrating such testimonial correspondence with the finger of John the Baptist in Matthias Grünewald's famous *Isenheim Altarpiece*.

Such an understanding ties back to a theological insight about knowledge of God, as well: That knowledge *of* God can never be reduced to knowledge *about* God. It does not merely exhibit an intellectual or noetic quality, but is in itself a practice and a relationship that has transformative effects for the subject of such knowledge and affects all areas of their life. We have too long neatly compartmentalized disciplines of dogmatics, as concerned with the noetic content or meaning of the faith, and ethics, as concerned with its corresponding life forms. The design lens challenges us to a more integrated treatment. It demands that we develop robustly *theological* accounts of, and criteria for, the "use" of theology. We might negatively use the lenses of falsehood, hubris, and sloth to diagnose at least some forms of inadequate theological design. *Better* design in theology will develop sensitivities for theological failures not only in theoretical but also in practical pitfalls, in order to avoid at least the more foreseeable failures. Neglecting to consider them in advance might in itself constitute a theological version of sloth.

Complexity and Humility

As Johan Redstrom remarks, "Design's capacity to deal with complexity and conflicting concerns is perhaps its most fascinating feature."[23] As we have seen, many things have to be considered when building a house—physical or conceptual—and the capacities design theory has developed to navigate such

23. Johan Redstrom, *Making Design Theory* (Cambridge: MIT, 2017), 2.

complexity makes it very appealing for the inevitably complex problems by which theology finds itself confronted. The material and grounded practices of design make it more resilient against the one-sidedness of cognitive system-atization or constructive contextualism alone while also resisting their easy dichotomization.

Of course, design is not free of the hubris, sloth, and falsehood—in short: sin—that attends all human endeavors. Hubris is the most obvious temptation for the designer, whether in material or conceptual work. Grandiose aspirations as to how to reshape life most effectively easily become totalitarian (not to men-tion ugly). Many ruins of design, overly optimistic as to the transformability of external conditions, have quickly turned out to be unlivable and litter our land-scapes with humbling reminders. Le Corbusier's highly efficient and uniform, but ecologically brutal, ideologically fascist, and practically unlivable cities may count among such heritages, to name just one example.[24]

One may critique such hubris on political, ethical, aesthetical, and yes, theological grounds. Interestingly enough, however, in design theory aspi-rations to optimized and uniform solutions quickly became questionable on epistemological grounds. If design has an advantage over theology, it might be the rate at which it has to confront reality checks. Earlier generations of design theorists wanted to understand design as a problem-solving endeavor, as rigorous optimization under conditions of bounded rationality. In order to "devise courses of action aimed at changing existing situations into preferred ones,"[25] they aspired to move almost mathematically from "soft, intuitive, informal, and cook-booky" descriptions to "a body of intellectually tough, analytic, partly formalizable, partly empirical, teachable doctrine."[26] The design was envisioned as a *Science of the Artificial* to promote objective, solution-oriented, and universal proposals based on epistemic individualism and mod-ernist rational optimism.[27]

The kinds of problems that design deals with were, however, quickly diag-nosed as "wicked problems": Their fundamental indeterminacy makes "opti-mal solutions" and "definite progress in achieving efficiency" impossible in all but the most trivial cases.[28] Part of the reason for such "wickedness"—a term that interestingly crosses practical intractability with associations of evil—were

24. Cf. Rae's excellent account and theological analysis of Le Corbusier's grandiose Plan Voisin in *Architecture and Theology*, 149–80.

25. Herbert A. Simon, *The Sciences of the Artificial*, third edition (Cambridge: MIT, 1969), 111.

26. Simon, *The Sciences of the Artificial*, 113.

27. For an account of this dominant frame, as well as a succinct overview of several generational shifts since, see Daniela K. Rosner, *Critical Fabulations: Reworking the Methods and Margins of Design*, Design Thinking, Design Theory (Cambridge: MIT, 2018).

28. Horst W. J. Rittel and Melvin M. Webber, "Dilemmas in a General Theory of Planning," *Policy Sciences* 4 (1973): 155–69.

identified in design's concern with particularity and the multiplicity of variables in any concrete situation. The possibility to calibrate any design issue at higher or lower levels of formulation introduces irreducible complexity, and design's orientation to the future, or the not-yet-existent, added layers of uncertainty. The fact that the solutions which design develops actively participate in shaping these futures creates both material path dependencies and epistemological complicities: The information needed to understand a problem depends on one's idea for *solving* it.[29]

In this sense, design—like theology—is in *practice* quickly disabused of the hubris (and subsequent inevitable frustration) that attends grand notions of progress and salvation, or revolution and modernization. The discipline of design studies has also found its condition to complicate any straightforward "scientific" methodology and started to formulate its endeavor in more open-ended and playful ways. As Donald Schön describes the peculiar condition of design,

> Designers put things together and bring new things into being, dealing in the process with many variables and constraints, some initially known and some discovered through designing. Almost always, designers' moves have consequences other than those intended for them. Designers juggle variables, reconcile conflicting values, and maneuver around constraints—a process where, although some design products may be superior to others, there are no unique right answers.[30]

Design solutions are not adequately conceptualized as "true-or-false, but good-or-bad . . . or, more likely, as 'better or worse' or 'satisfying' or 'good enough.'"[31] Slightly ironically, the *better* design will simply be *adequate* design, "good enough" design, in full awareness that adequacy already contains multitudes of complexities to take into account.

In sum, design might find itself in quite a similar position as theology. Both might invite—or be forced into—a similar posture of "ontological humility"[32] in light of their epistemological and ethical binds, both might have to continue their work without disavowing is ultimately irresolvable complexity. Their *better* versions know that they are always remedial, never universal, and never

29. Rittel and Webber, "Dilemmas in a General Theory of Planning," 161.

30. Donald A. Schön, *Educating the Reflective Practitioner: Toward a New Design for Teaching and Learning in the Professions* (San Francisco: Jossey-Bass, 1987), 40–41.

31. Rittel and Webber, "Dilemmas in a General Theory of Planning," 163.

32. Bruno Latour, "A Cautious Prometheus? A Few Steps Toward a Philosophy of Design (with Special Attention to Peter Sloterdijk)," in *Networks of Design: Proceedings of the 2008 Annual International Conference of the Design History Society (UK)*, ed. Jonathan Glynne, Fiona Hackney, and Minton Viv, 2–10 (Boca Raton: Universal, 2008), 3.

complete. Design responds to particular problems and tries to find limited, contextual solutions. Where it recognizes its complicated condition, designing thus virtually becomes "the antidote to founding, colonizing, establishing, or breaking with the past. It is an antidote to hubris and to the search for absolute certainty, absolute beginnings, and radical departure."[33] Might theology adopt a similar posture?

Since there is no singular "best" design in any given environment, more recent approaches have stressed the open and processual nature of design, describing its work as "*process*, a beginning point, rather than a measurable end"[34] or "as a permanent *striving toward*, an ongoing process of ideation, iteration, and revision."[35] Theology has of course similarly cultivated such a disposition. Thus Karl Barth spoke of the need to over and over "begin again at the beginning,"[36] and Marcella Althaus-Reid talked about the "nomadic movement"[37] of theology. But methodologically, such insight has often remained on the rather abstract level of a *semper reformanda*. Design, in turn, has had to come up with *concrete* strategies to navigate its condition practically. It has cultivated feedback loops and use reports to continue adapting design in its unforeseen entanglements and consequences. As more pertinent than illusions of objective solutions, design has turned to "reflective practices" of "thinking on one's feet" in "conversation with the material."[38] As more pertinent than fantasies of omnipotence and solutionism, design has developed iterative, multidimensional, and nonlinear processes of investigation, correction, and adaptation. What if we allowed theology to benefit from best practices that design has long developed to facilitate and structure its ongoing work, navigating complexity and ultimate insolubility in humility—concretely and materially?

Material Faithfulness and Poiesis

The remediability of design stands in contrast to a neighboring theological notion, that of creation. This explicit theological qualification puts design once more in a humbler, but also more realistic and promising position than other epistemic practices. While design is obviously a poietic process, the designer is just as obviously not a creator. A precursor of conceptual design,

---

33. Latour, "A Cautious Prometheus," 4.

34. Hamraie, *Building Access*, 249.

35. Costanza-Chock, *Design Justice*, 202.

36. Barth, *CD I.1*, xi.

37. Althaus-Reid, "Outing Theology," 49.

38. Donald A. Schön, *The Reflective Practitioner: How Professionals Think in Action* (New York: Basic Books, 1984).

Gilles Deleuze once observed that "concepts are not waiting for us ready-made, like heavenly bodies. There is no heaven for concepts. They must be invented, fabricated, or rather created and would be nothing without their creator's signature."[39] But against such claims, the design theorist will insist on the theologically relevant difference between *creation* and *design*: "Creation" is often imagined to underly the absolute and unrestrained control of their maker, whereas design is much humbler, always externally constrained and oriented by the purpose, the character of the given material, and ecological conditions.

Design distances itself both from the hubris and voluntarism of an unconstrained constructionism as well as from the relativism of which it is often accused: it is "never a process that begins from scratch: to design is always to *redesign*."[40] As opposed to creation *ex nihilo*, design always works with what is given, both in terms of problems and materials (in theology, think: texts and ideas, most prominently biblical canon and tradition). Better design knows that material is not inert matter that can be shaped and molded according to will. Materials have a character of their own, and better design (including better theological design) will be attentive to the specific quality of its materials, their substance, their history, their previous use, their structure, their possibilities, and their breaking points, attentive to the intentions and purposes to which they lend themselves.

When Feyerabend avers that "scientists are sculptors of reality,"[41] it might first sound like almost as grandiose a claim as creatorship. But the nuance in the imagery makes all the difference, theoretically as well as theologically: sculpting points less to the unlimited possibilities of theorization than to its restriction "by the properties of the material they use."[42] Feyerabend notes that the object of our inquiry, which he sometimes calls "Nature As She Is In Herself" or simply "Being," resists our modeling efforts even as it interacts with them in a kind of communicative process: "Being is like a person who shows a friendly face to a friendly visitor, becomes angry at an angry gesture, remains unmoved by a bore without giving an hint as to the principles that make Him (Her? It? Them?) act the way they do in the different circumstances."[43]

Such images of the agency of the object, to the point that it seems better described as a subject than as inert matter, might resonate even more with

39. Gilles Deleuze and Felix Guattari, *What Is Philosophy?* (New York: Columbia University Press, 1996), 5.

40. Latour, "A Cautious Prometheus," 20.

41. Feyerabend, *Against Method*, 284.

42. Feyerabend, *Against Method*, 284.

43. Feyerabend, *Against Method*, 285.

theologians than with natural scientists.[44] Theologians are acutely aware that their knowledge-making does not start *ex nihilo*, but with given material and objectives, and theology presumably comes closer than most other fields of study to assuming that the reality they conceptually model is not inert but engaged and responsive.

All theology is reworking of existing theology. Among its given material we find the community of the church and what it "traditions": Scripture, creeds and confessional statements, liturgical and diaconal practice, religious experiences of people past and present, and hopefully, somewhere behind it all: God. In theology as well, a good designer demonstrates their craftpersonship by working *with* their material rather than against it. What if we demanded that *better* theology be accountable to whether and how it has made use of its given materials in its conceptual design?

From Perception to Care

The complexity design inevitably encounters means that it cannot proceed without the exercise of great care and "attentiveness to details that is completely lacking in the heroic, Promethean, hubristic dream of action,"[45] as Bruno Latour observes. *Better* versions of design guard not only against hubris but also against sloth. There are certainly houses—material and conceptual ones—that are built on sloth, which in the case of architectural design might be seen in a resignation to the merely practical, or in the avoidance of the effort to go beyond functionality to a vision of *better* living. Sloth in conceptual design might consist in the refusal to take use and practical consequences into consideration, in an avoidance of caring for people and materials adequately, and in a lack of living up to its highest potentials of accountability and sustainability.

In any given environment, *better* design requires careful observation of *what has happened before* to understand *what will happen next* as consequence of even minute design changes. Such exercise of care is both a matter of intellectual acumen and ethical sensitivity. Design's accountability to the materials in (creative, and sometimes blasphemous) faithfulness is complemented by accountability on the side of the designed object's use. In design, Bruno Latour highlights, "materiality and morality finally coalesc[e]."[46] An inher-

44. Note, however, feminist and decolonial epistemologies that have long called the neat distinction of investigating subjects and investigated objects into question. Cf. Donna Haraway, "Situated Knowledges: The Science Question in Feminism and the Privilege of Partial Perspective," *Feminist Studies* 14, no. 3 (1988): 575–99.

45. Latour, "A Cautious Prometheus," 3.

46. Latour, "A Cautious Prometheus," 5.

ently ethical dimension arises in the weighing of bad design vs. good design—or, more realistically, "better" design: "Good design is responsible design."[47]

Elaine Scarry has artfully described artifacts as projections and "materializations" of human bodily parts, capacities, and desires. Artifacts are expressions of care for human pain, and mimetically respond to it. They translate one person's sentiment toward another person's need first into counterfactual, world-changing action, and, subsequently, into material structures that "deprive the external world of . . . its privilege of being irresponsible to its sentient inhabitants on the basis that it is itself nonsentient."[48] Design transforms affective sentiments into structures and "things" as self-perpetuating, durable, "objectified human compassion."[49] Rather than outsourcing and diminishing sentience, design has the potential to transform the world into one that is more caring and that increases the accountability of the world rather than merely offering functional solutions.

Arguably, the deconstructive redesign on which the four friends in Mark 2 embark goes in that direction. Barth, however, seems to miss the point when he sighs that the best method can do is "a turning of the sick man in his bed from one side to the other for a little diversion."[50] What if we understood such attention and care to be part of our responsibility as theologians, and translated it into conceptual structures, "compassion made effective"? What if our theologies avoided the temptation of sloth, and became materializations of perception and attention, not just to facts, but to needs and pain? What if we thus deprived our intellectual frameworks of the privilege of being irresponsive to suffering, and instead considered our conceptual work as a work of care for the world and its people, translating its perceptions into cognitive structures that remain attentive to it, even after the theologian's personal emotive response has run dry? Doing so might direct us to positive examples for *better* theology.

Communal Orientation and User Sensitivity

Design is an inherently communal endeavor, as is theology. Design has had to develop best practices to take into account the insights of multiple stakeholders, practices from which theology can only benefit. Once we take the expansion to use-related criteria seriously as requirements of theological design and seek to address them as part of its task, we have to acknowledge that in order

---

47. Susan S. Szenasy, "Ethical Design Education Confessions of a Sixties Idealist," in *Citizen Designer: Perspectives of Design Responsibility*, 20–24 (New York: Allworth, 2003), 24.

48. Elaine Scarry, *The Body in Pain: The Making and Unmaking of the World* (New York: Oxford University Press, 1985), 290.

49. Scarry, *The Body in Pain*, 291.

50. Barth, "The Word of God as the Task of Theology," 175.

to design *well* by any standards, we will be dependent on the insight of those who have to live in the house we build or those who are driven away. We will need to attend to those who tell us that our structures are inhospitable at best and uninhabitable at worst because our windows do not allow for the circulation of air, our doors will not let the Spirit enter, and the staircase is not wheelchair-accessible. Or, to put it in terms of theological virtues, that they undermine the building of trust rather than afford solidarity and commitment; that they twist relationships into destructive and harmful rather than loving dynamics; and that they engender despair rather than hope.[51]

Better design—from trial and error—comes with its fair share of hamartiological realism. The design lens allows theology to conceptualize an orientation to justice in critical practices rather than idealistic postulates. It is aware that innovation comes from the knowing-making of material engagement and involvement rather than idealistic top-down processes, often through user initiative in repurposing and tinkering that might seem out of place to the professional designers. Where it has learned to avoid the more idealistic utopianisms' tendency to totalitarian formation, design will orient itself toward diverse users in short-rhythmed cycles of envisioning, prototyping, and implementing feedback. Where it has learned to avoid the tendency of slicker versions of pragmatism to consumerist pleasing, design will develop self-reflective orientations investigating its non-neutrality, faithfulness, care, and attention. To counteract its own hardcoded biases, conceptual design will choose deliberately what and whom it pays attention to, examine the conditions of its own production, and ask critically investigative questions like

1. Who participated in the design process? And who was excluded from participation, whether deliberately or not?
2. Who benefited from the design, whether intentionally or unintentionally?
3. Who was harmed by the design?[52]

Everyone is a theologian just like everyone designs. But not everyone has to become a professional theologian and dedicate themselves to conceptual design. Design allows for a multi-stakeholder account. Those who by societal division of labor invest more time and resources to conceptual theological design are challenged to implement close feedback loops and to cultivate recursive publics with the means to create and maintain their own discursive, legal, technical, and conceptual infrastructure.[53]

---

51. Cf. Brandt, "Sünde."

52. Costanza-Chock, *Design Justice*, 223.

53. Christopher M. Kelty, *Two Bits: The Cultural Significance of Free Software* (Durham: Duke University Press, 2008).

As a critical function of the church, theology is already an inherently communal endeavor. All theology is, at its root, practical, communicative, and social: It serves the purpose of not only reflecting intellectually on but ultimately communicating Christian belief, its insights and values, goals and life forms. It engages in such communication even where it does not understand itself as primarily concerned with preparing, supporting, and correcting the literal communication of the gospel, proclamation. While theology *can* happen in a purely academic mode, its *better* versions attend not just to their potential rhetorical effect but also to their inherent pastoral function.[54] Design, too, is of course a form of communication:[55] it communicates perceptions and values, intentions and goals, postures and courses of action into material forms—*and* even its own materialized pedagogy in the possible uses it signals.

To achieve its purpose, to be effective, design is (almost) by necessity user-centered and makes usability a central goal.[56] As design seeks to intervene in and change an environment according to specific intentions and requirements, it will be putting effort into establishing a natural fit between the intended use and the established form. Objects have to be adept such that users are not only easily *able* to use them but also to *grasp* their meaning intuitively rather than having to accommodate and compromise, or even just think too hard in order to access and execute their functions.

Building—in design or in theology—is always a communal practice, relying on a variety of stake-holders and their insights, needs, and particularities. Users in particular are quite capable of assessing whether a design does its job, even without extensive training or technical expertise. Feyerabend observes, "Scientists [architects] are no better off than anybody else in these matters, they only know more details,"[57] and explicitly makes space for public deliberation and discernment. The most "natural" fit can only be achieved through an elaborate feedback loop, trial and error processes, and most importantly, a communication between designer and user in which misfits between form and context are excised. In this procedural sense as well, design is always redesign. What would it look like if theology more intentionally developed practices that involved and developed diverse publics, infrastructures, and resources? What if it critically centered the experience and voices of those traditionally excluded from its condition of production?

---

54. Ellen T. Charry, *By the Renewing of Your Minds: The Pastoral Function of Christian Doctrine* (New York: Oxford University Press, 1999).

55. Klaus Krippendorff and Reinhart Butter, "Product Semantics: Exploring the Symbolic Qualities of Form," *Innovation* 3, no. 2 (1984): 4–9, 5.

56. Cf. Donald A. Norman and Stephen W. Draper, *User Centered System Design: New Perspectives on Human-Computer Interaction* (Hillsdale: Erlbaum, 1986).

57. Feyerabend, *Against Method*, xx.

The demand of fit, however, does not indicate in any way that design is simply *determined* by subjective or contextual requirements (a concern the Systematic Theologian might voice). Quite the contrary: Design is always an active response to such contextual environment, materially altering the environment in order to reorient behavior. As has already been pointed out, however, the designer cannot simply *invent* uses artificially. She will be attentive to the dynamics of the particular environment for which she is forming the materials. Arguably, similar freedoms and constraints obtain in theological work. While we cannot rule out that theologians' conceptual designs will simply reflect their own intentions, experiences, and interests, theologians who are trying to do *better* will look for *fit* with users' needs and capabilities as much as aspiring to let their *intervention* align the existing reality with the reality of God. If the design is not usable, it does not achieve its effects. Or, in Barth's own terms: theological notions must be fitting both to the reality of God and the reality of the human being, not as two distinct realities, rather as one and the same: "the answer must be the *question*."[58] Ultimately, Barth suggests, it is the very definition of the incarnation that it is the point where fit and intervention, communication and transformation become one. What if we understood the incarnation itself as a design solution to a real-life problem, a divine design if ever there was one?

Utopian Pragmatism

Barth of course denies the possibility that our theologies would incarnate the word of God: in this sense, theology remains impossible. Only God can communicate God-self; theology can only point to this reality. But to do so effectively, it has to become an adequate reflection of this reality. In remembrance of the incarnation and anticipation of its fulfillment, the reality of faith is unseen, promised but only experienced ever partially. It demands as much to become manifest as it remains eschatological. Similarly, the double description of design according to "fit" and "intervention" demonstrates that design is as counterfactual as it is responsive to its environment, as pragmatic as it is utopian.

Design is not merely about making artifacts—whether industrial or software products, factory lines or houses. Design responds to perceived needs and reshapes the world to meet them. It projects a vision of human life— and makes it possible; design is not about portraying the world *as it is*, but about transforming it.[59] The realm of what *is* and what *ought to be*, the realm of

---

58. Barth, "The Word of God as the Task of Theology," 179.

59. Cf. Papanek, *Design for the Real World*, 17. Post-humanists have taken the insight that by "designing objects, spaces, tools, and experiences, we are in fact designing the human being itself" a step further in the notion of "ontological design," cf. Daniel Fraga, "The Manifesto of

"things" and the "realm of meanings" become entangled. Once seen through the design lens, nothing can be merely "matter of fact," rather, things become "matters of concern."[60] Opening everything up to interpretation also affords opportunities for discernment, intervention, and change. The design lens allows theology to question a binary distinction between positive and negative approaches, dogmatism and critique, not only to dialectical but also to reparative possibilities. Design is a laboratory for change. The work of critique becomes one of building rather than of tearing down, of offering alternatives and adding space for them to reality as it already exists, rather than diminishing our options. As Latour wisely discerns, the real critic

> is not the one who debunks, but the one who assembles. The critic is not the one who lifts the rugs from under the feet of the naive believers, but the one who offers the participants arenas in which to gather. The critic is not the one who alternates haphazardly between anti-fetishism and positivism like the drunk iconoclast drawn by Goya, but the one for whom, if something is constructed, then it means it is fragile and thus in need of care and caution.[61]

In this vein, design's language can quickly become quite explicitly theological, particularly eschatological: As design attends to the "real world,"[62] it prompts the questions "Which 'World'? What 'Design'? What 'Real'?"[63] Design opens up a horizon of possibilities as it "models alternative presents and possible futures in material and experiential form."[64] Design is thus fundamentally future-oriented—not only concerned with the way things are but also with how things *might be* different and *better*. In this sense, "design inquiry starts not from premise but with a promise. Importantly, the notion of a promise is not only about the risk of failing but also about hope."[65]

The work of design, then, consists in *present*ing alternatives, quite literally and materially: It is "a way to create alternative nows," in the here and now, a way of "making a more diverse set of possible nows more *present*."[66] As such an exercise in world-making, it elicits questions like, are there worlds that are

---

Ontological Design," *Medium*, May 27, 2022, https://medium.datadriveninvestor.com/the-manifesto-of-ontological-design-7fdb19169107.

60. Latour, "A Cautious Prometheus," 4.

61. Bruno Latour, "Why Has Critique Run Out of Steam? From Matters of Fact to Matters of Concern," *Critical Inquiry* 30, no. 2 (January 2004): 225–48, 246.

62. Papanek, *Design for the Real World*.

63. Arturo Escobar, *Designs for the Pluriverse: Radical Interdependence, Autonomy, and the Making of Worlds* (Durham: Duke University Press, 2018), 25.

64. Carl Disalvo, *Adversarial Design* (Cambridge: MIT, 2015).

65. Redstrom, *Making Design Theory*, 131.

66. Redstrom, *Making Design Theory*, 129–30.

more or less sustainable, intellectually, materially, ethically? Drawing on Jesus'
hospitable promise that in his "father's house, there are many dwelling places"
(John 14:2), we might thus ask, can we design—literally and conceptually—a
world "where many worlds fit"?[67]

In its world-building as well as un-worlding aspirations, design's pragmatic
orientation is highly utopian; in its material and practical grounding, its utopian orientation is highly pragmatic.[68] Design is just as counterfactual as it
is responsive to the real world—much like theology, whether in its Constructive or Systematic varieties. And while design suffers from the same concomitant weaknesses as theology—the impossibility of achieving perfection, and
the dangers of falling into totalitarian aspirations on the one hand (hubris) or
relativizing surrenders of responsibility (sloth) on the other—it also harbors
the same ethical challenge: to do *better*, and to keep doing better, drawn by a
promise that lies always beyond its possibility. Design is never done. What if
theology recognized a kindred spirit in design's dual pragmatic and utopian
commitment to the *world that is* out of an orientation toward the promise of
a *world to come*? What might theology learn from design in its deeply experi-
mental nature, its vulnerability to failure as well as its strategies to learn from
mistakes?

Epistemological Quality

We might be compelled by now by the insight that "knowledge . . . is a kind
of design."[69] But our pursuit is not merely that of a critique and deconstruction of theological knowledge. We posed the question, at first somewhat awk-
wardly, "what is the truth of a house?" In continued investment in theology as
a field of knowledge, we might reformulate this question to the epistemological
merit of designed structures now as, "what does design *know*?"

In contradistinction to the *mimetic* understanding of knowledge that dominated Western epistemologies, conceptual design draws on the *poietic* quality of
"maker's knowledge."[70] In his proposal of philosophy as conceptual design, Luciano Floridi returns to the neglected half of the Platonic distinction. We are used
to seeing the practically grounded, artisanal, and creative "maker's knowledge"
as epistemologically inferior to the detached, "objective," theoretical knowledge of

---

67. Escobar, *Designs for the Pluriverse*, 21. Escobar invokes the famous Zapatista motto as
a principle of utopian design, against capitalism's reproduction of "one world" ontologies.
Escobar argues for a decolonized approach to design that focuses on collaborative and place-
based practices and that acknowledges the interdependence of all people, beings, and the earth.

68. For the "dual pragmatic/utopic approach" of design justice, cf. Costanza-Chock, *Design
Justice*, 134, 219, et passim.

69. Hamraie, *Building Access*, 10.

70. Floridi, "Maker's Knowledge."

the observer. But once, "maker's knowledge" was considered as epistemologically superior—its practical disadvantage was merely that it ultimately applied only to the *one* true maker: God.

As already stated, human "making" can at best be imitation and redesign of given materials. But our dwelling in the world is inextricably bound up with our efforts to know and redesign it. And our knowledge of the world is facilitated more through our "exploratory habitation of it, rather than by withdrawing from it in Cartesian fashion to a realm of abstract and detached contemplation,"[71] as Murray Rae lays out. Just as there are different ways to withdraw from the world, there are obviously also different ways of inhabiting and redesigning it. *Better* design is attentive to the fact that the "fashioning of a place for human habitation is not first a work of invention but requires, to begin with, attentiveness to an order that is already there."[72] Design theory gives theology tools to embark on intentional processes of "hermeneutical reverse engineering"[73] of its own conceptions, where "exploration of afforded actions leads to discovery of the system, rather than knowledge of the system metaphor leading to expectations of affordances."[74]

In an age where humans are redesigning natural, cultural, and technological environments like never before, with devastating effects for human and more-than-human societies and the viability of planetary futures, conceptual design has already gone through conversions that theology might yet have to learn. At the same time, it retains the practical insight not just that the systematic ordering of knowledge is itself a constructive enterprise, one that guides material construction, but also that "manufacturing means the same as learning—i.e., acquiring, producing, and passing on information."[75] The epistemic quality of design might just afford a *better* knowledge through the process itself as well as a humbler position toward such knowledge, an "ontological humility" as flagged earlier.

Just like theology, design is highly conscious of the fact that it does not itself create, but with Plato's valuation of poietic knowledge it understands that material engagement affords a different kind of knowledge than mere observation. As we have stressed, design is not constructive in the sense of the relativist caricature that things could be randomly made up. It works with given materials according to requirements that orient and constrain its

71. Rae, *Architecture and Theology*, 154.

72. Rae, *Architecture and Theology*, 153.

73. Anne Balsamo, *Designing Culture: The Technological Imagination at Work* (Durham: Duke University Press, 2011), 15.

74. William W. Gaver, "Technology Affordances," in *Proceedings of the SIGCHI Conference on Human Factors in Computing Systems Reaching Through Technology - CHI '91*, 79–84 (New Orleans: ACM, 1991), 4.

75. Vilém Flusser, *The Shape of Things: A Philosophy of Design* (London: Reaktion, 1999), 50.

task. Its constructive potential is in actively shaping them in the best possible way for their intended purpose. In the process, it encounters resistance and responses, from its materials, from the environment it attempts to fit in, from its users, both the intended and the unintended one, as well as possibly from other affected parties. In this process, the designer learns a great deal about all of them.

As design brings the epistemic affordances of material realities into focus, it uncovers the material base of knowledge projects. From critical access studies to proposals in design justice, design has become a site of critical epistemologies in intense negotiations over what users know and whose practices count as innovation rather than disruption of design. Hamraie draws on poietic understandings of knowledge to uncover the epistemic agency and potential of disabled users. Navigating a world that does not accommodate their bodies, needs, and movements, they are constantly engaged in designing and adapting their own technologies. Just as in the Markean account of the four friends so in Hamraie's study, design turns out to be not just a question of access or materialization of social disablement, but also an epistemic site of what Hamraie calls—in implicit reference to Plato's poietic knowledge—"knowing-making." The epistemic activism of disabled and crip users not only challenges "the built arrangements of segregated spaces, but also the structures of knowledge production itself."[76]

Arguably, design is not only a distinctly epistemic practice but also a site of critical epistemology, epistemic negotiation, and epistemic activism: "Design is also a way of thinking, learning, and engaging with the world."[77] Costanza-Chock argues that reasoning through design is a mode of knowledge production that is abductive—"the best prediction given incomplete observations"—and speculative—"it is about envisioning, as well as manipulating, the future. Designers imagine images, objects, buildings, and systems that do not yet exist. We propose, predict, and advocate for (or, in certain kinds of design, warn against) vision of the future."[78]

A theologian, too, is less of a "maker" in Plato's (ultimately divine) sense and more of a "knower-maker" in Hamraie's sense, or maybe a "sculptor of reality"[79] in Feyerabend's: not the one true creator, but someone who through material engagement with resisting realities comes to understand them better and more truly, while also learning and inventing new ways of navigating, engaging, and transforming them. In the Christian tradition, knowledge of

---

76. Hamraie, *Building Access*, 10.
77. Costanza-Chock, *Design Justice*, 15.
78. Costanza-Chock, *Design Justice*, 15.
79. Feyerabend, *Against Method*, 284.

God has typically had such a practical meaning as well, afforded by prayer and study, community engagement and spiritual experiences.

If, with Karl Barth, we understand theology as the "scientific self-examination of the Christian Church with respect to the content of its distinctive talk about God,"[80] such critical and remedial self-examination might well be conceived in terms of conceptual design, beginning time and again "from the beginning," developing iterative loops of envisioning, implementation, evaluation, and redesign. If, with Marcella Althaus-Reid, we understand theology as a "materially based theology" in which "holiness becomes a project, and a strategy of resistance, . . . a utopia which gathers together the aspirations of many communities for an alternative,"[81] then, too, design theory might be an ally in the negotiations of intervention and utopian envisioning that aim to manifest glimpses of queerly divine justice.

Maybe by now we have a fuller appreciation for what Gibson meant when he noted that the theory of affordances marks "a radical departure from existing theories of value and meaning."[82] The debates over the guilt and innocence of theological concepts (or of the historical figures, movements, and institutions standing behind them) often gets ugly, as we have seen in chapter 1. Design theory's notion of affordances allows us to reframe some of the most vocal Constructive-theological critiques of (Systematic theological) doctrine: Constructive Theologians have called attention to the affordances of doctrine as apparent through the historical uses to which they had been put; they have analytically discerned dysfunctions and design failures on the basis of differential user interaction with doctrine; and they have constructively reappropriated traditional doctrines, redesigning tools that used to serve their oppression, creatively and sometimes subversively into tools for liberative, life-giving purposes.

Marcella Althaus-Reid's work can very well be understood as such a "queer use" of Systematic Theology, or, in her terminology, as its "per/version." Together with the immune reaction it elicits, her Constructive Theology painfully exposes the double failure of Systematic Theology: not only in its initial design process but also in failing to take responsibility for the uses its designs afford. The ensuing stand-off between Systematic and Constructive Theology can be described all too well by Ahmed's words: "The system is working by stopping those who are trying to transform the system. This means that to transform a system we have to stop it from working."[83]

80. Barth, *CD I.1*, 1.
81. Althaus-Reid, "Outing Theology," 153.
82. Gibson, *The Ecological Approach to Visual Perception*, 140.
83. Ahmed, *What's the Use*, 212, italics removed.

Understanding theology as conceptual design affords us an alternative to such a destructive deadlock. Beyond their critical epistemological value, Marcella Althaus-Reid's per/versions serve a distinctly (and declared) constructive-creative purpose: the creation of more versions of Christianity than the dominant orthodoxy, to make room for more versions of people to inhabit such Christianity, even as they might inhabit it otherwise and differently. In the words of the Zapatista revolution, such per/version works toward "a world in which many worlds fit." We might even be reminded of Jesus' claim that in our "father's house, there are many dwelling places" (John 14:2).

De facto, theology already *does* conceptual design. But consciously adopting such a design framework as a hermeneutic for our self-understanding and our task allows us to benefit from the qualities we have just discussed—design's ontological humility, its attention to complexity, its material faithfulness and user sensitivity, its utopian pragmatism and epistemological quality. Adopting a hermeneutic of design further enables us to take seriously a variety of requirements that come into view beyond cognitive systematization and its justification of faith vis-à-vis reason, and hands us a host of best practices to work with. What if by conceptually redesigning theological concepts in relation to their actual use, theological *praxis* as conceptual *poiesis* could deepen our understanding of God and, aspirationally, facilitate a use of theology that will be a better witness to its subject matter?

DESIGN . . . WILL NOT SAVE THEOLOGY

To paraphrase George Box's famous dictum about scientific models, all theologies are wrong, but some are useful.[84] The design lens allows us to recognize the work Constructive Theologies have been doing as creative redesign in response to epistemic activism, and it invites us to an expanded and more rigorous investigation into the *adequatio intellectus ad rem* of theological notions that includes an ethics of material effects and practical uses. It also offers us analytic tools to point out some particularly common types of "design failures" for which, beyond questions of intent, designers rather than users are to be held accountable. It might also raise some new contentions.

From a Systematic side of the conversation, looking at doctrine through the lens of affordances might provoke pushback and questions: is any meaningful theology even possible if it is reduced to affordances, and if the focus is shifted

---

84. Repeated in several variations throughout his work, the aphorism first appeared in published form in George E. P. Box, "Science and Statistics," *Journal of the American Statistical Association* 71 (1976): 791–99.

from *what it says* to *what it does*? Should theology not, at the end of the day, be about truth rather than usefulness? Indeed, theology must be *true to* the God it talks about, and *better* versions of theology have always understood that this must be the criterion to both their content and their form. Such faithfulness to theology's *Sache* prompted even as systematic a theologian as Karl Barth to resist the dictates of method, as we might remember. What the gospel *is* and what kind of theology therefore would be *true to* it and in what way remains to be worked out in detail, theologically, but in principle precisely that should be the criterion. Design, too, has to be true to its purposes and the requirements of the context, as we have seen. Its focus on functionality and usability do not imply the possibility of random invention. They are always in service to its purpose and requirements, which are for the most part given—relationally, thus partially negotiable—and then have to be worked out technically as well as communicatively, just like in theology. Feedback from theology's "users" about doctrinal affordances and their failures are thus crucial to improving theology's *adequatio ad rem*.

If from a Systematic side the anxiety might be whether there is *too much* constructivism in design, from a Constructive side of the conversation, the question might be raised: Is redesign *enough*? Will it not invariably remain caught up in and complicit with the logics it criticizes? Audre Lorde famously posited, "the master's tools will never dismantle the master's house,"[85] powerfully pushing back against working *with* the grain of the system, articulating critique in its own logics, trying to change it by reforming or redesigning it. She writes,

> The old patterns, no matter how cleverly rearranged to imitate progress, still condemn us to cosmetically altered repetitions of the same old exchanges, the same old guilt, hatred, recrimination, lamentation, and suspicion. For we have, built into all of us, old blueprints of expectation and response, old structures of oppression, and these must be altered at the same time as we alter the living conditions which are the result of those structures. For the master's tools will never dismantle the master's house.[86]

We ought to pay attention to the architectural and design metaphors that structure Lorde's scathing criticism. The lens of design might retain Systematic Theologians as the master-builders of the house we are continuing to build. Home improvement is an inherently conservative pastime. It is dubious whether we will be able to even discern the ways our designs are complicit in disaffordances and harm, and even more dubious whether we would be able

---

85. Lorde, "Age, Race, Class, and Sex," 291.
86. Lorde, "Age, Race, Class, and Sex," 291.

to design altogether differently. Lorde not only points us back to the already noted need for "outsider" intervention but also to the realistic insight that some houses might have to be taken down altogether because they are, by design, uninhabitable or because the ways they structure life together cannot be redeemed. There are limits not only to repair but also to repurposing. But mindful of Mark 2:1–12, we might think of such destruction without reconstruction as not in antithesis to, but indeed as one of the options of faithful commitment.

Lorde does not suggest instead a "starting from scratch," either. In material as in conceptual design, there are no pure beginnings. There are only inherited materials, contextual requirements, and the needs that chafe against them. Lorde points to the necessity to change not only the outside world but also the blueprints "built into us," ourselves, concurrently. The work of redesign is more arduous and complex than we might like. But the possibilities of creative repurposing are also greater than one might think. We have seen that "queer use" beyond the intentions of any designer might prompt processes of reevaluation and, potentially, redesign, to remedy obvious misfits between the conceptual objects we design, their purpose, and the uses they afford, helping theology to *do its job better* and thereby be a truer witness. But queer use does more than feed back into the work of the system and stabilize it in the constructive use of its criticism. It not only points to lack in fit, it can also open up discussion about the theological validity of the purposes that oriented the initial design. It exposes the irredeemable but also to some extent self-defeating powers at work in any construction, pointing to its cracks in order to allow some light and fresh air to get in. It registers the refusal of "getting used to it"—i.e., to the fact that the way systems work is by systematic exclusion. It is the defiant insistence against all experience that "it is possible for those deemed strangers or foreigners to take up residence in spaces that have been assumed as belonging to others, as being for others to use."[87]

Queer use can thus pry open conceptual systems and their tools to better accommodate the needs of previously unintended users, or even to deliberately make room for different kinds of uses rather than narrowly prescribing one: "Buildings can be built with queer uses in mind, which is to say, with a commitment to a principle that not all uses could or even should be foreseen."[88] The theologian might eventually suspect that maybe a cathedral is not the only and maybe not even the most *adequate* structure to reflect who God is; that a more flexible and temporal, functional and versatile structure,

87. Ahmed, *What's the Use*, 228.
88. Ahmed, *What's the Use*, 200.

like a nomadic shelter, might provide a resting place more befitting the wandering people of a wandering God.

As noted earlier, the design lens challenges us to ask the question about the ends of doctrine not just as a pragmatic or marketing question, but as a *theological* question: What implicit theologies do the practical uses of doctrine communicate? What would it mean for the uses of doctrine, in our understanding, to adequately reflect the realities these doctrines talk *about?* How might they be actively redesigned to achieve their theological purpose more effectively, minimizing the possibility and damage of misuse without being ever able to rule it out effectively? In this sense, Ahmed's "What's the use [of doctrine]?" might be read as critically reminding us of Melanchthon's challenge that to know Christ is to know Christ's benefits. What are the benefits of Christ, and how does theology—knowledge about Christ—convey such knowledge of Christ? Can doctrine be redesigned—not to redeem itself, but to communicate the benefits of Christ rather than withhold or actively negate them?

But Ahmed's critical investigation "what's the use of use?" also calls into question what uses the valuation of usefulness serves. And both the Constructive Theologian and the Systematic Theologian have ample reasons to be suspicious of "use" as a criterion—wary as the one is of that which neatly benefits the system, and suspicious as the other is of the temptation to prove theology's usefulness as a form of self-justification.

Of course, the design lens does not once and for all *solve* the problem of (bad) theology—nor is it intended to. Users are no less exempt from the human condition of sin than designers, design is not a more holy activity than other human enterprises, and a criterion like use is neither unambiguously good nor salvific. To circle back to the central metaphor of the previous chapter: Just as swords can be transformed into plowshares, thus plowshares can be transformed into swords. Neither are plowshares themselves, for that matter, unequivocal instruments of peace. Literal plowshares can be instruments of ecological exploitation, settler colonialism, and imperial expansion. Even metaphorically, they can be cover-ups for the supposedly benign use of deadly technologies, as in the US Operation Plowshare's use of nuclear bombs for civil "developments." Even early human history gives rise to the suspicion that agriculture and warfare go hand in hand rather than marking opposite options. Cain was reportedly a "tiller of the ground" (Gen. 4:2) and it is not farfetched that a plowshare could have been the weapon he used to kill his brother Abel.

God, we proclaim, can transform the cross into a tree of life, but maybe not even God can prevent that our theologies of the cross end up killing one another. Under conditions of finitude, ambivalence might be the price of freedom. No amount of attention and intention in crafting functionalities, affordances, and feedback loops can *guarantee* to what use the design can be put—use remains irredeemably ambiguous, for good and for bad. No designer can prevent that a pillow would be used to smother someone in their sleep, or a baseball bat to beat someone to pulp. Not even the most ingenious theologian can prevent the possibility that someone will use a doctrine of grace to turn it into an anxiety-producing *syllogismus practicus*, preach a terrorizing "prosperity gospel," or fall into despair over sin. Every problem that haunts the work of theology will still afflict it when conceived as conceptual design.

The design lens does not absolve us from the problem that "method cannot save theology." Not the most sophisticated theoretical lens, not the most critical practice could do so. But what they can do is (a) offer theoretical tools to *better* describe the shape of the bind in which theology finds itself—with more nuance and more honesty; (b) allow for an expansion of perception and criteria, a *better* attention to the theoretical as well as practical complexities inherent in any particular design challenge with solidarity and care; and (c) open up concrete possibilities for navigating them *better* without deluding itself about the possibility of perfection: what the tradition calls the *tertius usus legis*.

A theory of theological design would thus also help us move beyond the urge to reduce "queer use" and Constructive critiques to their *usefulness*—their structural functions for the consolidation and efficiency of our conceptual systems and their top-down design. In this sense, "queer use is just a start."[89] Theologians would do well to remain mindful of the ways in which both the reality of real human beings and the reality of God will never fit into neat categories nor be exhausted by whatever current use we are able to attribute to them. Queer use sounds the reminder that God will always remain a misfit in any system, and that this stubborn and vexing reality, at the end of the day, is our hope.

---

89. Ahmed, *What's the Use*, 198.

Conclusions

BEYOND "AGAINST" METHOD

It is clear, then, that the idea of a fixed method, or of a fixed theory of rationality, rests on too naive a view of man and his social surroundings. To those who look at the rich material provided by history, and who are not intent on impoverishing it in order to please their lower instincts, their craving for intellectual security in the form of clarity, precision, "objectivity," "truth," it will become clear that there is only one principle that can be defended under all circumstances and in all stages of human development. It is the principle: Anything goes.

—Paul Feyerabend[1]

All things are permitted for me. But not all things build up. All things are permitted for me. But I will not be controlled by anything.

—1 Cor. 6,12[2]

In light of certain frustrations with deep-seated divisions in my field along broadly methodological lines, I have been tempted to call this book *Against Method.* Some readers may recognize the reference to the *enfant terrible* of the philosophy of science Paul Feyerabend. But even as that title seemed rhetorically effective, it also seemed misleading. After all, I am not *against method* as such, whatever that would mean. Neither was Feyerabend, for that matter. The original title of his infamous book was *Wider den Methodenzwang*, which would more aptly be translated

1. Feyerabend, *Against Method*, 19.
2. Translation adapted from NRSVue.

241

as *Against the Tyranny of Method*, or *Against Being Bound by Method*. While maybe a bit less catchy than the unqualified *Against Method*, that is much more to the point.

Feyerabend's claim is closer to Paul's sentiment that, "Everything is permitted for me . . . . But I will not be controlled by anything" (1 Cor. 6:12). Far from antinomianism, anti-legalism, or even relativism, Paul's famous freedom does not mean that "everything" is, well, "permitted." Rather than pointing us toward "lawlessness," Paul challenges us to a recover a qualitatively different *use* of the law, one that lives and dwells in the space opened up by God's election, enfleshes grace in communal solidarity, and ultimately contributes to the pleasure of those around him and to the honor of God (1 Cor. 10:31).

Similarly, and contrary to many a superficial reference, Feyerabend's much cited slogan "anything goes" does not imply that "anything," well, "goes." It means that method cannot secure insight and epistemological success, and that *which* method will lead to insight cannot be determined in advance. It means that more often than not, new insight has been generated—in the sciences as much as in theology—by inadvertent or programmatic *dis*regard for whatever counted as good scientific method at the time, and had to be asserted over against it. Not only most new insights, but even most "good" scientific practice originally emerged as deviance, as an outlier idea or unorthodox proceeding, and *became* method and methodologically justified only in hindsight, when validated by its epistemic success.

Feyerabend has often been called (and called himself) a relativist or a pluralist, but these descriptions are misleading, too, if one takes them to mean that all approaches are equally valid or that different approaches might lead to the same insights. Rather, Feyerabend's call for epistemological anarchism is due to a profound *realist* commitment—maybe even stronger than what is typically called realism: Feyerabend is attentive to the ways in which the reality in question is not objective, inert, and passive to the form of engagement with it. Rather, the reality with which method engages, and which Feyerabend personifies at times as Nature, Being, or even God, responds differently to different forms of inquiry. Diverse approaches thus produce unique insights that cannot be achieved by other frames of reference. Nor can they ever be integrated into a unified account, even as all of them also come with their specific limitations and blind spots. Feyerabend's epistemic realism recognizes that any state of scientific theory can never be confused with reality.

His project remains deeply committed to the pursuit of knowledge—*better* knowledge than any single methodological paradigm might procure. It is this investment in *better* knowledge rather than "perfect" knowledge that makes Feyerabend hypercritical of method, anti-fundamentalist with regard to any particular epistemic paradigm, and adamant against the mythological idealization of (whatever counts as) "science" as objective truth. Feyerabend's push for epistemological anarchism is not about chaos and unruliness for their own sake. Rather, it is intent on overcoming the limitations that adherence to any scientific theory and its methodological framework would impose on the possibilities of discovering new and different insights. It is a counterprogram built on a realistic assessment of human nature as well: Seeing the human being drawn naturally toward repetition, regularity, and rationality, there is no need to further strengthen this tendency by prescriptions of methodological rigor. Instead, there is a need to counteract these tendencies deliberately in order to prevent them from becoming rigid and unperceptive. Against what he calls "law and order methodologies," Feyerabend proposes "epistemological anarchism" for the sake of *better* attending to the complexities of reality.[3]

Feyerabend is thus not the spokesperson of a "post-truth" age that doubts the science of epidemiology, climate change, or ballot counting, and it is deeply ironic that today he is sometimes cited by the political right. Yet it might not be unwarranted to ask, is it really still the case that the greatest danger to theological inquiry and human flourishing is methodological dogmatism and a narrow definition of what should count as true, as defined by an elite of experts? Has not this very notion of truth and method already come under attack from so many sides, and from politically highly dubious players? Will the "anything goes" of freedom from methodological control not give room to the "anything goes" of social Darwinism in an epistemic register, the freedom hailed by those reasserting their solipsistic rights undisturbed by ethical questions and the common good? Has the time not come to raise the banner of truth against falsehood, and of rigorous methodological standards against populist propaganda, "alternative facts," and conspiration theories?[4]

What if, however, we understand Feyerabend's "anything goes" less as a revolutionary rallying cry than as a sobering assessment and an anti-idealistic account of the de facto functioning of intellectual inquiry, in a word: their hamartiologically realistic description? Feyerabend himself clarifies, "'anything goes' is not a 'principle' I hold . . . but the terrified exclamation of a rationalist who takes a closer look at history."[5] Feyerabend's studies in the history of science demonstrate that the most applauded breakthroughs in science have often occurred not through a rigorous application of scientific method, but through a deliberate or unwitting departure from them, and their validation has often owed more to trickery and rhetorics than to strict methodological standards. In that sense, Feyerabend first of all challenges us to recognize that science *has always been* more diverse than any methodological framework would assume, and "much more 'sloppy' and 'irrational' than its methodological image."[6]

---

3. Feyerabend, *Against Method*, 9, 153.
4. Feyerabend explicitly reflects on these questions and admits for strategic concessions to reason over inhumanity, 5.
5. Feyerabend, *Against Method*, xvii.
6. Feyerabend, *Against Method*, 160.

This insight, admittedly terrifying to those who want to believe in the epistemic superiority and historical success of rationality, nevertheless is not without promise for the pursuit of *better* knowledge. Feyerabend even maintains that such deviations from methodological standards are "absolutely necessary for the growth of knowledge."[7] Importantly, there are three consequences that Feyerabend does *not* draw from this insight, even vigorously pushes back against: (1) abandoning science, (2) finding a new and superior method, and (3) methodological relativism.

Not a dismissal of science as mere humbug or made-up fantasy is called for, but rather *honesty* about its "unscientific" conditions and functioning—an honesty that might seem indecent to the defenders of method. Feyerabend's historic case studies demonstrate that real and substantial breakthroughs in understanding have been produced by the occasional-essential deviation from method. The consequence to be drawn, then, is not that no insight exists, that all is relative to one's world-view, and that science should be abandoned. The consequence to be drawn is that reality is much more complex, that the pursuit of knowledge is a much more complicated process than can be achieved by following a cookie-cutter-method, and that knowledge and science ultimately demand much more subtle negotiations of method than any generally prescribed and unified program would allow: *More* science, rather than less, and *more* methodological frameworks, not just adherence to one, might be the implication of Feyerabend's dives into historical and epistemological complexities of intellectual inquiry—not the dismissal of method but its pluralization, not the supersession and abrogation of one paradigm by another, but allowing method to grow "sideways," to accumulate different models that describe different aspects of reality, to proliferate tools that allow for a more fine-tuned engagement with reality.

Second, Feyerabend also dismisses the suggestion that his case for epistemological anarchism means replacing conservative standards with more liberal standards, or a previous epistemic paradigm with a newer one of greater explanatory power. Feyerabend pushed back against Karl Popper's falsificationism, which was state of the art in the philosophy of science of his day and which demanded that any scientific theories ought to include provision for concrete means by which they could be falsified, and if such instances occurred in practice they were to be discarded and replaced by new, superior models. Feyerabend vigorously objected: "No single theory ever agrees with all the known facts in its domain."[8] Furthermore, Feyerabend maintained that facts and observations within any epistemic paradigm are not theory-independent. What we understand as "facts" at any given time are merely the particular experiences and observations that are possible under the ontology

---

7. Feyerabend, *Against Method*, 7.
8. Feyerabend, *Against Method*, 33.

of the dominant epistemic paradigm. There can then be no neutral ground
to decide between rivaling theories that respectively account for different
sets of facts. If all theories with their accompanying methodological standards give only partial, and partially contradictory accounts of reality, their
adjudication by way of temporalization—which is the resolution falsificationism amounts to—creates a kind of epistemological illusion through
which the respectively newer paradigm seems more powerful than the one
it is overturning. But much of that is a trick of optics, so to speak. Figure 1
illustrates that the relationship between the explanatory power of different
paradigms is imagined to be like the first or second of the figures while in
fact, it is closer to the third.

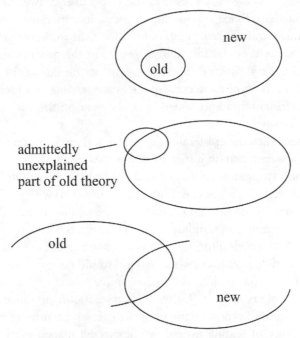

Figure 1: The epistemological illusion created by the new
theory regarding its assumed content.

Any hermeneutic comes with its own hermetics. In this sense, all theories
are not merely falsifiable, but outright *false*—even though they are false in different ways. The problem with falsificationism is that it is just too optimistic
about the possibility to curate the "better" theory on the basis of falsification.
We seldom have the privilege of choosing unfalsified theories over those that

have been falsified—rather, the need is to "choose between theories which we have already tested *and which are falsified*" by one another to some degree.[9] This is effectively the predicament we encountered in chapter 1, where Systematic Theology and Constructive Theology not only presented competing accounts of what "good theology" ought to look like but also disqualified *each other* on that basis, respectively. There is no objective ground from which to chose the best theory; the criteria of choice are always theory-dependent.

Falsificationism defaults to temporal precedence and antecedence to adjudicate between rival theories. But this is an arbitrary criterion that unduly reduces the complexity of reality, resulting in epistemological loss even as it supposedly pushes for progress. Falsificationism's temporalization of epistemic assessment disadvantagously pressures the respectively newer paradigm into dishonest practices. Since it now has to prove its superiority on all counts, it will minimize and conceal unaccounted-for facts and contradictory findings. At the same time, falsificationism results in the automatic dismissal of much that could still provide valuable insight on the side of the respectively older paradigm. Both of these consequences are terrible considered from the aspiration to insight and knowledge since they cut off the excess that reality inevitably presents.

The consequence the epistemic realist draws, then, is that no single methodological paradigm can do justice to reality, "After all, who can say that the world which so strenuously resists unification really is as educators and metaphysicians want it to be—tidy, uniform, the same everywhere?"[10] "Anything goes," then, means the firm conviction that the problem of method will not be "solved by a change of standards" for the better, but only by "taking a different view of standards altogether."[11] Rather than searching for a new and superior methodological framework—which would have different limitations than the old ones, but be just as limited—only "a new *relation* between rules and practices" offers hope.[12] Rather than resulting in pessimism against all method, this honest acknowledgment of the excessive nature of reality opens up the possibility of finding insight in unexpected places, even by virtue of methods that have been "abrogated" by newer developments, for the insights they might yet afford. Once more, it might be worth allowing method to grow sideways, to create loops and multiple presents that can be circled back to, rather than straightening them into past-present-future temporalities.

And finally, just as Feyerabend is not anti-science, so too does he not argue for the kind of relativism that abandons the common project of knowledge and

---

9. Feyerabend, *Against Method*, 45.
10. Feyerabend, *Against Method*, 257.
11. Feyerabend, *Against Method*, 242.
12. Feyerabend, *Against Method*, 242.

is resigned to a pluralism of isolated and irreconcilable theories. Instead, he pushes for a free society with open exchange between different views. Ongoing conversation may at the end of the day thus be the closest we can come to a scientific meta-method. Once more, this is not a romanticization of conversation or its supposedly open and democratic conditions, it is the acknowledgment of a vexing and frustrating reality and the constraints on knowledge that will continue to attend it. Under such conditions, the growth of knowledge will indeed resemble sideways thickenings and accumulation more than the straight line of progress, and scientific practice will resemble the searching and playful navigation of co-existing theories and methodological standards much more than their conclusive proving and disproving. Feyerabend suggests that anyone pursuing such growth "will adopt a pluralistic methodology, he will compare theories with other theories rather than with 'experience,' 'data,' and 'facts,' and he will try to improve rather than discard the views that appear to lose in the competition. For the alternatives, which he needs to make the contest going, may be taken from the past as well. As a matter of fact, they may be taken from wherever he is able to find them."[13] Academic training, or education in general consequently ought to enable people to use different kinds of methods, and equip them for the discernment needed "in a society that contains groups committed to various standards, *but only as one gets proficiency in a game*, that is, without serious commitment and without robbing the mind of its ability to play other games as well."[14]

For a long time, I settled on a more positive and affirmative (working) title: *Better Theology!* "Better Theology!" retains the urge and impetus toward which the dimensions of "against," "after," and "beyond" method gesture. It marks the aspiration to do *better* than any individual methodological paradigm, with its respective limitations and weaknesses, complicities, and blind spots, would allow. Rather than signaling superiority in any absolute sense, the comparative "better" refuses the idea of perfection or even linear progress: doing better is to be understood as an ongoing task of starting over, starting again and again with the beginning, as Barth might say, as one that poses itself anew in each epistemic ecology, in each particular encounter with grace as much as in each contextual encounter with the problem of method, while staunchly committed to the epistemological and ethical. "Better theology" is thus always relative, without being relativistic; aspirational while indexical; invested in beginnings while at the same time deeply an-archic; in theological terms, we would say that it marks an eschatological horizon, not a teleological one.

13. Feyerabend, *Against Method*, 28.
14. Feyerabend, *Against Method*, 165.

I have, however, after much back and forth, eventually decided to call the book *After Method* due to the struggle out of which it emerged, and to avoid triumphalistic misunderstandings. "After Method" does not signal my intention to do away with standards altogether or to leave the search for truth up for grabs and without criteria for its communal and—yes!—rational negotiation. Indeed, it is because I do not think that methodological dogmatism, whether on the "left" (liberationist orthopraxis?) or the "right" (dogmatic orthodoxy?) can overcome these pressing dangers, that I argue—much like Feyerabend!—not "against science" and not even "against method" but against the *tyranny* of any method, against being controlled by it, and against the myth that getting method "right" might *save* us—in theological terms: I am arguing for a desoteriologized understanding of method, a mindful and threefold use of it as an instrument of grace rather than its condition. "After Method" is humbler than "Better Theology," and implies a more complex relation than the antagonistic "Against Method," one that has moved through, and to some extent left behind, the commitment to method as method, while always continuing to find itself in its wake, potentially continuing to make use of it without being controlled by it. But both *after* and *beyond* might also remind us that we will never reach a point at which we can leave behind the "problem of method," resolved, and ready to move on. *After method* is instead of course always *before method*, including in its rather Kafkaesque sense. But such ongoing entanglement is not the only reality there is.

Rather than diluting the critical standards that method affords, I instead see promise for a *better* theology with both more generosity toward a variety of different epistemological paradigms and more rigorous conversation about the respective insights they afford. Such conversation can only take place on the basis of a discernment that is local and contextual and involves diverse stakeholders. Rather than abandoning critical standards, it ought to result in stronger critical standards, even if they are not as easy to translate into 1:1 cooking recipes or checklists against heresy or misuse. Precisely because reality is complex, "there are no general solutions"[15] in the form of whatever theory or methodological program. We would do better to be honest about this, and to forgo the temptation to resolve the question of truth in advance by adherence to any method. It is as simple as that. And as terrifying—unfettered pursuit of insight, wherever it may be found, striving forward as much as backward and sideways.

15. Feyerabend, *Against Method*, xxvii.

PROLEGOMENA, OR: A POSTSCRIPT ON THEOLOGY

> There is always an epistemological ceiling, called faith, or patriarchal faith, which is not removed. This I call the ceiling of decency.
> —*Marcella Althaus-Reid*[16]

> The question now, is whether theology can and ought to get out beyond being a prolegomena to Christology. It could also indeed be the case that with the prolegomena everything is already said.
> —*Karl Barth*[17]

Arguing for such a different view of theological method rather than a different theological method, this book has staged its pursuit *performatively* in what we might call "Feyerabend's wager": Rather than trying to find the one true method that would "make theology relevant again," give it back its sense of identity, and heal its moral injuries (cf. chapter 1), I have played on a couple of different theological paradigms that are often seen as mutually contradictory and often behave antagonistically. Looking through the lenses of a Reformed Systematic Theology and a Constructive Queer Theology, I have analyzed the tension between their respective intuitions and results and suggested why a stricter adherence to method will not solve the problem. Throughout the book, I have been conversing with Karl Barth and Marcella Althaus-Reid, a distinctly dogmatic theology and a distinctly queer one, a critically anti-systematic systematic theology and a critically indecent, materialist, constructive theology, taking both of them seriously while also holding them rather loosely. Disregarding their discursive deadlock, I have continued to wager that in the inferences between them, something *real* would show itself, and maybe even respond.

Design theory has functioned as a sideways interlocutor to get at a more pragmatic yet realistic use of method *after method.* My invocation of building, using, and cruising as central metaphors for such a use will surely elicit allergic reactions of their own. After all, *building* seems to give too much agency to human enterprises over against divine agency ("are we *building* the kingdom of God? Surely not"); *using* seems to instrumentalize epistemology to cater to human needs and desires ("is the truth, is the gospel always *useful*"?); and cruising, well . . .

Querying and queering use remains important, and the *uses of use* make a difference. Augustine famously distinguished between rightly directed and misdirected desires (a distinction that has often been put to anti-queer use).

---

16. Althaus-Reid, *Indecent Theology*, 167.
17. Barth, "The Word of God as the Task of Theology," 197–98.

The final goal of human life is to delight in God (*frui*); everything else should be seen as means that we use in order to attain that goal (*uti*). It is right to delight in created things insofar as in using them we enjoy God as the giver of these gifts. A problem arises when these relationships are inverted: when other things become goals and ultimate enjoyment in themselves, and when God becomes the means to achieve them. Is the desire to attend to the "uses" of theology, as well as the desire to "use" method in non-redemptive, slant, and *third* ways—misdirected? Are we throwing the door wide open to use God as a tool according to human need and desire, or are we on the contrary simply reminding ourselves that method, too, is a tool for free use, a means for delight in God, not an end in itself?

I opened the book with Melanchthon's claim that "*Christum cognoscere est beneficia eius cognoscere.*" Maybe the *beneficia Christi* have always been the place where *uti* and *frui* become indistinguishable as the ultimate incarnates in the penultimate and penultimate things are transfigured into ultimate goods. Rather than trying to generate, achieve, or secure grace, rather than trying to "get in" or "earn grace" or "grow up," the *beneficia Christi* as discerned by a searching exploration of the *uses* of theology can thus serve as an invitation to dwell in the landscapes of both grace and ruin, to explore and cruise the environments laterally rather than trying to enter, penetrate, find fulfillment, redemption, or escape, and, at the end of the day, to play, like children. Might such not be the more adequate mode of enjoyment and delight rather than the furrowed brow of the serious theologian?

Any *third use* is of course remarkably queer from the get-go. If Feyerabend uses political terms to describe his (anti-)methodology as "pluralistic" or "anarchic," we might also call it critically bisexual, as Althaus-Reid does (cf. chapter 4), or nonbinary as a denominator that traverses assumed either/or's of identity in favor of non-antagonistic both/and—before capaciously moving beyond. In this sense, "after method" moves beyond the binary "against method" antagonism, beyond the impasse between different supposedly conflicting methodologies, as well as beyond the distinction of the law's supposedly either "civil" or "theological" functioning (*primus/secundus usus legis*). Rather than abrogating both, it encompasses as well as opens them up in a radically dispossessive manner toward different, open, yet-to-be-determined ends.

While we might hold method more loosely rather than stake our salvation on it, we might also grow more skeptical of those who dedicate themselves to policing it as well as to those who are overconfident in getting it *right*. Every time I encounter my students I am reminded that those who are not quite at home—in a discipline, in the classroom, in the world—may have much to teach us. Conceptual design, as we practice in our theologies, demands close communication and iterative feedback loops of exploration and corroboration, trial and error, envisioning, correction, and development, with the actual *users* of theology—or anyone who would find themselves affected (or excluded) by the way theological structures are built. While "users" of theology in this sense might be pastors or lay Christians, teachers or preachers or readers, those affected by it might extend far beyond these groups, nor be defined by an affiliation to the church or Christianity. If we theologians give up on attempting to redeem ourselves by way of method, and instead venture to look around ourselves, we might just encounter grace in, with, and under the realities in which we live and which we are trying to conceptualize. Excessive commitment, messy solidarity, and indecent honesty may be pointers on the way.

It might seem ironic, to say the least, to write a book "against method" due to frustration over disciplinary debates and divides over method. "Too much sharpening of knives, not enough cutting the meat," as one of my theological mentors kept warning me. Rather than adding to the endless debate about theological method, rather than losing time on counter-method, anti-method, or un-method, ought we not move beyond reflections on method and instead embark on the *doing* of better theology that is so desperately needed?

But method is not about method. Karl Barth would not fail to remind the reader that the so-called *prolegomena* to theology are not something that can be said beforehand and independent of it—prolegomena are concerned not with the things that "can be known and said in advance," but simply with "the first part of dogmatics."[18] Laying out the condition of possibility for theology is not merely a transcendental investigation of human understanding, a genealogy of one's sources, or an analytic definition of warranted true belief. The condition for the possibility of theology, after all, is the reality of a God who scandalously reveals Godself, enters into kenotic solidarity with the creature, and remains stubbornly committed to their flourishing. Nothing in theology can thus ever be settled, decided once and for all, while merely talking prolegomena would also unfailingly get the theologian *in medias res* at substantial theological issues. Marcella Althaus-Reid, too, stipulated the non-independence of theological epistemology from the substance of theology. Her sexual theology was all about calling into question the dominant theological epistemologies in their apparent independence from the material conditions and contexts of its production.

In this book, too, I have wagered that the epistemological and the material, that method and substance of theology are no disjunct subject matters. This is one more sense in which the treatment of method will always be a case of "accidental theology." In the exploration of the shape of the problem of theological method, and in the rejection of its "tyranny," insights into human

---

18. Barth, *CD I.1*, 41.

finitude and sin, in divine grace, in the relative value of the law in an ethical, communal, and immanent rather than a soteriological and transcendent sense have surfaced:

Learning to inhabit, dwell in, and cruise our epistemic ecologies, without ever arriving at one, conclusive, definitive method is an expression of the eschatological itinerance of the Christian. The need for ongoing conversation and communal reasoning that foregrounds the witness of misfits and outsiders, of the most affected and the excluded, is an ecclesiological and pneumatological necessity. Paying attention to material conditions as well as material effects, ecological requirements as well as possible uses, is testament to the incarnational existence of all theo-logy in the flesh. The call to find God outside the gates of theology and thus to uplift marginalized and subjugated experiences to the primary site and expertise of theological reflection speaks to the staurological center of theology. The pointers to the ultimately ineffable nature of God's being, and thus to the non-possessive nature of any methodology, are epistemological versions of the resurrection and ascension: "He is not here!" The insistence on the pre-theological conditions of theology is an insistence on the created nature of all human reasoning. And the pointers to the always-already given materials of theology invoke Scripture as well as revelation, not as origins, but as nodes and preliminary effects of the ongoing work of theological reflection. Finally, a notion like "revelation" can never ground or explain theological insight; rather, it is the concept designed to name the fact that it happens, inexplicably, and for us, accidentally.

The renunciation of method for method's sake, the refusal of a redemptive use of method, then, articulates positive theological insights, even as it proceeds by way of critique and negation. The substance of epistemology is anthropology, but the substance of anthropology is soteriology, hamartiology, eschatology, and at the end of the day Christology. While this book may look like an extended sharpening of knives, my hope is that this process itself is an effect of, rather than a precursor to, the substance it is called to engage. The truth of the pudding will be in the eating. But until that time, it might indeed be the case that "with the prolegomena *everything* is already said."[19]

19. Barth, "The Word of God as the Task of Theology," 198.

Bibliography

Adorno, Theodor W. *Negative Dialectics*. Translated by E. B. Ashton. Routledge; Taylor & Francis. London, 2003.

Adorno, Theodor W. *Minima Moralia: Reflections from Damaged Life*. Translated by E. F. N. Jephcott. London: Verso, 2010.

Agamben, Giorgio. "The Messiah and the Sovereign: The Problem of Law in Walter Benjamin." In *Potentialities: Collected Essays in Philosophy*, 160–76. Stanford: Stanford University Press, 1990.

Ahmed, Sara. *Complaint!* Durham: Duke University Press, 2021.

———. *Queer Phenomenology: Orientations, Objects, Others*. Durham: Duke University Press, 2006.

———. *What's the Use? On the Uses of Use*. Durham; London: Duke University Press, 2019.

Alexander, Christopher. *The Timeless Way of Building*. New York: Oxford University Press, 1979.

Althaus-Reid, Marcella. "Class, Sex and the Theologian." In *Another Possible World*, edited by Marcella Althaus-Reid, Ivan Petrella, and Luiz Carlos Susin. Reclaiming Liberation Theology. London: SCM, 2007.

———. *Indecent Theology: Theological Perversions in Sex, Gender and Politics*. London: Routledge, 2000.

———. "Outing Theology: Thinking Christianity Out of the Church Closet." *Feminist Theology* 27 (2001): 57–67.

———. *The Queer God*. London: Routledge, 2003.

Althaus-Reid, Marcella, and Lisa Isherwood. "Thinking Theology and Queer Theory." *Feminist Theology* 15, no. 3 (2007): 302–14. https://doi.org/10.1177/0966735006076168.

Althaus-Reid, Marcella, Ivan Petrella, and Luiz Carlos Susin, eds. *Another Possible World*. London: SCM, 2007.

Anderson, Fiona. "Cruising as Method and Its Limits." *LUX*, August 23, 2017. https://lux.org.uk/cruising-method-limits-fiona-anderson/, 2017.

Ariès, Philippe. *Centuries of Childhood: A Social History of Family Life*. New York: Knopf; Random House, 1962.

Baard, Rachel Sophia. *Sexism and Sin-Talk: Feminist Conversations on the Human Condition*. Louisville: WJK, 2019.

Balsamo, Anne. *Designing Culture: The Technological Imagination at Work*. Durham: Duke University Press, 2011.

Barth, Karl. "Brief an einen Pfarrer in der DDR." In *Offene Briefe 1945–1968*, edited by Diether Koch, 35:401–39. GA. Zürich: TVZ, 1984.

———. *Church Dogmatics.* Edited by G. W. Bromiley and T. F. Torrance. 14 vols. Edinburgh: T&T Clark, 1936–1962.

———. *Evangelical Theology: An Introduction.* Translated by Grover Foley. Grand Rapids: Eerdmans, 1979.

———. "Evangelium und Gesetz." Edited by Lucius Kratzert and Peter Zocher, 55:172–220. GA. Zürich: TVZ, 2021.

———. *Fides Quaerens Intellectum: Anselms Beweis der Existenz Gottes im Zusammenhang seines theologischen Programms.* Vol. 3. Forschungen zur Geschichte und Lehre des Protestantismus. München: Kaiser, 1931.

———. "Gospel and Law." In *Community, State, and Church*, edited by David Haddorf, 71–100. Eugene: Wipf & Stock, 2004.

———. "The Christian in Society." In *The Word of God and Theology*, edited by Amy Marga, 31–70. London; New York: T&T Clark, 2011.

———. *The Christian Life: Church Dogmatics IV, 4 Lecture Fragments.* Edited by Geoffrey W. Bromiley. London; New York: T&T Clark, 2004.

———. *The Epistle to the Romans.* Translated by Edwyn C. Hoskyns. Oxford: Oxford University Press, 1968.

———. "The First Commandment as a Theological Axiom [1933]." In *The Way of Theology in Karl Barth: Essays and Comments*, edited by Martin Rumscheidt, 63–78. Allison Park: Pickwick, 1986.

———. *The Word of God and Theology.* Edited by Amy Marga. London: T&T Clark, 2011.

———. "The Word of God as the Task of Theology, 1922." In *The Word of God and Theology*, edited by Amy Marga, 171–98. London: T&T Clark, 2011.

———. *Theological Existence To-Day!: (A Plea for Theological Freedom) [1934].* Translated by R. Birch Hoyle. Eugene: Wipf & Stock, 2012.

———. "Wünschbarkeit und Möglichkeit eines allgemeinen reformierten Glaubensbekenntnisses. 1925." In *Vorträge und kleinere Arbeiten 1922–1925*, edited by Hinrich Stoevesandt, 19:604–43. GA. Zürich: TVZ, 1990.

Bauckham, Richard. *Jesus: A Very Short Introduction.* Oxford: Oxford University Press, 2011.

Bauke-Ruegg, Jan. "'Hoc est Christum cognoscere beneficia eius cognoscere': Melanchthons 'Loci Communes' von 1521 und die Frage nach dem Proprium reformatorischer Dogmatik. Ein Lektüreversuch." *Neue Zeitschrift für Systematische Theologie und Religionsphilosophie* 42, no. 3 (2000). https://doi.org/10.1515/nzst.2000.42.3.267.

Benjamin, Walter. "Charles Baudelaire. Ein Lyriker im Zeitalter des Hochkapitalismus, Zentralpark 1937." In *Gesammelte Schriften*, edited by Rolf Tiedemann and Hermann Schweppenhäuser, 1:509–690. Frankfurt / Main: Suhrkamp, 1991.

———. "Letter to Gershom Scholem on Franz Kafka." In *Selected Writings, Volume 3: 1935–1938*, edited by Edmund Jephcott and Howard Eiland, translated by Edmund Jephcott, 322–29. Cambridge: Cambridge University Press, 2002.

Berlant, Lauren. *Cruel Optimism.* Durham: Duke University Press, 2011.

Bersani, Leo. "Sociability and Cruising." *Umbr(a): A Journal of the Unconscious* no. 1 (2002), 9–23.

Best, Ernest. *Following Jesus: Discipleship in the Gospel of Mark.* Journal for the Study of the New Testament 4. Sheffield: JSOT Press, 1981.

Betcher, Sharon V. "Crip/Tography: Disability Theology in the Ruins of God." *JCRT* 15, no. 2 (2016): 98–115.

Boring, M. Eugene. *Mark: A Commentary*. New Testament Library. Louisville: WJK, 2006.

Box, George E. P. "Science and Statistics," *Journal of the American Statistical Association* 71 (1976): 791–99.

Brandt, Sigrid. "Sünde: Ein Definitionsversuch." In *Sünde: Ein unverständlich gewordenes Thema*, edited by Sigrid Brandt, Marjorie Suchocki, and Michael Welker, 13–34. Neukirchen-Vluyn: Neukirchener, 1997.

Bray, Karen. *Grave Attending: A Political Theology for the Unredeemed*. New York: Fordham University Press, 2019.

Brintnall, Kent L. "Desire's Revelatory Conflagration." *Theology & Sexuality* 23, no. 1–2 (2017): 48–66. https://doi.org/10.1080/13558358.2017.1341206.

———. "Who Weeps for the Sodomite?" In *Sexual Disorientations*, edited by Kent L. Brintnall, Joseph A. Marchal, and Stephen D. Moore, 145–60. New York: Fordham University Press, 2020. https://doi.org/10.1515/9780823277544-007.

Britzman, Deborah P. "Theory Kindergarten." In *Regarding Sedgwick: Essays on Queer Culture and Critical Theory*, edited by Stephen M. Barber and David L. Clark, 121–42. New York: Routledge, 2002.

Brunner, Emil, and Karl Barth. *Natural Theology: Comprising "Nature and Grace" by Emil Brunner and the Reply "No!" by Karl Barth*. Eugene: Wipf & Stock, 2002.

Buber, Martin. *Two Types of Faith*. Translated by Norman P. Goldhawk. Syracuse: Syracuse University Press, 2003.

Buchanan, George Wesley. *To the Hebrews*. Garden City: Doubleday, 1972.

Buddeus, Johann Franz. *Isagoge Historico-Theologica Ad Theologiam Universam Singulasque Eius Partes*. Leipzig: Fritsch, 1727.

Buell, Denise Kimber, and Caroline Johnson Hodge. "The Politics of Interpretation: The Rhetoric of Race and Ethnicity in Paul." *Journal of Biblical Literature* 123, no. 2 (2004): 235. https://doi.org/10.2307/3267944.

Butler, Judith. *Gender Trouble: Feminism and the Subversion of Identity*. New York: Routledge, 1990.

Cacciari, Massimo. *Icone Della Legge*. Milan: Adelphi, 1985.

Calvin, John. *Institutes of the Christian Religion*. Edited by John T. McNeill. Translated by Ford Lewis Battles. Philadelphia: Westminster Press, 1960.

———. *John Calvin's Commentary on the Letter to the Hebrews*. Translated by John Owen. Louisville: GLH, 2020.

Cappelen, Herman. *Fixing Language: An Essay on Conceptual Engineering*. Oxford; New York: Oxford University Press, 2018.

Chakrabarty, Dipesh. *Provincializing Europe: Postcolonial Thought and Historical Difference*. Princeton: Princeton University Press, 2000.

Chalamet, Christophe. *A Most Excellent Way: An Essay on Faith, Hope, and Love*. Lanham: Lexington; Fortress, 2020.

Chalmers, David J. "What Is Conceptual Engineering and What Should It Be?" *Inquiry*, (2020): 1–18. https://doi.org/10.1080/0020174X.2020.1817141.

Charry, Ellen T. *By the Renewing of Your Minds: The Pastoral Function of Christian Doctrine*. New York: Oxford University Press, 1999. https://doi.org/10.1093/acprof:oso/9780195134865.001.0001.

Clark, Hazel, and David Brody, eds. *Design Studies: A Reader*. Oxford; New York: Berg, 2009.

Cockerill, Gareth Lee. *The Epistle to the Hebrews*. New International Commentary on the New Testament. Grand Rapids: Eerdmans, 2012.

Code, Lorraine. *Ecological Thinking: The Politics of Epistemic Location*. Oxford: Oxford University Press, 2006.

Collins, Adela Yarbro, and Harold W. Attridge. *Mark: A Commentary*. Hermeneia: A Critical and Historical Commentary on the Bible. Minneapolis: Fortress, 2007.

Collins, Patricia Hill. *Intersectionality as Critical Social Theory*. Durham: Duke University Press, 2019.

———. "Learning from the Outsider Within: The Sociological Significance of Black Feminist Thought." *Social Problems* 33, no. 6 (1986): S14–32. https://doi .org/10.2307/800672.

Cone, Cecil Wayne. *The Identity Crisis in Black Theology*. Nashville: Barbour, 2003.

Cone, James H. *A Black Theology of Liberation*. 40th Anniversary edition. Maryknoll: Orbis, 2010.

Cornwall, Susannah. "'Something There Is That Doesn't Love a Wall': Queer Theologies and Reparative Readings." *Theology & Sexuality* 21, no. 1 (2015): 20–35. https://doi.org/10.1080/13558358.2015.1115596.

Costanza-Chock, Sasha. *Design Justice: Community-Led Practices to Build the Worlds We Need*. Cambridge: MIT, 2020.

Crenshaw, Kimberlé. "Demarginalizing the Intersection of Race and Sex: A Black Feminist Critique of Antidiscrimination Doctrine, Feminist Theory and Antiracist Politics." *University of Chicago Legal Forum* 1989, no. 1 (1989): 139–67.

Cronin, Micah. "Queer Grace: An Essay on the Task of Queer Theology." *Theology & Sexuality* (forthcoming).

Daly, Mary. *Beyond God the Father: Toward a Philosophy of Women's Liberation*. Boston: Beacon Press, 1973.

Daniels, Brandy. "Is There No Gomorrah? Christian Ethics, Identity, and the Turn to Ecclesial Practices: What's the Difference?" *JSCE* 39, no. 2 (2019): 287–302. https://doi.org/10.5840/jsce2019102313.

Davis, Jenny L. *How Artifacts Afford: The Power and Politics of Everyday Things*. Edited by Ken Friedman and Erik Stolterman. Cambridge: MIT, 2020.

De la Torre, Miguel A. *Embracing Hopelessness*. Minneapolis: Fortress, 2017.

Dean, Tim. *Unlimited Intimacy: Reflections on the Subculture of Barebacking*. Chicago; London: University of Chicago Press, 2009.

Dean, Timothy James. "An Impossible Embrace: Queerness, Futurity, and the Death Drive." In *A Time for the Humanities: Futurity and the Limits of Autonomy*. Edited by James J. Bono, Tim Dean, and Ewa Plonowska Ziarek. 122–40. New York: Fordham University Press, 2008. https://doi.org/10.5422/fso /9780823229192.003.0009.

Deleuze, Gilles, and Felix Guattari. *What Is Philosophy?* Translated by Hugh Tomlinson and Graham Burchell. New York: Columbia University Press, 1996.

Derrida, Jacques. "Before the Law." In *Acts of Literature*. Edited by Derek Attridge, 181–220. New York: Routledge, 1991.

Detmers, Achim. *Reformation und Judentum*. Stuttgart: Kohlhammer, 2001.

Disalvo, Carl. *Adversarial Design*. Cambridge: MIT, 2015.

Dorrien, Gary. "Theology and Socialism Intertwined and Held Apart: Social Democracy, Ragaz, Christian Socialism, and Barth." Unpublished talk at "Karl

Barth and the Political" hosted by Center for Barth Studies, Princeton, June 23, 2021.

Douglas, Kelly Brown. *The Black Christ*. Maryknoll: Orbis, 1994.

Duggan, Lisa. "Queer Complacency Without Empire." *Bully Bloggers*, September 22, 2015. https://bullybloggers.wordpress.com/2015/09/22/queer-complacency -without-empire.

Dussel, Enrique D. *Philosophy of Liberation*. Maryknoll: Orbis, 1985.

Edelman, Lee. *No Future: Queer Theory and the Death Drive*. Series q. Durham: Duke University Press, 2004.

Escobar, Arturo. *Designs for the Pluriverse: Radical Interdependence, Autonomy, and the Making of Worlds*. Durham: Duke University Press, 2018.

Feyerabend, Paul. *Against Method: Outline of an Anarchistic Theory of Knowledge*. Edited by Ian Hacking. London; New York: Verso, 2010.

Floridi, Luciano. "The Logic of Design as a Conceptual Logic of Information." *Minds and Machines* 27, no. 3 (2017): 495–519. https://doi.org/10.1007/s11023 -017-9438-1.

———. *The Logic of Information: A Theory of Philosophy as Conceptual Design*. Oxford: Oxford University Press, 2019.

———. "What a Maker's Knowledge Could Be." *Synthese* 195, no. 1 (2018): 465–81. https://doi.org/10.1007/s11229-016-1232-8.

Flusser, Vilém. *The Shape of Things: A Philosophy of Design*. London: Reaktion, 1999.

Foucault, Michel. *Discipline and Punish: The Birth of the Prison*. New York: Random House, 1977.

———. *Power/Knowledge: Selected Interviews and Other Writings, 1972–1977*. New York: Pantheon, 1980.

Fraga, Daniel. "The Manifesto of Ontological Design." *Medium*, May 27, 2022. https://medium.datadriveninvestor.com/the-manifesto-of-ontological-design -7fdb19169107.

Freedman, Joseph S. "Keckermann, Bartholomaeus." In *Encyclopedia of Renaissance Philosophy*, edited by Marco Sgarbi, 1–4. Cham: Springer, 2016.

Freud, Sigmund. "Eine Schwierigkeit der Psychoanalyse." *Imago: Zeitschrift für Anwendung der Psychoanalyse auf die Geisteswissenschaften* 5 (1917): 1–7.

Fricker, Miranda. *Epistemic Injustice*. Oxford: Oxford University Press, 2007.

Friedrich, Benedikt. "Gottes Resignieren." In *Verletzt Fühlen: Systematisch-theologische Perspektiven auf den Zusammenhang von Verletzung und Emotion*, edited by Lisanne Teuchert, Mikkel Gabriel Christoffersen, and Dennis Dietz, 219–43. Tübingen: Mohr Siebeck, 2022.

———. *Modelle der Erlösung: Eschatologische Denkformen im Anschluss an die Theologie Karl Barths*. Theologische Anstöße. Göttingen: Vandenhoeck & Ruprecht, forthcoming 2023.

Fulkerson, Mary McClintock. "Sexism as Original Sin: Developing a Theacentric Discourse." *Journal of the American Academy of Religion* 59, no. 4 (1991): 653–75.

Garcia, Kevin. *Bad Theology Kills: Undoing Toxic Belief & Reclaiming Your Spiritual Authority*. Independently published, 2020.

Garland-Thomson, Rosemarie. "Misfits: A Feminist Materialist Disability Concept." *Hypatia* 26, no. 3 (2011): 591–609. https://doi.org/10.1111/j.1527-2001.2011 .01206.x.

———. "The Story of My Work: How I Became Disabled." *Disability Studies Quarterly* 34, no. 2 (2014). https://doi.org/10.18061/dsq.v34i2.4254.

Gaver, William W. "Technology Affordances." In *Proceedings of the SIGCHI Conference on Human Factors in Computing Systems Reaching Through Technology - CHI '91*, 79–84. New Orleans: ACM, 1991. https://doi.org/10.1145/108844.108856.

Ghaziani, Amin, and Matt Brim. "Queer Methods: Four Provocations for an Emerging Field." In *Imagining Queer Methods*, edited by Amin Ghaziani and Matt Brim, 3–27. New York: New York University Press, 2019. https://doi.org/10.18574/nyu/9781479808557.003.0003.

Gibson, James J. *The Ecological Approach to Visual Perception*. Dallas; London: Houghton Mifflin, 1979.

Gilliss, Martha Schull. "Resurrecting the Atonement." In *Feminist and Womanist Essays in Reformed Dogmatics*, edited by Amy Plantinga Pauw and Serene Jones, 125–39. Columbia Series in Reformed Theology. Louisville: WJK, 2006.

Gogarten, Friedrich. "Die Krisis unserer Kultur [1920]." In *Anfänge der dialektischen Theologie*, edited by Jürgen Moltmann, 2:101–21. München: Kaiser, 1963.

Grant, Jacquelyn. *White Women's Christ and Black Women's Jesus: Feminist Christology and Womanist Response*. American Academy of Religion Academy Series 64. Atlanta: Scholars Press, 1989.

Gritsch, Eric W. *Martin Luther's Anti-Semitism: Against His Better Judgment*. Grand Rapids: Eerdmans, 2012.

Guthrie, George. "Hebrews' Use of the Old Testament: Recent Trends in Research." *Currents in Research: Biblical Studies* 1 (2003): 271–94.

Gutiérrez, Gustavo. *A Theology of Liberation: History, Politics, and Salvation*. Translated by John Eagleson and Caridad Inda. London: SCM, 1973.

Haddorf, David. "Karl Barth's Theological Politics." In *Community, State, and Church*, edited by David Haddorf, 1–69. Eugene: Wipf & Stock, 2004.

Halberstam, Jack. *Female Masculinity*. Duke: Duke University Press, 1998.

———. "Straight Eye for the Queer Theorist: A Review of 'Queer Theory without Antinormativity'." *Bully Bloggers*, September 12, 2015. https://bullybloggers.wordpress.com/2015/09/12/straight-eye-for-the-queer-theorist-a-review-of-queer-theory-without-antinormativity-by-jack-halberstam.

Halberstam, Judith. *The Queer Art of Failure*. Durham: Duke University Press, 2011.

Hamraie, Aimi. *Building Access: Universal Design and the Politics of Disability*. Minneapolis: University of Minnesota Press, 2017.

Haraway, Donna J. "Situated Knowledges: The Science Question in Feminism and the Privilege of Partial Perspective." *Feminist Studies* 14, no. 3 (1988): 575–99.

———. *Staying with the Trouble: Making Kin in the Chthulucene*. Durham; London: Duke University Press, 2016.

Harding, Sandra. "Introduction: Is There a Feminist Method?" In *Feminism and Methodology*, edited by Sandra Harding, 1–14. Bloomington: Indiana University Press, 1987.

Haslanger, Sally. "Gender and Race: (What) Are They? (What) Do We Want Them to Be?" *Noûs* 34, no. 1 (March 2000): 31–55. https://doi.org/10.1111/0029-4624.00201.

Heschel, Susannah. *The Aryan Jesus*. Princeton: Princeton University Press, 2010.

hooks, bell. "Choosing the Margin as a Space of Radical Openness." In *Yearning: Race, Gender, and Cultural Politics*, 145–53. Boston: South End, 1990.

Hunsinger, George. "Barth and Luther." In *Wiley Blackwell Companion to Karl Barth*, edited by George Hunsinger and Keith L. Johnson, 461–72. Wiley Blackwell Companions to Religion. Chichester: Wiley Blackwell, 2019.

Jagose, Annamarie. "The Trouble with Antinormativity." *Differences* 26, no. 1 (2015): 26–47. https://doi.org/10.1215/10407391-2880591.

Johnson, Luke Timothy. *Hebrews: A Commentary*. Louisville: WJK, 2006.

Jones, Serene. *Feminist Theory and Christian Theology: Cartographies of Grace*. Guides to Theological Inquiry. Minneapolis: Fortress, 2000.

Jongte, Rochhuahthanga. "The Being of the Electing God: The Relevance of Karl Barth's Doctrine of Election for a Liberationist Theological Ontology." PhD thesis, Princeton Theological Seminary, 2023.

Jordan, Mark D. *The Invention of Sodomy in Christian Theology*. Chicago: University of Chicago Press, 1998.

Kaalund, Jennifer T. *Reading Hebrews and 1 Peter with the African American Great Migration: Diaspora, Place, and Identity*. London: T&T Clark, 2019.

Kafka, Franz. *The Aphorisms of Franz Kafka*. Edited by Reiner Stach. Translated by Shelley Frisch. Princeton: Princeton University Press, 2002.

———. *The Trial: A New Translation Based on the Restored Text*. Translated by Breon Mitchell. New York: Schocken, 1999.

Kalinna, Hermann E. J. *War Karl Barth, „Politisch einzigartig wach"? Über Versagen politischer Urteilskraft*. Münster: LIT, 2009.

Kant, Immanuel. *Critique of Pure Reason*. Bohn's Philosophical Library. London: Bell, 1897.

Kaufmann, Thomas. "Luther, Martin." In *Handbuch des Antisemitismus: Judenfeindschaft in Geschichte und Gegenwart*, edited by Wolfgang Benz, 2.2:501–6. Berlin: De Gruyter, 2009.

———. *Luther's Jews: A Journey into Anti-Semitism*. Oxford; New York: Oxford University Press, 2017.

Keckermann, Bartholomaeus. *Systema S.S. Theologiae, tribus libris adornatum*. Hanau: Antonius, 1602.

———. *Systema systematum*. Hanau: Antonius 1613.

Kelty, Christopher M. *Two Bits: The Cultural Significance of Free Software*. Durham: Duke University Press, 2008.

Kranzberg, Melvin. "Kranzberg's Laws." *Technology and Culture* 27, no. 3 (1986): 544–60.

Krippendorff, Klaus, and Reinhart Butter. "Product Semantics: Exploring the Symbolic Qualities of Form." *Innovation* 3, no. 2 (1984): 4–9.

Krug, Steve. *Don't Make Me Think, Revisited: A Common Sense Approach to Web Usability*. Berkeley: New Riders, 2014.

Kuhn, Thomas S. *The Structure of Scientific Revolutions*. Chicago: University of Chicago Press, 1962.

Lacan, Jacques. *Écrits*. Paris: Seuil, 1966.

———. *The Seminar of Jacques Lacan: Book 1, Freud's Papers on Technique, 1953–1954*. Edited by Jacques-Alain Miller. Translated by John Forrester. New York: Norton, 1991.

Lane, William L., John D. W. Watts, and Ralph P. Martin. *Hebrews 9–13, Volume 47B*. Edited by David Allen Hubbard and Glenn W. Barker. Dallas: Word, 1991.

Latour, Bruno. "A Cautious Prometheus? A Few Steps toward a Philosophy of Design (with Special Attention to Peter Sloterdijk)." In *Networks of Design: Proceedings*

of the 2008 Annual International Conference of the Design History Society (UK), edited
   by Jonathan Glynne, Fiona Hackney, and Minton Viv, 2–10. Boca Raton:
   Universal, 2008.

———. "Why Has Critique Run Out of Steam? From Matters of Fact to Matters
   of Concern." *Critical Inquiry* 30, no. 2 (January 2004): 225–48. https://doi
   .org/10.1086/421123.

Lessing, Gotthold Ephraim. *Lessing: Philosophical and Theological Writings*. Translated by
   Hugh Barr Nisbet. Cambridge: Cambridge University Press, 2005.

Link, Christian. "Bleibende Einsichten von Tambach." In *Karl Barth in Deutschland*,
   edited by Michael Beintker, Christian Link, and Michael Trowitzsch, 333–46.
   Zürich: TVZ, 2005.

Linné, Carl von. *Systema Naturae*. 10. ed. Weinheim: Cramer, 1964.

Liska, Vivian. "'Before the Law Stands a Doorkeeper. To This Doorkeeper Comes a
   Man . . .': Kafka, Narrative, and the Law." *Naharaim* 6, no. 2 (2013): 175–94.
   https://doi.org/10.1515/naha-2012-0011.

Litz, Brett T., Nathan Stein, Eileen Delaney, Leslie Lebowitz, William P. Nash,
   Caroline Silva, and Shira Maguen. "Moral Injury and Moral Repair in War
   Veterans: A Preliminary Model and Intervention Strategy." *Clinical Psychology
   Review* 29, no. 8 (2009): 695–706.

Lloyd, Vincent. *The Problem with Grace: Reconfiguring Political Theology*. Stanford: Stanford
   University Press, 2011.

Long, Thomas G. *Hebrews: Interpretation: A Bible Commentary for Teaching and Preaching*.
   Louisville: WJK, 1997.

Lorde, Audre. "Age, Race, Class, and Sex: Women Defining Difference." In *Words
   of Fire: An Anthology of African-American Feminist Thought*, edited by Beverly Guy-
   Sheftall. New York: The New Press, 1995.

Love, Heather. *Feeling Backward: Loss and the Politics of Queer History*. Cambridge: Harvard
   University Press, 2009.

———. "Queer Messes." *Women's Studies Quarterly* 44, no. 3/4 (2016): 345–49.

———. "Truth and Consequences: On Paranoid Reading and Reparative Reading."
   Criticism 52, no. 2 (2010): 235–41.

Lowe, Mary E. "Sin from a Queer, Lutheran Perspective." In *Transformative Lutheran
   Theologies: Feminist, Womanist, and Mujerista Perspectives*, edited by Mary Streufert,
   71–86. Minneapolis: Fortress, 2010.

Luther, Martin. *Martin Luther, the Bible, and the Jewish People: A Reader*. Minneapolis:
   Fortress, 2012.

———. "Nr. 428 Luther and Melanchthon. Wartburg, 9. September 1521." In *WAB
   2 (1520–1522)*, edited by Joachim Karl Friedrich Knaake, 382–87. Weimar:
   Böhlaus, 1931.

———. *The Freedom of a Christian, 1520: The Annotated Luther*. Edited by Timothy J.
   Wengert. Paris: Fortress, 2016.

Mace, Ronald. "A Perspective on Universal Design." In *Designing for the 21st Century:
   An International Conference on Universal Design*, edited by Jan Reagan. Hofstra
   University, Hempstead, New York, 1998.

Maurer, Wilhelm. "Melanchthons Anteil am Streit zwischen Luther und Erasmus."
   Archiv für Reformationsgeschichte 49 (1958): 89–115.

McCain, Paul Timothy, Edward Andrew Engelbrecht, Robert Cleveland Baker, and
   Gene Edward Veith, eds. "The Formula of Concord, Solid Declaration (1577)."

In *Concordia: The Lutheran Confessions—A Reader's Edition of the Book of Concord*, 503–620. St. Louis: Concordia, 2007.

McLeod Campbell, John. *The Nature of the Atonement and Its Relation to Remission of Sins and Eternal Life*. Cambridge: Macmillan, 1856.

McSwain, Jeff. *Simul Sanctification: Barth's Hidden Vision for Human Transformation*. Eugene: Pickwick, 2018.

Melanchthon, Philip. *Commonplaces: Loci Communes 1521*. Translated by Christian Preus. Saint Louis: Concordia, 2014.

Melanchthon, Philipp. *Opera Quae Supersunt Omnia*. Edited by Karl Gottlieb Bretschneider. CR 1. Halle: Schwetschke, 1834.

Meyerhoff, Tina. "Affordances in the Work of Eve Kosofksy Sedgwick: Pedagogies of Writing, Reading, and Making." PhD thesis, City University of New York, 2019.

Migliore, Daniel L. *Faith Seeking Understanding: An Introduction to Christian Theology*. Grand Rapids: Eerdmans, 1991.

Mignolo, Walter. *The Darker Side of Western Modernity: Global Futures, Decolonial Options*. Latin America Otherwise: Languages, Empires, Nations. Durham: Duke University Press, 2011.

Moltmann, Jürgen. *The Crucified God: The Cross of Christ as the Foundation and Criticism of Christian Theology*. New York: Harper & Row, 1974.

———. *Theology of Hope: On the Ground and the Implications of a Christian Eschatology*. Minneapolis: Fortress, 1993.

Muller, Richard A. *Post-Reformation Reformed Dogmatics*. Vol. 1: Prolegomena to Theology. Grand Rapids: Baker, 1987.

Muñoz, José Esteban. *Cruising Utopia: The Then and There of Queer Futurity*. Sexual Cultures. New York: New York University Press, 2009.

———. "The Antisocial Thesis in Queer Theory." *PMLA* 121, no. 3 (2006): 819–28.

Nietzsche, Friedrich. *Thus Spake Zarathustra*. Translated by Thomas Common. Standard Ebooks, 2021.

Norman, Don. *The Design of Everyday Things: Revised and Expanded Edition*. New York: Basic, 2013.

Norman, Donald A., and Stephen W. Draper. *User Centered System Design: New Perspectives on Human-Computer Interaction*. Hillsdale: Erlbaum, 1986.

Nüssel, Friederike. *Bund und Versöhnung: Zur Begründung der Dogmatik bei Johann Franz Buddeus*. Vol. 77. Forschungen zur Systematischen und Ökumenischen Theologie. Göttingen: Vandenhoeck & Ruprecht, 1996.

Oelke, Harry, ed. *Martin Luthers "Judenschriften": Die Rezeption im 19. und 20. Jahrhundert*. Arbeiten zur kirchlichen Zeitgeschichte. Reihe B, Darstellungen, Band 64. Göttingen: Vandenhoeck & Ruprecht, 2016.

Office of the General Assembly, ed. Heidelberg Catechism. In *Book of Confessions: The Constitution of the Presbyterian Church (U.S.A.)*, 27–74. Louisville: Office of the General Assembly, Presbyterian Church (U.S.A.), 2014.

Ofield-Kerr, Simon. "Cruising the Archive." *Journal of Visual Culture* 4, no. 3 (2005). https://doi.org/10.1177/1470412905058353.

Osten-Sacken, Peter von der. *Martin Luther und die Juden: Neu untersucht anhand von Anton Margarithas „Der gantz Jüdisch glaub" (1530/31)*. Stuttgart: Kohlhammer, 2002.

Pangritz, Andreas. *Theologie und Antisemitismus: Das Beispiel Martin Luthers*. Frankfurt / Main: Lang, 2017.

Pannenberg, Wolfhart. *Systematic Theology*. Vol. 1. London; New York: T&T Clark, 2004.

———. *Systematische Theologie: Bd. 1*. Göttingen: Vandenhoeck & Ruprecht, 1991.

Papanek, Victor J. *Design for the Real World: Human Ecology and Social Change. With an Introduction by R. Buckminster Fuller*. Toronto; New York; London: Bantam, 1973.

Patton, Cindy, and Benigno Sánchez-Eppler, eds. *Queer Diasporas*. Durham: Duke University Press, 2000.

Peterson, Paul Silas. *The Early Karl Barth: Historical Contexts and Intellectual Formation, 1905-1935*. Vol. 184. Beiträge zur historischen Theologie. Tübingen: Mohr Siebeck, 2018.

Petrella, Ivan. "Theology and Liberation: Juan Luis Segundo and Three Takes on Secular Inventiveness." In *Another Possible World*, edited by Marcella Althaus-Reid, Ivan Petrella, and Luiz Carlos Susin, 162–77. London: SCM, 2007.

Rae, Murray. *Architecture and Theology: The Art of Place*. Waco: Baylor University Press, 2017.

Redstrom, Johan. *Making Design Theory*. Cambridge: MIT, 2017.

Rees, Geoffrey. *The Romance of Innocent Sexuality*. Eugene: Cascade, 2010.

Reichel, Hanna. "Conceptual Design, Sin and the Affordances of Doctrine." *International Journal of Systematic Theology* 22, no. 4 (October 2020): 538–61. https://doi.org/10.1111/ijst.12442.

———. "Swords to Plowshares: On Doing Election." *Stellenbosch Theological Journal* 8, no. 1 (2022): 1–14. https://doi.org/10.17570/stj.2022.v8n1.ad1.

Reinhard, Johannes. *Studien zur Geschichte der Altprotestantischen Theologie*. Leipzig: Deichert, 1906.

Rescher, Nicholas. *Cognitive Systematization: A Systems-Theoretic Approach to a Coherentist Theory of Knowledge*. Oxford: Blackwell, 1979.

Rittel, Horst W. J., and Melvin M. Webber. "Dilemmas in a General Theory of Planning." *Policy Sciences* 4 (1973): 155–69.

Roberts, J. Deotis. *Liberation and Reconciliation: A Black Theology*. Maryknoll: Orbis, 1994.

Rogers, Eugene. "Doctrine and Sexuality." In *The Oxford Handbook of Theology, Sexuality, and Gender*, edited by Adrian Thatcher, 53–66. Oxford: Oxford University Press, 2015.

Rosner, Daniela K. *Critical Fabulations: Reworking the Methods and Margins of Design*. Design Thinking, Design Theory. Cambridge: MIT, 2018.

Ruether, Rosemary Radford. *Sexism and God-talk: Toward a Feminist Theology*. Boston: Beacon, 1983.

Ruti, Mari. "Why There Is Always a Future in the Future." *Angelaki: Journal of The Theoretical Humanities* 13, no. 1 (2008): 113–26. https://doi.org/10.1080/09697250802156109.

Saiving, Valerie. "The Human Situation: A Feminine View." *The Journal of Religion* 40, no. 2 (1960): 100–112.

Sanders, E. P. *Paul and Palestinian Judaism: A Comparison of Patterns of Religion*. Minneapolis: Fortress, 1977.

Scarry, Elaine. *The Body in Pain: The Making and Unmaking of the World*. New York: Oxford University Press, 1985.

Schellong, Dieter. "Alles hat seine Zeit: Bemerkungen zur Barth-Deutung." *Evangelische Theologie* 45, no. 1 (January 1985): 61–80. https://doi.org/10.14315/evth-1985-0107.

Scholem, Gershom. *The Messianic Idea in Judaism: And Other Essays on Jewish Spirituality*. New York: Schocken, 1995.

Schön, Donald A. *Educating the Reflective Practitioner: Toward a New Design for Teaching and Learning in the Professions*. San Francisco: Jossey-Bass, 1987.

———. *The Reflective Practitioner: How Professionals Think in Action*. New York: Basic Books, 1984.

Schonfeld, Eli. "*Am-ha'aretz*: The Law of the Singular. Kafka's Hidden Knowledge." In *Kafka and the Universal*, edited by Arthur Cools and Vivian Liska, 107–29. Berlin: De Gruyter, 2016.

Sedgwick, Eve Kosofsky. *Between Men: English Literature and Male Homosocial Desire, Thirtieth Anniversary Edition*. New York: Columbia University Press, 2015.

———. *Epistemology of the Closet*. Berkeley: University of California Press, 1990.

———. "Paranoid Reading and Reparative Reading; or: You're So Paranoid, You Probably Think This Introduction Is about You." In *Novel Gazing: Queer Readings in Fiction*, edited by Eve Kosofsky Sedgwick, 1–39. Durham: Duke University Press, 1997.

Segundo, Juan Luis. *Liberation of Theology*. Maryknoll: Orbis, 1976.

Simon, Herbert A. *The Sciences of the Artificial*. Third edition. Cambridge: MIT, 1969.

Slenczka, Notger. "Flucht aus den dogmatischen Loci: Das Erbe des 20. Jahrhunderts. Neue Strömungen in der Theologie." *Zeitzeichen*, no. 8 (2013): 45–48.

Smit, Dirk J. "Paradigms of Radical Grace." In *On Reading Karl Barth in South Africa*, edited by Charles Villa-Vicencio. Grand Rapids: Eerdmans, 1988.

Smythe, Shannon. "Barth on Justification." In *Wiley Blackwell Companion to Karl Barth*, edited by George Hunsinger and Keith L. Johnson, 291–301. Wiley Blackwell Companions to Religion. Chichester: Wiley Blackwell, 2019.

Sobrino, Jon. *Christ the Liberator*. Translated by Paul Burns. Maryknoll: Orbis, 2001.

———. *The Principle of Mercy: Taking the Crucified People from the Cross*. Maryknoll: Orbis, 1994.

Solevåg, Anna Rebecca. *Negotiating the Disabled Body: Representations of Disability in Early Christian Texts*. Atlanta: Society of Biblical Literature, 2018.

Spivak, Gayatri Chakravorty. *A Critique of Postcolonial Reason: Toward a History of the Vanishing Present*. Cambridge; London: Harvard University Press, 1999.

———. "Can the Subaltern Speak?" In *Marxism and the Interpretation of Culture*, edited by Cary Nelson and Lawrence Grossberg, 271–313. Communications and Culture. Basingstoke: Macmillan, 1988.

Stein, Robert H. *Mark*. Baker Exegetical Commentary on the New Testament. Grand Rapids: Baker, 2008.

Steinfeld, Edward. "Barrier Free Access in the Man-Made Environment: A Review of Current Literature. Interim Report." Syracuse University, NY School of Architecture: Department of Housing and Urban Development, Washington DC, Office of Policy Development and Research, October 1975.

Stendahl, Krister. *Paul Among Jews and Gentiles and Other Essays*. Philadelphia: Fortress, 1976.

———. "The Apostle Paul and the Introspective Conscience of the West." *Harvard Theological Review* 56, no. 3 (1963): 199–215.

Stockton, Kathryn Bond. *The Queer Child, or Growing Sideways in the Twentieth Century*. Duke University Press, 2009.

Stoever, Dietrich Heinrich. *The Life of Sir C. Linnaeus; to Which Is Added a List of His Works, and a Biographical Sketch of the Life of His Son.* Translated by Joseph Trapp. London: White, 1794.

Szenasy, Susan S. "Ethical Design Education Confessions of a Sixties Idealist." In *Citizen Designer: Perspectives of Design Responsibility*, 20–24. New York: Allworth, 2003.

Terrell, JoAnne Marie. *Power in the Blood? The Cross in the African American Experience.* Maryknoll: Orbis, 1998.

Teuchert, Lisanne. *Gottes transformatives Handeln: Eschatologische Perspektivierung der Vorsehungslehre bei Romano Guardini, Christian Link und dem „Open theism."* Göttingen: Vandenhoeck & Ruprecht, 2018.

Theissen, Gerd. *The Miracle Stories of the Early Christian Tradition.* Edinburgh: T&T Clark, 1983.

Thomas Aquinas. *Summa Contra Gentiles: Book One: God.* Edited by Anton C. Pegis FRSC. Notre Dame: University of Notre Dame Press, 1975.

Tonstad, Linn Marie. "Ambivalent Loves: Christian Theologies, Queer Theologies." *Literature and Theology* 31, no. 4 (2017): 472–89. https://doi.org/10.1093/litthe/frw043.

———. "Everything Queer, Nothing Radical?" *Svensk Teologisk Kvartalskrift* 92, no. 3–4 (2016): 118–29.

———. *Queer Theology: Beyond Apologetics.* Eugene: Cascade, 2018.

———. "The Limits of Inclusion: Queer Theology and Its Others." *Theology & Sexuality* 21, no. 1 (2015): 1–19. https://doi.org/10.1080/13558358.2015.1115599.

Tracy, David. *Blessed Rage for Order: The New Pluralism in Theology.* New York: Seabury, 1975.

Troeltsch, Ernst. *The Absoluteness of Christianity and the History of Religions.* Louisville: WJK, 2005.

Tügel, Franz. *Unmögliche Existenz! Ein Wort wider Karl Barth.* Hamburg: Agentur des Rauhen Hauses, 1933.

Via, Dan Otto. *The Ethics of Mark's Gospel—in the Middle of Time.* Philadelphia: Fortress, 1985.

Von Hippel, Eric. "Lead Users: A Source of Novel Product Concepts." *Management Science* 32, no. 7 (1986): 791–805. https://doi.org/10.1287/mnsc.32.7.791.

Ward, Jane. "Dyke Methods: A Meditation on Queer Studies and the Gay Men Who Hate It." *Women's Studies Quarterly* 44, no. 3–4 (2016).

Warner, Michael. "Uncritical Reading." In *Polemic: Critical or Uncritical*, edited by Jane Gallop, 13–38. New York; London: Routledge, 2004.

Weber, Otto. *Foundations of Dogmatics.* Vol. 1. Grand Rapids: Eerdmans, 1981.

Webster, John. "Introduction: Systematic Theology." In *The Oxford Handbook of Systematic Theology*, edited by John Webster, Kathryn Tanner, and Iain R. Torrance, 1–15. Oxford Handbooks. Oxford: Oxford University Press, 2007.

Williams, Delores S. *Sisters in the Wilderness: The Challenge of Womanist God-Talk.* Maryknoll: Orbis, 1993.

Wilson, Bianca D. M., Soon Kyu Choi, Gary W. Harper, Marguerita Lightfoot, Stephen Russell, and Ilan H. Meyer. "Homelessness Among LGBT Adults in the US." UCLA School of Law, Williams Institute, May 2020.

Wingren, Gustaf. *Luther on Vocation.* Eugene: Wipf & Stock, 2004.

Winters, Joseph R. *Hope Draped in Black: Race, Melancholy, and the Agony of Progress.* Durham: Duke University Press, 2016.

Wittgenstein, Ludwig. *Philosophical Investigations.* Oxford: Blackwell, 1953.

Wolff, Hans Walter. *Joel and Amos: A Commentary on the Books of the Prophets Joel and Amos.* Hermeneia. Philadelphia: Fortress, 1977.

Woolf, Virginia. *A Room of One's Own.* London: Hogarth; Harcourt, 1929.

Zelizer, Viviana A. Rotman. *Pricing the Priceless Child: The Changing Social Value of Children.* New York: Basic Books, 1985.

Zwingli, Huldreich. *Auslegen und Gründe der Schlussreden: 14. Juli 1523.* Edited by Emil Egli and Georg Finsler. Huldrcich Zwinglis sämtliche Werke Vol. 2.. CR 89. Leipzig: Heinsius, 1908.

Index

Note: Scripture references can be found at "Old Testament" or "New Testament."

Printed in the USA
CPSIA information can be obtained
at www.ICGtesting.com
CBHW062139290124
3840CB00002B/2